Intellectual Capital in Organizations

In a global competitive economic environment, resources that are scarce or irreplaceable are a source of sustained competitive advantage for companies and organizations. Knowledge-based resources are a major and increasing driver of long-term competitive advantage. Most accounting standards, however, do not allow for knowledge-based resource calculations, including the most important of these, intellectual capital. Intellectual capital is the collective knowledge, documented and otherwise, of individuals in an organization. In the absence of accounting standards to numerically evaluate intellectual capital, some institutions have devised their own reports and statements. But why should companies, universities and research centers measure these resources? How are intellectual capital statements built? How does one set targets, and what indicators should they include?

This book reviews the development of the field of intellectual capital reporting, including core concepts, latest developments, the main components of intellectual capital, how a statement is built and key indicators of each component. It further analyzes experiences from a variety of pioneering companies and institutions around the globe in measuring intellectual capital, including case studies from educational and research institutions, and provides crucial transnational comparisons. Authors Ordóñez de Pablos and Edvinsson examine the challenges and next steps for the harmonization of intellectual capital reports, consider the creation of a special international agency for intellectual capital reporting standards and evaluate the weaknesses of current standards and how they might be overcome.

Patricia Ordóñez de Pablos is a professor in the Department of Business Administration and Accountability in the Faculty of Economics at the University of Oviedo, Spain. Her teaching and research interests focus on the areas of strategic management, knowledge management, intellectual capital and Chinese studies. She serves as an associate editor for the *Behaviour and Information Technology* journal and is editor-in-chief of the *International Journal of Learning and Intellectual Capital* and *the International Journal of Strategic Change Management*.

Leif Edvinsson is professor of intellectual capital at Lund University, Sweden and chair professor at Hong Kong Polytechnic University. He is a key pioneering contributor to both the theory and practice of intellectual capital. He is the author of numerous journal articles on service management and intellectual capital, and in 1997, co-authored (along with Michael S. Malone) one of the first books on intellectual capital. He serves as special advisor on societal entrepreneurship to the Swedish Governmental Foundation for Competence Development and to the Swedish Governmental Agency for Innovation.

Routledge Advances in Organizational Learning and Knowledge Management

Series Editor: Patricia Ordóñez de Pablos, University of Oviedo, Spain

Intellectual Capital in Organizations

Nonfinancial Reports and Accounts

**Edited by Patricia Ordóñez de Pablos
and Leif Edvinsson**

Routledge
Taylor & Francis Group

NEW YORK AND LONDON

First published 2015
by Routledge
711 Third Avenue, New York, NY 10017

and by Routledge
2 Park Square, Milton Park, Abingdon, Oxon OX14 4RN

*Routledge is an imprint of the Taylor & Francis
Group, an informa business*

Library of Congress Cataloging-in-Publication Data

   Intellectual capital in organizations : nonfinancial reports and accounts /
edited by Patricia Ordóñez de Pablos and Leif Edvinsson.
      pages cm. — (Routledge advances in organizational learning and
knowledge management ; 1)
   Includes bibliographical references and index.
  1. Intellectual capital.   2. Knowledge management.   3. Knowledge
economy.   4. Economic development.   I. Ordóñez de Pablos, Patricia,
1975–   II. Edvinsson, Leif.
  HD53.I5765 2015
  657'.7—dc23
  2014024862

ISBN: 978-0-415-73782-1 (hbk)
ISBN: 978-1-315-81778-1 (ebk)

Typeset in Sabon
by Apex CoVantage, LLC

Printed and bound in Great Britain by
TJ International Ltd, Padstow, Cornwall

Contents

PART I
Knowledge-Based Resources as the Basis for Competitive Advantage for Countries and Regions

PART II
The Importance of Measuring Knowledge-Based Resources

PART VI
Asian versus Western Approaches to Intellectual Capital Reports

PART VII
Trends and Challenges for Intellectual Capital Reports

Figures

Tables

Series Editor Foreword

Key topics such as intellectual capital (IC), organizational learning (OL) and knowledge management (KM) have received increasing interest, both from the academic community and companies facing an economic crisis worldwide. The influence of learning, innovation and entrepreneurship on the achievement of a competitive advantage for the companies, universities, research institutions, organizations and regions is well recognized. Literature on KM and IC suggests that competitive advantage flows from the creation, ownership, protection, storage and use of certain knowledge-based organizational resources.

The book series *Advances in Organizational Learning and Knowledge Management* aims to bring together a selection of new perspectives from leading researchers from around the world on topics like KM and learning in cities and regions; KM and IC reporting in universities, research centers and cities; IC reports trends and more, just to name a few.

The first book of this series, *Intellectual Capital in Organizations: Nonfinancial Reports and Accounts*, edited by Professor Leif Edvinsson and myself, presents an outstanding collection of fifteen chapters written by leading experts in the field of IC reports. I hope this first book of the series can be the starting point of a fruitful path in the publication of reference books in the field of IC, KM and OL.

Patricia Ordóñez de Pablos
Book Series Editor
Co-editor of the Book
Professor
University of Oviedo, Spain

Preface

In today's competitive environment, some knowledge-based resources can be the key to achieving a long-term competitive advantage. Resources that are rare, scarce, without complementary products and without substitutes are sources of sustained competitive advantage for companies and organizations. Accounting standards do not allow the inclusion of most knowledge-based resources, unlike the case with intellectual capital. Intellectual capital is formed by human capital, relational capital and structural capital. Because accounting standards do not permit reporting on these resources, some companies decided to make their own reports for their intellectual capital: the intellectual capital report or statement. Scandinavian countries were pioneers in the building and disclosure of their intellectual capital. Later, companies from Austria, Germany, Italy and Spain decided to follow them and built their own intellectual capital reports (ICRs). Now, some Asian companies and institutions are measuring and reporting their knowledge-based resources too. What is the usefulness of the ICRs? How are they built? What indicators do they include? Are there differences between reports published by European companies and Asian companies? What are the major challenges for ICRs? And the trends in this field? These and other issues will be addressed in the sections of the book.

Knowledge management and organizational learning topics use a dynamic approach to analyze knowledge-based resources and learning processes. However, it is important to analyze knowledge-based resources from a static view too: the intellectual capital approach.

The book starts with a description of the state of the art in the field of ICRs: core concepts, latest developments, main components of intellectual capital, main sections of the report and indicators of each component. The book will cover experiences from pioneering companies and institutions in measuring intellectual capital. Most books only focus on what is going on in European companies and organizations. This book will provide experiences about the building of intellectual capital in Asian and Latin America too. In addition, the book will discuss the usefulness of elaborating the ICR, as well as major trends and challenges.

Patricia Ordóñez de Pablos
Book Series Editor
Co-editor of the Book
Professor
University of Oviedo, Spain

WHERE IS THE VALUE CREATING EVOLVING? INSIDE OR OUTSIDE OR . . .

When I started to look into intellectual capital (IC) and hidden value potential, it was before the digital economy and Internet era. Today, we have new tools assisting us to go deeper into the search! But the starting point is still in the questioning, or *Quizzics*. The meaning of this Quizzics concept is the art and science of questioning, pioneered by the late professor Stevan Dedijer.

IC—or I see the hidden value—of opportunity! IC might even be seen as *capital in waiting!* The epistemological perspective of IC is derived from insights of hidden value. IC is about tools and metrics, but most of all about perspectives and dynamic navigation options of hidden values. Today, the subject of IC has evolved onto many levels and growing insights from both quantitative as well as qualitative research regarding IC of individuals, enterprises, regions, cities and nations. But still we are perhaps in a space of Ignoranz, as phrased by the late professor Ursula Schneider. In one of her final booklets, "Management of Ignorantz," she described four major areas; Positive Ignorantz, Protecting Ignorantz, Ignoring Ignorantz and Inspiring Ignorantz. This IC book is hopefully of the character of Inspiring Ignorantz!

So what is it in the IC that gives energy, inspiration and dynamics? In my view, it is, among things, the relational capital—in other words, the space in between. There we find the current, the electricity and dynamics. In Chinese, it might also labeled Quanxi. In urban planning, it is sometimes called the open public space . . . and in innovation management, it is sometimes called white space management! Today, it is often referred to a space for Open Innovation 2.0 (see https://twitter.com/OISPG).

Many IC tools are now available. I described some of this evolution in a 2013 article in the *Journal of Intellectual Capital* called "Reflections from 21 Years of IC Practice and Theory". The metrics of IC is often used to give a position, like in traditional accounting. But the IC dynamics require a perspective of reassuring, to provide trust in the evolution. This evolution I called *IC navigation* to address the position, direction and speed. IC dynamics is about this flow and velocity of, among other things, transforming human capital into structural capital to get both scaling up, as well as sustainability.

So perhaps the more intriguing IC metrics will be found in the navigation process, as well as in the transformation of volatile and constrained human capital into IC multiplier effects with relational capital and organizational capital.

The value dimension might be outside the firm boundaries. It is found more and more in the networking capability as an externalized variable. Today, this is often referred to as the relational capital. This is visible in the new so-called networking economy, or even more visible as in the *app economy*. This new phenomenon, according to the European Commission in a recent report on app ecology, is going to grow in Europe from close to two million jobs in 2013 to around five million jobs in 2018! And then look into What'sApp, with around fifty employees and with some 500 million daily active users (recently, its stock was valued at $USD16 billion by Facebook).

The recent case with Facebook and What'sApp indicate that the search area for the IC multiplier is in the relational capital and outside the traditional firm perspective. Challenging and innovative IC alliances leverage hidden value! just look at what BMW has been pioneering in terms of innovative relational capital by shaping the IC alliance of BMW Guggenheim Lab of Innovation.

The global outlook on IC indicates that we are now moving to a phase of IC 3.0. We are going beyond the initial pioneering that started twenty years ago. Look, for example, at the Internet of Things measuring interactivity in real time. The challenge is that the old economy's tools might become obsolete and be unable to capture and describe this value process shift. Therefore, initiatives are needed both on an enterprise level and a national and societal level. See more about the milestone IC metrics initiative in the U.S. at www.businessweek.com/articles/2013-07-18/the-rise-of-the-intangible-economy.

National IC (NIC) is going to give use new maps for social welfare as well as for peace processes. The evolution and growth of economies will be driven more and more by NIC investments. There is a high correlation between NIC and GDP per capita (purchasing power parity, ppp). That is, the stronger the NIC as a driver/input, the higher the GDP per capita (ppp). Investing in NIC is positively impacting GDP evolution, or people, society and wealth.

Special regions with high IC density are emerging. Just look at the IC of Singapore, Hong Kong, San Francisco, Stockholm, etc. For the evolutionary map patterns of NIC, see www.NIC40.org or www.nic4nations.com.

The development of NIC has been researched and traced in a unique database for more than forty-eight countries for seventeen years. NIC is represented in the refined Edvinsson, Lin, Stahle, Stahle (ELSS) model by four major categories: national human capital, market capital, process capital and renewal capital.

There is a lot of focus on today on innovation, but behind this is the deeper dimension of renewal, and especially of the organizational capital, both for enterprises as well as nations.

Based on the data of fifty-nine countries in 2010, total renewal capital explains about 37.6 percent of GDP per capita (ppp) according to research by Pirjo Stahle and Sten Stahle (see www.nic4.nations.com).

Consequently, IC work and prototyping on societal innovation will be a challenging IC policy area. This is also part of the knowledge agenda setting work by NCP (see https://www.facebook.com/pages/New-Club-of-Paris/289294509793).

So this book on IC might stimulate forthcoming society IC options or IC liability for present as well as future generations!

Happy IC future!

Leif Edvinsson
The World's First Director of Intellectual Capital
The World's First Professor of Intellectual Capital
Co-founder and Chairman of the New Club of Paris
Awardee 2013 for Thought Leadership by Peter
Drucker Foundation, European Commission and Intel

Part I

Knowledge-Based Resources as the Basis for Competitive Advantage for Countries and Regions

1 Identifying Knowledge-Based Factors Supporting Regional Development
Theoretical Frameworks and Systems of Indicators

Giovanni Schiuma and Antonio Lerro

1. INTRODUCTION

Academic and policy debate have widely recognized that *knowledge-based* factors increasingly play a fundamental role in territorial development dynamics (Boschma 2004; Budd and Hirmis 2004; Huggins and Izushi 2007; Lerro and Schiuma 2009; Pike et al. 2006). This acknowledgement is mainly linked to the recognition that territorial systems' success is no longer based only on "hard" productivity, but softer dimensions play a fundamental role as well (Asheim 1999; Dakhli and De Clercq 2004; Kitson et al. 2004; Maskell et al. 1998; Morgan 2004; Palma Lima and Ribeiro Carpinetti 2012; Valkokari et al. 2012).

Despite this wide acknowledgement, theory and practice highlight, there is still a lack of clear, coherent and shared frameworks for identifying, managing, assessing and reporting knowledge-based factors at a regional level.

In particular, two main issues emerge as relevant for academic and policy debate (Vieira et al. 2011). The first one deals with the objective difficulty in identifying and measuring knowledge-based factors within regional systems. The second one is related to the fact that although the quality and availability of data on different aspects of regional development have improved, there is still a significant lack of homogeneous and relevant data about the endowment and use of knowledge-based factors; moreover, there is a need to define and collect nonestablished data about knowledge sources in order to potentially explain the reasons behind the large differences in regional development patterns.

The aim of this chapter is to address these gaps. First, it briefly analyzes the role of the knowledge-based factors for regional development dynamics. Then, according to a knowledge-based interpretation of territorial strategic resources, the Knoware Tree framework identifies and classifies territorial knowledge-based factors, and the Knoware Dashboard framework drives the design of potential indicators and metrics to assess territorial knowledge-based factors. Finally, a set of key indicators for identifying and assessing the knowledge-based factors potentially supporting regional development paths is elaborated. We conclude the chapter by discussing the directions of future research.

2. KNOWLEDGE AND REGIONAL DEVELOPMENT: BACKGROUND

The first systematic attempts to study the relationships between knowledge and regional development were made by economic historians who wanted to understand why some territories managed to catch up with the richer ones while other territories continued to be poor (Gerschenkron 1962; Abramovitz 1986, 1994). The works of Gerschenkron and Abramovitz focused mainly on evidence from Europe and the U.S. However, from the 1970s onwards, several studies about the relevance of knowledge to development patterns emerged. Since the beginning of the 1970s, the most advanced economies in the world were undergoing structural changes, transforming from industrialized economies based on labor, tangible capital and material resources into economies based more and more on the creation, diffusion and exploitation of new knowledge (Bell 1973; Handy 1989; Mandel 2000). According to this perspective, different scholars highlighted the emergence of a so-called "knowledge-based economy" (D'Aveni 1995; Hitt et al. 1998). Specifically, the concept of a "knowledge-based economy" indicates a new phase of development in which technology, scientific knowledge and human resources represent the key strategic factors for the growth, and it is possible to identify a strict link among the learning processes, the innovation processes, the competitiveness and the economic development. At the same time, the climate of crisis in the manufacturing activities in most European countries, as well as in traditional policies to support economic development, determined a new interest in the local dimension of economic development. In turn, the emergence of a "knowledge-based economy" and the attention on models of *locally based* development brought about meaningful changes in the approaches to resources and the capabilities to activate and enhance value-creation dynamics. Accordingly, in the last decades, various theoretical and practical contributions have been produced, arguing that the more relevant factors to activate and support territorial development paths are more and more linked to the ownership and use of assets, resources and capabilities related—in a direct or indirect way—to the notion of knowledge.

By analyzing specifically the local systems literature, as well as territorial and regional development and competitiveness streams, several terms and concepts, which are frequently interchangeable due to ambiguous definitions and a juxtaposition of their meanings, have been coined to refer to and analyze territorial systems' cognitive resources and their role in activating dynamics of growth (Lerro and Schiuma 2011; Moulaert and Sekia 2003). It is possible to state that many convergent or competitive academic currents have taken part in the debate, such as the Italian *Industrial District School* (Albino and Schiuma 2003; Becattini 1987; Schiuma 2000), the French stream of *Innovative Milieux* (Ratti 1992; Camagni 2002), the *Learning Region* stream (Cooke 1998; Morgan and Nauwelaer 1998). Other scholars have highlighted, although often in a confused way, the relevance of quality and skills of the labor force; the extent, depth and orientation of social networks and institutional forms; the range and quality of cultural facilities and assets; the presence of an innovative and creative class and the scale and quality of public infrastructure (Lerro and Schiuma 2008).

More recently, according to the concepts expressed by the strategic management research stream, such as resource-based view, dynamic capabilities, competence-based view and knowledge-based view, the economic and regional sciences streams have also paid attention to these issues (Morgan 2004; Pinch et al. 2003). For example, Maskell et al. (1998) argue that the only economic production factors not subjected to ubiquification are localized, sticky knowledge, including collective tacit as well as disembodied codified knowledge (Asheim 1999). Storper's notion of "untraded interdependencies"—such as flows of tacit knowledge, technological spillovers, networks of trust and cooperation and local systems of norms and conventions—is also regarded as central to understanding the economic performance and the competitive advantage of a territorial system (Storper 1995). Carlsson and Jacobsson (1997) have underlined that the competitiveness of a region depends not only on the presence of a critical mass of qualified organizations within its boundaries, but also on its capacity to coordinate the actions of these organizations.

However, the observation that "soft" factors affect the process of economic development might also be taken as supporting the view that a broader, more systematic approach that takes such interactions into account is required. During the late 1990s, such concerns led to the development of a new systematic conceptualization to the study of territories' abilities and goods to generate and profit from knowledge—the so-called "knowledge asset" notion (Marr and Schiuma 2001). Traditionally, knowledge assets are grouped into three large components: human capital, structural capital and social and relational capital (Lerro and Schiuma 2008, 2009). The first comprises essentially the know-how characterizing the different actors operating within the territorial system (Dakhli and De Clercq 2004). Structural capital includes all those tangible and intangible assets relevant for the development, acquisition, management and diffusion of knowledge (Lerro and Carlucci 2007; Lerro and Jacobone 2013). Indeed, although knowledge assets have been fundamentally considered intangible in nature, it is essential to recognize that tangible assets also incorporate knowledge. Tangible assets are knowledge artifacts. However, we recognize that the intensity of the knowledge incorporated is different from asset to asset. Here, we consider tangible-knowledge structural assets those that are highly knowledge-based artifacts and that significantly contribute to knowledge management. With regard to social and relational capital, attention has been paid to other kinds of infrastructures related to relationships systems among the stakeholders, local culture, history, attitudes, norms, values, behaviors, image and other cultural dimensions characterizing the territorial systems (Kitson et al. 2004; Iyer et al. 2005; Tura and Harmaakorpi 2005). In the next section, we will discuss this issue more in detail.

3.   MODELING KNOWLEDGE-BASED FACTORS: THE KNOWARE TREE AND THE KNOWLEDGE DASHBOARD

In the last decade, most of the strategic literature has assumed that resources can be distinguished between traditional tangible resources and new, strategically valuable intangible resources. This distinction can be traced back to two fundamental microeconomic strategic approaches, that is, the resource-based view (RBV) and the competence-based view (CBV). Both approaches argue that institutions searching for a sustainable competitive position have to control and develop resources characterized by heterogeneity and immobility.

In particular, the RBV stresses that resources are of sustainable competitive advantage if they are hard to transfer and accumulate, inimitable, rare, not substitutable, idiosyncratic in nature, synergistic and not consumable because of their use (Barney 1991; Peteraf 1993). Along these lines, the CBV has focused attention on the relevance of core competencies, distinctive capabilities, absorptive capacity and dynamic capabilities as source of competitive advantage (Prahalad and Hamel 1990; Teece et al. 1997). These studies have resulted in an emphasis on the intangible resources instead of the more traditional tangible assets.

The KBV is a more comprehensive approach and argues that the critical source of growth and competitiveness is knowledge (Grant 1996, 1997). When adopting a knowledge-based approach, the relevance of a resource is related either to its embedded knowledge or to its role of stimulating and sustaining knowledge dynamics. This is consistent with the twofold interpretation of knowledge—"static" vs. "dynamic" and/or "stock" vs. "flow". Consequently, a resource can be analyzed as an entity embodying critical knowledge and/or as a catalyst for cognitive dynamics.

The assessment of knowledge resources as a stock of assets allows us to understand the value of an institution, as well as to evaluate its value creation capabilities, by understanding the knowledge domains grounding the competencies. This means that the criterion for defining and evaluating the value of a resource, both tangible and intangible, resides mainly with the cognitive role that it assumes, or, in other words, with its level of relevance in building a competency or a capability.

In accordance with a knowledge-based approach, we adopt the notion of a knowledge asset to denote those strategic resources driving and defining the value of a territorial system. We define a knowledge asset as any resource made of or incorporating knowledge that provides an ability to carry out a process or a function aimed at creating and/or delivering value. It can be a tangible or an intangible resource. Although, generally, intangible resources correspond to knowledge resources, not all knowledge resources are intangible. Many tangible resources can be interpreted as knowledge assets, since they embody knowledge variously codified that plays a fundamental role in creating and delivering value as well as in supporting knowledge development and management dynamics.

Knowledge assets provide abilities that, when specialized, define a competence that becomes "core" if distinctive and somehow unique, in addition to building up dynamic capabilities—that is, the ability to continuously renew and develop the knowledge domains at the basis of competencies.

The adoption of the knowledge-based approach allows an interpretation of territorial strategic resources as the group of knowledge assets that are attributed to a territorial system and that most significantly drive its value-creation mechanisms. This conceptualization of territorial knowledge assets means that the key interpretation of the analysis and assessment of such resources must not be the physical nature—distinguishing tangible and intangible resources—but rather, the nature of the knowledge characterizing a resource. In such a perspective, the evaluation models of the intangible resources proposed in the management literature hold a great deal of importance due to the fact that they have to be applied with the aim of identifying and evaluating the resource that really defines the knowledge domains of a territorial system.

However, most of the proposed models present two main limitations: they mainly adopt a taxonomy based on a resource-based approach, rather than on a KBV, and they generally disregard the tangible resources as possible relevant knowledge resources. In order to take into account the knowledge-based nature of territorial resources and to explicitly consider the tangible resources as knowledge assets, we propose the Knoware Tree. Starting with the recognition of the knowledge nature of the strategic territorial resources, the Knoware Tree, as a descriptive model, proposes a taxonomy of the knowledge asset categories building and representing the knowledge assets of the territorial systems.

The Knoware Tree has been proposed as a framework for the assessment of knowledge assets on the basis of value-definition and value-creation dynamics of a territorial system. The concept of Knoware—characterizing its definition—denotes all those resources that are made and/or embody knowledge resulting from the individual or collective cognitive activities. This concept allows us to stress that a knowledge asset is a strategic resource characterized by a knowledge nature, which can present different forms, being tangible or intangible, an alternative nature, being tacit or codified, diverse contents and aims related to its ability to satisfy specific wants and needs. The Knoware Tree is based on the recognition that for any territorial system, it is possible to distinguish two main components: its actors, both internal and external, and its structural components, that is, all those elements at the basis of the processes. Starting from this assumption, it defines two main categories of knowledge assets: the knowledge assets related to the stakeholders of a territorial system—named Stakeholder Knoware—and the knowledge assets related to the tangible and intangible infrastructures of a territorial system—named Structural Knoware. The two categories can be further divided into subcategories, specifically, Wetware and Netware for the Stakeholders Knoware, and hardware

8 *Giovanni Schiuma and Antonio Lerro*

and software for the Structural Knoware. This taxonomy shares the basic hypotheses of other frameworks for the identification and evaluation of the knowledge assets, which generally adopt three categories of intangible resources: the human resources, the structural or organizational resources and the relational resources (Edvinsson and Malone 1997; Roos et al. 1997; Sveiby 1997). However, this taxonomy has the ability to interpret them as knowledge assets, which can be tangible or intangible as well as codified or tacit in nature.

The Wetware perspective, originally introduced by Romer (2003), denotes all knowledge related to the human resources of a territorial system. It gathers all the knowledge that is at the basis and that influences the behavior and competencies of human resources. The Netware perspective represents the set of knowledge assets related to the relationships characterizing a territorial system. This category of capital has been described in the strategic management literature in different ways, such as relational capital, customer capital and social capital. These forms of capital can be either internal to the local context, for example, the stakeholders' networking dynamics taking place within a territorial systems, or they can be external, representing all possible ties linking a territorial system to its external economic, production and sociocognitive environment. The Hardware perspective includes all those assets relevant to the development, acquisition, management and diffusion of knowledge, but that are tangible in nature, as well as all the components linked to the structural features of the territorial system. This category involves two main subcategories: the physical infrastructures and the technological infrastructures. Finally, the Software perspective denotes the "soft externalities" (Kitson et al. 2004) affecting the economic growth and wealth creation of a territorial system. It comprises attitudes, norms, values, behaviors and other cultural dimensions of a territorial system and involves mainly aspects related to the social resources, which affects the territorial output by changing the manner in which human resources use their cognitive abilities to innovate and develop enterprise, to lever the tangible and financial resources and to develop relational resources.

In order to deliver policy and managerial actions based on the exploitation of knowledge assets, policymakers and managers need frameworks to identify, analyze, classify and measure the knowledge assets of a territorial system. The Knoware Tree as a descriptive framework can support the identification and understanding of the knowledge assets of a territorial system, both for interpretative as well as normative purposes. It represents a "lens" through which to analyze and interpret the key success resources and sources of local growth.

However, in order to make it operative, that is, to be used as a performance management tool, it needs to be populated with a set of measures that build an informative base to design, communicate, implement and review policies and actions aimed at developing and managing territorial knowledge assets. This means that the Knoware Tree has to be integrated with a measurement system, that is, a systematic body of metrics to perform a qualitative and quantitative evaluation. For this reason, the Knoware Tree is complemented with the Knoware Dashboard (Figure 1.1). The latter adopts the four knowledge asset categories identified by the Knoware Tree and, by consistently applying performance measurement systems, defines four balanced measurement perspectives: Wetware, Netware, Hardware and Software. Each perspective has to be populated with measures for evaluating the knowledge assets characterizing a specific local context. Regarding the definition of metrics, it is important to stress that knowledge assets are idiosyncratic and specific to their organizational context. This means that the definition of measures for their evaluation has to be mainly a context-related process. It has to take into account the properties of the context in which the evaluation is carried out, as well as the strategic intents of the policymakers and managers. The adoption of a high number of indicators could indicate a reduction of the managerial focus by the users and then reduce their managerial effectiveness (Marr and Schiuma 2001).

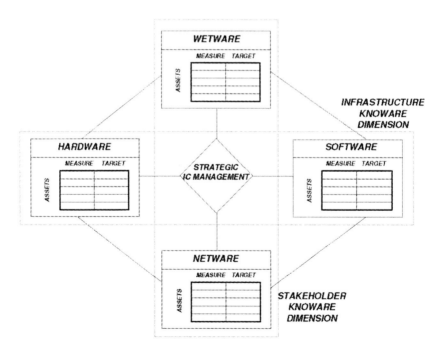

Figure 1.1 The Knoware Dashboard: The knowledge asset perspectives for identifying and assessing knowledge assets within regional systems

4. IDENTIFYING INDICATORS OF KNOWLEDGE-BASED FACTORS AT A REGIONAL LEVEL

Populating the Knoware Dashboard with a set of metrics acting as evaluation proxies lets researchers measure the knowledge assets driving regional development dynamics. Single indicators provide relevant and useful management information in order to understand specific and isolated performance issues and take action to manage them. However, in order to get a holistic view of a phenomenon, we need measures that can offer an integrated and systemic picture of the investigated object.

In this regard, by combining single measures with an appropriate algorithm, it could be possible to define aggregate *indices*. The definition of such indices is particularly important for the assessment of local knowledge assets, since it can provide not only more synthetic and richer information about the knowledge assets ownership of a regional system, but can also define a "thermometer" and a "benchmarking" instrument for the definition, management and review of territorial development strategies, as well as for performing statistical analysis.

In the last years, various scholars (Lerro and Schiuma 2008; Pasher and Shachar 2005) and a number of institutions—for example, the European Union (EU), the Organisation for Economic Co-operation and Development (OECD), the United Nations, the World Economic Forum and the Council of Competitiveness—have paid a great deal of attention to the identification and assessment of knowledge assets at territorial level, adopting different measurement indicators and proxies. Some examples of these attempts are the EU Regional Yearbook, the EU Scoreboard and the EU Report on Science & Technology Indicators; the EU Sustainable Development Indicators; the Global Competitiveness Report; the Regional Intellectual Capital Index and so on.

However, despite the different attempts to provide an informative base for the identification and assessment of the knowledge assets characterizing geographic areas, both at a meso-level and meta-level, there is still a lack of consensus about the measures to be adopted for identifying and assessing the knowledge assets of a territorial system, and specifically the regional ones. Even if indicators and metrics are defined on the basis of the specific informative needs driving their design, it is necessary to identify a set of standard indicators that can be used for identifying and assessing the ownership and use of knowledge assets.

This is a particularly important issue, since the definition of a list of standard measures can benefit both the assessment of the knowledge assets of a territorial system and the benchmarking evaluation, and more generally, the definition of an information platform to integrate the different knowledge assets measurement initiatives. Based on the discussion in the preceding section and on a review of previous sources (Fagerberg and Shrolec 2008; Castellacci and Archibugi 2008; Chaminade and Vang 2008), Table 1.1

presents an overview of the knowledge assets that we expect to be of particular interest for supporting regional development dynamics, along with examples of possible empirical indicators.

Table 1.1 Measuring knowledge assets of a regional system

Wetware (Human Capital):

Number of graduates/100 people 25 years old;

Number of science and engineering graduates/100 people 20–29 years old;

Number of graduates employed after three years from the degree/100 people;

PC users/100 people;

Number of professionals employed in public and private R&D activities/100 people employed;

Number of people with basic educational skills/100 people;

Number of PhDs/number of graduates;

Number of university students involved in a mobility program/number of university students;

Proxies about competence of public officials and public administration managers and employees;

Number of professional managers leading firms of the region/number of firms of the regions;

Number of participants in lifelong learning/100 people aged 25–64.

Netware (Relational Capital):

Number of firms associated in industry associations/total number of the firms of the region;

Number of agreements among universities and firms of the regions;

Number of agreements among universities and industry associations;

Number of university stages activated within firms/total number of university students;

Number of agreements among schools and firms of the region;

Number of agreements among schools and industry associations.

Hardware (Structural Capital):

Number of universities in the region;

Number of research centers in the region;

Number of technological districts in the region;

Proxies about scientific production of the researchers of the universities of the region;

(Continued)

Table 1.1   (Continued)

Proxies about scientific production of the researchers of the research centers of the region;

Internet access in schools;

Proxies about patenting;

Proxies about availability and use of e-government services and tools.

Software (Social Capital):

Number of conflicting labor-employer relationships;

Number of associations/100 people;

Proxies about civic activities, trust and tolerance;

Proxies about civil and political rights;

Rate of irregular work;

Crime rate;

Gender pay gap;

Proxies about citizens' confidence in EU institutions;

Voter turnout in local elections;

Voter turnout in national and EU parliamentary elections;

Proxies about quality of governance: reputation, corruption, law and order, independence of courts, property rights, business-friendly regulation.

5.   FINAL REMARKS

This chapter has briefly analyzed the role of knowledge-based factors in regional development dynamics. Then, according to a knowledge-based interpretation of territorial strategic resources, the Knoware Tree as a framework for identifying and classifying territorial knowledge-based factors and the Knoware Dashboard as a framework for driving the design of potential indicators and metrics to assess territorial knowledge-based factors were presented. Finally, a set of potential key indicators for identifying and assessing the knowledge-based factors that potentially support regional development paths were described.

We recognize some limitations of this study that need to be highlighted in order to constraint the generalization of its implications, as well as to drive further research on the identification and the assessment of the knowledge assets within a territorial system. Unfortunately, there is a lack of data collected with the specific aim of capturing information about the knowledge assets characterizing regional systems. However, the national institutes of statistics and various institutions at a macro level, even if they do not gather data with specific attention to the knowledge dimensions, collect a great amount of data that, if screened, can be used to assess the knowledge dimensions. For this reason, it is critical to review and refine further the definition of a set of appropriate and standard indicators about knowledge assets at a territorial level. Based on an analysis of the theory and practitioner literature, we have identified a list of significant potential indicators, which is not comprehensive, but does represent a meaningful starting point for more rigorous analysis. Of course, different indicators of knowledge assets can be further elaborated and defined, specifically in terms of building indicators on the basis of primary sources. Finally, we call for further empirical investigations of the role and relevance of territorial knowledge assets for value creation within specific territorial systems in order to analyze differences and analogies about their various development paths, as well as to refine the policy tools for the identification and the management of such particular territorial resources.

REFERENCES

Abramovitz, M. 1986. "Catching up, forging ahead and falling behind". *Journal of Economic History,* 46, 406–419.

Abramovitz, M. 1994. The origins of the post-war catch-up and convergence boom. In Fagerberg, J., Verspagen, B. and von Tunzelman, N. (Eds.), *The Dynamics of Technology, Trade and Growth.* (Aldershot: Edward Elgar).

Albino, V., and Schiuma, G. 2003. New forms of knowledge creation and diffusion in the industrial district of Matera-Bari. In Belussi, F., Gottardi, G. and Rullani, E. (Eds.), *The Net Evolution of Local Systems—Knowledge Creation, Collective Learning and Variety of Institutional Arrangements.* (Dordrecht, the Netherlands, Kluwer).

Asheim, B.T. 1999. "Interactive learning and localised knowledge in globalising learning economies". *GeoJournal,* 49 (4), 345–352.

Barney, J.B. 1991. "Firm resources and sustained competitive advantage". *Journal of Management Studies,* 17, 99–120.

Becattini, G. 1987. *Mercato e Forze Locali: Il Distretto Industriale.* (Bologna: Il Mulino).

Bell, D. 1973. *The Coming of Post-Industrial Society.* (New York: Basic Books).

Boschma, R.A. 2004. "Competitiveness of regions from an evolutionary perspective". *Regional Studies,* 38 (9), 991–999.

Budd, L. and Hirmis, A. 2004. "Conceptual framework for regional competitiveness", *Regional Studies,* 38 (9), 1015–1028.

Camagni, R. 2002. "On the concept of territorial competitiveness: sound or misleading?". *Urban Studies,* 39, 2395–2411.

Carlsson, B. and Jacobsson, S. 1997. Diversity creation and technological systems: a technology policy perspective. In C. Endquist (Eds.), *Systems of Innovation: Technologies, Institutions and Organizations.* (London/Washington D.C.: Frances Pinter).

Castellacci, F. and Archibugi, D. 2008. "The technology clubs: The distribution of the knowledge across nations". *Research Policy,* 37, 1659–1673.

Chaminade, C. and Vang, J. 2008. "Globalisation of knowledge production and regional innovation policy: Supporting specialized hubs in the Bangalore software industry". *Research Policy*, 37, 1684–1696.

Cooke, P. 1998. Introduction. In Braczyk, H.J., Cooke, P. and Heidenreich, M. (Eds.), *Regional Innovation Systems*. (London: UCL Press).

Dakhli, M. and De Clercq, D. 2004. "Human capital, social capital, and innovation: a multi-country study". *Entrepreneurship & Regional Development*, 16, 107–128.

D'Aveni, R. 1995. "Coping with hypercompetition: Utilizing the new 7S's framework". *Academy of Management Executive*, 9, 45–60.

Edvinsson, L. and Malone, M.S. 1997. *Intellectual Capital: The Proven Way to Establish Your Company's Real Value by Measuring Its Hidden Values*. (London: Piatkus).

Fagerberg, J. and Srholec, M. 2008. "National innovation systems, capabilities and economic development". *Research Policy*, 37, 1417–1435.

Gerschenkron, A. 1962. *Economic Backwardness in Historical Perspective*. (Cambridge, MA: The Belknap Press).

Grant R. 1997. "The knowledge-based view of the firm: Implications for management practice", *Long Range Planning*, 30 (3), 450–454.

Grant R. 1996. "Towards a knowledge-based theory of the firm". *Strategic Management Journal*, 17 (Special Issue), 109–122.

Handy, C. 1989. *The Age of Unreason*. (Boston, MA: Harvard Business School Press).

Hitt, M.A., Gimeno, J. and Hoskinsson, R.E. 1998. "Current and future research methods in strategic management". *Organizational Research Methods*, 1, 6–44.

Huggins, R. and Izushi, H. 2007. *Competing for Knowledge. Creating, Connecting, and Growing*. (London and New York: Routledge).

Iyer, S., Kitson, M. and Toh, B. 2005. "Social capital, economic growth and regional development". *Regional Studies*, 39 (8), 1015–1040.

Kitson, M., Martin, R. and Tyler, P. 2004. Regional competitiveness: An elusive yet key concept?, *Regional Studies*, 38 (9), 991–999.

Lerro, A. and Carlucci, D. 2007. "Intellectual capital and regions: origins, theoretical foundations and implications for decision-makers". *International Journal of Learning and Intellectual Capital*, 4, 357–376.

Lerro, A. and Jacobone, F.A. 2013. "Technology Districts (TDs) as driver of Knowledge-Based Development (KBD): Defining performance indicators assessing TDs' effectiveness and impact". *International Journal of Knowledge Based Development*, 4(3), 274–296.

Lerro A. and Schiuma G. 2011. "Editorial. Knowledge-based dynamics of local development: a position paper". *International Journal of Knowledge-Based Development*, 2(1).

Lerro, A. and Schiuma, G. 2009. "Knowledge-based dynamics of regional development: the case of Basilicata region", *Journal of Knowledge Management*, 13, 287–300.

Lerro, A. and Schiuma, G. 2008. "Knowledge-based capital in building regional innovation capacity", *Journal of Knowledge Management*, 12, 21–36.

Mandel, M.J. 2000. *The Coming Internet Depression*. (New York: Basic Books).

Maskell, P., Eskelinien, H., Hannibalsson, I., Malberg, A. and Vatne, E. 1998. *Competitiveness, Localized Learning and Regional Development*. (London, New York: Routledge).

Marr, B. and Schiuma, G. 2001. Measuring and managing intellectual capital and knowledge assets in new economy organisations. In Bourne, M. (Ed.), *Handbook of Performance Measurement*. (London: Gee).

Morgan, K. 2004 "The exaggerated death of geography: learning, proximity and territorial innovation systems". *Journal of Economic Geography,* 4, 3–22.

Morgan, K. and Neuwelaer, C. 1998, Eds. *Regional Innovation Strategies: The Challenge for Less Favoured Regions.* (London: Jessica Kingsley).

Moulaert, F. and Sekia, F. 2003. "Territorial innovation models: A critical survey". *Regional Studies,* 37 (3), 289–302.

Palma Lima, R.H. and Ribeiro Carpinetti, L.C. 2012. "Analysis of the interplay between knowledge and performance management in industrial clusters". *Knowledge Management Research & Practice,* 10(4), 368–379.

Pasher, E. and Shachar, S. 2005. The intellectual capital of the state of Israel. In Bounfour, A. and Edvinsson, L. (Eds.), *Intellectual Capital for Communities.* (Boston: Elsevier Butterworth-Heinemann).

Peteraf, M.A. 1993. "The cornerstones of competitive advantage: A resource-based view". *Strategic Management Journal,* 14, 179–191.

Pike, A., Rodriguez-Pose, A. and Tomaney, J. 2006. *Local and Regional Development,* 1st edition. (London: Regional Studies Association-Routledge).

Pinch, S., Henry, N., Jenkins, M. and Tallman, S. 2003. "From 'industrial districts' to 'knowledge clusters': A model of knowledge dissemination and competition in industrial agglomerations". *Journal of Economic Geography,* 3, 373–388.

Prahalad, C.K. and Hamel, G. 1990. "The core competence of the corporation". *Harvard Business Review,* 68 (3), 79–91.

Ratti, R. 1992. *Innovation Technologique et Développement Régional.* (Lausanne: Meta-Editions).

Romer, P. 2003. The soft revolution: Achieving growth by managing intangibles. In Hand, J. and Lev, B. (Eds.) *Intangible Assets.* (Oxford: Oxford University Press).

Roos, J., Roos G., Dragonetti, N.C. and Edvinsson, L. 1997. *Intellectual Capital: Navigating the New Business Landscape.* (London: Macmillan).

Schiuma, G. 2000. "Dinamiche Cognitive nei Distretti Industriali in Evoluzione". *Economia e Politica Industriale,* 106.

Storper, M. 1995. "Competitiveness policy options: The technology-regions connection". *Growth and Change,* Spring, 285–308.

Sveiby, K.E. 1997. "The intangible asset monitor". *Journal of Human Resource Costing & Accounting,* 2 (1), 73–97.

Teece, D.J., Pisano, G. and Shuen, A. 1997. "Dynamic capabilities and strategic management". *Strategic Management Journal,* 18 (7), 509–533.

Tura, T. and Harmaakorpi, V. 2005. "Social capital in building regional innovative capability". *Regional Studies,* 39 (8), 1111–1125.

Valkokari, K, Paasi J. and Rantala, T. 2012. "Managing knowledge within networked innovation". *Knowledge Management Research& Practice,* 10(1), 27–40.

Vieira E., Neira I. and Vazquez E. 2011. "Productivity and innovation economy: comparative analysis of European NUTS II 1995–2004", *Regional Studies,* 45(9), 1269–1286.

2   A New Theory of Value
The New Invisible Hand of Altruism

Thomas J. Housel, Wolfgang Baer and Johnathan Mun

1.   THE NEW AGE OF ALTRUISM

Adam Smith (1776, cited in Khalil 2001) coined the phrase and general philosophy of capitalism with his reference to the "invisible hand" that kept the market in equilibrium while also fomenting capital formation and new wealth. As such, this invisible hand is thought of as a self-regulating (Sorzano 1975) or self-correcting mechanism for the market.[1] This viewpoint doesn't go far enough, however, in that it begs the question of whether the invisible hand is influencing market making or, based on our current understanding, is a self-regulating force that moves markets toward equilibrium. It does not explain market making in an open system where continued disequilibrium as shaped by moral meaning (Fourcade and Healy 2007) may be the only constant. Market making in the current age is shaped by the new invisible hand of altruism (McMahon 1981).[2] We hypothesize that it is this new invisible hand of altruism that is motivating the making of new markets, such as the high-technology industry, necessitating a new theory of value to explain market making and related value creation in the twenty-first century.

Evidence of the force of altruism surrounds us, from the "Occupy Wall Street" movement driven by a desire for wealth redistribution, to the triple-balance-sheet thinking that includes social welfare, to the offering of free massive online open courses (MOOCs) (McCluskey and Winter 2013),[3] as well as the general societal pressure to feed and nurture the poor.

We can see this move toward altruistic motivations in the social media sector with companies such as WhatsApp, Inc., which offers a range of smartphone apps, and others in the same market sector focusing on generating new forms of value for their users and, most likely, also for their *twenty-something* millennial-generation programmers. These companies are essentially giving away services while creating the infrastructures that will help them reach out to new, underserved users and markets worldwide.

Altruistic or prosocial behaviors appear to generate greater happiness in the giver than in the receiver of the generosity (Keltner 2009; Post 2005).

The third richest man in the world, Warren Buffett, is touting the benefits of altruism by promising to give away 99 percent of his accumulated multiple billions when he passes on (with 85 percent of that going to the Gates Foundation [CNN-Money 2006]). Buffett's altruism is being matched by a string of wealthy, well-known media figures, individuals such as Pierre Omidyar of eBay, Mayor Michael Bloomberg, musician Gene Simmons, and Bill Gates, among others (Business Insider 2013). Even people in the poorer countries in the world who give of the little they have to others find greater happiness or a "warm glow"[4] (Hamilton 1963; Andreoni 1990; Sussman and Cloninger 2011).[5] Not surprisingly, the leaders of the dominant religions in the world are calling for a return to their altruistic roots. For example, the new pope has been agitating for a return to the Church's original, altruistic, Christian roots in filling the need for food and care for the less fortunate.

The new period we are entering is characterized by a movement toward producing *non–zero sum* opportunities to produce value for all involved. Most successful entrepreneurs of this new age have been driven by the need to generate value for their audiences in addition to the eventual financial gains they will receive from attracting their audiences (Avolio and Locke 2002).[6] Examples include Bill Gates, who, during the early years of Microsoft, was seeking to move computing from behind a glass wall to the desktop, and Google that provides free e-mail, social networking, document storage, and productivity applications and that maintains the popular "Don't Be Evil" philosophy (Thompson 2006)[7] in its public and intraorganizational communications. Those social and business entrepreneurs who focus solely on how to generate monetized value will succeed at a slower rate than those who begin their journeys with a focus on generating various forms of altruistic value. They will also be more likely to burn out faster than their more altruistically motivated counterparts (Maslach and Jackson 1982).

While altruism may be understood as motivating the creation of a public good or a personal desire to benefit others, recent studies using game theory suggest that altruism or generosity strategies perform better in large evolving populations and explain, in part, the evolution of cooperation in society (Stewart and Plotkin 2012;[8] Rude 2004[9]). This new invisible hand of altruism[10] necessitates a reformulation of how new markets form and create value in nonmonetized, prosocial terms. The assumption we make is that this new form of nonmonetized value, which we call *proto-value,* precedes the traditional monetized value that it will eventually propagate.

Intuitively, we have known that there are forms of nonmonetizable value provided by not-for-profit institutions whose purpose is inherently altruistic. For example, public libraries have existed since the days of the pharaohs, providing valuable services to their various constituencies. National roadways have been central to building value in societies since

Roman times. More recently, social media and smartphone apps provide citizens with public service announcements or with situational awareness and access to resources during times of crisis. For example, the U.S. Geological Service's "Did You Feel It?" app allows the public to input and receive, in real time, information about an earthquake just seconds after such a geological event.

Over the past centuries, the development of the field of physics has been motivated primarily by altruistic activities, with the general goal of obtaining a better understanding of our world and the universe in general. The spin-off benefits to society of this altruistic development process have been immeasurable.

More recently, the ARPANET, built to ensure fail-safe redundant communications should a nuclear war decimate telecommunications infrastructure in the U.S., resulted in the ubiquitous Internet that has been one of the most powerful engines of value creation in the history of civilization. Other more recent examples of altruism seeking to advance a public good include the emergence and rapid growth of MOOCs, offered for free unless the student wants to earn course credits toward a degree, at an increasing number of large universities promoting the worldwide sharing of knowledge.

The recently founded WhatsApp, Inc., is a poster child in the social media sector for generating proto-value. The company's mission statement includes references to protecting its users from advertisers, protecting their privacy by not sharing their click behavior, charging them a minimal fee for the use of the service (i.e., $1 per year), and the desire to reach the millions who may not be connected. Another example is the movement of Google to create a new broadband infrastructure to reach those millions of potential Internet users who cannot get access due to lack of infrastructure. Whereas Google may receive monetized benefits in the long run, investments in broadband telecommunications infrastructure are not for the faint of heart. Facebook's acquisition of WhatsApp, Inc., for the seemingly insane price tag of $19 billion, could not be justified on purely monetized value terms, especially since Facebook's leadership claimed that they would be protecting WhatsApp from any intrusions by Facebook management.[11]

The typical approaches used to value companies that do not have impressive revenue-generating track records, such as WhatsApp, Inc., include comparing them to similar companies that have established track records for generating revenue and that produce similar services. By using the standard valuation technique of market comparables, it becomes possible to generate discounted cash flows to forecast future revenues (see Pratt, Reilly and Schweihs 2000 for a review of the standard valuation techniques, including market comparables). Another valuation approach is to forecast how much revenue the company will derive from "getting a piece of the action" from any revenue it facilitates through sales for another party, akin to eBay, which facilitates transactions via its exchange infrastructure. In the case of WhatsApp, Inc., the only current source of revenue is the $1 per year it charges its users. Either the user base and/or the subscription charge would have to be substantially increased to justify the phenomenal price tag Facebook paid for the company.

Lest we become maudlin about the good intentions of companies in a world still dominated by unadulterated capitalist philosophy, we must also include a discussion of how these altruistic activities would lead to monetized value. By focusing on increasing proto-value, these companies are benefiting users while enlarging the world market for all their services. With a larger market mass, the companies can project their services on a larger scale, thus increasing their potential field of influence that will, in turn, lead to a larger potential use of services or energy that can be converted into work, that is, monetized value. Surely, there will be free riders who did not contribute to this opening of the underserved world to all players. However, due to the purported altruistic motivations of the bigger players, and even the smallest players, every player stands to benefit.

2.   THE PROTO-VALUE APPROACH

The real challenge is to develop a more comprehensive framework that will allow us to move from anecdotal accounts to a better understanding of the primary forces affecting proto-value production. We begin by mapping this value production process according to physics concepts. The connection between physics concepts and economic theory has been well documented (Mirowski 1989) and along with it implications for business (Beinhocker 2007).

As each company projects its *potential field* of services on to a larger *mass* of potential users, some of those users become actual users, resulting in a production of total *energy*. As the *momentum* of usage builds, so does energy. In our physics-to-economics analogy, energy is equivalent to proto-value. As the total amount of proto-value increases, the probability of extracting larger amounts of *work* (i.e., akin to kinetic energy that represents monetized value in our scheme) increases, leading to a virtuous cycle whose *velocity* is ever increasing as long as the companies stick to a focus, first, on producing proto-value and, second, on extracting monetized value. As an example, when Google releases new products such as Google Glass, it increases access to its existing applications by a larger mass of users. Consequently, an increase in the potential field of its applications results in increasing momentum and energy production. Since energy, in the physics-to-economics analogy, equals proto-value, as the total amount of proto-value derived from use of Google Glass increases, the probability of extracting larger amounts of work, that is, monetized value, from Google Glass increases.

The risk is that companies such as Google, WhatsApp and Facebook will be pulled back into the nonaltruistic motivations of the zero-sum game of "we have your money, and now you don't." This force to generate revenue immediately or before they have generated significant proto-value will lead to failure. A focus on proto-value, however, leads to a new non–zero sum game. The services these companies project to the consumer market assume that "we have your eyeballs for a while, but you still have your eyeballs" whereby users maintain their reservoir of attention even though they have temporarily given some of it to the company's services.

MySpace, after being acquired by Rupert Murdock, provides a recent example of how shifting from producing proto-value to focusing on monetized value can lead to a dramatic failure. After Murdock acquired the company for $535 million, the focus was on monetizing and exploiting the user base, which was larger than Facebook's or Google's in 2008. Murdock's MySpace tried to do this by cramming more of its content and advertising on its users. The desire to immediately generate various forms of revenue on the backs of its user population became the goal. Not surprisingly, in short order, the company began to lose users, resulting in fewer advertising dollars and fewer eyeballs to view its offerings. The layoffs in the company happened quickly as the old economy zero-sum game model kicked into high gear (i.e., lower revenues leads to cutting costs, which in this case was the talent that made the company successful in producing proto-value in the first place), resulting in the classic cost-cutting death spiral.[12] What was left of the company was eventually sold for $35 million.

The original goal of Bitcoin was to provide a means for the poor to engage in microtransactions (Arias and Shin 2013). This goal was a form of altruism, although it was attempting to supplant standard monetization that was eventually hijacked by the single goal of monetizing the value of Bitcoin. It was also hijacked by those with less-than-altruistic intents who used it to facilitate their illicit, and arguably unethical, needs and wants. The digital currency became the coin of the realm for illicit sex, drugs and other black market businesses (Moore 2013). The more recent troubles encountered by the leadership of Bitcoin emanate from these problems, as well as attempts by professional hackers, in an example of a true zero-sum game motivation, to break into the Bitcoin "bank" and steal its monetized value (Grinberg 2011).

The future of Bitcoin has been set in motion as its momentum in the production of proto-value wanes, the potential field of its offerings is reduced and, subsequently, its customer base declines, leading to a reduction in the potential energy it can generate. The combination of these forces will ultimately lead to a dramatic reduction in the total energy (proto-value) it creates, resulting in the probability of a much lower extraction of work (standard monetized value) and its ultimately reaching an equilibrium state of no value of any kind. Along with the MySpace case, Bitcoin's situation is an example of how initial altruistic motivation for the production of proto-value does not ensure success in a monetized world.

The public library is an example of nonmonetized proto-value in action. "Libraries offer the public the chance to gain knowledge, improve their job prospects and learn how to use computers, as well as get their complex reference questions answered by professionals. The public library is the center of culture in most small towns as well as larger cities" (M. B. Housel, 2014, personal communication with the director of the Santa Maria, CA Public Library System). As such, its central altruistic goal is to serve the public's needs and wants with no expectation for future monetized revenue. One can hardly count late book fines as a serious source of revenue. Of course, tax dollars support this institution, as well as most of the other common nonprofit organizations that provide basic services to the public. However, the sole focus of the public library is on creating proto-value, and as such, it can be compared to for-profits that have production of proto-value as a central focus. In this way, our approach provides a pathway to track the value production of not-for-profits to begin to benchmark and identify the top performers and best proto-value–producing practices.

In what follows, we provide a framework for structuring the identification and tracking of the production of proto-value using analogies to physics concepts. This framework will also provide a means to begin the process of estimating how monetized value is extracted from proto-value. We include a series of examples of how the framework can be operationalized so that it can be applied to any organization interested in identifying and tracking its production of proto-value.[13]

We proceed from a simplified approach that can be applied relatively quickly to a more precise and detailed approach that will require greater effort by the organization. For the simplified and more precise frameworks, we provide examples of how each can be operationalized, requiring the organization to supply its own numbers.

3. NEWTON IS STILL RELEVANT

Before we present our frameworks pertaining to proto-value, we feel we should revisit the connection between physics concepts—specifically the Newtonian model—and economic theory. There is a reason that the Newtonian model is still prominent in economics: It is because most of us intuitively think in Newtonian cause-effect terms. Even with the problems that arise from applying this framework to modern companies such as WhatsApp, Google and Facebook, the Newtonian model substantially simplifies the complexities of economics with its many moving parts and apparently capricious human participants. The concepts of *mass, velocity, force, potential energy, momentum, work,* and *kinetic energy,* to name a few, are still in use in a wide variety of estimation problems, such as in meteorological predictions, predicting the movements of asteroids, getting the rocket to the moon and many other typical business prediction problems. As such, a Newtonian-based framework is useful to organizational leaders as they grapple with the complexities of the modern economy.

In the following example of a notional Silicon Valley start-up, we have aggregated a number of the physics concepts into a simplified form to show how it is possible to use the resulting framework for an analysis of the velocity of innovativeness of the example company. We do not use standard physics notation for the simplified example. However, in the section presenting the WhatsApp, Inc. example, we use the more standard physics notation in our analysis to allow for a more precise mapping to standard physics terminology.

4. SIMPLIFIED EXAMPLE: A NOTIONAL SOCIAL MEDIA START-UP

We begin our simplified example with a definition of the mapping of the physics to organizational concepts as shown in Table 2.1. Operationally defining these concepts in economic terms presents a number of challenges that must be surmounted before the framework proves useful to decision makers. In many cases, the operational definition will depend on the specific context of the company, customer base, market, competitors, regulatory restrictions and other relevant conditions.

Using a notional Silicon Valley start-up that operates in the social media market niche as an example, we can apply these concepts and derive quantifiable proto-value outputs and indicators of market making, as well as other insights that may prove useful to management. In this example, the company leadership was concerned about the innovativeness of the company's employee talent pool and how quickly the company could bring new applications to its market. We begin the process by generating surrogates for the concepts shown in Table 2.2.

A great concern for organizational leaders, especially in Silicon Valley companies, is how well they can stimulate their talented employees to be innovative and how quickly the innovations can be brought to the marketplace. Nonprofit organizations, such as those involved in homeland security, are equally motivated to stimulate innovation within their organizations in

Table 2.1 Concept definitions

- **Mass {M}** is the relative richness of services, measured in common units of complexity.
- **Position of M {b or c}** is the name of the node in a network of the entity that is offering the service established by the force, that is, the push of the business and the pull of the customer for the service.
- **Business Mass {Mb}** has a given offering strength of push of the service M.
- **Customer Mass {Mc}** is the need pull strength of the customer on the service offered by the business.
- **Number of services {N}** is the total number of services M at a given point in time (e.g., e-mail, social networking and search).
- **Velocity {V}** is the rate of position change of M.
- **Momentum {Mo}** is the rate at which service M moves from *b* to *c*.
- **Work** is the total monetized value extracted from proto-value.
- **Force** is the push of the mass of the company Mb times the pull of the customer Mc divide by a function of distance.
- **Constant {k}** equals the fit or appropriateness of the business offering with the customers' desire.
- **Distance {r}** is the barrier between Mb and any potential customer or the number of services of a given complexity M offered by an organization to a field of customers.
- Using the following definitions, we can determine the following relationships:

$$Force = \frac{k + Mb + Mc}{r^2}$$

$$Total\ Potential\ Field\ \{TPF\} \approx M \times N \times \frac{Mb}{r}$$

$$Total\ Energy\ \{E\} = TPF \times Mc \approx Protovalue$$

Table 2.2 Framework for estimating organizational innovativeness

- **Mass {M}** is the relative complexity of services.
- **Number of Services {N}** is the total number of services at a given point in time (i.e., e-mail, texting, image sharing).
- **Potential Field (PF)** = $M \times N$ the number of services of a given complexity M offered by the organization to a field of customers/clients/users.
- **Velocity** is the change in the rate of PF over a period of three years.

an effort to outsmart potential foes or competitors. These concerns make tracking the innovation cycle a high priority. The simplified physics framework can be used to structure this problem.

5. VELOCITY

In our example social media start-up company, the first thing the company leadership wants to know is how rapidly the talent pool is creating new services for its market niche. The velocity (i.e., change in rate) of introduction of the new services is presumed by management to be a reasonable surrogate for employee innovativeness. We use relative complexity (i.e., scale from 1–10) of the service as a surrogate for the mass of the services the employees create. This approach allows for a rough estimate that is consistent within the simplified framework used for the example.[14] Table 2.3 illustrates the kind of data this framework would generate. Figure 2.1 graphically depicts that the velocity of introduction of new applications is rising from Year 1 to Year 2 and falling precipitously from Years 2 to 3—not a good indicator of the relative innovativeness of the company's talent pool.

As can be seen from Table 2.3, the velocity of introduction of services over the three-year examination period declines, and thus it appears that the company employees are losing innovation steam. Clearly, the innovativeness momentum is headed in the wrong direction. Having this new information would prompt company management to investigate to determine the reasons for this negative change in the velocity of innovation.

One implication from the use of this framework to estimate rate of change of innovation is that there is a correlation between the velocity of

Table 2.3 Social media company example

Year	E-mail (EM) $8 \times N$	Texting (T) $6 \times N$	Image Sharing (IS) $4 \times N$	Potential Field (PF) $EM + T + IS$	Velocity (V)	Potential Users/ Uses (PU)	Total Energy (E) $PF \times PU$
2010	56	12	100	168	90	100	16800
2011	80	24	180	284	116	120	34080
2012	80	18	150	248	−36	125	31000
Total	216	54	430	700		345	81880

Mass per service weightings		(N = number of new applications)
EM = 8	T = 6	IS = 4

introduction of new services/products and the rate of innovativeness of the organization's creative minds. Increasing velocity of introduction of new services would represent an increasingly larger potential field for customers, while decreasing velocity would represent users moving away from the potential offerings of the organization.

6.   MASS

Operationally defining mass is particularly challenging. There is need for a surrogate for weighting to establish an operational definition of mass, and there are several different kinds of potential kinds of mass, as presented in Table 2.1. The definition will depend on the context. There are several possibilities when considering candidates for mass, including:

- Complexity: Lines of code (bits) and embedded algorithms.
- Innovativeness: Amount of knowledge embedded in the *IT* (learning time) created from intellectual-social capital.
- Scale: Using a 1–10 complexity scale in the Services example in Table 2.3.
- Clustering of Knowledge Stocks: Clusters can range in density as measured by a clustering coefficient.

These are a few of the possibilities for quantifying mass. Empirical evidence will be needed for each context to determine the usefulness of the given operationalization of mass.

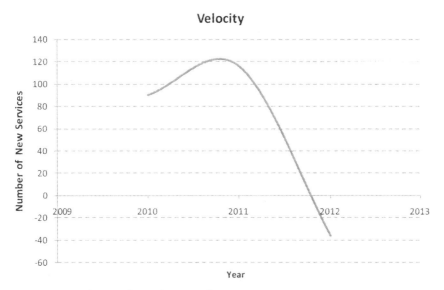

Figure 2.1   Velocity of introduction of new services

7.   FORCE AND DISTANCE

Force is one of the most complex concepts in the framework and requires a number of simplifying assumptions to make it usable for decision makers. Force is a result of the push and pull of the customer and the company in the context of a given service. For example, in the automobile industry, GM exerts a force, or push, on its product while the auto buyer exerts a pull based on his or her desire to possess the car. The car itself has a given mass determined by the combination of the pull of GM and the auto buyer. The distance of the customer from the car is eliminated when he or she buys the car from GM. In the simplified example noted earlier, we have aggregated the various types of mass into the mass of the service type.

In the case of Google, WhatsApp, or for-profit the company's goals are to push its services to the users to reduce the distance from the customers as the customers exert their force (Mc) on the service based on their desire to use the service. Making it easy for the customer to reduce the distance between him and the service by an appealing and easy-to-use interface serves to greatly increase the customer's force, or desire to use the service. It follows, then, that Google, WhatsApp, and for-profit will try to reduce customer distance by reducing the number of clicks needed to make use of the desired service.

The success of this click reduction depends on both the company's and the individual customer's infrastructure. For example, Google's current strategy of offering inexpensive laptops (i.e., Chrome books) and tablets that need only be used to access all of Google's services further reduces the distances of its services from the customer. By reducing distance, Google avoids a potential slowing of momentum in the usage of its services. If the customer had to buy a laptop operating system, standard applications and lots of processing power and random access memory (RAM) for video applications, a much greater distance would exist and, hence, a much lower customer force, resulting in a slower adoption rate momentum.

Amazon has a variety of ways to reduce the distance from its customers. It often offers free shipping that increases the customer force, or pull, of their desire for given products. It also provides customers with a variety of information aimed at their reservoir of desire by suggesting other products that were bought by other customers who purchased the particular product. The Kindle platform and tablet have provided a means to reduce the push of the company and increase the pull of the customer by removing impediments to ordering and using (e.g., books and soon movies) its products. In the future, Amazon may provide customers with the means to generate products at their own residences using 3D printing machines that it may sell at a loss with the purpose of decreasing customer distance and, hence, increasing customer force for its products.

An example of product-oriented companies that failed miserably in the heydays of the dot.com era was e-grocery shopping services. The purported strategy appeared to be that such services would reduce customer distance from company products via home delivery, and thus increase customer force, or desire, for those products. The exact opposite actually happened. These companies increased customer distance by making it harder for customers to do their shopping and receive the desired products in a timely manner. These companies made extravagant investments in infrastructure (e.g., delivery trucks, warehouses) and personnel to fulfill customer orders. Customers reduced the distance themselves by actually visiting the grocery stores because they wanted to price and compare items, browse or get out of the house for a while and wanted the items in their possession immediately.

These e-grocery stores might have reduced the distance by offering customers preprogrammed, easy-to-use terminals for free (e.g., an e-grocery Kindle), offering options to partners with brick-and-mortar stores so that customers could pick up the products at the store themselves, showing customers the best deals or qualities on given products, offering cooking tips for quick or elaborate meals and offering customers the chance to evaluate and vote for given products and share that information with other customers, as well as other ways to reduce customer barriers and thereby increase customer force for their products and services. They simply neglected the need to produce more proto-value via these kinds of "free" services, failing to realize that the monetized value would follow.

Companies can explore a number of options to increase customer force for their products and services. However, the burden is greater on the product-oriented companies to reduce their force on their products and reduce customer distance from their offerings. The need for these companies to "possess" the products creates a number of disadvantages when compared to companies that seemingly give away their services such as Google, WhatsApp, Facebook, and Twitter. These service companies not only try to reduce their force on their services, but also actually try to push their services to customers, thus greatly reducing the service provider–customer distance and greatly increasing customer force on their services.

8.   DISTANCE-FORCE PARADOX

However, there is a catch, even for those companies seeking to increase customer force. Rather than increasing customer force, many companies are actually trying to extract customer attention and information from their service offerings, which they can sell to advertisers and other interested parties to quickly monetize existing products and services. As they ramp up their advertising to their customer base and sell (monetize) customer behavior information, the distance from their customers increases. Thus, they risk increasing their company's force on their services indirectly and thereby reduce their customers' force, or desire, for their services. Focusing on quickly monetizing customer attention, companies are increasing customer distance with more advertising and the sale of customer behavioral information. This action draws these modern companies backwards into the old economic model based on the need for those companies to monetize value immediately. They risk focusing on short-term monetization efforts and ignoring the production of proto-value that results in alienating customers, increasing customer distance and reducing customer force on services. The idea is that the old economic models require companies to monetize value first and foremost, often replacing a push to produce more proto-value with a push to immediately produce monetized value.

9.   POTENTIAL FIELD & VELOCITY

Another challenge in fully utilizing this physics framework is in operationally defining potential field. One promising candidate is the number of potential services that the creative minds of the organization offer to a given field of users via the services they produce. In the case of Google, it would represent all the various services (e.g., Gmail, search) and, more recently, physical products (e.g., Google Glass) that the company offers its users. When combined with the quantification of mass, PF would represent the total number of services of a given mass offered to the customer base at a given point in time.

With the quantification of mass and potential field, all that is left to determine force, momentum and total energy is the quantification of velocity. Curiously, this term signifies different things to companies in the same market sector. For example, Facebook quantifies velocity in terms of the rate of change in users, and Google, in terms of the rate of change in page views. For this reason, Facebook is doomed to reach a saturation point once all users in the world have adopted Facebook, but, in Google's case, the velocity in page views is virtually unlimited. This difference in calculation of velocity has a profound impact on the computation of total energy and the subsequent extraction of work because:

- Momentum = Velocity *x* Mass
- Momentum *x* Potential Field = Rate of Total Energy Flows (business customer)

10.   WORK

Extracting work from total energy might be represented as the eventual monetized value of the work. For example, Facebook and Google eventually were able to extract advertising revenues from the total energy—proto-value—it created for its users. The revenue curves for both companies compared to the velocity curves, per their definitions, have similar shapes (after a bit of smoothing) per Figure 2.2. The notable difference is that the velocity curve inflection points for the users or uses precede the revenue curves by one to two years. This difference provides some preliminary evidence for the hypothesis that proto-value precedes the production of monetized value.

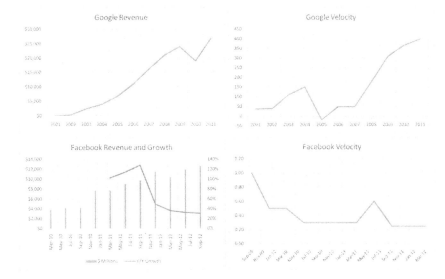

Figure 2.2   Facebook uses and Google's uses and revenue curves

11.   SIMPLIFIED FRAMEWORK FOR ESTIMATING PROTO-VALUE AND WORK

Let's assume that the example company's management would like a quick, rough estimate of the amount of proto-value and work (monetizable value) being produced over the three-year period. Using the simplified framework, it is possible to model the production of proto-value and monetized value by quantifying customer usage (as in Google's example in Figure 2.2) or users (as in Facebook's example in Figure 2.2) of company services in terms of the potential uses (*PU*) for the services and the actual uses (*AU*) of the services. In this example, we selected customer usage and potential usage, deeming them more meaningful representations of the company's outputs. Quantifying *PU*, *AU*, and *PF* (potential field) allows quantification of total energy, or proto-value, as well as the work, or monetized value, of the services.

Table 2.4   Customer usage of service offerings

- **Number of Potential Uses of Services** {*PU*} is the number of potential uses of service products within the time frame of the service offerings.
- **Number of Actual Uses of the Services** {*AU*} is the number of actual downloads, e-mails, clicks and page views within the time frame of the availability of the services.
- *PU x PF* = Total Energy = Proto-Value
- *AU x PF* = Work ≈ Monetized Value ≈ Future Revenue from Services

AU is representative of how many times customers actually used the services of given *weight mass*. The equation *AU x PF = W* is representative of the yield, or *work*, that is, future revenue (eventually extracted via advertising, selling user click behavior or some other means), extracted from proto-value. The difference between *PU* and *AU* is representative of the unused capacity of the organization's services or the opportunities forgone to provide monetizable value to the customer base. We are keeping the results in usage form to enable this comparison.

It is not difficult to translate the *AU* results into monetized revenue by assigning a given dollar amount per click, time at a web site or click-through to advertisements. Using the example of the social media company, we can generate a hypothetical table of values (Table 2.5) based on the results from Table 2.3 and the new equations.

Comparing total proto-value (i.e., total energy) with total work (i.e., total potential monetized value) provides a simple yield ratio of 46,080/81,880, or 56 percent yield for the three-year period. In the future, this ratio could be compared with the industry average for this business segment, as well as for other companies in direct competition with the start-up company in this example. Knowing these yields would be beneficial for investors, as well as management, in tracking the conversion of the proto-value to potential monetized value performance. A simple tracking of the velocity of actual usage would then be useful in estimating the volatility of actual usage, the *PU*-to-*AU* conversion ratio for purposes of forecasting future production of *PU* and *AU*.

In the example, the velocity of *AU* changed in a negative direction from Year 1 (2010) to Year 2 (2011) as seen in Figure 2.3. It appears that while the company's production of proto-value was increasing from Year 1 to Year 2, its work yield during that period decreased. This decrease may have been a result of a lag effect, that is, monetized value (work) lags production of proto-value. Given these trends, management should consider trying to increase proto-value from Year 3 to Year 4, with the potential of monetized value increasing afterward.

Table 2.5 Social media company example

Year	*PU*	*AU*	*PF*	Total *E*	Total *W*	Velocity of Usage
2010	100	40	168	16,800	6,720	40
2011	120	60	284	34,080	17,040	20
2012	125	90	248	31,000	22,320	30
Total	345	190	700	81,880	46,080	90

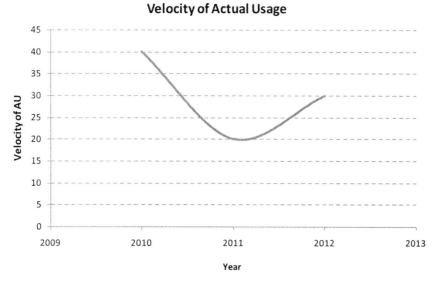

Figure 2.3 Velocity of actual usage

12. PRECISE APPLICATION OF PHYSICS CONCEPTS: WHATSAPP EXAMPLE

WhatsApp Messenger is a cross-platform instant-messaging subscription service that allows users to send text messages, images, video, audio and their location information to other smartphone users using client software installed for a subscription fee of $1 per year. At that nearly free price, the company claimed to have 400 million active users each month, and on February 19, 2014, it was bought for $19 billion by Facebook.

The eventual monetized value in addition to the subscription price extracted from 400 million active users can be characterized in several ways. One possibility is that the users' *attention* has a value to the business, since it could be sold to advertisers or anyone who wishes to direct social behavior. Two other possibilities include the users' knowledge or effort required to *learn* how to operate the services, and users' experience of the services' *benefits*. These three possibilities are assumed to sustain a need for the services in the future. This need may later be satisfied in exchange for a higher subscription price. For example, if only $10 per year is charged to 400 million users, the business will generate $4 billion in revenue per year. Thus, user *attention, learning* and awareness of service *benefits* from using WhatsApp services are possible value entities for any business in WhatsApp's market space. These three value categories can be mixed, sliced and packaged in a myriad of ways; however, first we must calculate value using these three factors. We will label these value sources as proto-value (i.e., energy in the physics analogy) in the analysis and equations that follow.

The equation used for proto-value calculations is:

Equation 2.1: $E[B,x] = Q_{f'}[B] \times k_{f;f} \times \dfrac{q_f[x]}{r[B,x]}$

Where:

- $Q_{f'}[B]$ is the quantity of potential satisfaction of type f projected by the business B (i.e., WhatsApp), formerly Mb in Table 2.1
- $q_f[x]$ is the quantity of potential need for services of type f' by user x, which was formerly known as Mc in Table 2.1
- $k_{f',f}$ is the fit matrix that matches need f' to satisfaction f [15]
- $r[B,x]$ is the distance between the need of x and its satisfaction by B
- $E[B,x]$ is the energy (i.e., proto-value) generated between x and B
- f is an index for the generic type of services

In what follows, we demonstrate how to estimate the values for each of the input parameters in Equation 2.1. The generic type of messaging services might be subdivided into text, image, video, audio or location services and each given an individual index. In this case, $k_{f',f}$ becomes a matrix, and the satisfaction and need quantities are vector arrays. However, to simplify the algorithm, we can group all individual services under the generic messaging service (*ms*) category to simplify the matrix to $f = f' = ms$. The distance created between the B offering of *ms* and x is a result of initial subscription applications, the installation of client code on a user's smartphone and the learning time required to become proficient with the applications.

This can be modeled by an exponentially decreasing function of the form:

Equation 2.2: $r(n) = t_{exp} + t_{init} \times 2^{\frac{n}{lh}}$

Where:

- $r(n)$ is the user time as a function of the number of service executions
- n is the number of service executions
- lh is the learning half-time (the number of service executions decreasing the user time by a factor of 1/2)
- t_{exp} is the operational time required to use the service for a proficient user
- t_{init} is the initial, or first-use, learning time investment

The time required to install and learn the service t_{init} will be a barrier to entry, but once allocated by the user, it will be a deterrent to switching service providers. The operational time investment in using the service t_{exp} daily will be determined by the quality of the user interface. If we assume a proficient user will spend, on average, say, 10 seconds per message, then $n = \infty$, $t_{exp} = 10$ *seconds*, and $r(n) \geq r(\infty) = 10$ *seconds*.

The *user need* parameter $q_{ms}[x]$ measures the strength of the need for *ms* by the user. For well-established services, this is measured by the time the user is willing to invest in acquiring and using a service, and would be an empirical constant. For the economy as a whole, this time investment can be character- ized with a demand curve. However, if established alternatives are available (e.g., a typical time investment and need strength is empirically established), then the measures would vary only slightly from an equilibrium metric.

For new services, the situation is substantially more complex because it is difficult to predict what benefits will actually accrue from the use of a new capability. Factors such as our need for novelty or cultural dreams, among oth- ers, may make a new capability valuable simply because it has been unavail- able. For example, if a levitation device were invented, one might be willing to pay a lot for it. But after trying it for a while, one might find that floating around is not as useful as it initially appeared to be, and the price might reach a much lower general equilibrium than an initial offering might fetch.

In the case of WhatsApp, we are not talking about a new set of services. Messaging services have been around for quite a while, so we are actu- ally talking about messaging services that satisfy an existing and recognized demand. It follows, then, that one might expect a demand curve could be established; however, the use of smartphones and nearly free applications introduces new dynamics. If something is nearly free, the demand curve reaches a free-use limit determined by forces different from those determin- ing the shape of the curve near a typical equilibrium operating point. A free service, such as e-mail, is only used to the level that a user has a genuine

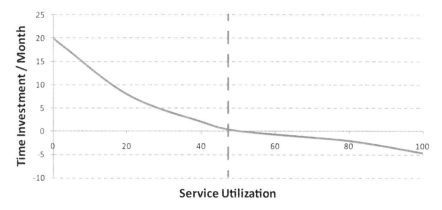

Figure 2.4   Typical demand curve for full message service users

need to exchange messages and chooses to devote the time to do so. Figure 2.4 shows the free-use limit as a dashed vertical line.

The region to the left of the dashed line shows the service executions the customer is willing to allocate time for. As the cost to the user decreases, the service utilization increases until the free-use limit is reached. Beyond that limit, to the right of the dashed line, the user needs to be paid for additional uses. Though not shown, the shape of the demand curve eventually turns sharply negative because even if paid, the user can only spend so much time on the service before needing to rest.

Data on WhatsApp active users and what services they used were available as of November 10, 2013. At that time, WhatsApp had over 190 million monthly active users, 400 million photos were shared each day and the messaging services infrastructure handled more than 10 billion messages each day. Those numbers translate into two photos per user per day and more than fifty messages per user per day. Thus, in the WhatsApp case, the user need for messaging services is only a single data point at the free-use limit of the demand curve. This fact raises the question of whether there is a way to estimate the absolute need for messaging services.

A rough estimate of that need can be derived by looking at the possible activities WhatsApp supports. Humans are social animals and have an innate need to communicate. If a human being spends eight hours at work, eight hours sleeping and several hours eating, traveling, shopping and housekeeping, he or she might end up with one hour to allocate to messaging services. If we assume half of that time is reserved for face-to-face friend and family communication, then a half-hour per day is left for messaging services. The exact number can be established only from behavioral studies. Here, the estimate is used for the purpose of demonstrating the techniques of the analysis.

Assuming that the user's messaging services need measure is a constant of 1/2 hour, we have:

Equation 2.3: $q_{ms}[x] = 0.5 \dfrac{hr}{user} \, per \, day$

To be clear, this parameter is intended to define the need the customer has for the messaging services if the services were supplied for free or nearly free. It is assumed to be a single constant value that defines the average amount of time the average user is willing to allocate in order to communicate in a society, given that demands of time pull him or her toward many other activities. This parameter is the time a typical user can afford to spend, not the additional monetary cost of the services the customer is willing to pay to achieve her or his needs. This additional time allocation investment shows up as the vertical axis in the demand curve and is included in the concept of "distance" discussed previously because it is a barrier (i.e., difficulty separating a user need and her or his satisfaction of the need).

The next parameter that must be discussed is the quantity Q of satisfaction of type f for messaging services (*ms*) projected by WhatsApp, Inc. (i.e., company *B*), or $Q_f[B]$). This parameter defines the amount of satisfaction WhatsApp is able to supply when delivering its package of messaging services.

This parameter is identified as the quality of the messaging services, which is measured by the reciprocal of the number of tries the user must initiate in order to send a message successfully multiplied by the delivery time per try. The measure of satisfaction is then the ratio of the quality of service to the quality level when success is achieved on every attempt.

Assume that a perfect service delivers every message and only has a delivery time as provided by the underlying network. Then the formula for $Q_f[B]$ in this case is:

Equation 2.4: $Q_f[B] = \dfrac{network\ delay}{\#\ of\ tries} \times (delivery\ time\ per\ try)$

If, for example, the servers are slow or they lose a message packet, the user will be forced to spend more time to actually get the result he or she wants from the service and, hence, the proto-value of the service is diminished. If one out of ten messages is lost and the typical delivery time is 2 seconds but the underlying network delay is 1 second, then the $Q_f[B]$ parameter is 1/2.2 seconds.

The last parameter to be defined is the fit matrix $k_{f,f}$ showing the user's need for a messaging service and the appropriateness of the business offering to supply a service that will satisfy that need. In general, this matrix, not the quality of the offering per se, is a result of how well the offering matches the user's needs. In the WhatsApp case, the matchup is dominated by one simple criterion: that the offered messaging service can actually deliver the message to the person to whom it is addressed. A person with ten friends with whom he or she has a need to spend a half-hour per day communicating to maintain a comfortable social environment will find a messaging service appropriate only if it can actually deliver the message to each friend. If only three out of ten of his or her friends are signed up, we have $k_{f,f} = 0.3$. If they are all signed up, we have $k_{f,f} = 1$. If the service has the capability to introduce new friends, then $k_{f,f}$ could become greater than 1, but this situation would be handled by an increase in the need parameter, since enlarging a friendship circle may be considered an expansion of the need.

Substituting the sample values discussed in the paragraphs earlier into Equation 2.1 gives the following proto-value results for a proficient user:

Equation 2.5: $E[B,x] = Q_{f'}[B] \times k_{f',f} \times \dfrac{q_f[x]}{r[B,x]} = 0.3 \times 0.5 \times \dfrac{360}{2}.2$

Where:

- $Q_{f'}[B] = \dfrac{1}{2.2}$ is the

- $k_{f',f} = 0.3$ is the fit matrix
- $q_f[x] = 0.5$ hour/day
- $r[B,x] = 10$ seconds or 1/360 hours
- $E[B,x] = 24.55$ proto-value/energy units

In the next section, WhatsApp's proto-value is compared to proto-values calculated for different situations; the relative unit-independent ratios should be of interest.

13.   TOTAL PROTO-VALUE CALCULATIONS

We have thus far presented the methodology and formula for estimating the proto-value $E[B,x]$ of the messaging services offering from business B (in this example, WhatsApp) to a typical user x. This is a single proto-value number. In business, almost all useful information requires the use and comparison of many business entities. The first calculation would be the proto-value provided by the business to all 400 million users per month of the messaging services. Since users have different needs, the calculation should sum up all the individual needs expressed as a sum over all users. Performing this calculation would require a survey and classification of many user categories.

For demonstration purposes, we have defined the user need $q_f[x]$ as an average user need and, hence, the number of users can be factored out of the summation as follows:

Equation 2.6: $$\sum E[B, x] = 4 \times 10^8 \times Q_{f'}[B] \times k_{f',f} \times \frac{q_f[x]}{r[B, x]}$$

$$\sum E[B, x] = 4 \times 10^8 \times 24.55$$

The total proto-value of $E[B] = 98.16 \times 10^8$ resulting from this calculation is overstated because each of the 400 million users per month does not have the same unit of need at 1/2 hour per day. Note that user x is no longer in the definition of $E[B]$ because it has been summed over all users and the result is the proto-value the business supplies to the marketplace. If the typical user used the service only once a month, he or she would still be counted in the 400 million figure. What we need is the average number of users per day. In the absence of these data, the best that can be done is to calculate a range. The users can use the service every day or only once a month, decreasing the proto-value by 1/30.

The total proto-value delivered to the user market by WhatsApp is bounded as follows:

Equation 2.7: $$E[B, x] = 98.16 \times 10^8 > E[B] > 3.27 \times 10^8 \frac{\text{proto - value}}{\text{energy}} \text{ units}$$

The single business-to-user calculation in Equation 2.6 assumes only a single business B is involved (e.g., Telegram, Threema, TextSecure, Black-Berry Messenger, Viber, LINE, KakaoTalk or WeChat). Including Whats-App, there are more than nine major competitors in the global market for mobile phones and a host of older technologies, including File Transfer Protocol (FTP) and wireline phone service, as well as the U.S. Postal Service.

The actual total proto-value would then be calculated as a sum over all the competing business alternatives:

Equation 2.8: $E[B] = \sum_{x1} E[B_1, u_1 x_1] + \sum_{x2} E[B_2, u_2 x_2] + \cdots = \sum_i \sum_{xi} [EB_i, u_i x_i]$

Where:

- B_i is the ith competitor
- x_i is the total number of users per day using the ith competitor services
- u_i is the fraction of the users' need actually satisfied by the ith competitor

Most users would divide their messaging needs among all these services so that the user need for a specific service is reduced by the fraction of time a user used another service to satisfy the need.

Assuming each of the 400 million users use some other service half the time, the limit calculation in Equation 2.7 would be reduced by half and the total value/energy supplied by WhatsApp would be bounded by:

Equation 2.9: $49.08 \times 10^8 > E[B] > 1.63 \times 10^8$ proto-value/energy units

14. PROTO-VALUE OF INVESTING TO IMPROVE SERVICES

The number of users claimed by a business and the fraction of those claimed who also satisfy their need through competitors' offerings are after-the-fact numbers and often difficult to obtain. It is useful to compare two different businesses using more fundamental parameters in the proto-value/energy equation. Such a comparison will lead to market proto-value comparisons and predict the market share a company may achieve with a particular technology.

Let's assume we have two nearly identical companies, B_1 and B_2, there are N users in the market and the fractional use for both companies is split evenly $use_1 = use_2 = 0.5$. Let's further assume that the same values for parameters used in Equation 2.4 apply. Now let's assume that B_2 makes an investment to double the quality of its service to $Q_{f'}[B_2] = \dfrac{1}{1.1}$ by reducing the time it takes for the user to learn how to use the service. Let's also assume that the user interface is improved. The resulting comparative estimates are listed in Table 2.6.

Table 2.6 Comparative estimates with changes in quality and distance

- $Q_f[B_1]$ = 1/2.2 quantity of potential satisfaction
- $Q_f[B_1]$ = 1/1.1 quantity of potential satisfaction
- $q_f[x_1] = q_f[x_2]$ = 0.5 hour/day for messaging
- $k_{f,f}$ = 0.3 fit matrix
- $r[B_1,x_1]$ = 10/3600 distance
- $r[B_2,x_2]$ = 5/3600 distance
- $N = 4 \times 10^8$ users in the market
- $u_1 = u_2$ = 0.5 market share
- $E[B_1,x_1]$ = 49.0^8 x 10^8 proto-value or energy units
- $E[B_2,x_2]$ = 196.36 x 10^8 proto-value or energy units

At the instance of introduction, the proto-value/energy calculations would be as shown in Equations 2.10A and 2.10B:

Equation 2.10A: $$\sum E\left[B_1, x_1\right] = u \times N \times Q_{f'}\left[B_1\right] \; k_{f',f} \times \frac{q_f\left[x_1\right]}{r\left[B_1, x_1\right]}$$

$$= 49.08 \times 10^8 = 0.5 \times 4 \times 10^8 \times 0.3 \times 0.5 \times \frac{360}{2.2}$$

Equation 2.10B: $$\sum E\left[B_2, x_2\right] = u_2 \times N \times Q_{f'}\left[B_2\right] \times k_{f',f} \times \frac{\left[q_f x_2\right]}{r\left[B_2, x_2\right]}$$

$$= 196.36 \times 10^8 = 0.5 \times 4 \times 10^8 \times 0.3 \times 0.5 \times \frac{720}{1.1}$$

B_2 now provides four times the proto-value/energy compared to B_1 which did not invest in such improvements. The market share at the instant of introduction has not changed, since the same users with the same habits are using the same two services. However, the users recognize the advantage of the better-quality user interface and will not only have a tendency to switch, but also to tell their friends to switch. As a function of time, the switch is depicted by an adoption curve in Figure 2.5.

Adoption curves are typically slow to increase initially, followed by an exponential rise and flattening out as the market is saturated. Initially, the total proto-value/energy is *245 x 10⁸* units, since half the population is getting the new, improved service introduced by B_2 to its existing customer base, while the other half is still getting the value of the old service. If all the old users switch to the new service, the total proto-value/energy is

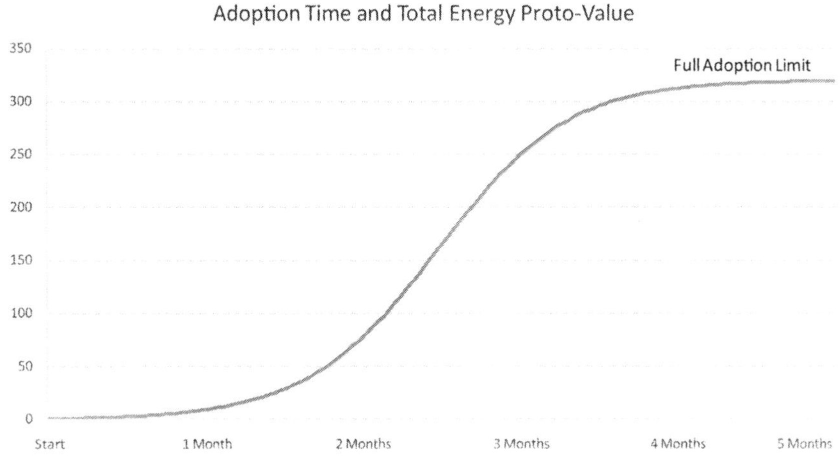

Adoption Time and Total Energy Proto-Value

Figure 2.5 Typical adoption curve for service switching

392 x 10⁸, since now both populations will receive the benefit of the new service.

A rule of thumb from physics that might apply is that the size of the energy change times the transaction time is a constant: $\Delta E \times \Delta t = adoption\ constant$

In other words, the larger the proto-value/energy increase for an action, the shorter the time it takes to make the switch. If such a rule applies to these kinds of businesses, then the graph would indicate the constant is $\Delta E \times \Delta t = 147 \times 3 = 441 = proto\text{-}value\ months = adoption\ constant.$

Once the adoption constant is known, the adoption rate and, consequently, the number of users for a service can be calculated as a function of time.[16] For example, if the proto-value difference gained by adopting the improved service is only *73* proto-value units, the adoption time would be 6 months.

15. CALCULATION OF MONETIZATION STRATEGIES

As mentioned previously, user *attention, learning* and awareness of service *benefits* are three potential indicators of proto-value for a business like WhatsApp, Inc. These categories of proto-value can be converted into income and profits, and this section provides the basic methodologies used to estimate the monetized value to the business.

Let's start with awareness of service benefits because this is directly related to the subscription price a business may charge a customer. The proto-value for the messaging services to a customer was described by Equation 2.1 and numerically calculated to *24.54* proto-value/energy units when inserting the parameters shown in Equation 2.4. Assuming all these parameters stay the same except for the amount charged for the service, how much can WhatsApp, Inc., charge before the users abandon their offering?

The traditional approach is to use a demand curve to calculate the demand for a product or service at a given price. An example of such a curve was shown in Figure 2.4. However, as mentioned, the traditional demand curve does not handle cases of free or nearly free services. What we first need to do is convert the service offered from the number of messages per day to a flat-rate service for a specific number of messages. We know that in WhatsApp's case there are *400* million customers who may use a service to send approximately *50* messages per day if it costs nothing to do so. In February 2010, there were *six* billion mobile phone subscribers (see "ITU releases latest global technology development figures," ITU 2010). Since the world population is approximately *seven* billion people today, the penetration level of cell phones may be saturated. As all cell phones become enabled to transmit audio, text, messages and so forth, all cell phone users will become part of the user market. Figure 2.6 shows a hypothetical demand curve for full message service users with a flat-rate package.

The kink in the curve corresponds to WhatsApp's *400* million users within the context of a full cell phone market. If this hypothetical curve was accurate and all *400* million users was WhatsApp users, the total yearly income from service fees would be *$2.8* billion per year.

The primary threat to such a business is from competitors who could provide a similar service for less or for free. As a free service, all six billion cell phone users will have the messaging package and none of them would be using WhatsApp if the company's services created a large distance from the user.

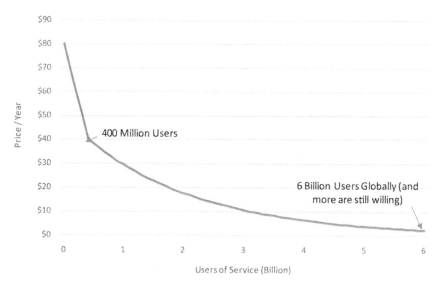

Figure 2.6 Typical demand curve for full message service users

16. CONSEQUENCES OF INCREASING WHATSAPP SUBSCRIPTION PRICE

The question to be asked is what can WhatsApp, Inc., do to retain users if it starts to exact a price for its service? The answer can be given in terms of the tools we have been developing by assuming there are two businesses: WhatsApp as B_1, and B_2 representing all of its competitors. The tale of these two businesses starts with WhatsApp, Inc., developing a loss-leader service that is given away for free, is easy to use (i.e., the distance $r[B_1, x_1]$ is very low) and is of excellent quality, so $Q_f[B_1]$ is high and the fitness matrix $k_{f',f}$ rapidly approaches *1* as the user community adopts the service. Therefore, the proto-value/energy $E[B_1, x_1]$ is very high for an individual user and continues to increase as all cell phone users adopt the service. Soon, WhatsApp has saturated the market of *six* billion cell phone users, as indicated on the right side of Figure 2.6, and may have a great reputation but generates less-than-optimal revenue.

The proto-value/energy is given by the following calculation of Equation 2.11:

Equation 2.11: $$E[B_1, x] = Q_{f'}[B_1] \times k[B_1]_{f',f} \times N \times \frac{q_f[x]}{r[B_1, x]}$$

$$E[B_1, x] = 1 \; x \; 0.99 \; x \; 6 \; x \; 10^9 \; x \; 0.5 \; x \; 360 = 1{,}069 \; x \; 10^9$$

Where:

- $Q_{f'}[B_1] = 1$, the
- $q_f[x] = 0.5$ hour/day, the quantity of need for messaging
- $k[B_1]_{f',f} = 0.99$, the fit matrix
- $r[B_1, x] = 10$ seconds $= 1/360$ hours
- $N = 6 \; x \; 10^9$ users in the market
- $E[B_1, x] = 1{,}069 \; x \; 10^9$ proto-value or energy units

The large number of users has now attracted competitors (bundled as B_2), and B_2 owners would like to see a profit. Let's assume B_2 develops a set of services of equal quality so that at market introduction, the fitness matrix is nearly zero: $k[B_1]_{f,f} = 0.001$. The parameter in the fitness matrix is some finite proto-value, since local markets can be developed with special incentives.

At the same time, WhatsApp, Inc., has decided to raise its price to *$7/ year*, which would bring in *$42* billion per year in revenue if all users paid that new price. This cost to users adds distance to the energy calculation for WhatsApp and its user base. For the sake of the example, let's assume time and money are related by the average wages. According to BBC News (Alexander 2012), the total world income is approaching *$70* trillion per year and there are *seven* billion people, so the average income is approaching *$10,000* per person per year.

Assuming a *2,000*-hour work year, we give the value of one second as *$10,000 / (2,000 x 3,600) = $0.0013* dollars per second, or *720 seconds per dollar*. The barrier to use, or distance, in our physics analogy will increase from *10 sec* by adding *r[B,x] = 720 x 7 / 365 = 13.8 sec/day*. This figure means that the distance value increases to *23.8* seconds, thus decreasing WhatsApp, Inc.'s proto-value by more than *50 percent*—not significant when confronted with a competitor who offers a proto-value a thousand times less. This simple calculation, however, does not tell the true story.

A further correction to the time–dollar estimate would suggest the median rather than the average. The global median income is only *$1,225/year*. This is probably a better number to use, since we are assuming almost all the people on the earth are using cell phones are from the lower-income populations. If the median of *$1,225/year* is used instead of the *$10,000* in the previous calculation, then the value of *$1* is *2,000 x 3,600 / 1,225 = 5,877 seconds per $*. Then, the distance is *r[B,x] = 5,877 x 7/365 = 112.7 seconds per day*, and the distance barrier increases to *112.7 + 10 = 122.7 seconds = 3,600 seconds per hour / 122.7 seconds = (1/29.3) per hour*. Using this distance, the proto-value/energy is calculated for WhatsApp, Inc., when it begins to charge *$7/year* as follows:

$$E[B_1,x] = Q_{f'}[B_1] \times k[B_1]_{f;f} \times N \times \frac{q_f[x]}{r[B_1,x]}$$

E[B₁,x] = 1 x 0.99 x 6 x 10⁹ x 0.5 x 29.3 = 87

A similar calculation for the competitor set *B₂* that has managed to build the same quality of service but remains free would be lower because its initial user base (as measured by the fitness matrix) is smaller than WhatsApp's service. The proto-value/energy calculation for *B₂* under these assumptions is:

$$E[B_2,x] = Q_{f'}[B_2] \times k[B_2]_{f;f} \times N \times \frac{q_f[x]}{r[B_2,x]}$$

E[B₂,x] = 1 x 0.001 x 6 x 10⁹ x 0.5 x 360 = 1

Thus, right after introducing the new subscription price of *$7*, there is an *87* to *1* advantage for WhatsApp, Inc., as measured by the proto-value/energy. But, how long would this advantage last?

The answer lies within a complex problem of social interactions and will depend on how the service is bundled, when the payment is requested and the topology of user network connections. To get an estimate of the effect, consider that the proto-value/energy on a single user is *1/6 x 10⁹ = 0.16* for *B₂* and *87/6 x 10⁹ = 14* for *B₁*. The ratio of *1* to *87* holds because we have simply eliminated the large number of users in considering the effect of collecting the service fee from a single user.

However, the topology of the friendship network is critical. Assume that a user of the B_1 service is confronted with having to pay $7. For the median user, this payment is approximately *30 percent* of his weekly wages, a considerable sum producing a considerable psychological impact. Assume this user has *ten* friends he would most like to share messages with, representing 80 percent of his messaging need. If he tells his friends about the free service available from B_2 and they all install it, his individual fitness parameter would jump from *0.001* to nearly *0.8*, and his personal proto-value/energy would jump from $E[B_2,x] = 1$ to $E[B_2,x] = 800$, a considerable jump in proto-value. In addition, he could save *30 percent* of his money and would thus feel a considerable force to move in the direction of encouraging his friends to switch services.

However, the proto-value/energy does not end there. While each of the *ten* friends is likely to have shared friends, each probably has some exclusive friends. Assume the ratio of shared to exclusive friends is *50 percent*; then each of the ten friends prompted to switch will see his or her fitness for using the B_2 product increase from $k[B_2]_{f,f} = 0.001$ to 0.4 and his or her proto-value/energy change from $E[B_2,x] = 1$ to $E[B_2,x] = 400$. Now *ten* users see the *400* to *87* proto-value/energy advantage for using the B_2 service rather than B_1. News of such advantages goes viral very rapidly—more on the order of a few days than years. If our adoption constant of *441* is accurate, the difference between *87* and *400* is *313* proto-value units, and the switch time in months would be calculated by

Adoption time in months = 441 / 313 = 1.4 months

The bottom line is that if WhatsApp, Inc., has a secret business plan to make money by raising service payments in an environment where free services of equal quality and accessibility are available, it will most likely lose all its users within less than the year in which it wishes to raise rates. The only way to avoid such a loss of users is if WhatsApp, Inc.'s product is of higher quality and substantially easier to use, the payment is hidden or the user is a member of a small segment of the world economy for whom a $7 payment at a point of sale is immaterial compared with the installation time of the new software. (If it takes *fifteen* minutes to install, this would represent people earning more than *$28/hour,* which is less than *1 percent* of the population, or less than 70 million people.) If this fraction could be maintained, WhatsApp, Inc., would make *7 x 70 = 490* million dollars a year. While not a trivial amount, with such a small user base, the fitness parameter would drop and even those users who are not influenced by the price of the service would probably use the equal-quality, and free, B_2 alternative.

Ultimately, then, if WhatsApp, Inc., wants to increase subscription pricing, it must add a barrier, keeping the distance between it and its user base small, and keep the fitness of its services to the user's needs high in comparison to the competition. If the distance and fitness problems are not addressed before rates are raised, WhatsApp, Inc., is likely to enter a death spiral. This example, then, demonstrates the need to have a comprehensive framework that connects the causes and effects of changes to the critical parameters in the model.

17.   CONCLUSIONS

We fully expect organizations to select and adjust the proposed frameworks in a way that best suits their purposes. The hope is that the users of the frameworks will maintain the consistency of the logic of each framework to ensure more accurate results.

As to where to begin, one suggestion is that the leadership begins with the simplified framework to obtain a rough view of their organization's proto-value production and then move to the more precise framework by involving employee teams. Using one, or both, of these frameworks will be useful in developing strategies for producing value in its various forms, monitoring the production of that value and better understanding the interconnectedness of all the variables that lead to proto-value production and eventual monetized value.

If organizations focus on the potential benefits of altruistic motivations and the production of proto-value, then the traditional economic value will follow. The same can be said for not-for-profit organizations, who will benefit from meeting the needs of their various constituencies. The leading organizations will be at the forefront of this new age and will reap the rewards accordingly.

NOTES

1. Smith's desire is, therefore, to remove the mercantilist restraints and to allow what he regarded as the self-regulating "natural tendencies" of the economic system to work themselves out and to produce "the full complement of riches" (J. S. Sorzano, David Easton and the invisible hand, *The American Political Science Review*, 1975, p. 25) that the society can attain. In other words, Smith viewed the economic system as being automatically and efficiently regulated by the forces of the market.
2. First, the sociologists we cite in this introductory paragraph are typically concerned with the social sources of moral ideas and not the development of a positive moral theory. Second, at the level of particular markets, sociologists of science have begun to treat the social technologies of market making in the same way that they examine life in laboratories. In this work, the persistent tension in economics between normative and descriptive theory is shown to be resolved in practice through the development of social technologies that bring the behavior of markets in line with the demands of theory. Third, at

the macro level, economic rules turn out to be filled with explicit moralizing, whether concerning the creditworthiness of nations or their degree of corruption and cronyism, or the extent of corporate social and environmental responsibility. All these approaches aim to show that market exchange is saturated with moral meaning—that is, that it involves more or less conscious efforts to categorize, normalize and naturalize behaviors and rules that are not natural in any way, whether in the name of economic principles (e.g., efficiency, productivity) or more social ones (e.g., justice, social responsibility).

3. *The Chronicle of Higher Education* surveyed those professors who create MOOCs to answer the question: Why did they do it? Their answer seems to lend support to the presupposition that MOOCs were designed to expand access and level the playing field. It is worth quoting in full: "Professors who responded to *The Chronicle* survey reported a variety of motivations for diving into MOOCs. The most frequently cited reason was altruism—a desire to increase access to higher education worldwide." F. B. McCluskey and M. Winter, MOOCs, ethics and the economics of higher education, *e-mentor*, 4:51, 91–94, 2013.

4. According to Elizabeth Dunn and Michael Norton (How Money Actually Buys Happiness, HBR Blog Network, June 28, 2013): "And our research shows that even in very poor countries like India and Uganda—where many people are struggling to meet their basic needs—individuals who reflected on giving to others were happier than those who reflected on spending on themselves. What's more, spending even a few dollars on someone else can trigger a boost in happiness. In one study, we found that asking people to spend as little as $5 on someone else over the course of a day made them happier at the end of that day than people who spent the $5 on themselves. Smart managers are using the power of investing in others to increase the happiness of their employees. Google, for example, offers a compelling 'bonus' plan for employees. The company maintains a fund whereby any employee can nominate another employee to receive a $150 bonus. Given the average salaries at Google, a $150 bonus is small change. But the nature of the bonus—one employee giving a bonus to another rather than demanding that bonus for himself—can have a large emotional payoff."

5. Sussman and Cloninger note: "The traits of altruism and cooperation often are assumed to be among humanity's essential and defining characteristics. However, it has been difficult to account for the origins and evolution of altruistic behavior. Recently, scientists have found data on cooperative behavior in many animal species, as well as in human societies, that do not conform to evolutionary models based solely on competition and the evolutionary drive to pass on selfish genes. In this volume, recent debates about the nature and origins of cooperative behaviors are reviewed. The hypothesis that unselfish cooperative behavior has evolved in animals that live in social groups is discussed. Many of the mechanisms that primates and humans have evolved for protection against predators, including cooperation and sociality, are explored.

"Social animals, including primates and humans, are not forced to live socially but do so because it benefits them in numerous ways. Through natural selection, primates and humans have developed areas of the brain that respond with pleasure and satisfaction to being cooperative and friendly, even if cooperation involves personal sacrifice. Data are presented supporting the idea that the normal pattern for most diurnal primates and for humans is to be social. Selfishness and aggression are expressions of adaptive responses that are well regulated in mature and healthy people with the benefit of mechanisms of social evolution in primates. People become noncooperative and express antisocial behavior as a result of faulty or incomplete development of their natural potential for cooperation and altruism. It is human nature to want to work together and cooperate. A hypothesis is developed and explored that positive social interaction is related to well-being in both nonhuman primates and in humans." R. W. Sussman and C. R. Cloninger, 2011, *Origins of Altruism and Cooperation*, New York: Springer.

6. As stated in the abstract to Avolio and Locke's 2002 article: "In this series of letters, Avolio and Locke compare and contrast their different views on leadership motivation, considering how selfish and self-sacrificing altruistic behavior influences leaders' and followers' motivation and performance. Locke bases his main arguments in both letters on the premise that leaders should act and think in a rational way, with selfish interest as the basis for action. By accomplishing their selfish interests, leaders will exhibit their highest principles and performance. Avolio argues that Locke's view on selfish interest is simply too idealistic. Since leadership is seen as being in the eye of the beholder, there is a point where all of the rational decision making in the world does not change the subjective views followers have of their leaders. Moreover, there are numerous situations where everyone's self- or selfish interests cannot be satisfied." B. J. Avolio and E. E. Locke, Contrasting different philosophies of leader motivation: Altruism versus egoism. *The Leadership Quarterly*, 13:2, 169–191, 2002.

7. "Lee has been with Google since only last summer, but he wears the company's earnest, utopian ethos on his sleeve: when he was hired away from Microsoft, he published a gushingly emotional open letter on his personal Web site, praising Google's mission to bring information to the masses. He concluded with an exuberant equation that translates as 'youth + freedom + equality + bottom-up innovation + user focus + don't be evil = The Miracle of Google'." C. Thompson, Google's China problem (and China's Google problem), *New York Times Magazine*, April 23, 2006.

8. According to Stewart and Plotkin, "Cooperative behavior seems at odds with the Darwinian principle of survival of the fittest, yet cooperation is abundant in nature. Scientists have used the Prisoner Dilemma game, in which players must choose to cooperate or defect, to study the emergence and stability of cooperation. Recent work has uncovered a remarkable class of extortion strategies that provide one player a disproportionate payoff when facing an unwitting opponent. Extortion strategies perform very well in head-to-head competitions, but they fare poorly in large, evolving populations. Rather, we identify a closely related set of generous strategies, which cooperate with others and forgive defection, that replace extortionists and dominate in large populations. Our results help to explain the evolution of cooperation. . . . Recent work has revealed a new class of 'zero-determinant' (ZD) strategies for iterated, two-player games. ZD strategies allow a player to unilaterally enforce a linear relationship between her score and her opponent's score, and thus to achieve an unusual degree of control over both players' long-term payoffs. Although originally conceived in the context of classical two-player game theory, ZD strategies also have consequences in evolving populations of players. Here, we explore the evolutionary prospects for ZD strategies in the Iterated Prisoner's Dilemma (IPD). Several recent studies have focused on the evolution of 'extortion strategies,' a subset of ZD strategies, and have found them to be unsuccessful in populations. Nevertheless, we identify a different subset of ZD strategies, called 'generous ZD strategies,' that forgive defecting opponents but nonetheless dominate in evolving populations. For all but the smallest population sizes, generous ZD strategies are not only

robust to being replaced by other strategies but can selectively replace any noncooperative ZD strategy. Generous strategies can be generalized beyond the space of ZD strategies, and they remain robust to invasion. When evolution occurs on the full set of all IPD strategies, selection disproportionately favors these generous strategies. In some regimes, generous strategies outperform even the most successful of the well-known IPD strategies, including win-stay-lose-shift." A. J. Stewart and J. B. Plotkin, Extortion and Cooperation in the Prisoner's Dilemma, *Proceedings of the National Academy of Sciences*, 109:26, 10134.

9. W. Rude has this to say: "The results presented here empirically quantify the relationship between servant leadership, job burnout and job satisfaction. When there is the presence of the positive aspects of servant leadership, and the absence of power and pride, subordinates report higher levels of job satisfaction, professional efficacy and lower levels of emotional exhaustion and cynicism." W. Rude, The connection between servant leadership and job burnout, doctoral dissertation, Trinity Western University, p. 74, 2004.

10. Another article presents the idea of "impure altruism" versus "pure altruism." Based on the author's work, it appears that distribution of wealth and a sense of fairness are among those contributing to a public good. In his article, W. D. Hamilton observes: "The overall conclusion is that the 'pure altruism' model is extremely special, and its predictions are not easily generalized. On the other hand, the impure altruism model is consistent with observed patterns of giving . . . . When people make donations to privately provided public goods, they may not only gain utility from increasing its total supply, but they may also gain utility from the act of giving. However, a simple application of the public goods model ignores this phenomenon. A consequence of this omission is that the theoretical predictions are very extreme and implausible: total provision of the public good is independent of the distribution of income among contributors, government provision completely crowds out private provision and subsidies are neutral. On the other hand, the impure altruism model leads to predictions that are intuitive and that are consistent with empirical regularities. By assuming that individuals are not indifferent between gifts made by themselves and gifts made by other individuals or the government, we conclude that redistributions to more altruistic people from less altruistic people will increase total provision, that crowding out will be incomplete and that subsidies can have the desired effect." W. D. Hamilton, The evolution of altruistic behavior, *The American Naturalist*, 97:896, 354–355.

11. It has been unclear to most of the financial world as to how Facebook hopes to make money from the acquisition. The typical cynical Wall Street explanation is that Facebook will get access to all of WhatsApp's growing audience of users and somehow exploit the new connections. However, the purported agreement between the leadership of Facebook and WhatsApp, Inc., is that Facebook will not interfere with WhatsApp's current relationship with its user base. This relationship is built on the trust that WhatsApp will not share any usage behavior or personal information, or will not allow advertising to access its users.

12. The Financial Times Lexicon web site [http://lexicon.ft.com/Term?term=death-spiral-(costing_based)] defines "cost cutting death spiral" as follows: "Some of an entity's overhead costs are either fixed (in that they remain the same irrespective of the volume of production or service-providing activity) or are semi-variable (in that a portion of the cost is fixed). Eliminating a product or service can increase the overhead rate used to cost products or services

because these fixed or semi-variable costs (the numerator in the overhead rate) remain the same or decrease more slowly than the cost allocation base (the denominator), which is often related to the expected number of products or services offered. The higher overhead rate increases the overhead cost to remaining products or services. If any products or services are subsequently eliminated, the burden rate may increase again. In theory, the product eliminations and the subsequent increases in the overhead rates could continue until all products become too expensive and are therefore eliminated, resulting in no products left to sell." Cost cutting often results in cutting the value a company is producing, as in the MySpace case, leading to the cost cutting death spiral.

13. As there is no magic, there will be a need to create new categories for common units of value such that they can transcend organization boundaries. One promising common unit candidate for proto-value is a unit of complexity (T. J. Housel, and V. A. Kanevsky, Reengineering business processes: A complexity theory approach to value added, *INFOR,* 33:4, 248–262, 1995; T. J. Housel, and A. Bell, *Measuring and Managing Knowledge,* New York: McGraw-Hill, 2001). A unit of complexity represents a unit of change (Housel and Kanevsky 1995) and can be operationally defined as an information theory bit, in terms of lines of code or learning time (Housel and Bell 2001). The assumption is that in organizations, energy changes inputs into outputs, and it follows that a unit of energy, that is, proto-value, may be represented as a unit of complexity. Complexity theory has been touted as foundational for a new theory of economics (E. D. Beinhocker, *The Origin of Wealth: The Radical Remaking of Economics and What It Means for Business and Society,* Boston: Harvard Business School Press, 2007). For any theory that purports to measure anything, positing a unit of measurement is central.

14. One study found that relative innovativeness of an organization's employees is related to their ability to share and exchange knowledge among themselves (K. G. Smith, C. J. Collins, and K. D. Clark, Existing knowledge, knowledge creation capability, and the rate of new product introduction in high-technology firms, *Academy of Management Journal,* 48:2, 346–357).

15. It is traditional in physics to compensate for changes in units within the fitness matrix $k_{f,f}$. So, for example, if distance were measured in meters instead of hours, then a velocity related to Einstein's speed of light constant c would be imbedded in $k_{f,f}$ and its units would be proto-value/meters per hour per need, f per satisfaction, f'. If time were measured in years instead days so that a need was defined in hours per year, then the units of value would change to satisfaction/year.

16. A further wrinkle to be added is the fact that switching services usually involves learning and setup time. This phenomenon is handled in the distance function shown in Equation 2.1. The calculations in this equation only compared proficient users and ignored the learning time. Thus, if learning and setup time are taken into account, the initial distance r will not be reduced by 1/2, but might actually increase, thus acting as a barrier that slows down the adoption rate. For popular services on cell phones, the definition of a better user interface implies that it is both easy to use and easy to learn and set up. For more complex products such as operating systems, the promise of easier use and better product results may not be enough to entice users, and eliminating the option to remain with traditional interfaces causes customer loss. This is a lesson Microsoft has encountered as it tries to force new, and possibly better, versions of Office and Windows on its users.

REFERENCES

Alexander, R. 2012. "Where are you on the global pay scale?" *BBC News Magazine* March 29, 2012. http://www.bbc.com/news/magazine-17512040.

ANACOM—UTI. URL http://www.acacom.pt/render.jsp?contentId=1141492.

Andreoni, J. 1990. "Impure altruism and donations to public goods: A theory of warm-glow giving". *The Economic Journal*, 100(June), 464–477.

Arias, M. A., and Shin, Y. 2013. "There are two sides to every coin—even to the Bitcoin, a virtual currency". *The Regional Economist* (October). http://www.stlouisfed.org/publications/re/articles/?id=2427.

Avolio, B. J., and Locke, E. E. 2002. "Contrasting different philosophies of leader motivation: Altruism versus egoism". *The Leadership Quarterly*, 13:2, 169–191.

Beinhocker, E. D. 2007. *The Origin of Wealth: The Radical Remaking of Economics and What It Means for Business and Society.* Boston: Harvard Business School Press.

Business Insider. 2013. "15 tycoons who won't leave their fortunes to their kids." http://finance.yahoo.com/news/15-tycoons-who-won-t-leave-their-fortunes-to-their-kids-195610442.html.

CNN-Money. 2006. "Warren Buffett gives away his fortune." http://money.cnn.com/2006/06/25/magazines/fortune/charity1.fortune/.

Dunn, E., and Norton, M. 2013. "How money actually buys happiness", *HBR Blog Network,* June 28. http://blogs.hbr.org/2013/06/how-money-actually-buys-happiness/.

Fourcade, M., and Healy, K. 2007. "Moral views of market society". *Annual Review of Sociology*, 33(August), 285–311.

Grinberg, R. 2011. "Bitcoin: An innovative alternative digital currency". *Hastings Science & Technology Law Journal*, 4(Dec. 9), 160. http://hstlj.org/articles/bitcoin-an-innovative-alternative-digital-currency/2/.

Hamilton, W. D. 1963. "The evolution of altruistic behavior". *The American Naturalist*, 97(896), 354–356.

Housel, T. J., and Bell, A. 2001. *Measuring and Managing Knowledge.* New York: McGraw-Hill.

Housel, T. J., and Kanevsky, V. A. 1995. "Reengineering business processes: A complexity theory approach to value added". *INFOR*, 33(4), 248–262.

Keltner, D. 2009. *Born to Be Good: The Science of a Meaningful Life.* New York: WW Norton & Company.

Khalil, E. L. 2001. "Adam Smith and three theories of altruism". *Recherches Économiques de Louvain*, 67(4), 421–435.

Maslach, C., and Jackson, S. E. 1982. *Burnout: The Cost of Caring.* Englewood Cliffs, New Jersey: Prentice-Hall.

McCluskey, F. B., and Winter, M. 2013. "MOOCs, ethics and the economics of higher education". *E-mentor*, 4(51), 91–94.

McMahon, C. 1981. "Morality and the invisible hand". *Philosophy & Public Affairs*, 10(3), 247–277.

Mirowski, P. 1989 *More Heat than Light: Economics as Social Physics, Physics as Nature's Economics.* Cambridge, UK: Cambridge University Press.

Moore, T. 2013. "The promise and perils of digital currencies". *International Journal of Critical Infrastructure Protection*, 6(3), 147–149.

Post, S. G. 2005. "Altruism, happiness, and health: It's good to be good". *International Journal of Behavioral Medicine*, 12(2), 66–77.

Pratt, S. P., Reilly, R. F., and Schweihs, R. P. 2000. *Valuing a Business: The Analysis of Closely Held Companies.* New York: McGraw-Hill.

Rude, W. 2004. "The connection between servant leadership and job burnout". Doctoral dissertation, Trinity Western University.

Smith, A. 1937. *The Wealth of Nations* (1776). New York: Modern Library, 740.

Smith, K. G., Collins, C. J., and Clark, K. D. 2005. "Existing knowledge, knowledge creation capability, and the rate of new product introduction in high-technology firms". *Academy of Management Journal*, 48(2), 346–357.

Sorzano, J. S. 1975. "David Easton and the invisible hand". *The American Political Science Review*, 69(1), 91–106.

Stewart, A. J., and Plotkin, J. B. 2012. "Extortion and cooperation in the Prisoner's Dilemma". *Proceedings of the National Academy of Sciences*, 109(26), 10134–10135.

Sussman, R. W., and Cloninger C. R., eds. 2011. *Origins of Altruism and Cooperation*. New York: Springer.

Thompson, C. 2006. "Google's China problem (and China's Google problem)". *The New York Times Magazine*, April 23.

Part II

The Importance of Measuring Knowledge-Based Resources

3 Toward Measurement of Intangible Capital

Assessment of the Methods Presented by Baruch Lev

Pirjo Ståhle and Sten Ståhle

1. INTRODUCTION

The focus of wealth creation in developed countries has shifted increasingly from mass production to a knowledge economy, where the key drivers of economic growth are ever more intangible. The value-creating mechanisms of knowledge capital are profoundly different from those in the manufacturing era. The growing interest in intangibles lies in the belief that these are a crucial source of future wealth creation in business (Stewart 1997). The empirical evidence that companies with the greatest share of intangible-driven earnings perform better than others in the long term is also compelling (Gu and Lev 2002). Thus, it is an important challenge—both from a practical and an academic perspective—to recognize knowledge as an economic driver, to understand its behavior and to be able to measure its economic impact.

Intangibles as competitive business advantages have never been a mainstream interest in management research, but nor are they a completely novel topic. For instance, there have been attempts to explain the existence, creation and growth of multinational enterprises based on intangible assets ever since the earliest studies in international business strategy. The results of this research showed that in order to achieve international success, firms needed to possess advantageous intangible assets that they could leverage in a variety of foreign environments (Buckley and Casson 1976; Hymer 1976). Research in the 1990s typically used research and development (R&D) and advertising intensities as proxies for such firm-level advantages (e.g., Caves 1996; Morck and Yeung 1991, 1992). In the 2000s, the resource-based view turned the focus to firm-specific resources, especially knowledge resources (e.g., Hall 2000), and their role in helping the firm achieve sustainable competitive advantage. The deployment of firm-specific knowledge often requires that key employees make specialized human capital investments that are not easily redeployable to other settings. The effective use of governance mechanisms also allows firms to obtain greater performance from their efforts to deploy firm-specific knowledge resources. (Wang et al. 2009).

Scientific research literature on intangible resources began to accumulate with the emergence of the intellectual capital (IC) research tradition. The first wave of IC research started in the mid-1990s, adopting mainly a microeconomic perspective. Its principal focus was on how IC can be modeled, measured and reported. This early work proposed a range of different models and taxonomies; examples include the contributions of Edvinsson and Malone (1997), Sveiby (1997), Stewart (1997), Bounfour (1998, 2003), Roos et al. (1998), Canibano et al. (1998), and Mouritsen, Bukh and Larsen (2001). They were particularly useful for the purposes of studying IC within companies and organizations, and helped to establish a relatively homogeneous taxonomy.[1] At around the same time, several other scholars addressed the issue of IC management from a more dynamic perspective. The roots of this dynamic approach to IC lie in the Resource-Based View (RBV) of the firm and in the dynamic capability approach. RBV regarded the firm as a bundle of (mainly intangible) resources (Barney 1991; Grant 1996; Peteraf 1993; Wenerfelt 1984). The resources within this framework that are considered particularly relevant to competitive advantage are those that are valuable, rare, inimitable and nonsubstitutable (the so-called VRIN attributes).

The dynamic capabilities approach to IC aimed at addressing some of the RBV weaknesses, in particular, by providing a more operational analytical framework. Teece, Pisano and Shuen (1997) defined dynamic capability as "the firm's ability to integrate, build and reconfigure internal and external competencies to address rapidly changing environments"—a concept similar to the "combinative capabilities" defined earlier by Kogut and Zander (1992).

The understanding of intangibles expanded to comprise the effects of the level of firm-specific knowledge and other intangible resources, including R&D and patenting intensities. It was shown that firm-specific knowledge had positive and statistically significant effects on firm performance, indicating that firms with higher levels of firm-specific knowledge assets are more likely to achieve better economic performance. Godfrey et al. (2009) showed that both R&D spending and patenting intensity were positively and significantly related to performance.

It is often emphasized that IC is a useful concept for setting corporate goals and strategies (e.g., Robinson and Kleiner 1996), and that value can be extracted from IC only when it is linked with the strategic objectives of the company (e.g., Sullivan (1998). Roos et al. (1998) say that the theoretical roots of IC lie in two streams of thought: the strategic school, which studied the creation and use of knowledge for enhancing the value of the organization, and the measurement school, which aimed at constructing reporting mechanisms that enable nonfinancial, qualitative items to be used along with financial data.

The concept of IC refers to a rather diffuse entity that is not easy to grasp. It is not tangible, but rather embedded in organizations and in society's structures, processes and procedures. One interesting economic perspective on IC is provided by the angle of drivers, including the question of how IC creates successful economic dynamics.

Corrado, Hulten and Sichel (2005, 2006, 2009) developed an experimental method to measure gross fixed capital formation for a large number of intangibles, and furthermore extended the standard growth accounting framework to identify the contribution of IC to economic growth. They estimated that between 1998 and 2000, U.S. investment in intangibles averaged U.S. $1.1 trillion (1.2 times the tangible capital investment), or 12 percent of gross domestic product (GDP), and they showed that *U.S. productivity acceleration since the mid-1990s can largely be attributed to the growth of intangible assets.*

The direct expenditure-based approach was first adopted by Nakamura (1999, 2001), who measured gross investment in intangible assets by means of a series of measures, including R&D expenditure, software, advertising and marketing expenditure, and wages and salaries of managers and creative professionals. He found that in 2000, U.S. investment in intangibles was U.S. $1 trillion (approximately equal to investment in nonresidential tangible assets), with an intangible capital stock of at least U.S. $5 trillion.

Baruch Lev had another approach to IC. He wanted to measure a company's *managerial quality,* or what he calls *organization capital* (OC) (Lev and Kasnik 1995). According to Lev, OC consists of such items as information technology outlays, employee training costs, brand enhancement activities, payment to systems and strategy consultants, and the cost of setting up and maintaining Internet-based supply and distribution channels (Lev and Radhakrishnan 2004, 8). OC is thus closely related to the firm's capacity to generate growth. Accordingly, high market-to-book value companies are intangible intensive, that is, rich in OC that captures a major component of the firm's intangible assets or growth potential.

Lev also identifies five drivers of *intangible-driven earnings:* R&D, advertising (brand enhancement), capital expenditure (intangibles embedded in physical assets management), information technology and technology acquisitions (Lev 2001, 10). According to Lev and Radhakrishnan (2005), OC can serve as a proxy for managerial quality, and their measure of firm-specific OC is developed as an indicator of managerial quality. This measure empirically captures the "abnormal efficiency" in using the firm's resources (capital, labor, R&D) relative to competitor firms and reflects managerial quality.

2. AIM OF THE CHAPTER

In this chapter, our interest lies in the measurement and value generation of IC with a special focus on the methods developed by Baruch Lev, professor of accounting and finance at New York University. Lev is interestingly positioned between the two main streams of IC thought: the strategic school and the measurement school. Lev is one of the first authors to underscore the explicit need to incorporate general and firm-specific intangibles into the production function, arguing that their omission will give rise to critical inaccuracies.[2]

Another more recent model by Lev focuses more specifically on organizational capital and the effects of R&D investments on economic performance, as outlined in the book *The Valuation of Organization Capital* (Lev and Radhakrishnan 2004). This model is unique in that it dissects OC into two parts: first, a *company-specific* part and second, a general *economy-wide and common* part that is available to all companies.

Our main concern in this paper is to assess the validity and accuracy of Lev's methods in measuring IC. What do they tell us about intellectual capital and value generation? Can they reliably shed light on aspects of business performance that cannot be directly inferred from economic indicators?

3.   BACKGROUND OF LEV'S METHODS

Developed for the calculation of OC, the first of Lev's methods is essentially an application of the Cobb-Douglas form of a production function. In economics, the Cobb-Douglas form of production functions is widely used to represent the relationship of an output to inputs. It was originally proposed by Knut Wicksell and tested against statistical evidence by Charles Cobb and Paul Douglas in 1928. In 1928, Cobb and Douglas published a study in which they modeled the growth of the American economy during the period from 1899 to 1922 (Cobb and Douglas 1928). They considered a simplified view of the economy in which production output is determined by the amount of labor involved and the amount of capital invested. Whereas there are many other factors affecting economic performance, their model proved to be remarkably accurate.

The production function is an input-output model used for the calculation of business turnover. The function is generally denoted as

$Y = AL^{\alpha}K^{\beta}$, where:

- Y = total production (the monetary value of all goods produced in a year)
- L = labor input (hours/year)
- K = capital input (dollars/year at purchasing power parity, PPP)
- A = total factor productivity (TFP)
- α and β are the output elasticities of labor and capital, respectively. These values are constants determined by the technology available. Furthermore, $\alpha + \beta = 1$ is considered to denote a stable state of the economy and return to scale (e.g., increase or decrease in capital or labor input is reflected equally in output).

It is necessary to note that total factor productivity A (TFP) comprises all the factors that impact productivity and efficiency, as well as all the economic drivers that benefit the company in its production or its services: this will also include the impacts of IC. In general, *A* is considered to reflect the overall level of technology and general market conditions.

Since the publication of "Technical change and the aggregate production function" by Robert M. Solow (Solow 1957), the focus of interest has shifted from the original Cobb-Douglas production function to the so-called augmented Solow production function. Here the *augmentation*, enforcing or strengthening (*AG*), generally means that total factor productivity (*A*) is broken down into two parts, one of which is usually linked to labor:

$$Y = A'(AG)^\alpha L^\alpha K^\beta$$

Solow's original formula has been used to examine various augmenting entities, including human capital, social capital, innovation, R&D and value added. The augmented models have no doubt helped to shed light on TFP by introducing human or social capital, innovation, etc., as components in the production function and explaining how they affect productivity in general. However, there is still no consensus on *how* the augmenting part should be incorporated into the production function, nor is it properly understood how the augmenting entity should be *quantified* and *normalized*. Generally, the augmenting part is connected to labor and receives the corresponding elasticity, α or β, that is, the augmentation is effective via labor. This is the case, for example, when human capital has been used as an augmenting entity. Many studies have used three elasticities, α, β and γ, which means that the augmented part is an *independent* productivity variable. However, most suggestions put forward so far have been rather unique, and therefore, there exists no standard application.

Lev's organization-based model is basically a Solow model augmented with OC (implemented as TFP) and R&D as an independent variable, for example, with its own elasticity (b_3) in the production formula. As mentioned, his method dissects OC into two different parts: a firm-specific part and a general economy part available to all firms. This is an important distinction in that it acknowledges the key impact of the operational environment on productivity. This can also be seen *as a step toward recognizing the effects of national IC components on general productivity.*

Lev's other model that focuses on economic performance and intangible-driven earnings is also, by nature, a production function. However, it is neither a Cobb-Douglas nor a Solow type of function, but instead, Lev has created a specific type of general linear production function[3] focused on intangible-driven earnings as shares of overall earnings. His method is *supposed to indicate the proportion of net profit contributed by intangible*s.

4. LEV'S METHODS AND THEIR RESULTS

Lev's organization-based production function models the firm's output (denoted by SALE) as a function of three major inputs: physical capital (PPE: property, plant and equipment), labor (EMP: number of employees) and R&D capital (RND), where RND represents the firm's innovative activities (research and development), that is, its intangible assets, whereas (a) stands for OC:

$$(3.1.1.)^4 \ldots \text{SALE} = (a)\,(\text{PPE})^{\beta_1}\,(\text{EMP})^{\beta_2}\,(\text{RND})^{\beta_3}\varepsilon$$

The OC variable is represented as follows:

$$(3.1.2.) \ldots \log(a) = b_0 + b_{0_s}\log(\text{SGA})$$

where SGA is the firm's sales, general and administrative expenses in year t. Regarding the choice of SGA as the basis for OC, Lev observes (2004, 8):
"This major income statement item includes most of the expenditures that generate organization capital, such as IT outlays, employee training costs, brand enhancement activities, payment to systems and strategy consultants, and the cost of setting up and maintaining Internet-based supply and distribution channels."

As pointed out earlier, the unique characteristic of this model is that it allows for two types of OC, that is, an economy-wide, common organization capital b0, which is available to all firms (e.g., a certain level of population education, the prevailing legal and institutional setting), and second, a firm-specific organization capital b0s log(SGA), which is developed and maintained by each firm individually (e.g., coded knowledge, production blueprints, business processes and procedures, marketing networks and channels).

Lev's results are based on 57,258 (non-R&D) and 32,979 (R&D) firm-year observations over the period from 1978 to 2002 and show remarkable results. The findings introduce OC as part of the production function, and are summarized as follows (Lev and Radhakrishnan 2004):

1. Organization capital by itself explains a quarter (25 percent) of the cross-sectional variation in the difference between market and book values of equity. This suggests that organization capital is strongly related to the firm's capacity to generate growth. Accordingly, high market-to-book value companies are intangible-intensive, i.e., rich in organization capital.

2. The contribution of organization capital in a given year to the present value of *future* unusual earnings lasts for about two to three years for high market-to-book value companies and up to one year for low market-to-book value companies. This indicates that organization

capital captures a major component of the firm's intangible assets or growth potential, when reflected by the gap between the market and book values of companies.

3. Whereas the estimated average contribution of organization capital to sales volume is 4 percent for firm-specific and 3 percent for economy-wide organization capital, the contribution to sales *growth* is almost 100 percent, indicating the importance of both types of organization capital as an economic driver.

4. Non-R&D firms sustain their competitive edge through organizational processes and designs, generated by SGA expenditures (organization capital) to compensate the absence of R&D.

Lev's other method for measuring the value of intangible business assets is based on the thinking that economic business performance (net profit earnings) is produced by the three major classes of inputs: physical, financial and intangible. Here, Lev is quite simply dividing the source of (all) economic performance into these three categories. He transforms *intangible-driven earnings* into financial figures by reducing the effects of physical and financial-driven earnings on total earnings. Therefore, the effects of intangibles cannot be measured directly, but they can instead be measured as a residual by reducing the effects of physical and financial-driven earnings from total earnings. As a result, intangible-driven earnings, thus identified, are ratios or percentages of overall earnings. From this line of thought, Lev extracts the following production formula:

(3.2) . . . . Economic Performance = α(Physical Assets) + β(Financial Assets) + δ(Intangible Assets)

α, β and δ represent the contributions of a unit of asset to the enterprise performance.

Lev's two models are obviously related, although the latter takes a narrower perspective than the former one because it is exclusively focused on net profits. One critical advantage of Lev's organization model (3.1.1.–3.1.2.) over the general production function is that it allows a more accurate determination of the impacts of staff and R&D investment. Also, and importantly, IC is not included in Lev's economic performance model in Equation 3.2. as a given variable, but it is extracted from the following equation:

IDE = EP – α(Physical Assets) – β(Financial Assets)

Where:

IDE = Intangible-Driven Earnings

EP = Economic Performance = Net Profit

All the variables on the right side are known entities and can be derived from balance sheet figures (α and β empirically through regression analysis). *Ultimately, the assessment of the firm's IC is obtained via the capitalization of IDE.*

Empirical results have shown that companies within the same industry that have the greatest share of intangible-driven earnings also perform better in the long term, from five to twelve years (Gu and Lev 2002). Several scholars have applied Lev's economic performance model to national stock markets (e.g., Colwell et al. 2001 and 2007), and this work has consistently confirmed Lev's main results.

This is noteworthy for two reasons. First, Lev is the first author to have reliably shown the influence of intangibles on future earnings, and second, the same dependency between intangible-driven earnings and economic performance has been verified by other researchers as well. Furthermore, even though intangibles remain a black box in Lev's model, five drivers among intangible-driven earnings have been identified in R&D, advertising (brand enhancement), capital expenditure (intangibles embedded in physical assets management), information technology and technology acquisitions (Lev 2001, 10).

5. ASSESSMENT OF LEV'S METHODS

Lev's approach has been analyzed, developed and applied by several researchers in recent years (e.g., Miyagawa and Kim 2008; Eisfeldt and Papanikolaou 2009; and Piekkola 2010a, 2010b). Miyagawa and Eisfeldt have rather straightforward applications of Lev's OC model, whereas Piekkola incorporates the concepts of capitalization and follows the principles suggested by Corrado and colleagues in their Corrado-Hulten-Sichel (CHS) model (Corrado et al. 2006).

Most of these and other similar studies have confirmed the findings by Lev, further highlighting the importance of OC as an economic driver and significantly establishing sales, general and administrative expenses (SGA), as a good enough proxy for OC. In his latest study entitled "Is doing good good for you? How corporate charitable contributions enhance revenue growth" (Lev et al. 2010), Lev still uses SGA as a proxy for OC. In a recent paper focusing on the relation between (sales) volatility and OC, Che concludes that "imperfect as it is, SG&A expenditure is arguably the best approximate for OC investment by far, considering data availability and accuracy" (Che 2009, 12).

Lev's organization based model (see Equation 3.1.1.) is, in fact, a direct Solow model augmented with R&D investments (RND) and OC. It can easily be rewritten in the Solowian mode as follows:

(3.1.1b.) ... $Y = A\ K^{\beta_1}\ L^{\beta_2}\ (RND)^{\beta_3}\varepsilon$
with
$Y = SALE$, $K = PPE$, $L = EMP$ and
$\log(A) = b_0 + b_{0s} \log(SGA)$; SGA = sales, general and administrative expenses.

In fact, rewritten in this way, the model can be described as a Solow model augmented with three distinct parts: RND, internal OC [b0s log(SGA)] and external OC (b0). Interpreted this way, the model can be used to assess R&D investments and the effects of OC on productivity in an augmented Solow model.

However, the TFP component has now vanished, or—to be more precise—it is embedded in the external OC component b_0^5 and the error component ε. Lev concludes:

> It is possible to estimate organization capital from the residual of expression (3.1.1.), either by extracting the systematic component of ε, or by inserting firm-specific dummy variables in (3.1.1.). This approach was followed in the early attempts to estimate "total factor productivity" (TFP) in macroeconomic growth models (Solow 1957). The downside of estimating TFP, or our firm-specific organization capital, from the residual of a growth model is that a residual estimate is essentially a black box, reflecting random shock and various omitted variables along with organization capital, or TFP. (Lev 2004, 8)

Lev's economic performance model in Equation 3.2 is, in essence, a production function, albeit one that is rather heuristic by nature. His approach focuses on measuring the real *effects of active intangibles,* rather than the intangibles themselves. This is, in fact, at once the strength and the weakness of his model. In one sense, it is indisputable that the sources of economic performance are physical (e.g., plants, properties and equipment), financial (e.g., cash, stocks or financial instruments) or intangible (e.g., brands, processes and human resources). On the other hand, the weakness of Lev's model is that it lacks detailed indicators of intangibles. The very concept of intangibles therefore remains unexplained and hidden, and consequently, we do not really know what it is that is measured. Lev (2001, 2) defines intangibles as "a source of future benefits that doesn't have a physical embodiment", but in practice, it is difficult to know what kind of elements he is referring to. In any case, Lev's concept of intangibles is more extensive than the established IC taxonomy of three factors (human, structural and relational capital), and it also includes such elements as strategic position and market demand that are not included in the categories of physical or financial-driven earnings.

Another problematic aspect of Lev's thinking lies in his assumption that *excess* profit—more than ordinary profit—originates in intangibles only. The same assumption is made in Stewart's calculated intangible value (CIV). In an earlier paper (Aho, Ståhle and Ståhle 2011), we have argued that this line of thinking only yields performance indices that cannot be linked back to intangibles. In fact, it is impossible to know whether these results actually describe intangibles or general performance conditions.

6. CONCLUSIONS

Our aim in this chapter has been to assess the validity and accuracy of Baruch Lev's methods in measuring IC. We wanted to find out what these methods tell us about IC and value generation, and whether they can shed light on aspects of business performance that cannot be directly inferred from economic indicators.

We discovered that Lev's methods offer a genuine approach to IC measurement. There is no question that Lev's two models contribute to our understanding of both the significance and dynamics of intangibles as drivers of economic performance. A major advantage of Lev's models is their inherent simplicity and general applicability. Both models work from the premise that 1) productivity is driven by labor as well as by intangible and physical assets, and 2) that all the key variables can be identified in the company's financial statements.

An important strength of Lev's organization model is that it exposes both the effects of OC on TFP and the effects of IC on production. Both models support the notion that production functions and augmented Solow models can successfully be used by applying IC entities. In this sense, *both models are ground-breaking in that they upgrade IC measures from mere IC indicators to active variables in a production function.*

Furthermore, since the variable of OC is divided into two parts, general and firm-specific, this represents a significant departure from the focus on firms' *internal IC drivers* to acknowledging the importance of *external IC drivers*. This recognition may prove extremely useful in cross-country and cross-regional comparisons. To that extent, Lev has taken a noteworthy step toward a greater understanding of the drivers of the economy.

However, Lev's models also involve some serious shortcomings:

1. The models fail to establish which variables are connected to different drivers and how. The general and firm-specific parameters remain numeric variables and do not allow us to assess the real impacts of identifiable drivers on business performance. This is a clear drawback in terms of applicability, because the results tend to remain rather general and it is difficult to grasp the true meaning of the measurements or to draw any concrete conclusions.
2. Some of Lev's conceptual definitions lack in theoretical rigor and are more heuristic. For example, 1) SGA expenses are used as a proxy for OC; b) a certain level of education, the prevailing legal and institutional setting are used as proxies for social capital; and 3) coded knowledge, production blueprints, business processes and procedures, marketing networks and channels are used as proxies for firm-specific OC.
3. Lev's economic performance model fails to explain why IC impacts net profits only, and not negative or zero profits (or is calculated and estimated using positive net profits only).[6]

Even though Lev makes important progress by breaking down TFP into its constituent parts, he unfortunately fails to link those constituents with different economic and IC drivers. For useful applications, it would be important to be able to link IC indicators with capital and labor entities in a general production function, that is, an augmented Solow model. This applies most particularly to the general part of OC, which would need to be firmly anchored in explicit IC measures. In this respect, the model has some serious shortcomings.

Even though Lev's models, as we have pointed out, mark an important step forward and in the right direction, they still fail to specify what the intangible economic drivers are. The models can have practical value only if they can accurately identify and measure the drivers and if they can establish the true effects on production. One of the challenges for further research, therefore, is to unravel the IC concepts so that they can be both satisfactorily measured and further explained by the IC entities incorporated into the production function. In other words, an input-output analysis of investments in drivers and their contribution to productivity can only be conducted if the drivers are specific and we have a clear and detailed understanding of the economic drivers.

NOTES

1. One of the most commonly used classifications is the breaking down of intellectual capital into three main elements: human capital, structural capital and relational capital.
2. Corrado later highlights the additional need for *accurate and expanded capitalization* of intangibles over time, where *all* expenditures in intangibles are treated as investments, and following the production function and flow account for each of three different sectors: consumption, investments and intangibles (Corrado et al., 2006; 6–7).
3. A general linear production function has the form $Y = a + bX(1) + cX(2) + \ldots$ where a, b, c . . . determines the contributions of $X(1)$, $X(2)$ . . . to production Y.
4. The production function is somewhat simplified, with the time variable (t) and company identifier (i) omitted for the sake of clarity.
5. Following the logarithms for $A'=eb0$
6. The same assumption is made by Stewart in the CIV model (see Aho, Ståhle and Ståhle 2011).

REFERENCES

Aho, S., Ståhle, S. & Ståhle, P. 2011. "Critical analyses of the calculated intangible value (CIV) method". *Measuring Business Excellence*, 4, 27–35.

Barney, J.B. 1991. "Is the resource-based view a useful perspective for strategic management research? Yes". *The Academy of Management Review*, 26 (1), 41–56.

Bounfour. A. 1998. *Intangible Investments,* Single Market Review Series, Kogan Page, London, and Office for Official Publications of the European Communities, Luxembourg.

Bounfour, A. 2003. "The IC-dVal approach". *Journal of Intellectual Capital,* 4 (3), 393–413.

Buckley, P.J. and Casson, M.J. 1976. "Analyzing foreign market entry strategies: Extending the internationalization approach". *Journal of International Business Studies,* 29 (3), 539–561.

Canibano, L., Sanchez, M.P., Garcia-Ayuso, M. and Dominguez, C.C. 1998. "Guidelines for managing and reporting on intangibles (intellectual capital report)", EU MERITUM Project. Top of Form.

Caves, E.R. 1996. *Multinational Enterprise and Economic Analysis.* New York: Cambridge University Press.

Che, N.X. 2009. *The Great Dissolution: Organization Capital and Diverging Volatility Puzzle.* Georgetown University. Available at: http://mpra.ub.uni-muenchen.de/13701/1/The_Great_Dissolution_Organization_Capital_and_Diverging_Volatility_Puzzle.pdf (08.03.2013).

Cobb, C.W. and Douglas, P.H. 1928. "A theory of production". *American Economic Review,* 18 (Supplement), 139–165.

Colwell, D., Liu, Y. and Sim, A.B. 2001, 2007. *The Effect of Intangible Assets on Jumps in Stock Returns.* School of Banking and Finance, The University of New South Wales Sydney, NSW 2052 Australia. Available at http://www.fmpm.ch/docs/10th/papers_2007_web/C2a.pdf (08.03.2013).

Corrado, C., Hulten, C. and Sichel, D. 2005. "Measuring capital and technology: An expanded framework." In *Measuring Capital in the New Economy, Studies in Income and Wealth,* C. Corrado, J. Haltiwanger & D. Sichel (Eds.), Vol. 65, Chicago: The University of Chicago Press.

Corrado C, Hulten C and Sichel D. 2006. "Intangible capital and economic growth", *Finance and Economics Discussion Series No. 24.* Washington D.C.: The Divisions of Research & Statistics and Monetary Affairs, Federal Reserve Board.

Corrado, C, Hulten, C. and Sichel, D. 2009. "Intangible capital and U.S. economic growth", *Review of Income and Wealth,* 55, 661–685.

Edvinsson, L. and Malone, M. 1997. *Intellectual Capital: Realising Your Company's True Value by Finding Its Hidden Brainpower.* New York: Harper Collins.

Eisfeldt, A.L. and Papanikolaou, D. 2009. *Organization Capital and the Cross-Section of Expected Returns.* Available at SSRN: http://ssrn.com/abstract=1359320 (08.03.2013).

Godfrey, P.C., Merrill, C.B. and Hansen, J.M. 2009. "The relationship between corporate responsibility and shareholder value: An empirical test of the risk management hypothesis", *Strategic Management Journal,* 30, 425–445.

Gu, F. and Lev, B. 2002. "Intangible assets: Measurement, drivers, usefulness", Working paper, Stern School of Business, New York University.

Grant, R.M. 1996. "Toward a knowledge-based theory of the firm." *Strategic Management Journal.* 17 (Winter, Special Issue), 109–122.

Hall, R.E. 2000. "E-capital: The link between the stock market and the labor market in the 1990s", *Brookings Papers on Economic Activity,* 2, 73–102.

Hymer, S. 1976. *The International Operations of National Firms.* Cambridge, MA: MIT Press.

Kogut, B. and Zander, U. 1992. "Knowledge of the firm, combinative capabilities and the replication of technology", *Organization Science,* 3, 383–397.

Lev, B. 2001. *Intangibles: Management, Measurement and Reporting.* Washington, D.C.: The Brookings Institution.

Lev, B. and Radhakrishnan, S. 2003. "The measurement of firm-specific organization capital", National Bureau of Economic Research (NBER), Working Paper No. 9581. Available at: http://www.nber.org/papers/w9581 (08.03.2013).

Lev, B. and Radhakrishnan, S. 2004. *The Valuation of Organization Capital.* New York: New York University, Stern School of Business.

Lev, B. and Radhakrishnan, S. 2005. "The valuation of organizational capital". In Corrado, C., Haltiwanger, J. & Sichel, D. (Eds.), *Measuring Capital in the New Economy.* National Bureau of Economic Research, Studies in Income and Wealth, Chicago and London: The University of Chicago Press, 65, 73–110.

Lev, B., Petrovits, C. and Radhakrishnan, S. 2010. "Is doing good good for you? How corporate charitable contributions enhance revenue growth", *Strategic Management Journal*, 31, 182–200.

Miyagawa, T. and Kim, Y. 2008. "Measuring organization capital in Japan—an empirical assessment using firm-level data", JCER discussion paper No.112. Japan Center for Economic Research.

Morck, R. and Yeong, B. 1991. "Why investors value multinationality," *Journal of Business*, 64 (2), 165–187.

Morck, R. and Yeong, B. 1992. "Internalization: An event study method", *Journal of International Economics,* 33, 41–56.

Mouritsen, J., Bukh, P. and Larsen. H. 2001. *Guideline for Intellectual Capital Statements: A Key to the Knowledge Management,* Agency for Trade and Development, Copenhagen. Available at: www.efs.dk/icaacounts (08.03.2013).

Nakamura, L. 1999. "Intangibles: What put the new in the New Economy", *Federal Reserve of Philadelphia Business Review,* July/August, 3–16.

Nakamura, L. 2001. "What is the U.S. gross investment in intangibles? (At least) one trillion dollars a year!" Federal Reserve of Philadelphia Working Paper 01–15. Available at: http://www.philadelphiafed.org/research-and-data/publications/working-papers/2001/wp01-15.pdf (08.03.2013).

Peteraf, M.A. 1993. "The cornerstones of competitive advantage: A resource-based view", *Strategic Management Journal*, 14 (3) 179–191.

Piekkola, H. 2010a. "Intangibles: Can they explain the unexplained?" INNO-DRIVE Working Paper No 2. Available at: http://innodrive.org/publications. php (08.03.2013).

Piekkola, H. 2010b. *Making the Difference: The Organization Capital.* University of Vaasa, Department of Economics. Available at: http://www.ceriba.org.uk/pub/CoInvest/COINVESTCostevent/PiekkolaOrgCapital2009_02_05-APA_5th-1.pdf (08.03.2013).

Robinson, G. and Kleiner, B. 1996. "How to measure an organisation's intellectual capital", *Managerial Auditing Journal* 11, 8.

Roos, J., Roos, G., Edvinsson, L. & Dragonetti, N.C. 1998. *Intellectual Capital: Navigating in the New Business Landscape.* New York: New York University Press.

Stewart, T.A. 1997. *Intellectual Capital: The New Wealth of Organizations.* New York: Doubleday.

Solow R. 1957. "Technical change and the aggregate production function", *The Review of Economics and Statistics,* 39 (3), 312–320.

Sullivan, P. 1998. *Profiting from Intellectual Capital: Extracting Value from Innovation.* New York: John Wiley and Sons.

Sveiby, K.E. 1997. *The New Organizational Wealth: Managing & Measuring Knowledge-Based Assets.* San Francisco: Berrett-Koehler Publishers.

Teece, D.J., Pisano, G. and Shuen A. 1997. "Dynamic capabilities and strategic management", *Strategic Management Journal*, 18 (7), 509–533.

Wang, H.C., He, J. and Mahoney, J.T. 2009. "Firm-specific knowledge resources and competitive advantage: The roles of economic- and relationship-based employee governance mechanisms", *Strategic Management Journal*, 30, 1265–1285.
Wernerfelt, B. 1984. "A resource-based view of the firm", *Strategic Management Journal*, 5 (April-June), 171–180.

4 Intellectual Capital Disclosure and Market Valuation

Abdifatah Ahmed Haji and Nazli Anum Mohd Ghazali

1. INTRODUCTION

Intellectual capital (IC) has grown as a central and strategic resource, both at the national (Lin and Edvinsson 2010; Seleim and Bontis 2013) and organizational level (Wang 2008; Zéghal and Maaloul 2010; Edvinsson 2013; Mention and Bontis 2013). For instance, in the wake of the recent global financial turmoil, countries with a higher amount of national IC recorded quicker recovery from the recent financial meltdown (Lin et al. 2013). At the organizational level, it had been preliminarily suggested that mobilizing IC resources could have mitigated the extent of the financial turmoil, with IC having "the potential to be the deciding factor in surviving difficult market conditions" (Henry 2013, 98). Evidently, the share price of a firm is largely determined by its IC resources. For instance, Edvinsson (2013) in his reflections from 21 years of IC practice and theory, demonstrates how Apple, a firm of huge IC resources and few physical assets, became the most valuable company in human history, with a market value of more than $U.S. 600 billion in August 2012. In the knowledge-based economy, there are a plethora of similar examples, such as Nokia, Google, Samsung and many more, that create value principally from intangible resources.

Despite the significance and strategic importance of IC resources in an organizational setting (Ghosh and Wu 2007; Mention and Bontis 2013), it is known that it is difficult to account and manage IC resources. For example, current accounting standards do not adequately address accounting for intangibles, and thus IC remains largely unaccounted for and unreported in the financial reports of a firm. However, IC is reported in an unsystematic format through narratives in a bid to complement the deficiencies associated with the financial reports. For instance, an investor of Apple or a similar firm will not expect a significant amount of physical assets in its statement of financial position; but rather, such an investor could be attracted to narratives of IC through advances in technology, potential introduction of new innovative brands, secured contracts with key business partners and human capital skills in the other sections of the annual report. Release of narrative

IC information such as this are to a firm in "the knowledge economy" what land and equipment were to a firm in "the old economy".

To this end, established, capital market–based research had already indicated the importance of releasing IC information to a firm's market value (Abdolmohammadi 2005; Orens et al. 2009; Vafaei et al. 2011; Anam et al. 2011; Gamerschlag 2013), with investors and financial analysts using such information to complement weakness associated with the traditional financial reporting (Petty et al. 2008; Arvidsson 2011; Holland et al. 2012). A review of this chain of research suggests that the overall amount, as well as subcomponents of IC information (e.g., human capital development and brands), have a significant positive impact on market value and is useful to market participants (Abhayawansa and Guthrie 2010). However, the extant IC literature does not examine how the market reacts to IC information during a financial crisis. We argue that narratives of IC information could be useful to address a crisis situation to ease and restore investors' confidence during the economic uncertainty, consequently resulting in a favorable impact on a firm's market value. Given that IC information is used to explain the widening gap between book and market values of a firm (Whiting and Miller 2008), such information could provide the necessary leeway for companies to address the recent financial meltdown.

Existing traditional theories provide competing predictions as to the potential role of narrative IC information in firm value during an unstable economy. Proprietary costs theory suggests firms would withhold information concerning new and innovative brands, strategic partnerships, human capital capacity building and technologically advanced internal systems to protect their competitive edge and avoid other firms mimicking a firm's IC. On the other hand, signaling theory predicts firms would release additional information to the market to avoid misevaluation and attract more investors. While the proprietary costs theory suggests firms tend to avoid any potential costs with increased disclosure, the signaling theory focuses on the potential benefits from increased disclosures. During an economic crisis, it is unknown which theoretical prediction prevails, and this is our first motivation to undertake this study.

Our study intends to investigate how the market reacts to release of narrative IC information in light of the recent financial crisis. In doing so, contrary to most prior studies, we examine the effects of prior and current-year IC information on the market capitalization, controlling for governance attributes, ownership structure patterns and firm-specific characteristics. To monitor the way the stock market reacts to releases of IC information, we follow the firms' release of IC information to the market over time and benchmark the corresponding market capitalization of the selected firms. For a number of reasons, but mainly due to their huge IC resources and market visibility, we investigate top listed companies in terms of market capitalization to evaluate the market reactions to releases of IC information. Large companies also have more analysts following the yearly corporate reports.

The empirical evidence is drawn from Malaysia, one of the most interesting and growing economies in Asia, as evidenced by continuous corporate governance development and quick economic resilience from recurring financial crises. Malaysia set its sights to become a developed nation by the year 2020, and the vision is seemingly strategized to be accomplished by transforming the economy into a knowledge-based one. Similar to several European and other Asian countries such as Japan, Hong Kong and China (Edvinsson 2013), and in line with its 2020 vision, Malaysia developed an IC project in Multimedia Super Corridor (MSC) for managing IC (Kamaluddin and Abdul Rahman 2007). Consequently, at the organizational level, huge investments in IC and a growing trend of intangible assets are observable in the Malaysian market (Salamudin et al. 2010; Kweh et al. 2013) with the government en route to its 2020 vision, offering significant financial backing for IC development to small, medium enterprises (SMEs), as well as large corporations, through government linked enterprises (Tan et al. 2009). The growing IC resources in the market have been reflected through IC disclosures in the corporate landscape, with recent studies showing an increasing trend of IC-related disclosures of Malaysian-listed companies (Ahmed Haji and Mohd Ghazali 2012). However, it is unknown how the market values react to release of IC information, particularly during economic uncertainty.

Our findings show that release of both previous and current-year IC information has a significant positive impact on the market capitalization of a firm. In particular, the market most significantly reacts to prior-year IC information. In terms of IC subcomponents, the market reacts the most to human capital information and to a lesser extent to external capital information. The results are robust to controls for governance attributes, ownership structure elements, firm-specific characteristics and different IC information measures. The positive role of IC information is parallel to a firm's profitability and size, with the results indicating that the market reacts negatively to highly leveraged firms during the financial meltdown. Overall, our findings support the notion that narratives of IC information could be useful to address a turbulent economic situation in the stock market.

The results of this study provide several interesting theoretical as well as policy implications. First, our results provide support to the signaling theory's conjecture, as opposed to the proprietary costs theory, that companies would benefit from an increased amount of disclosures to the market, in this case, during difficult market conditions. Second, our findings suggest that the stock market fully reacts to IC information, particularly human capital information. This finding is in partial support of the observations made by Edmans (2011), who documented that the stock market reacts to intangibles conditionally, that is, when the intangibles subsequently manifest the related tangible. However, he found that the stock market fully appreciates human capital information. Third, this study presents an alternative method to examine the value-relevance of IC information. Most prior studies assess the impact of current-year IC information against the same-year market value (Orens et al. 2009; Vafaei et al. 2011; Anam et al. 2011). In our case, and in similar to the study by Dumay and Tull (2007) in Australia, we argue that the market reactions to IC information can only be noticed after the information is released;

thus, the effects of such information on market value can be captured in a subsequent year's market capitalization. In pursuing this hypothetical scenario, we assessed the impact of both current-year and prior-year IC information on the market value of a firm and show that the impact is stronger in the prior year's IC information. Finally, our study circles the market reactions of IC information in the context of an unstable economy, particularly in the context of an emerging economy where the creation of IC is significantly growing, yet is not as systematic as in other parts of the world such as European countries.

The remainder of the paper is structured as follows. The next section reviews prior literature and draws on the usefulness of IC information to the capital markets. It also presents the research hypotheses. The ensuing section details the research methods and data collection procedures. This is then followed by presentation of the research findings, and conclusions are provided in the last section.

2.   INTELLECTUAL CAPITAL INFORMATION AND THE CAPITAL MARKET

The recent global financial meltdown, as can be seen from the annual report extractions later, has undoubtedly shaped and changed the way many companies report information to relevant stakeholders, particularly voluntary information, including IC narratives to address the surrounding economic uncertainties:

> Ranked 8th out of Malaysia's Top 10 Most Valuable Brands 2008, with a brand value of RM2.0 billion. The ranking was done by Brand Finance, an independent brand valuation advisory firm, based on publicly available information. (Extraction from Annual Report)

> In facing these challenges, it is imperative that the Company continues to be innovative and undertake changes to ensure that it remains relevant and ahead of competitors. Customers' service will be continuously improved and higher quality products meeting the needs of consumers will be regularly introduced. The quest for operational excellence will remain unabated. Human capital development will continue to be the focus. Various community programs will be introduced. (Extraction from Annual Report)

Although disclosures do not come without cost, companies may derive economic benefits from a well-executed disclosure policy pertaining to IC information (Williams 2001). IC information, for instance, enables firms to avoid misevaluation and allows stakeholders to better evaluate a firm's capabilities, consequently leading a firm's cost of equity to decline (Williams 2001; Marr 2003). As a result, companies are under pressure to report their hidden IC capabilities to gain competitive advantage (Edvinsson and Malone 1997; Marr 2003). Subsequent research reveals that market participants, such as financial analysts, fund managers and investors, value IC information (Petty et al. 2008; Arvidsson, 2011; Holland et al. 2012; Abhayawansa and Guthrie 2012). These studies identify that market participants use IC information for two major reasons. First, IC information is used to balance the incompleteness of the traditional financial statements (Thomas 2003; Arvidsson 2011). Second, IC narratives are used to estimate earnings and firm valuation (Holland et al. 2012). Invariably, firms use IC information to explain the differences between the book value and market capitalization (Whiting and Miller 2008).

In terms of the relevance of IC information to a firm's share price, although studies suggest a perceived association between IC information and share price, this is difficult to examine given the complexity of IC elements (Mouritsen 2003). A chain of recent empirical studies provide an apparent link between a firm's share price and IC disclosures (Abdolmohammadi 2005; Dumay and Tull 2007; Orens et al. 2009; Vafaei et al. 2011; Anam et al. 2011; Abeysekera 2011; Uyar and Kiliç 2012; Gamerschlag 2013). These studies identify a significant positive association between IC disclosures and market value of a firm in several countries. As a result, there has been an increasing amount of companies reporting IC elements in the corporate information channels internationally, with an increasing trend of IC disclosures (Williams 2001; Abdolmohammadi 2005; Sihotang and Winata 2008; Ahmed Haji and Mohd Ghazali 2012).

We identify two research gaps in the existing IC literature pertaining to the usefulness of IC information in relation to firm valuation. First, the existing literature has drawn evidence from a stable economy. It is therefore unknown how the market values and reacts to IC information during a financial meltdown. Despite the reported positive role of IC information in firm valuation, companies still face two critical dilemmas as to whether or not their hidden capabilities of IC should be released to the market, and this could be particularly the case during a financial crisis. The first scenario, as posited by the signaling theory, relates to the benefits associated with a higher amount of IC disclosures, such as reduction in cost of equity, increased market capitalization and more analysts following the company. Signaling theory assumes that the capital markets interpret more disclosure as "good news" and less disclosure as "bad news" (Abhayawansa and Abeysekera 2009). Henry (2013) observed that IC narratives can be crucial during difficult market conditions such as the recent economic recession. Hence, given the surrounding economic uncertainty, companies would endeavor to release an increased amount of disclosures to avoid misevaluation and incorrect interpretation by the market participants. Therefore, this theoretical stance suggests that during a financial downturn, companies would adopt a different IC disclosure strategy, which tends to increase information tremendously in an endeavor to avoid misevaluation.

The second contrasting theoretical prediction belongs to the proprietary costs theory. This theory propounds that the costs associated with an increased amount of IC disclosures include preparation costs, competitive disadvantage and possible litigation costs. Of particular relevance to

IC information is the potential competitive disadvantage associated with increased IC disclosures pertaining to *inter alia* new brands, innovative products, internal systems and human capital development programs. Companies may not be willing to release information that could spur or aid their competitors. Williams (2001), who found an inverse relationship between a firm's IC performance and disclosure level, suggests that companies are aware of the competitive disadvantage associated with an increased amount of IC disclosures, particularly when a certain threshold of IC level is reached. However, it is unknown which strategy companies would choose when they have to make a choice. This study intends to examine these two competing theories in light of the recent global financial crisis.

Our second motivation to undertake this study concerns a methodological concern associated with the majority of the existing literature that examines the link between IC information and market value of a firm. The extant literature examines the impact of the current-year IC information on the same-year market value. Dumay and Tull (2007) question the issue of IC information immediacy because the effects of IC information can only be realized once the information is released, thus logically having an effect on a subsequent year's market valuation. As a result, in a departure from the existing literature, we examine the effects of last-year as well as current-year IC information on a firm's market value. Hence, we develop the following research hypotheses to examine the market reactions to IC information during the recent economic crisis:

> **H1a:** Previous year's overall IC disclosure is positively related to this year's market capitalization.
> **H1b:** Previous year's external capital disclosure is positively related to this year's market capitalization.
> **H1c:** Previous year's internal capital disclosure is positively related to this year's market capitalization.
> **H1d:** Previous year's human capital disclosure is positively related to this year's market capitalization.
> **H2a:** Current year's overall IC disclosure is positively related to the same year's market capitalization.
> **H2b:** Current year's external capital disclosure is positively related to the same year's market capitalization.
> **H2c:** Current year's internal capital disclosure is positively related to the same year's market capitalization.
> **H2d:** Current year's human capital disclosure is positively related to the same year's market capitalization.

3. RESEARCH METHOD

Data Collection and Sample

The data for this study were collated from top companies listed on Bursa Malaysia based on their market capitalization for the years 2008, 2009 and

2010. The data were mainly retrieved from annual reports through individual corporate web sites. Additional data in the form of market capitalization were obtained from Bloomberg Database. The years under investigation correspond to a period in which the Malaysian business environment weathered significant incidents, including policy changes, as well as the recent global financial meltdown. The policy changes, which came in the form of a corporate governance amendment in 2007, is in line with ongoing corporate governance development[1] in Malaysia as part of a wider national policy en route to the 2020 vision of a developed nation. Corporate governance development is suggested to have a major role in IC improvement (Keenan and Aggestam 2001; Burgman and Roos 2007; Cerbioni and Parbonetti 2007; Li et al. 2008), particularly in the emerging economies (Abeysekera 2010; Ahmed Haji and Sanni 2012; Abdul Rashid et al. 2012; Ahmed Haji and Mohd Ghazali 2013). In addition, the period corresponds to the recent global financial turmoil in which Malaysia was not spared. These significant incidents are expected to change the disclosure policy of listed companies, in particular, information concerning IC.

Large companies were the target of this study for several reasons. First, larger companies possess a significant amount of IC resources (Guthrie and Petty 2000). With this amount of IC assets, large companies would want to release IC information to explain the widening gap between book value and a firm's market capitalization. Such information can also be used to ease and restore investors' confidence given the surrounding economic uncertainty. Second, the ownership structure in the Malaysian market is highly concentrated, and much of the ownership is in the hands of family businesses, government-linked institutions and other institutional shareholding. Larger companies are closely monitored by the substantial shareholders; thus, release of IC information would make more meaningful sense to institutional investors. Third, top companies are highly visible in the market and have more analysts following their annual report announcements. As such, larger companies are aware of the importance of IC narratives and may use disclosure of IC information to deflect additional scrutiny.

The initial sample consisted of the largest sixty companies across seven sectors (construction, finance, consumer products, industrial products, plantation, property, and trading and services). Due to the amount of missing data as a result of the longitudinal coverage of the study, the final sample comprises fifty-one companies, producing 153 firm-year observations over the three-year period (51 × 3 = 153 observations).

Variables Measurement

Dependent Variable: Market Value

The dependent variable of this study is the market capitalization of the firms for the years 2008–2010, computed as the number of outstanding shares multiplied by the share price. Rather than computing manually, the market capitalization values were obtained from the Bloomberg Database. Due to variations in the market capitalization of the firms, the natural logarithm of market capitalization was used as the dependent variable, in line with several prior studies (e.g., Abdolmohammadi 2005; Anam et al. 2011).

Independent Variables: IC Disclosures

The overall amount and subcomponents of IC disclosures are the main independent variables of this study. This study relies on a comprehensive IC disclosure index constructed by Ahmed Haji and Mohd Ghazali (2012) to measure both the extent and quality of IC disclosures. The checklist was tested in the Malaysian context and was derived from multiple sources, including award-winning Malaysian corporate annual reports as well as the extant IC literature. The index also contains items of the three IC subcomponents of internal, external and human capital, with an overall tally of forty IC items. Of the forty items, nine are internal capital elements, seventeen items represent external capital and the remaining fourteen are human capital elements. Appendix I provides a detailed list of the IC disclosure index.

Control Variables

To address the fact that other variables may have an impact on a firm's market capitalization, we control a number of variables, including corporate governance attributes, ownership structure patterns and firm-specific characteristics.

Corporate Governance Attributes

We include several corporate governance attributes emphasized by the revised Malaysia Code of Corporate Governance (2007), namely board size, independent nonexecutive directors, audit committee financial expertise, audit committee size and board meetings. We argue that an effective corporate governance structure plays a key role in enhancing the market capitalization of a firm by identifying and executing key strategic investment opportunities. The market will in turn respond favorably to these strategic choices made by the governing board. The corporate governance code in Malaysia was recently revised to restructure and re-emphasize the role of corporate governance bodies in the value creation process of a firm. Studies in Malaysia have already shown an improved governance atmosphere following the revised code of corporate governance toward IC disclosure practices (Ahmed Haji and Mohd Ghazali 2013).

Ownership Structure Patterns

The ownership structure in Malaysia is highly concentrated, and much of the ownership is in the hands of managing directors and institutions, usually government-affiliated institutions. Therefore, institutional shareholding and director ownership are included in the regression models to reduce any possible impact of these variables on the interplay between IC disclosures and market value of a firm.

Firm-Specific Characteristics

In line with the mainstream literature, we control the effects of firm size, profitability and leverage. Larger and more profitable companies are able to attract more investors through their visibility, dividend payout and brand. Hence, large and profitable companies tend to have higher market capitalization. On the other hand, highly leveraged companies struggle to attract investors due to debt covenants to pay interest costs and as a result will likely have lower market capitalization (Williams 2000).

Data Analysis Techniques

Several data analysis techniques were performed. Descriptive statistics were first computed to show the mean scores as well as the overall distribution of the data. Second, to evaluate the trend of IC information over time, the parametric approach of "one-way repeated measures analysis of variance (ANOVA)", as well as the alternative nonparametric technique of the Friedman test, were computed. Third, the correlation analyses (not tabulated due to space limitation) were undertaken to check the existence of multicollinearity among the independent variables, the results of which have shown that there are no multicollinearity problems among the independent variables included in the study, as the highest correlation coefficient among the independent variables is below the 0.7 cutoff point.

Finally, panel data regression analyses were employed to examine market reactions to IC disclosure in light of the recent financial crisis. Panel data analyses have more advantages over cross-sectional data analysis, including the ability to control heterogeneity problems (Moulton 1987) and can mitigate the yearly differences of the pooled data (Wang et al. 2013). A number of preliminary tests were conducted to choose the most appropriate regression model for the data of this study between the two common approaches of the "fixed effects model" and the "random effects model". We have conducted the Hausman test to choose the appropriate approach of panel data. We confirm that the random effects model is the most suitable test for the data of this study. As a result, the following equations are formulated:

$$\text{Model 1:} \quad \text{MCAP}_{it} = \beta_0 + \beta_1 \text{OICD}_{it-1} + \beta_2 \text{BSIZE}_{it-1} + \beta_3 \text{IND}_{it-1} + \beta_4 \text{ACFE}_{it-1}$$
$$\beta_4 \text{ACSIZE}_{it-1} + \beta_5 \text{BMEET}_{it-1} + \beta_6 \text{DOWN}_{it-1}$$
$$+ \beta_7 \text{IOWN}_{it-1} + \beta_8 \text{SIZE}_{it-1} + \beta_9 \text{ROA}_{it-1} + \beta_{10} \text{LEV}_{it-1} + \varepsilon_{it}$$

$$\text{Model 2:} \quad \text{MCAP}_{it} = \beta_0 + \beta_1 \text{OICD} + \beta_2 \text{BSIZE} + \beta_3 \text{IND} + \beta_4 \text{ACFE} + \beta_4 \text{ACSIZE}$$
$$+ \beta_5 \text{BMEET} + \beta_6 \text{DOWN} + \beta_7 \text{IOWN} +$$
$$\beta_8 \text{SIZE} + \beta_9 \text{ROA} + \beta_{10} \text{LEV} + \varepsilon_{it}$$

Table 4.1 Research variables shows operationalization of the variables included in the models.

Acronym	Definition	Type	Operationalization	Source of Data
MCAP	Market Capitalization	Dependent	Market capitalization (natural logarithm of market capitalization)	Bloomberg
OICD	Overall Intellectual Capital Disclosures	Independent	Extent of the OICD is computed as number of items in the checklist disclosed divided by the maximum possible score (i.e., 40). Quality of OICD is calculated as the number of items in the checklist (40) (based on the scale of 0–3) disclosed divided by the maximum possible score (i.e., 40 × 3 = 120).	Annual Reports
INCD	Internal Capital	Independent	Extent of INCD is computed as number of items in this category disclosed divided by the maximum possible score (9). Quality of INCD is computed as the number of items in this category (9) (based on the scale of 0–3) disclosed divided by the maximum possible score (9 items × 3 = 27).	Annual Reports
EXCD	External Capital	Independent	Extent of EXCD is computed as number of items in this category disclosed divided by the maximum possible score (17). Quality of EXCD is computed by the number of items in this category (17) (based on the scale of 0–3) disclosed divided by the maximum possible score (17 items × 3 = 51).	Annual Reports
HCD	Human Capital	Independent	Extent of HCD is computed as the number of items in this category disclosed divided by the maximum possible score (14). Quality of HCD is computed as the number of items in this category (14) (based on the scale of 0–3) disclosed divided by the maximum possible score (14 items × 3 = 42).	Annual Reports

BSIZE	Board Size	Control Variable	Total number of directors on the board	Annual Reports
IND	Board Independence	Control Variable	Proportion of independent directors to total number of directors	Annual Reports
ACFE	Audit Committee Financial Expertise	Control Variable	Proportion of audit committee members with accounting/finance qualification or experience to the total number of audit committee members	Annual Reports
ACSIZE	Audit Committee Size	Control Variable	Number of audit committee members	Annual Reports
BMEET	Board Meetings	Control Variable	Total number of board meetings held during the year	Annual Reports
DOWN	Director Ownership	Control Variable	Percentage of shares held by executive and nonindependent directors including their deemed interests	Annual Reports
IOWN	Institutional Ownership	Control Variable	Percentage of equity shares owned by institutional investors with 5% or more	Annual Reports
SIZE	Company Size	Control Variable	Total assets (log of total assets)	Annual Reports
ROA	Return on Assets	Control variable	Total assets to net income	Annual Reports
LEV	Leverage	Control variable	Total debt to total assets	Annual Reports

4.   RESEARCH FINDINGS

Descriptive Statistics: IC Disclosures over Time

We follow the release of IC information to the market over the crisis period to see the extent, quality, nature and trend of IC information. Table 4.2 presents descriptive statistics for the extent and quality of IC disclosures over the three-year period under investigation. The results show that the mean scores in the extent of IC disclosures increased from 42.25 percent in 2008 to 44.12 percent in 2009 to 46.37 percent in 2010. Similarly, the table shows increases in the average scores in the quality of IC disclosures, from 20.31 percent in 2008 to 21.05 percent in 2009 to 22.12 percent in 2010. In terms of the IC components, the results show that external capital disclosures was the most disclosed category for both the extent and quality of IC information in all three years. The dominance of the external capital disclosure category, attributed to a corporate tendency to enhance external relations, has been widely documented in previous IC research in several countries (e.g., Guthrie and Petty 2000; Goh and Lim 2004; Whiting and Miller 2008). However, the pattern of IC information was highly qualitative and contained large amounts of "good news", perhaps as a way to address the ongoing financial turmoil.

Our investigation extends to examining the trend of IC information to observe whether the increases in the mean scores in the extent and quality of IC disclosures were statistically significant. The results in Table 4.3 reveal that the extent and quality of the overall amount of IC disclosures increased significantly at the 1 percent level (p = 0.009) over the three-period. In terms of the IC disclosure categories, only the human capital disclosures increased significantly at the 1 percent level (p = 0.003) over time, showcasing the increasing importance of human capital programs within the Malaysian market.

Further analyses show that although IC information increased over time, the increase in IC disclosures was only significant from 2008 to 2010 and from 2009 to 2010. Malaysian companies may have released an increased amount of IC disclosures to reflect their IC investments as a form of explaining the increasing gap between market and book values to key stakeholders, thereby avoiding potential misevaluation. Such endeavors could also restore the confidence of investors and other key stakeholders, thereby enhancing their market capitalization, particularly during a period of economic uncertainty.

Panel Regression Analyses: Market Reactions to Previous Year's IC Information

This section presents the market reactions to a prior year's IC information. The results are presented in Tables 4.4 and 4.5. The tables present the market reactions to the *extent* and *quality* of the prior year's IC information, with each of the tables separately incorporating the subcategories of internal, external and human capital information.

Table 4.4 presents the market reactions to the extent of the overall amount and subcategories of IC information in the prior year, robust for

Table 4.2 Descriptive results—Main independent variables (IC disclosure)

IC disclosures over the three-year period

	Year 2008			Year 2009			Year 2010		
	Min	Max	Mean	Min	Max	Mean	Min	Max	Mean
Extent of ICD (%)	5.00	87.50	42.25	15.00	82.50	44.12	15.00	82.50	46.37
Quality of ICD (%)	3.33	50.00	20.31	5.00	45.83	21.05	6.67	43.33	22.12

IC Categories—Extent of ICD

IC Categories	Year 2008		Year 2009		Year 2010	
	Score	%	Score	%	Score	%
Internal Capital	198	23	199	22	208	22
External Capital*	409	47	417	46	421	44
Human Capital	255	30	284	32	317	34
Total	862	100.00	900	100.00	946	100.00

IC Categories—Extent of ICD

IC Categories	Year 2008		Year 2009		Year 2010	
	Score	%	Score	%	Score	%
Internal Capital	259	21	259	20	277	20
External Capital*	630	51	625	49	634	47
Human Capital	354	28	404	31	443	33
Total	1243	100.00	1288	100.00	1354	100.00

* The highest disclosed category

Table 4.3 Trend of IC disclosures over time: One-way repeated measures ANOVA

Extent of ICD Mean (%)			
Dimension	2008	2009	2010	p-value
Overall ICD	42.25	44.12	46.37	0.009***
Internal Capital	43.14	43.35	45.32	0.379
External Capital	47.17	48.10	48.56	0.719
Human Capital	35.71	39.78	44.40	0.003***
Quality ICD Mean (%)			
Overall ICD	20.31	21.05	22.12	0.013**
Internal Capital	18.81	18.81	20.12	0.124
External Capital	24.22	24.03	24.38	0.874
Human Capital	16.53	18.86	20.68	0.006***

** The increase is significant at the 5% level.
*** The increase is significant at the 1% level.

the control variables. The regression models for the extent of IC information produce an explanatory power ranging from 59.6 percent to 57.4 percent, indicating that the set of variables included in the models is able to explain approximately 60 percent of the variance in the respective dependent variables. The results indicate that the extent of the overall amount of IC information in a prior year has a significant positive impact on the share price in the following year at the 1 percent level. Last year's external and human capital information also show a significant positive impact on the subsequent year's market capitalization of a firm, at the 5 percent and 1 percent levels, respectively. However, the stock market does not respond to a prior year's internal capital information. As for the control variables, larger companies and prior year's profitability lead to higher market capitalization on the following year, with both being statistically significant and positive at the 1 percent level in all regression models. On the other hand, last year's leverage has a significant negative implication on the subsequent year's market capitalization at the 1 percent level in all models. The stock market, surprisingly, is not sensitive to governance and ownership structure attributes of the firms, most likely due to the ongoing financial turmoil, which may have relegated the role of governance attributes in the eyes of investors to a peripheral role.

Table 4.5 shows the market reactions to the quality of IC information as well as its subcomponents in the prior year. Similar to the previous models, the explanatory power of the models presented in Table 4.5 range from

Table 4.4 Panel least square—Market reactions to prior year's ICD: Extent

Variables	Overall ICDs (Model 1)		Internal Capital (Model 2)		External Capital (Model 3)		Human Capital (Model 4)	
	Coefficient	Sig	Coefficient	Sig	Coefficient	Sig	Coefficient	Sig
$OIC_{t-1}/INC_{t-1}/EXC_{t-1}/HC_{t-1}$	0.011064	0.0039***	0.002774	0.3171	0.007432	0.0389**	0.007153	0.0028***
$BSIZE_{t-1}$	0.031268	0.3485	0.037239	0.2849	0.04396	0.1823	0.03368	0.3162
IND_{t-1}	0.432888	0.36	0.392073	0.4239	0.522186	0.2783	0.358617	0.4467
$ACEXPERTISE_{t-1}$	0.402844	0.2208	0.469052	0.1668	0.360606	0.2811	0.563459	0.0917*
$ACSIZE_{t-1}$	-0.12506	0.1288	-0.09996	0.2361	-0.12091	0.1457	-0.10864	0.1859
$BMEETINGS_{t-1}$	-0.01326	0.4416	-0.01323	0.4583	-0.01503	0.3879	-0.01217	0.4806
$DIROWN_{t-1}$	0.004254	0.3284	0.002538	0.563	0.003251	0.4363	0.003661	0.4094
$IOWN_{t-1}$	0.002836	0.4035	0.003966	0.2506	0.003695	0.2648	0.002532	0.4659
$SIZE_{t-1}$	0.650256	0.000***	0.689718	0.000***	0.659464	0.000***	0.663782	0.000***
$PROFITABILITY_{t-1}$	3.775233	0.000***	3.926749	0.000***	4.13258	0.000***	3.623502	0.000***
$LEVERAGE_{t-1}$	-1.10125	0.0013***	-0.99548	0.0041***	-1.09399	0.0012	-1.00788	0.0032***
R-squared	0.596		0.574		0.594		0.589	
Adjusted R^2	0.546		0.522		0.545		0.538	
F-statistic	12.051		11.008		11.983		11.712	
Prob. (F-statistic)	0.000		0.000		0.000		0.000	

***Significant at the 1% level   **Significant at the 5% level   *Significant at the 10% level

Table 4.5 Panel least square—Market reactions to prior year's ICD: Quality

Variables	Overall ICDs (Model 1)		Internal Capital (Model 2)		External Capital (Model 3)		Human Capital (Model 4)	
	Coefficient	Sig	Coefficient	Sig	Coefficient	Sig	Coefficient	Sig
$OIC_{t-1}/IINC_{t-1}/EXC_{t-1}/HC$	0.021009	0.0032***	0.00672	0.201	0.011138	0.0726*	0.013477	0.0023***
$BSIZE_{t-1}$	0.035114	0.2871	0.036665	0.289	0.044851	0.1726	0.038055	0.2529
IND_{t-1}	0.38319	0.4148	0.300749	0.5415	0.47111	0.3268	0.425515	0.3634
$ACEXPERTISE_{t-1}$	0.41331	0.2056	0.450429	0.184	0.423748	0.1994	0.536291	0.1052
$ACSIZE_{t-1}$	-0.10444	0.1982	-0.0865	0.305	-0.10813	0.1892	-0.10051	0.2171
$BMEETINGS_{t-1}$	-0.01438	0.4014	-0.01371	0.4401	-0.01377	0.4287	-0.01455	0.395
$DIROWN_{t-1}$	0.003834	0.3704	0.002623	0.5524	0.002686	0.514	0.003332	0.4488
$IOWN_{t-1}$	0.003268	0.3301	0.004273	0.2186	0.003862	0.2407	0.002722	0.43
$SIZE_{t-1}$	0.645511	0.000***	0.682778	0.000***	0.669104	0.000***	0.658292	0.000***
$PROFITABILITY_{t-1}$	3.739475	0.000***	3.81988	0.000***	4.147036	0.000***	3.597361	0.000***
$LEVERAGE_{t-1}$	-1.07804	0.0014***	-0.97294	0.0048***	-1.08518	0.0013***	-0.97589	0.004***
R-squared	0.598		0.572		0.594		0.588	
Adjusted R^2	0.549		0.520		0.544		0.538	
F-statistic	12.169		10.933		11.953		11.689	
Prob. (F-statistic)	0.000		0.000		0.000		0.000	

***Significant at the 1% level   **Significant at the 5% level   *Significant at the 10% level

59.8 percent to 57.2 percent; hence, the models are able to capture a good amount of the variances in the dependent variables. The results largely concur with the previous models that the quality of the overall amount of IC information in a prior year has a significant positive impact on the following year's market capitalization at the 1 percent level. External and human capital information in the prior year remained sensitive to the stock market, producing a significant positive impact at the 10 percent and 1 percent levels, respectively. Again, the prior year's internal capital information does not show a significant impact on the following year's market value.

Consistent with the previous models, firm size and last year's profit margin continue to be significant for the subsequent year's market value, with last year's leverage level similarly producing a contrasting negative impact on the market capitalization of a firm. In the second stream of models, none of the governance and ownership structure attributes shows significant association with the market value of a firm.

Panel Regression Analyses: IC Information and Current-Year Market Value

Having seen the market reactions to a prior year's IC information in terms of market capitalization of a firm, we examine the relationship between current-year IC information and same-year market capitalization to investigate whether IC information immediately influences a firm's share price. The same regression models are repeated here, only replacing the prior year's IC information and its components with the current year's IC information. All control variables (corporate governance, ownership structure and firm characteristics) are also the current year's in this model. The results are presented in Tables 4.6 and 4.7. The regression models produce explanatory powers of approximately 50 percent of the variation in the dependent variables.

Table 4.6 shows the extent of the overall amount of IC information in the current year has a significant positive impact on the same-year market capitalization at the 5 percent level. Only the extent of human capital information in the current year has a significant positive impact on the same-year market capitalization at the 1 percent level. In contrast to the previous models, the extent of external capital disclosures in the current year is no longer significant in determining the same-year market capitalization of a firm. The extent of the current year's internal capital disclosures continues to be insignificant in relation to the market capitalization of a firm, as was the case in the previous models. Firm size and profitability continue to be positive and significant in explaining the current-year share price at the 1 percent level, in all regression models, with leverage having a significant negative impact on the market capitalization at the 1 percent level. Interestingly, and in contrast to previous models, independent directors have a significant positive relationship with the current-year market capitalization at the 1 percent level in all regression models, suggesting that outside directors can only influence the current-year market value of a firm.

Table 4.6 Panel least square—Extent of IC information and current year's market value

Variables	Overall ICDs (Model 1)		Internal Capital (Model 2)		External Capital (Model 3)		Human Capital (Model 4)	
	Coefficient	Sig	Coefficient	Sig	Coefficient	Sig	Coefficient	Sig
OIC/INC/EXC/HC	0.008443	0.0141**	0.003456	0.1469	0.002048	0.4951	0.005737	0.0044***
BSIZE	0.008447	0.7598	0.012452	0.6591	0.020637	0.4522	0.00946	0.7292
IND	1.040191	0.0077***	1.089403	0.0061***	1.1113	0.005***	1.039778	0.007***
ACEXPERTISE	0.024672	0.9237	0.065133	0.8036	0.067885	0.7994	0.135415	0.5966
ACSIZE	-0.09669	0.1414	-0.08326	0.2119	-0.08919	0.1842	-0.08407	0.195
BMEETINGS	0.006495	0.6661	0.004773	0.7552	0.00485	0.7497	0.007278	0.6261
DIROWN	0.003402	0.4245	0.002315	0.5854	0.001803	0.6592	0.003332	0.436
IOWN	0.001872	0.5539	0.002551	0.4236	0.002541	0.4166	0.001824	0.5656
SIZE	0.697418	0.000***	0.728102	0.000***	0.729103	0.000***	0.705244	0.000***
PROFITABILITY	4.07843	0.000***	4.262148	0.000***	4.415446	0.000***	3.942346	0.000***
LEVERAGE	-1.52242	0.000***	-1.44474	0.000***	-1.45082	0.000***	-1.49674	0.000***
R-squared	0.530		0.523		0.526		0.530	
Adjusted R²	0.493		0.486		0.489		0.494	
F-statistic	14.4655		14.06583		14.21801		14.47482	
Prob. (F-statistic)	0.000		0.000		0.000		0.000	

***Significant at the 1% level **Significant at the 5% level *Significant at the 10% level

Table 4.7 Panel least square—Quality of IC information and current year's market value

Variables	Overall ICDs (Model 1)		Internal Capital (Model 2)		External Capital (Model 3)		Human Capital (Model 4)	
	Coefficient	Sig	Coefficient	Sig	Coefficient	Sig	Coefficient	Sig
OIC/INC/EXC/HC	0.013307	0.0458**	0.005845	0.2227	0.002214	0.6881	0.009398	0.0155**
BSIZE	0.013411	0.6264	0.014033	0.616	0.021527	0.4324	0.013361	0.6262
IND	1.048039	0.0076***	1.036006	0.0094***	1.115526	0.0049***	1.102286	0.0046***
ACEXPERTISE	0.035391	0.8913	0.046696	0.8583	0.094413	0.72	0.098371	0.7018
ACSIZE	-0.09155	0.165	-0.07729	0.2445	-0.08515	0.2026	-0.08941	0.1723
BMEETINGS	0.006508	0.667	0.00502	0.7416	0.005019	0.7419	0.006044	0.6879
DIROWN	0.002768	0.5121	0.001863	0.6601	0.001647	0.6861	0.002905	0.4961
IOWN	0.002185	0.489	0.00251	0.432	0.002656	0.3948	0.002039	0.5216
SIZE	0.705319	0.000***	0.728685	0.000***	0.733648	0.000***	0.712297	0.000***
PROFITABILITY	4.120095	0.000***	4.165253	0.000***	4.434046	0.000***	3.994253	0.000***
LEVERAGE	-1.50556	0.000***	-1.43194	0.000***	-1.44212	0.000***	-1.47557	0.000***
R-squared	0.526		0.517		0.525		0.526	
Adjusted R^2	0.489		0.480		0.488		0.489	
F-statistic	14.25347		13.77528		14.18742		14.25302	
Prob. (F-statistic)	0.000		0.000		0.000		0.000	

***Significant at the 1% level   **Significant at the 5% level   *Significant at the 10% level

In terms of the quality of IC information, as presented in Table 4.7, the results are largely similar. The quality of the overall amount of IC information in the current year has a significant positive impact on the same-year market capitalization at the 5 percent level. The quality of human capital information shows a significant and positive impact on firm value at the 5 percent level. However, both internal and external capital information are insignificant. The results further support the role of firm size and profitability in market capitalization of a firm, with all the models showing a consistent significant positive association at the1 percent level, whereas leverage significantly hinders the market capitalization at the 1 percent level. Independent directors maintain a significant positive association with the same-year market capitalization at the 1 percent level in all the models when the quality of IC information is incorporated.

5.   DISCUSSION AND CONCLUSIONS

Drawing upon contrasting theoretical predictions purported in signaling and proprietary costs theories, as well as practical issues based on capital market research on IC, we have formulated several research hypotheses to predict the market reactions to releases of IC information in the wake of the recent global financial meltdown. To frame the discussion and see the immediacy of market reactions to IC information, we have evaluated whether the market reacts mostly to last-year or same-year IC information. The results are robust in terms of controlling for the effects of governance attributes, ownership structure patterns and firm-specific characteristics.

The results indicate that although the overall amount of IC information in the prior year and the current year both yield a significant positive impact on a firm's market capitalization, the stock market reacts most significantly and is more sensitive to a prior year's IC information (as shown by the respective significance levels of 1 percent and 5 percent). With regard to the subcomponents of IC information, the findings show that the market capitalization of the companies is positively sensitive to the release of external and human capital information in the prior year, with the market being more sensitive to human capital disclosures. However, only human capital information in the current year is shown to have a significant impact on the same-year market capitalization. The market does not respond to the release of internal capital information in the prior year, nor in the current year. In short, our results suggest that the market fully reacts to IC information during a period of economic uncertainty, both the current year's and the prior year's IC information. However, as time passes, market reactions to releases of IC information change, particularly information concerning human and external capital disclosures. Capital market–based research has already shown a significant positive role in terms of IC information in the market value of a firm in several countries (Abdolmohammadi 2005; Dumay and

Tull 2007; Orens et al. 2009; Vafaei et al. 2011), although this research drew on evidence from a stable economy.

Our findings contribute to three strands of research. First, we contrast conflicting traditional theoretical predictions (i.e., proprietary and signaling theories) of the role of IC information in terms of firm value during economic uncertainty. Our results indicate that companies choose to release an increased amount of IC disclosures to signal their capabilities in a bid to attract more investors and to avoid misevaluation. Hence, the results support the signaling theory's conjecture, as opposed to the proprietary costs theory, that companies opt to signal strategic information to the market during economic crisis, thus choosing to sacrifice any potential competitive costs that the IC information may result in. Henry (2013) identified that IC narratives can be critical and could prove to be a deciding factor in surviving difficult market conditions. Communicating IC narratives can therefore help companies go through the financial turmoil and ease investors' confidence in the company's long-term strategy.

Second, our results show that the stock market fully reacts to human capital information (Gamerschlag 2013), particularly during difficult market conditions. This observation supports the recent increasing trend of the importance of human capital in the knowledge economy (Edmans 2011). This is in line with the recent governmental initiatives in Malaysia regarding human capital development and indicates that the ongoing governmental initiative toward transforming the economy into a knowledge-based one through human capital capacity building is becoming a reality in the economy.

Finally, the findings asserted in this study show that the capital market does not appreciate IC information components equally and at the same time. In contrast to Dumay and Tull (2007), who found the Australian capital market to be most sensitive to internal capital information, we find human capital information, and to a lesser extent external capital information, are most appreciated in the Malaysian stock market, with the prior-year information most strongly relating to the market value of the firm. This suggests that different markets value information differently. Human capital information is a major issue in most developing countries, and companies tend to use information relating to their human development programs as a competitive advantage to differentiate themselves from the rest. Similarly, prior studies had shown that companies in the emerging economies use external capital information to compete with big foreign corporate brands entering their markets, thus explaining the sensitivity to external capital information in the Malaysian stock market.

The results of this study should be interpreted within the scope of several limitations. First, the scope of the study is restricted to the Malaysian capital markets and, therefore, the results may not be generalizable to countries with different business and cultural settings. The results of the study nonetheless could serve as a case in point for current and future researchers intending to further investigate market reactions to IC information. Second, the study draws evidence from an unstable economy. Market reactions to IC information could change along with changes in the overall economy. Future studies should extend the coverage of the study to after the recent economic crisis, thus permitting an observation of market reactions to IC information under different economic climates. Finally, the perceived association between share price and IC information has been criticized by some researchers as flawed (Mouritsen 2003), who argue that the complexity of IC elements does not permit one to easily examine such association from a distance, seemingly suggesting a closer examination of the interactions between IC and stock market reactions through action research, which may provide a more solid evidence of such association (Dumay and Roslender 2013). Future researchers should therefore adopt a different approach in case studies to closely observe the role of IC in the market capitalization of a firm.

NOTE

1. The corporate governance code was revised again recently in 2012, replacing the earlier version, which was introduced in 2007.

REFERENCES

Abdolmohammadi, M.J. 2005. "Intellectual capital disclosure and market capitalization". *Journal of Intellectual Capital*, 6 (3), 397–416.
Abdul R., Azwan, M.K.I., Radiah O. and Kok Fong S. 2012. "IC disclosures in IPO prospectuses: Evidence from Malaysia". *Journal of Intellectual Capital*, 13 (1), 57–80.
Abeysekera, I. 2010. "The influence of board size on intellectual capital disclosure by Kenyan listed firms". *Journal of Intellectual Capital*, 11 (4), 504–518.
Abeysekera, I. 2011. "The relation of intellectual capital disclosure strategies and market value in two political settings". *Journal of Intellectual Capital*, 12 (2), 319–338.
Abhayawansa, S. and Abeysekera I. 2009. "Intellectual capital disclosure from sell side analyst perspective". *Journal of Intellectual Capital*, 10 (2), 294–306.
Abhayawansa, S. and Guthrie, J. 2010. "Intellectual capital and the capital market: A review and synthesis". *Journal of Human Resource Costing & Accounting*, 14 (3), 196–226.
Abhayawansa, S. and Guthrie, J. 2012. "Intellectual capital information and stock recommendations: Impression management?". *Journal of Intellectual Capital*, 13 (3), 398–415.
Ahmed Haji, A. and Mohd Ghazali, N.A. 2012. "Intellectual capital disclosure trends: Some Malaysian evidence". *Journal of Intellectual Capital*, 13 (3), 377–397.
Ahmed Haji, A. and Mohd Ghazali, N.A. 2013. "A longitudinal examination of intellectual capital disclosures and corporate governance attributes in Malaysia". *Asian Review of Accounting*, 21 (1), 27–52.
Ahmed Haji, A. and Sanni, M. 2012. "The trends of intellectual capital disclosures: Evidence from the Nigerian banking sector". *Journal of Human Resource Costing & Accounting*, 16 (3), 184–209.

Anam, O. Abdulrahman, F.A.H. and Rashid, H.M.A. 2011. "Effects of intellectual capital information disclosed in annual reports on market capitalization: Evidence from Bursa Malaysia". *Journal of Human Resource Costing & Accounting,* 15 (2), 85–101.

Arvidsson, S. 2011. "Disclosure of non-financial information in the annual report: A management-team perspective". *Journal of Intellectual Capital,* 12 (2), 277–300.

Burgman, R. and Roos, G. 2007. "The importance of intellectual capital reporting: Evidence and implications". *Journal of Intellectual Capital,* 8 (1), 7–51.

Cerbioni, F. and Parbonetti, A. 2007. "Exploring the effects of corporate governance on intellectual capital disclosure: An analysis of European biotechnology companies". *European Accounting Review,* 16 (4), 791–826.

Dumay, J.C. and Tull, J.A. 2007. "Intellectual capital disclosure and price-sensitive Australian stock exchange announcements". *Journal of Intellectual Capital,* 8 (2), 236–255.

Dumay, J.C. and Roslender, R. 2013. "Utilising narrative to improve the relevance of intellectual capital". *Journal of Accounting and Organizational Change,* 9 (3), 248–279.

Edmans, A. 2011. "Does the stock market fully value intangibles? Employee satisfaction and equity prices". *Journal of Financial Economics,* 101 (3), 621–640.

Edvinsson, L. 2013. "IC 21—Reflections from 21 years of IC practice and theory". *Journal of Intellectual Capital,* 14 (1), 163–172.

Edvinsson, L. and Malone, M.S. 1997. *Intellectual Capital: The Proven Way to Establish Your Company's Real Value by Measuring Its Hidden Brainpower.* New York: HarperCollins Publishers.

Gamerschlag, R. 2013. "Value relevance of human capital information." *Journal of Intellectual Capital,* 4 (2), 325–345.

Ghosh, D. and Wu, A. 2007. "Intellectual capital and capital markets: Additional evidence". *Journal of Intellectual Capital,* 8 (2), 216–235.

Goh, P.C. and Lim, K.P. 2004. "Disclosing intellectual capital in company annual reports: Evidence from Malaysia". *Journal of Intellectual Capital,* 5 (3), 500–510.

Guthrie, J. and Petty, R. 2000. "Intellectual capital: Australian annual reporting practices". *Journal of Intellectual Capital,* 1 (3), 241–251.

Henry, L. 2013. "Intellectual capital in a recession: Evidence from UK SMEs". *Journal of Intellectual Capital,* 14 (1), 84–101.

Holland, J., Henningsson, J. Johanson, U., Koga, C. and Sakakibara, S. 2012. "Use of IC information in Japanese financial firms". *Journal of Intellectual Capital,* 13 (4), 562–581.

Kamaluddin, A. and Abdul Rahman, R. 2007. "Intellectual capital reporting in Malaysia". *Accountants Today,* April, 18–20.

Keenan, J. and Aggestam, M. 2001. "Corporate governance and intellectual capital: Some conceptualizations". *Corporate Governance: An International Review,* 9 (4), 259–275.

Kweh, Q.L., Chan, Y.C. and Wei Kiong Ting, I. 2013. "Measuring intellectual capital efficiency in the Malaysian software sector". *Journal of Intellectual Capital,* 14 (2), 310–324.

Li, J., Pike, R. and Haniffa, R. 2008. "Intellectual capital disclosure and corporate governance structure in UK firms". *Accounting and Business Research,* 38 (2), 137–159.

Lin, C.Y. and Edvinsson, L. 2010. "What national intellectual capital indices can tell about the global economic crisis of 2007–2009." Proceedings of the 2nd European Conference on Intellectual Capital, Lisbon, Portugal, March 29–30.

Lin, C.Y., Edvinsson, L., Chen, J. and Beding, T. 2013. *National Intellectual Capital and the Financial Crisis in Greece, Italy, Portugal, and Spain.* New York: Springer.

Marr, B. 2003. "Why do firms measure their intellectual capital?". *Journal of Intellectual Capital,* 4 (4), 441–464.

Mention, A-L. and Bontis, N. 2013. "Intellectual capital and performance within the banking sector of Luxembourg and Belgium". *Journal of Intellectual Capital,* 14 (2), 286–309.

Moulton, B.R. 1987. "Diagnostics for group effects in regression analysis." *Journal of Business and Economic Statistics,* 5, 275–282.

Mouritsen, J. 2003. "Intellectual capital and the capital market: The circulability of intellectual capital". *Accounting, Auditing & Accountability Journal,* 16 (1), 18–30.

Orens, R., Aerts, W. and Lybaert, N. 2009. "Intellectual capital disclosure, cost of finance and firm value". *Management Decision,* 47 (10), 1536–1554.

Petty, R., Ricceri, F. and Guthrie, J. 2008. "Intellectual capital: A user's perspective". *Management Research News,* 31 (6), 434–447.

Salamudin, N., Bakar, R., Kamil Ibrahim, M. and Haji Hassan, F. 2010. "Intangible assets valuation in the Malaysian capital market". *Journal of Intellectual Capital,* 11 (3), 391–405.

Seleim, A. and Bontis, N. 2013. "National intellectual capital and economic performance: Empirical evidence from developing countries". *Knowledge and Process Management,* 20 (3), 131–140.

Sihotang, P. and Winata, A. 2008. "The intellectual capital disclosures of technology-driven companies: Evidence from Indonesia". *International Journal of Learning and Intellectual Capital,* 5 (1), 63–82.

Tan, K.S., Chong, S.C., Lin, B. and Eze, U.C. 2009. "Internet-based ICT adoption: Evidence from Malaysian SMEs". *Industrial Management & Data Systems,* 109 (2), 224–244.

Thomas, A. 2003. "A tale of two reports". *European Business Forum,* 16, 79–81.

Uyar, A. and Kiliç, M. 2012. "Value relevance of voluntary disclosure: Evidence from Turkish firms". *Journal of Intellectual Capital,* 13 (3), 363–376.

Vafaei, A., Taylor, D. and Ahmed, K. 2011. "The value relevance of intellectual capital disclosures". *Journal of Intellectual Capital,* 12 (3), 407–429.

Wang, J-C. 2008. "Investigating market value and intellectual capital for S&P 500". *Journal of Intellectual Capital,* 9 (4), 546–563.

Wang, Z., Ali, M.J. and Al-Akra, M. 2013. "Value relevance of voluntary disclosure and the global financial crisis: Evidence from China". *Managerial Auditing Journal,* 28 (5), 444–468.

Whiting, R.H. and Miller, J.C. 2008. "Voluntary disclosure of intellectual capital in New Zealand annual reports and the 'hidden value'". *Journal of Human Resource Costing & Accounting,* 12 (1), 26–50.

Williams, S.M. 2001. "Is intellectual capital performance and disclosure practices related?". *Journal of Intellectual Capital,* 2 (3), 192–203.

Zéghal, D. and Maaloul, A. 2010. "Analysing value added as an indicator of intellectual capital and its consequences on company performance". *Journal of Intellectual Capital,* 11 (1), 39–60.

Part III

Intellectual Capital Reports in Europe

5 Intellectual Capital Statement as a Strategic Management Tool
The European Approach

Markus Will

1. INTRODUCTION

Today's economy is characterized by continuous globalization of markets, shorter product life cycles and dynamic changes in the business environment. In this context, a company can only achieve business success if it can exploit its particular competitive advantages, represented by its ability to offer either the same products as the competitors at a lower price or better products at the same price (Hungenberg 2004).

Regarding the sources of competitive advantages, two major theoretical streams within strategic management research exist. On the one hand, the Market-Based View (MBV) identifies a dominant market position as a major source of competitive advantages (Porter 1991). On the other hand, the Resource-Based View (RBV) argues that the specific resource base of a company offers the source of competitive advantages (Barney 1991). By now, MBV and RBV are considered complementary approaches in order to identify competitive advantages (Mahoney and Pandian 1992). In conclusion, the major objective of strategic management is to identify and to exploit competitive advantages possibly conceptualized from an external perspective (MBV) or an internal perspective (RBV), and ideally developed by integrating both perspectives.

Furthermore, the critical success factors of economic growth changed toward the generation, application and exploitation of knowledge. The key to competitiveness increasingly reveals itself to be the way people combine, master and commercialize their know-how. Thus, managing their specific intellectual capital (IC) becomes more and more important for future-oriented organizations. Systematically reporting those intangible assets to customers, partners and investors has become a critical factor of success in the context of the globalization process (Mertins et al. 2006; Will et al. 2006).

First efforts to measure intangibles and to evaluate their potential started in the 1960s with Schultz (1961) and Becker (1964). They focused on how investing in human capital affects the growth of national economies. Within the following human resource accounting approach, Hermanson (1964), Flamholtz (1974) and Fitz-enz (1984) developed models that aimed at calculating the costs as well as the value of human resources in order to support more effective management within companies. At the end of the 1980s, comprehensive management information systems had already been developed, but financial indicators still dominated. The already developed knowledge about "soft" factors did not regain prominence until the development of the Balanced Scorecard (BSC) (Kaplan and Norton 1996).

The integration of formerly independent strategic management approaches, such as BSC, managerial accounting (Society of Management Accountants of Canada 1998) and customer relations management (CRM) (Shapiro 1974), had been furthered mainly in Scandinavia. In particular, practitioners such as, for example, Edvinsson and Malone (1997) and Sveiby (1997, 2002) influenced the development during the 1990s. They developed two different models, the "Skandia Navigator" (Edvinsson and Malone 1997) and the "Intangible Asset Monitor" (Sveiby 2002), to measure the components of IC by using both qualitative and quantitative indicators, and to communicate the results in an intellectual capital statement (ICS). Both models aimed at identifying and evaluating intellectual capital in order to outweigh deficits primarily in finance-oriented management. Edvinsson subdivided IC into human capital, structural capital and relational capital. This structure is currently the most frequently used to describe intangible assets (Alwert 2006).

More recent approaches emphasize the effective management of IC regarding the overall value creation within a company. The ICS model by the Austrian Research Centers Seibersdorf (ARCS 1999; Koch et al. 2000), as well as delineated models by Deutsches Luft- und Raumfahrtzentrum (DLR) (Blum and Borrmann 2004), the Austrian university statement (Republic of Austria 2002a, 2002b), Netzwerk Öko-Energie Steiermark (NOEST). 2004. Wissensbilanz, Graz, Joanneum Research (2003), the Value Chain Scoreboard (Lev 2004) or Intellectual Capital Statement—Made in Germany (Alwert al. 2004), integrate aspects from value-creating models (Porter 1985, EFQM 2003) with a structural perspective of IC. Framing IC in an input-process-output relation, these approaches stress the importance of IC for developing strategies and the operational implementation of the most important business processes (Leitner 2005). At the same time, models have been developed that integrate the evaluation of IC by using indicators depicting the monetary evaluation of the particular components of IC (Andriessen 2004; Mertins et al. 2005; Alwert 2005).

2. INTELLECTUAL CAPITAL STATEMENT:
THE EUROPEAN APPROACH

In recent years, different national approaches to the management of IC have been developed and tested. Financed by the German Federal Ministry of Economics and Technology, the project consortium "Arbeitskreis Wissensbilanz," led by Berlin-based Fraunhofer IPK, developed the methodology

"Wissensbilanz—Made in Germany" (Alwert et al. 2008). The consortium conducted a pilot project to adjust the preparation of IC statements to the German Small and medium-sized enterprise(s) (SME) situation and to test it practically. The results and the experiences of the project led to the first German guideline for implementing ICS in SMEs (Alwert et al. 2004; Bornemann and Alwert 2007; Alwert, Bornemann and Will 2009). By the end of 2007, more than fifty ICSs had been implemented in the course of the pilot project. The German ICS guideline and the supporting software had been retrieved 60,000 times, but a European-wide standard regarding the measurement and management of IC was still missing.

The emerging need for a consistent method and a European standard was the starting point for the European Union (EU) project "Intellectual Capital Statement—Made in Europe (InCaS)". The intention of InCaS was to harmonize the different national ICS approaches and to develop and test this European ICS methodology in twenty-five SMEs in five core countries. Target groups of InCaS were SMEs that depended decisively on their IC to ensure success, that is, that were based on so-called knowledge-intensive business models. National SME associations in those countries acted as dissemination partners and aimed at targeting 1,000 EU SMEs using the InCaS model and tools by the end of the project (December 2008). By 2011, the harmonized ICS methodology (European Commission 2008) was implemented by trained ICS moderators in over 1,000 companies in Germany and Europe, using a software created for this purpose, the "ICS Toolbox", developed by Fraunhofer IPK. At the same time, Fraunhofer Academy is responsible for the training and certification of ICS moderators, as well as for the quality assurance of the applications using a specifically developed ICS audit approach.

Following the most frequently used structure to describe intangible assets, the InCaS approach divides IC into three dimensions: human, structural and relational capital. Human capital (HC) includes the staff's competencies, skills, attitudes and the employees' motivation. HC is owned by the employees and can be taken home or to the next employer. Structural capital (SC) comprises all structures and processes needed by the employees in order to be productive and innovative. According to a sloppy but useful definition, it "consists of those intangible structures which remain with the organization when the employee leaves" (Edvinsson and Malone 1997). Relational capital (RC) sums up the organization's relations with customers, suppliers, partners and the public.

Based on the results of the German pilot project, fifteen standard IC factors have been extracted "bottom up" from the actual ICSs of the fifty pilot SMEs. This set of harmonized IC factors has been used and continuously reviewed during later stages of the German project and during the European project. The results from practice proved that approximately 80 to 90 percent of individual IC elements could be harmonized on an aggregated level, whereas the remaining 10 to 20 percent are completely individual (Mertins and Will 2008).

Within the European Guideline for Intellectual Capital Statements (European Commission 2008), these harmonized IC factors were agreed upon as a basic standard set of factors that were relevant to the major part of companies when assessing and analyzing IC. On the basis of a firm's assessment of a set of standardized IC factors, strengths and weaknesses of IC can be compared between different companies, for example, the respective industrial sector, different branches, size, regions, etc., and can reveal the specific IC strategy of a sector, branch, region or any other group of companies.

The method is applied by trained ICS moderators and supported by the software "ICS Toolbox", capturing the relevant data and producing analysis results in diagrams. The procedural model (see Figure 5.1) defines eight steps and different assessment instruments applied while going through the process of ICS implementation in detail (Mertins, Will and Meyer 2009; Bornemann and Will 2009). It starts with the formulation of the company's business model, aimed at aligning intangible resources with significant value-generating processes and, crucially, with the objectives and desired business success of the company. This information is the basis for the other steps that complete the procedure for applying the method, ending with the establishment of the actions and indicators, which are then summarized in an ICS report and a management presentation to be used as management tools for monitoring change and reporting results.

The summarizing visualization, derived from the ICS Toolbox, is a portfolio of IC factors that have the greatest impact on company results compared to their current assessment in a four-quadrant matrix. The IC management portfolio displays the IC factors identified and assessed in step 2 in a four-quadrant matrix according to their relative importance in achieving the company's strategic objectives (impact analysis) and the assessment of their current status (QQS Assessment). Figure 5.2 gives an example.

The portfolio represents, on a consolidated basis, the results of the evaluation of each IC factor. The Y axis displays the relative weight or impact of the factors on the results of the organization. As a tool for analyzing each factor compared to its significance in relation to the organization's results, the impact matrix generates this weighting measure, which is called "relative influence". The X axis represents the consolidation of the assessment of IC factors in three dimensions—quantity, quality and systematic (QQS Assessment)—and the extent to which the company treats each of the factors. Thus, through easy and realistic illustrations, managers can manage their intangible assets and objectively assess the results over time, as shown in Figure 5.2.

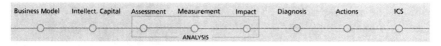

Figure 5.1   The procedural model
Source: ICS Toolbox

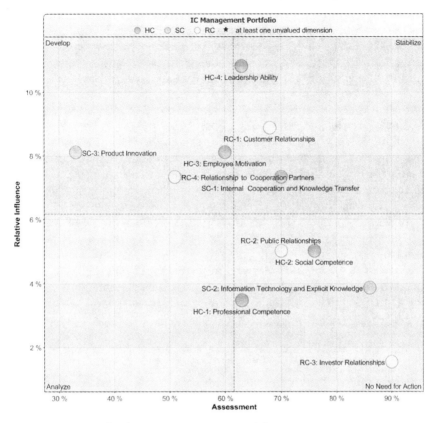

Figure 5.2 Example of an IC management portfolio
Source: ICS Toolbox

In general, IC factors in the upper-left section represent future fields for intervention. If a factor appears in this section, according to the QQS Assessment, the status quo is rather poor, whereas its relative importance is rather high. Therefore, it is crucial to develop these IC factors, as they have the highest potential of intervention. By systematically searching for those factors with the highest potential for intervention, the top management can answer the following essential questions: "Where should we start to invest?" and "Where can we get the maximum impact at minimum costs?"

An ICS outcome is a defined set of actions aimed at the systematic development of particular IC factors, as well as a set of indicators that helps monitor these factors. This set of measures can be viewed as an initial, rough IC strategy that can be elaborated over time. Based on those findings, managers might expand their business strategy, taking into account IC-related objectives and the opportunities deriving from systematic IC development.

The impact map represents the factors with their mutual influences and their delays. In order to develop a comprehensive understanding of the investment results in one of the IC factors—for instance, product innovation—it is necessary to understand how long this factor takes to affect the financial results. This is a powerful tool to formulate strategies in the medium and long term. Managers assess future scenarios and prioritize their investments and actions to achieve clearly connected goals in each of the prioritized IC factors, as shown in Figure 5.3.

The ICS method can be considered an indicator that reveals critical factors, which can determine the failure or success of the company, in an early stage of its life cycle. Companies often fail to focus on aspects of general business management to such a point where they even diminish growth and trigger financial strangulation. This explains, for example, the high mortality rate of start-ups. ICS helps companies become aware of their lack of management skills or structure necessary to allow organic growth. The companies also reported that the method's biggest gains derive from the ICS evidence of possible failure mechanisms of coordination within the enterprise and internal communication, as well as some rigidity factors or counterproductive effects of corporate culture. In general, according to

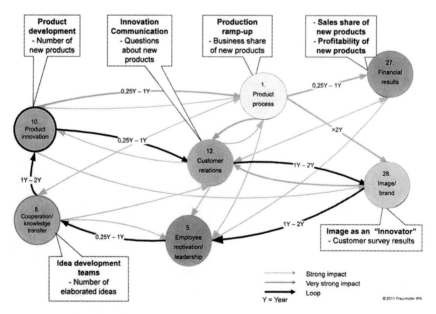

Figure 5.3   Example of an impact map with an IC loop and measurable actions
Source: Alwert, K., Bornemann, M. and Will, M. 2008. *Wissensbilanz—Made in Germany. Leitfaden 2.0.* Berlin: German Federal Ministry for Economics and Technology Germany.

the results of the pilot project, the IC factor that shows the greatest development potential is the human capital factor "management competence". In most companies, it appeared to be the factor with the greatest relative impact on business results, but with relatively low assessment. This means that by investing in the development of this factor with the highest intervention potential, the results arising from this investment are expected to be the greatest.

3. EXEMPLARY EVIDENCE OF THE KNOWLEDGE-BASED ECONOMY: THE GERMAN IC MANAGEMENT SURVEY

Using the mentioned standard set of IC factors and additional questions with regard to strategy, Fraunhofer IPK and Arbeitskreis Wissensbilanz conducted an online survey of over 1,000 German enterprises across different industry sectors. The results of this survey (Alwert et al. 2010) are based on the "Wissensbilanz-Schnelltest" (IC Quick Check). The "Wissensbilanz-Schnelltest" provides enterprises with a quick overview of the status quo of their IC, as well as initial action recommendations to manage their soft factors. From July 2009 through December 2010, 2,300 data sets were captured through the web sites www.wissensbilanz-schnelltest.de, www.wiwo.de and www.impulse.de. The participating enterprises were asked how important certain factors were with regard to their business success (impact) on a scale from 0–10. Furthermore, they were asked to estimate how well these factors were developed in their enterprise at present (rating). After the revision of all data sets, 947 questionnaires could be used for evaluation.

The survey's sample comprises 947 enterprises. Eight hundred twenty-eight of these enterprises answered the questions regarding the sector they are active in. In this context, 287 enterprises (34.7 percent) stated that they belong to the production sector, and 541 (65.3 percent) stated that they were part of the service sector. Nine hundred two enterprises answered the question regarding the number of employees (see Figure 5.4).

Of the 947 enterprises surveyed, 795 stated their annual turnover. The majority of the companies participating in the survey (38.9 percent) quoted an annual turnover of up to 2 Mio. €. About one-fifth stated that it has an annual turnover of more than 50 Mio. € (20.4 percent).

As part of the study, the most important enterprise resources were assessed with regard to the factors' individual impact on the enterprises' business success. Based on the assessment, it was possible to derive the importance of the specific factors for different groups of enterprises.

Overall, the different types of IC are already of higher importance for business success than the material resources (see Figure 5.5). In addition, the

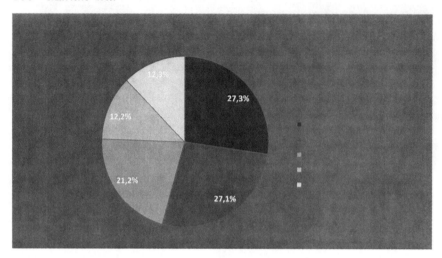

Figure 5.4   Sample according to the number of employees
Source: Alwert, K., Bornemann, M., Meyer, C., Will, M. and Wuscher, S. 2010. *Wissensstandort Deutschland—Deutsche Unternehmen auf dem Weg in die wissensbasierte Wirtschaft.* Berlin: Fraunhofer IPK.

IC is rated better by the surveyed enterprises. The impact of HC on business success is by far the greatest (8.2) and has the best rating (6.7) as well. The factors of the SC (7.2) are seen as the second most important type of capital by the surveyed participants and were rated with 6.1 in the mean.

When analyzing the difference between rating and impact, it becomes obvious that the rating of the factors is in most cases lower than their impact on business success. The biggest difference is to be found in the HC (−1.5) followed by the SC (−1.1) and the RC (−0.4). The factors of the material resources only show slight differences. In conclusion, the highest demand for action by knowledge-based corporate management constitutes itself in the HC.

If one compares the ratings of the enterprises from the service sector with those of the production sector, differences can be determined. Significant differences in the HC area show that the service sector is one step ahead of the production sector with regard to structural and employee-related organizational development.

On the one hand, the impact, and thereby the importance, of HC (8.3) is rated significantly higher than that of the participating production enterprises (7.9). On the other hand, the material resources are more important to the production enterprises (6.7) than to the service enterprises (4.7). These results confirm the dependency of production enterprises on machinery, plants and raw materials and on the capital needed to finance these, whereas

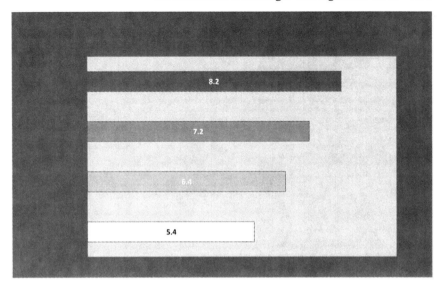

Figure 5.5 Impact and rating of the different types of capital with regard to business success

Source: Alwert, K., Bornemann, M., Meyer, C., Will, M. and Wuscher, S. 2010. *Wissensstandort Deutschland—Deutsche Unternehmen auf dem Weg in die wissensbasierte Wirtschaft.* Berlin: Fraunhofer IPK.

the service enterprises strongly depend on the abilities of their employees. Although material resources are of great importance for the business success of production enterprises, they are seen as less important than the HC. Hence, the employees are the most important type of capital in the production sector.

The IC as a whole, and especially the HC, impacts the business success of the surveyed enterprises more heavily than the material resources do. Figure 5.6 shows which IC factors are of greatest importance and thereby critical for corporate success. In addition, the figure shows how well the enterprises are presently doing with respect to the critical factors for business success (rating).

Professional competence (8.5), customer relationships (8.3), motivation of employees (8.3), social competence (8.1) and leadership ability (7.8) are the factors with the highest impact on business success, followed by the SC factors, such as internal cooperation and knowledge transfer (7.7), information technology (IT) and explicit knowledge (7.6), corporate culture (7.4) and management instruments (7.0).

The material factor with the highest impact is that of financial resources (6.8), which ranks in the midfield. Material factors such as machinery, plants and buildings (4.5) and material and raw material (4.4) have the relatively lowest impact on business success.

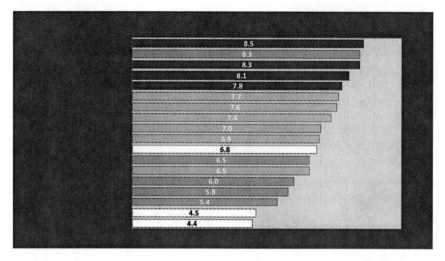

Figure 5.6   Impact and rating of the success factors of knowledge-based corporate management
Source: Alwert, K., Bornemann, M., Meyer, C., Will, M. and Wuscher, S. 2010. *Wissensstandort Deutschland—Deutsche Unternehmen auf dem Weg in die wissensbasierte Wirtschaft.* Berlin: Fraunhofer IPK.

Surprisingly, process innovation (6.9) and product innovation (6.5) show a relatively low importance as well. Hence, innovative products or improved processes do not seem to be the focus of German enterprises and are seen as less critical for business success.

Another interesting fact is that the impact of the investor relationships ranks last within the RC (5.4), as has been shown by previous surveys on the importance of the IC (Mertins et al. 2007b). A reason for this could be found in the fact that enterprises are currently holding back investments, and thus the importance of investor relationships seems minor. On the other side, the low impact could also be based on enterprises' expectations with regard to the support to solve financial problems.

Furthermore, the surveyed enterprises assign a relatively low impact to the factors of the RC in general, except customer relationships. This allows the conclusion that the participating enterprises rate their internal resources as more important than public relationships, supplier relationships or investor relationships.

4.   CONCLUSIONS AND OUTLOOK

Figure 5.7 illustrates which components of the German method have been valued most by the SMEs. Of the participating companies, 70 to 90 percent evaluated the benefits of the ICS implementation process as "Very high" or "High" regarding all analyzed categories. In particular, the benefits of "Development or reflection of business strategy", "Strategy and Intellectual Capital becomes transparent", "Corporate Culture benefits from open discussions" and "Enhanced understanding about how the organization works" have been perceived as "Very high".

In general, all SMEs participating in the InCaS project were satisfied with the ICS implementation and the organizational arrangements. One of the most cited benefits of the ICS implementation was the "verification of gut feeling", that is, most SME managers had some intuitive image of their strategic IC factors and their particular strengths and weaknesses, but were not able to structure, visualize and communicate this implicit knowledge within their company. The ICS process helped them to identify the relevant IC factors and to precisely detect their strategic potential for improvement.

On the other hand, it became obvious that SMEs need to pay greater attention to strategy development in general. During the course of InCaS, it became apparent that the first implementation was hindered by the fact that some SMEs did not have a well-defined strategy at all. For this reason, it is necessary to complement the method with modules devoted to strategy development issues, for example, business model definition and competitive analysis. Derived from this analysis and from practical experiences

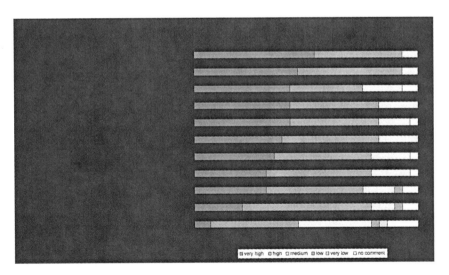

Figure 5.7   Benefits of implementing an ICS (perceived level of benefit from very high to very low)

Source: Will, M., Wuscher, S. and Bodderas, M. 2006. *Wissensbilanz—Made in Germany—Nutzung und Bewertung der Wissensbilanz durch die Pilotunternehmen.* Berlin: Fraunhofer IPK.

with numerous SMEs in Europe, the methodological requirements for an integrated approach to strategy development can be summarized as follows:

- Integrate the internal and external perspective on intangibles, and, by that, link the concept of IC as a Resource-Based View with the concept of customer value as a Market-Based View.
- Integrate the theoretical concept of IC with a methodology for comprehensive strategy development.
- Integrate the formulation and implementation of business strategies, taking into account the actual practice in SMEs.

As a first hint of what kind of external aspects of strategy development should be taken into account when drafting further modules and enhancing the methodology, the additional questions of the German online survey described earlier give some insights.

The question regarding the enterprises' prime markets was answered by 900 enterprises. The distribution is relatively homogenous, whereby slightly more enterprises (38.1 percent) sell their products and services nationwide. In contrast, only 26.2 percent of the enterprises are operating on international markets. A reported 74.7 percent of the 894 companies that answered the question concerning corporate objectives stated that they aim at future

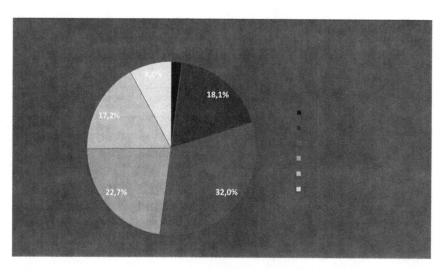

Figure 5.8   Sample according to competitive strategy

Source: Alwert, K., Bornemann, M., Meyer, C., Will, M. and Wuscher, S. 2010. *Wissensstandort Deutschland—Deutsche Unternehmen auf dem Weg in die wissensbasierte Wirtschaft.* Berlin: Fraunhofer IPK.

growth, whereas 24.4 percent stated that they aim at maintaining their current position. Around one-third of the enterprises that answered the question regarding their competitive strategy stated that they pursue a niche strategy (see Figure 5.8). The minority (2 percent) said that they are concentrating on cost leadership.

Nine hundred forty-seven enterprises answered the question regarding their competitive differentiation. Customer orientation is the most important factor to differentiate from competition (66.8 percent). In this context, factors such as price (20.1 percent), additional product value (16.9 percent) and process innovations (15.5 percent) are considered less important by the enterprises in order to stand out from the competition (see Figure 5.9).

The results of the study indicate that one-dimensional strategy types such as cost leadership or market leadership do not sufficiently reflect the actual conditions SMEs are facing in competition. Rather, a multidimensional individual differentiation is required in order for them to be able to meet competition successfully. Furthermore, the study shows that already today, intangible resources have a significantly higher impact on German enterprises' success than material resources such as machinery, facilities and buildings.

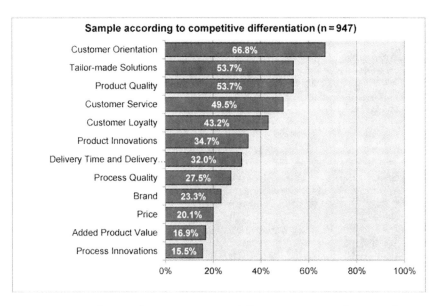

Figure 5.9 Sample according to competitive differentiation (no. of companies per strategy type in %)

Source: Alwert, K., Bornemann, M., Meyer, C., Will, M. and Wuscher, S. 2010. *Wissensstandort Deutschland—Deutsche Unternehmen auf dem Weg in die wissensbasierte Wirtschaft.* Berlin: Fraunhofer IPK.

REFERENCES

Alwert, K., Bornemann, M., Meyer, C., Will, M. and Wuscher, S. 2010. *Wissensstandort Deutschland—Deutsche Unternehmen auf dem Weg in die wissensbasierte Wirtschaft.* Berlin: Fraunhofer IPK.

Alwert, K., Bornemann, M. and Will, M. 2008. *Wissensbilanz—Made in Germany. Leitfaden 2.0.* Berlin: German Federal Ministry for Economics and Technology Germany.

Alwert, K., Bornemann, M. and Will, M. 2009. "Does intellectual capital reporting matter to financial analysts?". *Journal of Intellectual Capital,* 10 (3), 354–368.

Alwert, K. 2006. *Wissensbilanzen für mittelständische Organisationen.* Stuttgart: Fraunhofer IRB Verlag.

Alwert, K. 2005. Die integrierte Wissensbewertung: ein prozessorientierter Ansatz. In *Wissensbilanzen—Intellektuelles Kapital erfolgreich nutzen und entwickeln.* Berlin: Springer, 253–277.

Alwert, K, Bornemann, M. and Kivikas, M. 2004. *Intellectual Capital Statement—Made in Germany.* German Federal Ministry for Economics and Technology: Berlin. http://www.bmwi.de/BMWi/Redaktion/PDF/W/wissensbilanz-made-in-germany-leitfaden, property=pdf,bereich=bmwi,sprache=de,rwb=true.pdf, accessed December 14, 2013.

Andriessen, D. 2004. *Making Sense of Intellectual Capital: Designing a Method for the Valuation of Intangibles.* Burlington MA: Butterworth-Heinemann.

Austrian Research Centers Seibersdorf. *Wissensbilanz.* 1999, 2000, 2001, 2002 and 2003. http://www.arcs.ac.at/publik/fulltext/wissensbilanz, accessed March 8, 2004).

Barney, J.B. 1991. "Firm resources and sustained competitive advantage". *Journal of Management,* 17 (1), 99–120.

Becker, G.S. 1964. *Human Capital.* Chicago: University of Chicago.

Blum, J. and Borrmann, R. 2004. "Wissensbilanzen zur internen Steuerung und externen Berichterstattung von Forschungsorganisationen". In *Intangibles in der Unternehmenssteuerung.* München: Vahlen.

Bornemann, M. and Alwert, K. 2007. "The German guideline for intellectual capital reporting: Method and experiences". *Journal of Intellectual Capital,* 8 (4), 563–576.

Bornemann, M. and Will, M. 2009. "Preliminary experiences with InCaS". In *Proceedings of the IFKAD 2009.* Matera.

Edvinsson, L., and Malone, M.S. 1997. *Intellectual Capital.* New York: Harper Business.

European Commission. 2008. *InCaS: Intellectual Capital Statement—Made in Europe.* European ICS Guideline. www.incas-europe.org, accessed 14 December 2013.

EFQM. 2003 *European Foundation for Quality Management: "EFQM Excellence Model",* http://www.efqm.org/Default.aspx?tabid=35, accessed 14 December 2013.

Fitz-enz, J. 1984. *How to Measure Human Resources Management.* New York: McGraw-Hill.

Flamholtz, E. 1974. *Human Resource Accounting.* Encino: Dickenson.

Hermanson, R.H. 1964. *Accounting for Human Assets.* Michigan State University: Bureau of Business and Economic Research.

Hungenberg H. 2004. *Strategisches Management in Unternehmen. Ziele—Prozesse— Verfahren.* Wiesbaden: Springer.

Joanneum Research. 2003. *Wissensbilanz.* http://www.joanneum.at., accessed 14 December 2013.

Kaplan, R.S. and Norton, D.P. 1996. *The Balance Scorecard—Translating Strategy into Action.* Boston: Harvard Business School Press.

Koch, G.R., Leitner, K.H. and Bornemann, M. 2000. "Measuring and reporting intangible assets and results in a European contract research organization". In *Proceedings of the Joint German-OECD Conference Benchmarking Industry-Science Relationships*. Berlin.

Leitner, K.H. 2005. Wissensbilanzierung für den Forschungsbereich: Erfahrungen der Austrian Research Centers. In *Wissensbilanzen—Intellektuelles Kapital erfolgreich nutzen und entwickeln*. Berlin: Springer, 203–224. .

Baruch, L. 2004. *Sharpening the Intangibles Edge*. Boston: Harvard Business Review.

Mahoney, J.T. and Pandian, R.J. 1992. "The resource-based view within the conversation of strategic management". *Strategic Management Journal*, 13 (5), 363–380.

Mertins, K., Alwert, K. and Heisig, P. 2005. *Wissensbilanzen—Intellektuelles Kapital erfolgreich nutzen und entwickeln*. Berlin: Springer.

Mertins, K., Alwert, K. and Will, M. 2006. "Measuring intellectual capital in European SME". In *Proceedings of I-KNOW '06, 6th International Conference on Knowledge Management)*, 21–25. Graz.

Mertins K., Will, M. and Wuscher, S. 2007b. "Erfolgsfaktoren des Intellektuellen Kapitals in mittelständischen Unternehmen", Paper read at the *KnowTech 2007*. Frankfurt am Main.

Mertins, K. and Will, M. 2008. "InCaS: Intellectual Capital Statement—Made in Europe; Strategic relevance of intellectual capital in European SMEs and sectoral differences". In *Proceedings of the 9th European Conference on Knowledge Management*. Southampton.

Mertins, K., Will, M. and Meyer, C. 2009. "InCaS: Intellectual capital statement. Measuring intellectual capital in European small and medium sized enterprises. In *Proceedings of the European Conference on Intellectual Capital*. Haarlem.

Netzwerk Öko-Energie Steiermark (NOEST). 2004. Wissensbilanz, Graz.

Porter, M.E. 1985. *Competitive Advantage*. New York: Free Press.

Porter, M.E. 1991. "Towards a dynamic theory of strategy". In *Strategic Management Journal*, 12 (S2), 95–117.

Republic of Austria. 2002a. § 13 Leistungsvereinbarung, Absatz 6. In *Bundesgesetzblatt für die Republik Österreich*. Vienna.

Republic of Austria. 2002b. Erläuterung zu § 13 Leistungsvereinbarung. In *Bundesgesetzblatt für die Republik Österreich*. Vienna.

Shapiro, P. 1974. *Manage the Customer, Not Just the Sales Force*. Harvard Business Review: Boston.

Schultz, Theodore W. 1961. *Investment in human capital*. In American Economic Re-view 51(1), 1–17.

Society of Management Accountants of Canada. 1998. *The Management of Intellectual Capital: The Issue and the Practice*. Hamilton.

Sveiby, Karl E. 2002. Die Messung immaterieller Vermögenswerte. In *Praxishandbuch Wissensmanagement: Strategien—Methoden—Fallbeispiele*. Symposium: Düsseldorf.

Sveiby, Karl E. 1997. *The New Organizational Wealth. Managing & Measuring Knowledge-Based Assets*. Berrett-Koehler: San Francisco.

Welge, Martin K. and Andreas Al-Laham. 2001. *Strategisches Management. Grundlagen—Prozesse—Implementierung*. Springer: Wiesbaden.

Will, Markus. 2012. *Strategische Unternehmensentwicklung auf Basis immaterieller Werte in KMU—Eine Methode zur Integration der ressourcen- und marktbasierten Perspektive im Strategieprozess*. Stuttgart: Fraunhofer Verlag.

Wheelen, T. and Hunger, D.J. 1995. *Strategic Management and Business Policy.* Reading, MA: Addison-Wesley.

Will, M., Alwert, K., Bornemann, M. and Wuscher, S. 2007. *Wissensbilanz—Made in Germany—Auswirkungen eines Berichts über Intellektuelles Kapital auf die Unternehmensbewertung.* Berlin: Fraunhofer IPK. http://www.akwissensbilanz.org/Projekte/070201_Finanzmarkt_Wirkungstest_Teil2_V17.pdf, accessed 14 December 2013.

Will, M., Wuscher, S. and Bodderas, M. 2006. *Wissensbilanz—Made in Germany—Nutzung und Bewertung der Wissensbilanz durch die Pilotunternehmen.* Berlin: Fraunhofer IPK. http://www.akwissensbilanz.org/Projekte/KMUWirkungstest Teil 2.pdf, accessed 14 December 2013.

6 Overview of IC Reporting Models within Serbian Industries

Sladjana Cabrilo

1. INTRODUCTION

In the last twenty years we have witnessed an increasing interest in intellectual capital (IC) measurement, management and reporting (Lerro and Schiuma 2013; Chiucchi 2013; Ax and Marton 2008; Karagiannis et al. 2009; Janosevic et al. 2013a). Managers have become aware that the competitiveness of their organizations no longer resides solely in tangible resources (Lerro and Schiuma 2013), and that today, the creation of economic value is based mainly on IC (Drucker 1993; Grant 1996; Stewart 1997; Sveiby 1997a; Edvinsson and Malone 1997; Carlucci et al. 2004; Schiuma et al. 2008; Kianto et al. 2010).

Because IC is completely different from its tangible counterparts (Cabrilo et al. 2009; Cabrilo 2009), it is not being monitored by the traditional bookkeeping system (Burgman and Roos 2007; Cabrilo et al. 2009). However, without IC measuring and reporting, companies are neither able to manage intangible and knowledge dimensions of their business nor to represent companies' values to the stakeholders, which leads to internal management and external communication problems (Marr et al. 2003; Ax and Marton 2008; Cabrilo and Grubic Nesic 2010). Thus, there is a pressing need for a set of metrics by which managers and companies' stakeholders (especially investors) can account for intangible resources that significantly affect the value creation (Low 2000).

Despite the difficulties in accurately measuring IC (Choo and Bontis 2002; Tovstiga and Tulugorova 2009; Cabrilo et al. 2009), in addition to severe limitations associated with the IC measuring paradigm (Dumay 2009a; Mouritsen 2006, 2009; Marr et al. 2004; Yu and Humphreys 2013), great interest has resulted in a plethora of frameworks for IC measuring and reporting (Edvinsson and Malone 1997; Sveiby 1997a; Roos et al. 1997; Stewart 1997; Bontis 1999; Sanchez et al. 2000; Andriessen 2004, Chiucchi 2013; Cabrilo et al. 2009). These new measurement frameworks differ widely in objectives, methodology and solutions (Cabrilo et al. 2009).

Serbia is a rather turbulent environment, apart from the existing global economic crisis. The country has also undergone a transition from an industrial to a knowledge economy, from a nonmarket to a market economy, and is still in the process of privatization (Cabrilo et al. 2009). In order to foster the transition to the knowledge and innovation-driven economy, Serbia must focus its economic activities on resources that have the potential to create value in the long run. Therefore, Serbian companies have to develop their IC. Unfortunately, most Serbian companies have traditionally measured economic, financial and operational performances, whereas they have disregarded the immaterial component of their business. In order to overcome the lack of relevant information in traditional financial statements, it is necessary to raise awareness of the importance of IC in the Serbian business environment and initiate a strong call for IC reporting in Serbia.

Although there has been some research on IC assessment and measurement in transition countries (Bozbura 2004; Clark 2003; Deol 2009; Kamath 2007; Tovstiga and Tulugurova 2009; Xiao and Lo 2003), the European Union's (EU's) members from Central and Eastern Europe (Ederer et al. 2007), little has been written about IC within the Serbian business environment. Some authors have explored the impact of IC on the financial performance of Serbian companies (Janosevic et al. 2013a; Janosevic et al. 2013b; Bontis et al. 2013), whereas others have focused on IC reporting in Serbian companies (Cabrilo 2009; Cabrilo et al. 2009; Kontic and Cabrilo 2009; Cabrilo and Grubic-Nesic 2010).

The first IC research conducted on a Serbian company comprised the application of two IC measuring methods and indicated a necessity to modify the existing IC measuring methods, particularly in the field of indicators, pertaining to characteristics of the environment, industry and the company (Cabrilo 2005). Wide-ranging research of IC in the Serbian business environment has followed, with the primary objectives being to provide an appropriate model for IC reporting in the transitional economic system of Serbia (Cabrilo et al. 2009) and to facilitate IC reporting in Serbian companies. In addition to this model for IC reporting on the macro level, the research has resulted in other important results related to IC analysis and reporting in Serbian industrial companies (Kontic and Cabrilo 2009) and the Serbian service industry (Cabrilo and Grubic-Nesic 2010), as well as results related to the comparison of Serbian industries from the perspective of IC (Cabrilo 2009).

Because many research works are focused on adjusting IC reporting to national (Andriessen and Stam 2004; Stam and Andriessen 2009; Bontis 2004; Pulic 2002; Pasher 1999, Lin and Edvinsson 2008; Lin and Edvinsson 2011) and regional clusters (EC 2006), as well as cities (Bounfour and Edvinsson 2005), in order to increase report accuracy by including their specific features, this chapter is aimed at analyzing IC from different Serbian industries in order to facilitate the fine-tuning regarding the particular facets of the Serbian industries, that is, to define adequate IC reporting models within different Serbian industries.

The chapter is organized as follows. It will first illustrate the literature review related to IC and IC reporting methods (Section 2); then, attention will be turned to research questions and the method chosen to address the issues (Section 3). After analysis of IC, as well as the key value drivers and specific features of IC within different industries (Section 4), the models of IC reporting within each particular industry will be presented (Section 5). Finally, the most important research findings (Section 6), theoretical and practical implications, as well as the research limitations, will be discussed (Section 7) and the conclusions drawn (Section 8).

2. THEORETICAL BACKGROUND

Definition and Nature of IC

The field of IC is multidisciplinary, and views of the nature and taxonomy of IC tend to vary from one author to another. The term "intellectual capital" emphasizes a combination of intellect and capital in order to point out the importance of knowledge (Serenko and Bontis 2013). IC is often viewed as intangible assets or knowledge resources that can create value for companies as well as achieve and maintain a competitive edge for them (Sharma et al. 2007; Stewart 1997; Sveiby 1997a; Yi and Davey 2010). According to many definitions in the literature, IC includes only productive knowledge, which can be transformed into value. Intellectual resources or ability that can contribute to value creation can be categorized as IC (Stewart 1997; Edvinsson and Malone 1997; Sullivan 1998; Kong 2008).

IC can be categorized in different ways (Kaufmann and Schneider 2004). Given that IC refers to the collective knowledge that is embedded in employees, organizational routines and relations with the external environment (Bontis 2002), in this chapter, we follow the well-accepted IC taxonomy in which IC encompasses three interrelated components: human capital (HC), structural capital (SC) and relational capital (RC) (Saint-Onge 1996; Roos et al. 1997; Stewart 1997; Bontis 1998; MERITUM 2002; Roos 2004; Marr 2004; Tovstiga and Tulugurova 2007). HC consists of various human-based resources and capabilities, including experience, skills, competences, attitude, intuition, creativity and innovativeness of people (Bontis 2002; Choo and Bontis 2002; Roos et al. 1997). SC is the nonhuman knowledge that lies in databases, processes, strategies, routines, organizational culture, brands and copyrights (Bontis et al. 2000; Guthrie et al. 2006). RC represents a company's relations with its external stakeholders and their perceptions about it (Bontis 1998; Bontis 2002; Fletcher et al. 2003; Marr and Roos 2005).

IC Measuring and Reporting

The reasons for fostering IC measuring and reporting practices are many (Marr et al. 2003; Andriessen 2004). According to many authors (Andriessen 2004; Sveiby 1997a; Kaplan and Norton 1996, Roos et al. 1997; Edvinsson and Malone 1997), the basic motives of IC measuring and reporting are the following: (1) *to improve internal management,* because IC statements provide an insight into vital intangibles, which determine future success (Kaplan and Norton 1996); (2) *to improve external reporting,* because IC statements help companies disclose the value's attributes to stakeholders outside the company (Pike et al. 2002); and (3) *to enable legal protection and transaction of intangibles,* because IC statements help companies sell or buy some intangibles as intellectual property. Lönnqvist et al. (2009) find the benefit of the IC measuring and reporting within the change process, and Lerro and Schiuma (2013) find it in managing organizational value-creation capabilities. Measuring and reporting IC brings managerial (Dumay 2012; Chiucchi 2013), cultural (Chiucchi 2008) and organizational changes (Mouritsen and Roslender 2009) and might foster creativity, imagination, energy and passion within organizations (Lerro and Schiuma 2013) and IC mobilization (Chiucchi 2013). Perhaps the best reason to measure IC is to consider the risks of not measuring it (Cabrilo and Grubic Nesic 2010), such as unpredicted labor shortages, skills mismatches that curtail growth, talent fleeing to competitors and productivity levels that are only 70 percent of what they could be (Schiemann 2008).

By analyzing the literature that examines IC measuring and reporting, it is possible to conclude that there has been a minor explosion in the IC metrics industry over the last two decades (Edvinsson 2013; Guthrie et al. 2012; Cabrilo and Grubic-Nesic 2010). One recent study categorized fifteen different approaches to measuring IC (Karagiannis and Nemetz 2009), and another identified more than thirty (Pike and Roos 2004; Andriessen 2004).

According to the main objective (to define groups of relevant IC indicators within different industries), the "scorecard-based" approach to IC measuring and reporting is the focus in this chapter. According to Karagiannis and Nemetz (2009), scorecard methods are inductive-analytical (Daum 2003) and nonmonetary reporting methods aimed at identifying main IC areas for assessment and defining a set of key measures for each area (Lerro and Schiuma 2013). Certain methods refer to those relevant IC areas as key IC influencing factors—for example, Wissensbilanz (Arbeitskreis Wissensbilanz 2004), key success factors—for example, IC index (Roos et. al. 1997) or critical IC intangibles—for example, MERITUM Guidelines (MERITUM 2002). In this chapter, they are referred to as the key IC value drivers and are related to intangible value drivers that affect the performance and success of an organization the most.

The IC questionnaire in this research was designed based on the theoretical and practical guidelines of the following IC reporting methods: Intangible Assets Monitor (Sveiby 1997a, 1997b), Danish Guidelines (DATI 2000), MERITUM Guidelines (MERITUM 2002) and Wissensbilanz (Arbeitskreis Wissensbilanz 2004). These methods measure each particular IC component (human, structural and relational), as well as specific value drivers within particular IC components.

Intangible Assets Monitor (IAM) was developed by Sveiby (1997a, 1997b). The intangible part of the balance sheet is classified as individual competence (people's capacity to act in various situations, including skills, education, experience, values and social skills); internal structure consisting of a wide range of patents, concepts, models, and computer and administrative systems; and external structure consisting of relationships with customers and suppliers, brand names, trademarks and reputation or image. Danish Guidelines provide "a status of the company's efforts to develop its knowledge resources through knowledge management" (DATI 2000, 14), and do so in "text, figures and illustrations" (14). MERITUM Guidelines is a project that results in the system of indicators communicating the company's business success and helping to manage its stock of intangibles (MERITUM 2002). Finally, Wissensbilanz is a German project that has incorporated a great number of small as well as large German companies. According to this method, the IC statement "is an instrument to precisely assess and to develop the intellectual capital of an organization" (Arbeitskreis Wissensbilanz 2004, 11) in which the influencing IC factors are "highlighted with measurable IC indicators in the shape of numbers and facts" (28).

3. RESEARCH DESIGN

Method

The questionnaire was designed to assess the relevance of defined IC value drivers and identify the key IC value drivers and specific features of IC, as well as the knowledge processes, such as knowledge creation/acquisition, sharing and codification, in Serbian companies from different industries. Within the group of IC value drivers suggested in the initial methods (IAM, Danish Guidelines, MERITUM Guidelines, Wissensbilanz), thirty-two value drivers were chosen—twelve of HC, ten of SC, and ten of RC.

According to Tovstiga and Tulugurova (2009), the HC analysis encompassed all three attributes of employee HC: competence (knowledge, skill sets and experiential knowledge), attitude (level of motivation, behavioral patterns) and intellectual agility (innovation, creativity, flexibility, adaptability). The categorized questions included the following four items: (1) managers' competence development, (2) managers' attitudes toward employees' desirable characteristics, (3) managers' attitudes toward employees'motivational factors and (4) the relevance of the defined HC value drivers and identification of the key HC value drivers. Other attributes of HC were explored by thirty-five Likert-type items and factor analysis.

The analysis of SC included knowledge-related processes, such as processes and procedures, organizational routines and attributes (including the attributes of organizational culture), managerial mechanisms and SC value drivers. The categorized questions included managers' attitudes toward the following: (1) knowledge transformation for innovation, (2) knowledge codification, (3) knowledge storing and knowledge base and (4) the relevance of the defined SC value drivers and the key SC value drivers. Other attributes of SC were explored by eighteen Likert-type items and factor analysis.

During the analysis of the RC of organizations, external relations with stakeholders were carefully examined. The categorized questions included managers' attitudes toward (1) key stakeholders (customers were excluded, as they were considered separately), (2) key sources of competitiveness, (3) key sources of knowledge acquisition and (4) the relevance of the defined RC value drivers and the key RC value drivers. Other attributes of RC were explored by seventeen Likert-type items and factor analysis.

Each of the IC value drivers was determined by a group of questions. Moreover, questions were clustered around three primary IC categories (human, structural and relational) and the value drivers they comprised. The final version of the questionnaire consisted of eighty-seven questions. The first five questions were factual questions, thirty-nine questions were related to HC value drivers, twenty-seven questions to SC value drivers and sixteen questions to RC value drivers. Out of the total number, seventy questions were applied by the scaling technology. All Likert-type items were measured on a five-point Likert scale, where "1—strongly disagree" and "5—strongly agree". The remaining seventeen questions were categorical, most of which were the "closed" type.

The first draft of the questionnaire was pretested by ten managers from diverse industries, regions and company sizes. During the interviews, they pointed out some difficulties regarding a few questions. Their feedback significantly improved the final version of questionnaire.

Sample

In this survey, the responses were given by top- and medium-level managers, as it was assumed that they were most familiar with the intangible success drivers of their companies. In order to overcome a general lack of survey participants, the research team compiled a list of Serbian companies (following the criteria of good financial performance according to the data drawn from the financial statements of each of these companies) where the team members had business contacts or friends in managerial positions. These business contacts were "survey insiders". Because these business contacts were used successfully, the response rate was outstanding—90 percent. Such a high response rate can also be attributed to additional steps that were undertaken. The questionnaire provided a degree of anonymity, whereas different forms/versions of the questionnaire were offered for the convenience of respondents.

A total of 554 managers from sixty-seven Serbian companies from seven different industries participated in the survey. Selected companies were diverse with regard to ownership structure, number of employees and geographic location. The number of respondents varied across companies, according to the company size (number of available managers) and the willingness of managers to be included in the survey. The respondents from a particular company differed in their hierarchical and functional positions.

The sample structure is presented in Table 6.1. The respondents are distributed between seven industries, that is, utility services (20.9 percent), industry (19.7 percent), mining and energy (17 percent), services (14.3 percent), media (9.9 percent), information-communication technology (ICT) (9.2 percent) and banking (9.0 percent).

The share of respondents from small, medium and large companies within industries is presented in Table 6.2.

Table 6.1 The sample structure

Industry	Number of respondents	Number of companies	% in the sample
Utility services	116	13	20.9%
Industry	109	13	19.7%
Mining and energy	94	3	17.0%
Services	79	12	14.3%
Media	55	9	9.9%
ICT	51	10	9.2%
Banking	50	7	9.0%
TOTAL	554	67	100%

Table 6.2 The share of respondents from small, medium and large companies within industries

% of respondents from	Utility services	Industry	Mining and energy	Services	Media	ICT	Banking
Large companies	69.82	56.07	100	27.85	30.91	19.60	40.82
Medium-size companies	23.28	43.93	0	31.64	29.09	49.03	22.45
Small companies	6.90	0	0	40.51	40.00	31.37	36.73

Data Analysis

Pareto analysis of cumulative frequencies and the analysis of the percentage of occurrence have been used in all categorized questions. In the Likert-type questions, the data have been analyzed by using factor analysis of principal components (Kaiser criteria). After extracting the factors, the orthogonal analytical rotation (varimax criterion) has been applied. Pareto analysis has been used to determine the impact level of particular IC value drivers on goal achievement and business success. Measures of suggested drivers' importance in Serbian companies have been identified based on their impact level. The principal component factor analysis has identified the most relevant factors to describe IC of organizations from each industry and the level of presence (presence measure) of these IC factors in the companies from the surveyed industries. The analysis of the identified factors and their presence measure has recognized the dominant characteristics and numerous specific features of the IC within specific industries.

4.   OVERVIEW OF INTELLECTUAL CAPITAL WITHIN DIFFERENT SERBIAN INDUSTRIES

The results and the discussion are presented in seven separate sections, with each section including the IC analysis, identification of the key value drivers and strengths and weaknesses, as well as the specific characteristics of IC within the particular industry. Only the most important results are represented in this section, because they are the basis for the defined group of IC indicators relevant to each industry.

Analysis of Intellectual Capital in Serbian Utility Services

A total of 116 top- and medium-level managers from thirteen companies within Serbian utility services participated in the survey (see Table 6.1). Most of the respondents (69.82 percent) were from large organizations, 23.28 percent were from midsize organizations and only 6.9 percent of respondents were from small organizations (see Table 6.2). The majority of respondents were in utility services (33.6 percent), belonged to the 36 to 45 age group, with 21 to 30 years length of service (33.6 percent), and had university education (58.6 percent).

The analysis of managers' competence development in Serbian utility services reveals that only half of them participate in professional development trainings once or twice a year, whereas nearly half of them take the trainings less frequently or do not take them at all. More than a quarter of respondents (28 percent) from the utility sector participated in the development training less than six months ago, 27 percent had been there more than six months but less than one year ago and 26 percent had been at the training more than one year ago. It is alarming that as many as 19 percent of managers have never attended professional development training.

The managers were asked to rank employees' personal and work characteristics (efficiency, experience, expertise, cooperativeness, innovativeness, commitment, education, initiative, loyalty, continuous competence development) they appreciated the most. According to managers in Serbian utility services, the key employee competences in this industry are expertise, commitment and cooperativeness.

In order to assess the relevance of defined HC value drivers, the participants in the survey were asked to choose, without ranking, five out of nine offered HC value drivers, which according to them, had the greatest impact on their company's business success. The following ranking of HC value drivers (in decreasing order) is developed: (1) efficiency, (2) experience, (3) motivation, (4) strategic alignment, (5) managing competence and leadership, (6) expertise, (7) education and knowledge-sharing, (8) innovativeness, and (9) social skills. *The most relevant HC value drivers in Serbian utility services (the "Pareto rule") are efficiency, experience and motivation.*

The analysis of attitudes toward innovation is based on the question related to the treatment of inventions (novel ideas) in their companies. The results show that inventions are exploited to the largest extent spontaneously—47 percent. About 39 percent of novel ideas are codified in explicit form, whereas 14 percent remain in tacit form. Only 5 percent of innovations are patented (transformation of HC into SC through intellectual property).

The analysis of employee databases is focused on identifying whether and to what extent these companies create knowledge bases. According to the results, employee databases in Serbian utility companies mainly contain the employee's personal information and information on formal education and service length, whereas information on the employee's actual experience, knowledge and skills, as well as their psychological profiles, is not as well documented. In order to create a knowledge base that leads to a better HC management, the observed companies have to focus on real knowledge and skills of employees rather than on their formal education, on their work experience rather than on their years of service.

By looking at what employees document in their work process, the level of knowledge codification can be determined. The results show that employees in Serbian utility services mostly document the work process (61 percent) that is significant only for process innovations. In 49 percent of cases, employees write down specific experiences (specific problems and ways of dealing with them), and in 44 percent of cases, they document the way they work. This is how employee experiences get codified and may be shared within the company. In only 16 percent of cases do employees write down novel ideas for the work process improvement, which is a small percentage of codification.

Based on relevance, the following ranking of SC value drivers (in decreasing order) is developed: (1) managerial processes, (2) employees' communication and interaction, (3) ICT, (4) process and procedural innovation, (5) databases, (6) research and development (R&D), (7) product innovation development, (8) brands and trademarks, (9) corporate culture and (10) technological opportunities for knowledge transfer and acquisition. *The key SC value drivers are managerial processes, employees' communication and interaction, ICT, and process and procedural innovation development.*

Organizations from the utility sector cooperate the most with business partners and local governments, which is logical, given that these public enterprises are under the jurisdiction of local governments. These companies cooperate with research institutes, universities and shareholders the least. Little cooperation with stakeholders is an expected result, given that all the observed companies are still considered nonprivatized (no shareholders). On the other hand, the small extent of cooperation with research institutes and universities reveals that these companies are not focused on innovating their services, research and development, probably because of the monopoly position they have in the market.

The utility companies generally obtain the knowledge they lack by cooperating with the users of their products and services, by recruiting people with appropriate competences and by training and education of their employees. Faculties are the least important source of knowledge acquisition for these organizations. According to the managers' opinions, customers appreciate the quality of their products and service, reliability and long tradition the most and their innovation the least.

In order of decreasing relevance, the ranking of defined RC value drivers is the following: customer relationship, relationship with local community, relationship with media, supplier relationship, relationship with financial institutions, perceived image, relationship with shareholders and investors, social involvement, relationship with competitors and integration of external knowledge. *The key RC value drivers in Serbian utility services are customer relationship and relationship with local community.* The external knowledge integration and relationships with competitors affect business results and success of their organizations the least, which is a logical result, given the monopoly position of these companies in Serbia. The public utility companies in Serbia quite logically orient their relational capital to local communities.

Setting aside the key value drivers of human, structural and relational capital, the key IC value drivers in Serbian utility services are defined and presented in Table 6.4. These value drivers are the following: employee efficiency, experience and motivation, managerial processes, employees' communication and interaction, ICT, process and procedural innovation, customer relationship and relationship with local community. According to managers, these items impact business achievements and success in Serbian utility services to the greatest extent.

Table 6.3 The Cronbach's alpha in different industries

	Utility service	Industry	Mining & energy	Services	Media	ICT	Banking
Cronbach's alpha	0.7464	0.7542	0.7725	0.8099	0.8669	0.8587	0.8612

Because the Cronbach's alpha is 0.7464 (Table 6.3), the questionnaire is suitable for researching IC of companies in the utility sector. The most relevant statistical factors in the utility sector are shown in Table 6.4.

HC is a dominant part of IC of public utilities, whereas innovation and experience of employees have particular significance within the HC. Because of the high degree of rewarding and encouraging employee innovation, the management of communal organizations is aware of the increasing importance of innovation and the lack of this HC key driver. The SC in the surveyed organizations is characterized by the information technologies (IT) impact on cooperation and communication among employees. In the analyzed companies, it is possible for a part of the HC to be codified by the IT and to use IT to support knowledge sharing. Because the atmosphere in these companies is generally stimulating, conditions for successful knowledge sharing exist. In utility companies, the dominant characteristics of RC are their relationships with suppliers and other utility companies, as well as a clear presentation to the public. These companies do not attach great importance to professional training and transfer of knowledge after training courses, which together with the organizational competence based solely on the competence of several key experts, indicate improper understanding of professional development goals. The employees do not sufficiently accept the goals of the organization as their own. They are, to some extent, uncommitted and believe that the success of an organization is not the responsibility of all employees, so the dominance of the leaders in the public utilities is obvious and it creates leader–follower problems.

Analysis of Intellectual Capital in Serbian Industry Sector

A total of 109 managers holding key positions in thirteen industrial enterprises represented the Serbian industry sample (see Table 6.1). The vast majority of respondents (56.07 percent) came from large organizations, while 43.93 percent came from medium-sized ones (see Table 6.2). The majority of respondents in Serbian industrial companies (46 percent) belonged to the 46 to 55 age group (there were no respondents under 25 years of age in the sample), had 21 to 30 years of service (37 percent) and had university education (53 percent).

The analysis of managerial competence development reveals that more than half of the managers in the Serbian industrial enterprises insufficiently develop their competences and neglect training and education. Almost a quarter of them (23 percent) have never improved their competence after completing formal education. In the current environment with the lifelong learning imperative and the role of management as a key to competitiveness, managers from Serbian industrial companies insufficiently develop their competencies, which is certainly an important cause of the lack of competitiveness of these companies.

Managerial attitudes toward characteristics of employees reveal that the most desirable ones in Serbian industrial companies are experience, cooperativeness, commitment and efficiency. On the other hand, employee innovativeness and continuous competence development, which are the most important employees' personal and work characteristics in the knowledge era, are considered the least important.

The analysis of motivational factors shows that managers see money as the key motivational factor for employees in Serbian industry. Other stated factors are insignificant in terms of employee motivation.

Assessing the relevance of defined HC value drivers in Serbian industrial companies, the following ranking (in decreasing order) is acquired: (1) efficiency, (2) experience, (3) motivation, (4) managing competence and leadership, (5) education and knowledge sharing, (6) expertise, (7) strategic alignment, (8) innovativeness and (9) social skills. *The key HC value drivers in Serbian industrial companies are efficiency, experience and motivation.* It is disappointing that expert knowledge and training and sharing of knowledge are not HC key value drivers in the industry and that, according to managers' opinions, innovation (which is the key to competitiveness in the knowledge era) has almost the least impact on the success of their organizations.

The results related to the transformation of novel ideas into innovation and exploitation of inventions in Serbian industrial companies show that inventions are exploited to the largest extent according to formal procedures and rules—39 percent, while 24 percent are implemented spontaneously. In 40 percent of cases, good ideas are always implemented, and 61 percent of novel ideas are codified in explicit form. Around 10 percent of innovations are patented (codified, implemented and protected as intellectual property).

In this chapter, formal education is not a comprehensive and accurate measure of employees' knowledge and skills, and service length is not a comprehensive and precise measure of experience. If a company creates a knowledge base containing real knowledge, experience and skills, it is able to realize what it knows and what it doesn't know. A knowledge base can contribute to knowledge creation, acquisition and sharing. In Serbian industrial companies, the key data in employee databases are employee's personal information and information on service length and formal education, whereas information on the employee's actual experience, knowledge and skills, as well as their psychological profiles, are much less documented.

The ranking of defined SC value drivers according to decreasing relevance to Serbian industrial companies is as follows: (1) employees' communication and interaction, (2) managerial processes, (3) process and procedural innovation, (4) brands and trademarks, (5) ICT, (6) R&D, (7) product innovation development, (8) technological opportunities for knowledge transfer and acquisition, (9) databases and (10) corporate culture. *The key SC value drivers in Serbian industry are employees' communication and interaction, and managerial processes.* Further analysis of how employees interact and communicate within companies indicates that these interactions are based mainly on direct verbal communication rather than on technology usage. Neither product and process innovation development, nor R&D is seen as the key SC value driver. These results indicate that innovations and R&D are neglected again, which is in line with the rankings of HC value drivers, in which innovativeness and competence development are omitted. These findings reveal obvious deficiencies in innovation in Serbian industrial enterprises because of the lack of managing initiatives aimed at encouraging and supporting the innovation process.

Key stakeholders for industrial companies in Serbia are partners, banks and the state administration. This is to be expected, because partners are directly involved in the process of value creation, banks have financial resources and the state administration determines import and export quotes, custom rates, legal roles, etc. These companies rarely cooperate with local administration, shareholders and research institutes. The main reason for undeveloped cooperation with shareholders is the relatively recent privatization of the companies in the sample (Kontic and Cabrilo 2009). The rare cooperation with research institutes and universities reveals that industrial enterprises are not oriented to product innovation or have their own internal R&D activities.

These companies acquire the knowledge they lack mostly through cooperation with customers, employing individuals with proper competence, training and education and benchmarking. The key sources of competitiveness most appreciated by users/consumers are the quality of products and its long tradition in the market and the reputation of its products and services.

Finally, the ranking of defined RC value drivers according to decreasing relevance for industrial companies is the following: (1) customer relationship, (2) supplier relationship, (3) perceived image, (4) relationship with financial institutions, (5) integration of external knowledge, (6) relationship with competitors, (7) relationship with shareholders and investors, (8) relationship with media, (9) social involvement and (10) relationship with local community. *The key RC value drivers are customer relationship and supplier relationship.*

The key IC value drivers comprising the key HC, SC and RC value drivers in Serbian industrial companies are presented in Table 6.4.

Since the Cronbach's alpha is 0.7542 (see Table 6.3), the questionnaire is suitable for IC research in industrial companies. The most relevant statistical factors in industrial companies are shown in Table 6.1. Based on them and on the weighted factor values, the dominant characteristics and numerous IC specificities in the industry can be perceived. The results show that HC is more important than the other two categories of IC. Responsibility and experience of the employees are the characteristics of HC that dominate when compared with expert knowledge and social skills of employees (empathy and the ability to quickly and easily interact with others). The organizational culture supports open communication, interaction and cooperation between employees, and thereby encourages knowledge sharing within the organization. Relations with customers and suppliers are focused on acquiring new knowledge, which suggests that the structural and relational capitals of industrial enterprises are in the function of learning (knowledge acquisition) from the external environment. Employees in industrial organizations are, to some extent, uncommitted (because they generally do the job without too much energy), which indicates employee dissatisfaction. These companies prefer experience in the organization less than professional experience. The analysis of IC in industry still reveals some business dependence on key experts in these companies and the willingness and motivation of employees for training and interagency cooperation.

Analysis of Intellectual Capital in the Serbian Mining and Energy Sector

Ninety-four top- and medium-level managers from three companies within the Serbian mining and energy sector participated in the survey (see Table 6.1). All companies in the sample were large (see Table 6.2). Considering that 89.59 percent of total employees in the Serbian mining and energy sector were employed in three Serbian companies included in the survey, the sample can be considered reliable for the analysis of IC in this industry. Most of the respondents (41 percent) were between 36 and 45 years old, had university education (60 percent) and had 11 to 20 years of service (33 percent).

Concerning managers' competence development, the results obtained were alarming. The fact that 22 percent of respondents have never participated in any professional training and that 39 percent did it more than a year ago points out that managers in the mining and energy sector have been insufficiently professionally competent. Insufficient managerial competence development in the observed Serbian companies certainly denotes a lack of modern leadership and management concepts and practices, which could seriously undermine the competitiveness of these companies.

The analysis of managers' attitudes toward desirable characteristics of employees reveals that the key employee competences are expertise, cooperativeness, commitment and efficiency. On the other hand, they find the least important employee competences to be innovativeness and loyalty.

According to the opinion of the managers, money is nearly the only motivating factor in the mining and energy industry. These results are logical taking into account that money has significant impacts on employees' motivation and their work-related behavior (Opsahl and Dunnette 1966; Whyte 1995), especially on employees with low incomes occupying nonmanagerial positions (Kovach 1987) and that Serbian citizens have a living standard and gross salary per hour much lower than the EU average.

The assessment of the relevance of defined HC value drivers results in the following ranking according to decreasing importance: (1) employee efficiency, (2) employee motivation, (3) employee experience, (4) employee expertise, (5) education and knowledge-sharing, (6) employee innovativeness, (7) managerial competence and leadership, (8) strategic alignment, and (9) social skills. The *key HC value drivers are efficiency, motivation and experience.* It is interesting that, among the most influential HC value drivers in the mining and energy sector, employee expertise, education and knowledge sharing, as well as innovativeness, do not exist. However, these HC value drivers are the key to company competitiveness in the knowledge economy.

Research on an organization's ability to innovate must encompass individual innovativeness and the organization's potential to "catch" employees' ideas, codify them and systematically incorporate them into the organizational processes. In the observed companies, employees mostly implement ideas spontaneously (46 percent), whereas in 13 percent of cases, the organizations have defined procedures for systematic implementation of inventions. The results show that 34 percent of ideas are codified (patented, reported and a procedure defined), whereas only 3 percent of innovations are patented. In 20 percent of cases, employees do not disclose their ideas.

The employee bases usually consist of personal information and data on education and service length. In order to create a knowledge base that leads to better-organized human resources, the observed organizations must focus on real knowledge and skills of employees rather than on their formal education, on their work experience rather than on their years of service. The employees in the mining and energy sector mainly annotate the work process, specific experiences and the way they work. They record new ideas for improving the work process much less.

The following is the ranking of SC value drivers, relative to their importance in decreasing order: (1) employees' communication and interaction, (2) managerial processes, (3) ICT, (4) process innovation, (5) databases, (6) R&D, (7) technological opportunities for knowledge transfer and acquisition, (8) product innovation, (9) brands and trademarks and (10) corporate culture. The following SC value drivers are highlighted as the key ones: employees' communication and interaction, managerial processes and ICT. These findings might be the primary cause of deficiencies in innovation in the Serbian mining and energy sector.

The observed companies mostly cooperate with business partners, state institutions, and associations and business alliances. This choice is a logical consequence of the fact that these companies are state-owned enterprises (or the state has a large share of the enterprise package). The companies from the mining and energy sector gain knowledge they lack mainly by cooperating with the scientific research institutes and through training and education. A small portion of missing knowledge is acquired through cooperation with customers, universities, employment of people with relevant knowledge and experiences of more successful companies. It is logical that managers rate that consumers are not the major source of new knowledge, given specificities of the observed companies' activities and products. According to the opinion of managers from the mining and energy companies, their customers rate the quality of their products/services, their long tradition and their reliability the highest, and the image of the company and its innovativeness the lowest. However, together with previously presented results, these results indicate the negative relationship of surveyed managers toward innovation, because they think innovation is not important for their consumers.

The relevance of RC value drivers on business achievements and success in the mining and energy sector is as follows: (1) customer relationship, (2) supplier relationship, (3) relationship with financial institutions, (4) perceived image, (5) relationship with local community, relationship with competitors, (6) relationship with media, (7) social involvement, (8) integration of external knowledge and (9) relationship with shareholders and investors. *The key RC value drivers in Serbian mining and energy companies are customer relationships and supplier relationships.*

Setting aside only the key value drivers of human, structural and relational capital, the group of the key IC value drivers for the mining and energy sector in Serbia are identified and presented in Table 6.4.

The questionnaire is appropriate for investigating phenomena of IC in Serbian companies from mining and energy sectors, because Cronbach's alpha is 0.7725 (see Table 6.3). In the observed companies, the generation of new knowledge through R&D activities; an organizational culture that promotes satisfaction, motivation and knowledge sharing within organizations; and IT support processes of knowledge sharing are dominant within IC. SC (investment in R&D) and RC (acquiring new knowledge from consumers and suppliers) mainly serve as a support to HC—the new knowledge created in order to increase employee competence. This result reveals the orientation of these organizations to manage HC and knowledge flows, which is an entirely appropriate strategy in terms of knowledge economy. The greatest potential of the human capital is represented by the experience of employees. Although some activities for encouraging employee innovation (remuneration, motivation, professional development) are identified in the observed companies, the lack of employee innovativeness (or lack of implementation of new ideas) is also a cause of the lack of product/process/procedure innovation. In the RC of the surveyed organizations, the relevant dependence of the business performance on a small number of key customers is identified, which always points to some instability of RC.

Although employees are rewarded according to their contribution to business results, they are not sufficiently focused on creating added value. In the HC, employees lack social skills that are important for communication, cooperation and teamwork, codification processes and knowledge sharing. The atmosphere in the observed enterprises is partially characterized by employees' fear and insecurity, which cause a lack of motivation and focus for their work.

Analysis of Intellectual Capital in the Serbian Services

Seventy-nine managers holding key managerial positions in twelve service companies participated in the survey (see Table 6.1). The vast majority of participants (40 percent) came from small organizations, 32 percent from medium-size organizations and 28 percent from large organizations (see Table 6.2). The results of manager profile examinations showed that the managerial structure in the Serbian service industry comprised mostly people ages 26 to 55 with an university education and between 11 and 20 years of working experience. Considering the previous results, the sample can be seen as representative.

Related to managers' competence development in Serbian service companies, a high percent of managers who have never taken part in a competence development program (16 percent) is particularly worrying. In addition, when managers rank employee characteristics they appreciate the most, the results include the following: competence, cooperativeness, commitment, efficiency, experience, education, initiative, innovativeness, loyalty and competence development. According to these results, top managers do not seem to recognize the importance of innovativeness and continuous competence development, so it is possible to conclude that top managers in the Serbian service industry still largely apply principles typical of the industrial era in that the level of awareness of changes in the environment and new demands of knowledge management are very low in this industry. In addition, the reasons for the lack of competitiveness within the Serbian service industry as a whole are examined in the obtained results.

Based on cumulative frequencies (Pareto analysis), the following ranking of HC value drivers (in decreasing importance) is acquired in the service industry: (1) employee efficiency, (2) employee motivation, (3) employee experience, (4) employee expertise, (5) management competence and leadership, (6) education and knowledge sharing, (7) employee innovativeness,

(8) strategic alignment and (9) social skills. *The key HC value drivers are employee efficiency, employee motivation and employee experience.* Efficiency being on top of the list and innovativeness close to the last position reflect the existence of an industrial rather than a knowledge era in Serbian services. Furthermore, managers find education and knowledge sharing, as well as innovation, to be less important for business performance, and that is quite discouraging. Such attitudes are certainly not in accordance with the modern economy in which innovation and lifelong learning have become ultimate tools for companies in their attempts to cope with the dynamics and global competition in business.

The results of managers' attitudes toward transforming knowledge into innovation, as well as the creation of a knowledge base, show that innovations in Serbian service industries are exploited to the largest extent spontaneously— 53 percent. About 37 percent of innovations in services are codified, but only 7.5 percent of innovations are patented. Concerning the creation of a knowledge base, the results show that employee databases in Serbian service companies mostly contain information on formal education, personal information and information on service length. They reveal that Serbian service companies are still not focused enough on identifying valuable knowledge, skills and experience, as well as their codification and storage, through the knowledge base creation. Finally, related to the level of knowledge codification in this industry, the results show that employees in the services industry mostly document the work process, specific experiences and the way they work. In only 20 percent of cases, employees write down new ideas for the work process improvement, which is a very small percentage of innovation codification.

The following is the ranking of SC value drivers, relative to their importance in decreasing order: (1) employees' communication and interaction, (2) managerial processes, (3) ICT, (4) databases, (5) process and procedural innovation development, (6) brands and trademarks, (7) product innovation development, (8) R&D, (9) corporate culture and (10) technological opportunities for knowledge transfer and acquisition. *The key SC value drivers are employees' communication and interaction and managerial processes.*

The key stakeholders in the Serbian service industry are business partners, industrial associations and unions, and state and local administration. Banks and unions are significantly less important stakeholders, whereas the observed companies have the least degree of cooperation with shareholders, research institutes, investors and universities. Because most observed companies have just recently finished or not yet finished the process of privatization, they have not developed the proper relationship with shareholders and investors so far, unaware that these relationships are extremely important for their business activities. A small degree of cooperation with scientific research institutes and universities reveals that service companies in Serbia are not sufficiently geared toward innovation and knowledge updating.

According to top managers from the observed companies, the key sources of competitiveness most appreciated by users/consumers are the following: the service quality, long tradition and reliability. Among the key sources of competitiveness, image and innovativeness are not listed.

The ranking of RC value drivers, according to decreasing influence on business success includes the following: (1) customer relationships, (2) perceived image, (3) relationships to media, (4) relationships to local community, (5) integration of external knowledge, (6) relationships with competitors, (7) supplier relationships, (8) social involvement, (9) relationships with financial institutions and (10) relationships with shareholders and investors. *The key RC value drivers are customer relationships and image.* It is strange that image is not a key source of competitiveness, but it is the key value driver with a significant influence on business performance and success. This finding reveals that managers are aware of the positive impact of image (it is also revealed by the high rank of relationship with media), but they are not aware of its relevance for competitiveness.

Based on the key value drivers of human, structural and relational capital, the key IC value drivers of the Serbian service companies can be established (Table 6.4).

The questionnaire is adequate for investigating phenomena of IC in service companies, because Cronbach's alpha is 0.8099 (see Table 6.3). The knowledge sharing potential, in terms of encouraging organizational culture and empathetic employees, is the dominant feature of IC organizations in the service sector. Organizational culture is characterized by trust and good relationships. Rewarding employees, expert knowledge and experience of employees dominate the HC, and the IT impact on the cooperation of employees and business results dominate the SC and knowledge acquisition from the external environment is the most significant feature within RC. Therefore, the relationships of the organizations with customers, suppliers and competitors are aimed at acquiring new knowledge.

The organizations in the service sector reward innovation and initiative of employees and their contribution to business performance to a greater extent, which is positive, because these initiatives encourage innovation and focus employees on value creation. The analysis perceives a problem with a lack of innovation, and the main reason is that employees are not motivated to improve. Regarding the process of sharing knowledge within these organizations, the problem is in the HC because employees are not willing to share their knowledge, and in the organizational culture in which trust between employees is undermined to some extent by fear and uncertainty. The observed organizations should increasingly encourage knowledge sharing, not by greater application of IT, because communication and work of employees is not based on IT, but by building satisfaction and trust in employees and encouraging teamwork and informal communication.

Analysis of Intellectual Capital in Serbian Media

The IC survey included fifty-five top- and medium-level managers from nine Serbian media companies (see Table 6.1). Most respondents were from small organizations (40 percent), followed by a group of respondents from large organizations (31 percent) and midsize organizations (29 percent) (see Table 6.2). The largest percentage of respondents (38.18 percent) was aged 36 to45 years, with less than five years of experience (36.36 percent) and university graduates (36.36 percent). A significantly less percentage of college-educated managers in the media compared with the previous industries may partly be due to the fact that the appropriate colleges for the media sector in Serbia began to work after the year 2000 (except for journalism).

Considering the professional development of managers, the media situation is alarming. The result showing that 60 percent of respondents have either never been in training or were there more than one year ago reveals that managers in the media do not have the relevant managerial and leadership knowledge and skills because that knowledge quickly becomes obsolete. Learning capability improves the business performance of an organization (Senge 1990; Stewart 1997; Nahapiet and Ghoshal 1998; Bontis et al. 2002; Prieto and Revilla 2006). Thus, the lack of managerial learning capabilities certainly significantly affects the performance of the surveyed companies. The most desirable employee personal and work characteristics for managers in media are expertise, cooperativeness, efficiency and commitment. However, the least important are innovation and continuous improvement of employees, which is absolutely inconsistent with the requirements of the modern media, where innovation is the basis for competitiveness improvement, and continuous development is the foundation of innovation.

The following is the ranking of HC value drivers relative to their importance in decreasing order: (1) efficiency, (2) experience, (3) motivation, (4) expertise, (5) managing competence and leadership, (6) innovativeness, (7) strategic alignment, (8) social skills, and (9) education and (10) knowledge sharing. *The key ones in the Serbia media are employee efficiency, experience, motivation and expertise.* The unexpected result is that innovation and social skills (such as communication skills or teamwork skills), as well as staff training, are not in the group of key drivers of HC in the media.

The results of managers' attitudes toward transforming knowledge into innovation, as well as the creation of a knowledge base, show that inventions in Serbian media companies are exploited to the largest extent spontaneously—32 percent. In 23 percent of cases, inventions are continuously implemented according to the formal procedures. Half of all novel ideas are codified in explicit form, whereas 18 percent remain in tacit form. The encouraging fact is that the best ideas in the media are patented in 12.7 percent of cases.

Most of the observed media organizations have personal information—information on education and working experience—in their employee databases. The results on the codification process in media companies reveal that the work process and experience of employees are most codified, while new ideas are less codified.

The ranking of defined SC value drivers according to their relevance for business success of media companies is as follows: (1) ICT, (2) employees' communication and interaction, (3) databases, (4) managerial processes, (5) process and procedural innovation, (6) brands and trademarks, (7) product innovation development, (8) R&D, (9) technological opportunities for knowledge transfer and acquisition and (10) corporate culture. *The key SC value drivers in the observed industry are ICT and employees' communication and interaction.* All SC value drivers related to innovation, such as product innovation development, process and procedural innovation and R&D, are not seen as the key drivers in media. These results reflect the rankings of HC value drivers, where innovativeness and competence development are omitted.

The results on key stakeholders of media companies are very interesting. The key stakeholders are universities, local government (which is logical, because the majority of respondents are from local and regional media), business unions and associations, and government organizations. It is worrying that business partners are not key stakeholders in the media organizations. According to the opinion of the managers, the companies collaborate with business partners, investors and shareholders the least. The key sources of competitiveness are quality of service, reliability, long tradition and image. Knowledge is mainly acquired by employing people with the appropriate competences, and by employee training and education.

The following is the ranking of RC value drivers: (1) customer relationship, (2) perceived image, (3) relationship with local community, (4) relationship with media, (5) social involvement, (6) supplier relationship, (7) integration of external knowledge, (8) relationship with financial institutions, (9) relationship with shareholders and investors and (10) relationship with competitors. *The key RC value drivers in Serbian media companies are customer relationship and image.*

Based on the key value drivers of human, structural and relational capital, the key IC value drivers of Serbian media companies are established as shown in Table 6.4.

The questionnaire is adequate for investigating phenomena of IC in media companies, because Cronbach's alpha is 0.8669 (see Table 6.3). In the framework of IC, the impact of technology on collaboration and operation of employees, an organizational culture characterized by openness and good relations (SC), concern with the satisfaction and loyalty of customers, and monitoring and learning from suppliers and competitors (RC) are dominant factors. Branding and quality systems are highly relevant to SC, whereas acquiring new knowledge in dealing with customers (market research) in order to improve the product or service (program schedule, content, etc.) is significant for RC. In terms of HC, the employees' responsibility and innovativeness are dominant, which is a consequence of rewards programs focused on individual contributions to innovations and overall results. Employee creativity is very important to the success of media organizations, but they do not encourage creativity because employees do not have enough freedom in expressing opinions and new ideas, which is an important precondition for creativity development. The employees are experienced, yet committed to a lesser extent, which raises the issue of motivation. Leaders do not dominate in the observed companies, except in the area of change. Although teamwork is present in the observed organizations to some extent, the collaboration of employees is insufficient.

Analysis of Intellectual Capital in the Serbian ICT Industry

Fifty-one managers from ten ICT Serbian companies participated in the survey (see Table 6.1). Most respondents were from midsize organizations (49 percent), followed by the group of respondents from small organizations (31 percent), whereas 20 percent of respondents were from large ICT companies (see Table 6.2). The largest percentage of respondents (55 percent) was aged 36 to 45 years, had a college education (65 percent) and 11 to 20 years of work experience (41 percent).

Since the ICT field changes dramatically fast, it is important to analyze the development of managerial competence (managerial trainings indirectly indicate their attitudes toward the development of employee competences). The situation in the ICT sector in Serbia is better than in the previously discussed industries, but considering the specificities of the area, it is not satisfactory. Forty-nine percent of respondents attended a professional development event less than six months ago; ten percent did done so more than six months but less than one year ago. However, 41 percent of managers improve themselves considerably less frequently, which is certainly not enough for the competence of managers in the ICT sector, knowing the intensity and frequency of change in this field. Managers in the ICT sector appreciate the most the following characteristics of their employees: expertise, dedication, cooperation and efficiency. On the other hand, they care the least about education, innovation, loyalty and continuous improvement. Because it is impossible to innovate only by applying existing knowledge, learning about and creating new knowledge is the driving force of innovation (Cabrilo and Grubic Nesic 2012b). Nevertheless, employee competence development through training and education is at the end of the list of desirable characteristics of employees. Without innovation and development of employee competences, ICT companies cannot survive in the market, even in the short term.

The following is the ranking of HC value drivers, relative to their importance in decreasing order: (1) efficiency, (2) expertise, (3) experience, (4) motivation, (5) managing competence and leadership, (6) education and knowledge sharing, (7) innovativeness, (8) strategic alignment and (9) social skills. *The key HC value drivers in the Serbian ICT industry are effi-ciency, expertise, experience, motivation, and managing competence and leadership.*

The analysis of managers' attitudes toward transforming knowledge into innovation and exploiting that innovation in their companies shows that novel ideas in the Serbian ICT sector are exploited to the largest extent spontaneously (51 percent). In 33 percent of cases, inventions are imple-mented according to formal procedures. It is discouraging that only 4 per-cent of innovations are patented in the observed ICT companies. Innovation makes continual contributions only within organizations that either have an innovation system, that is, formal procedures and rules, or if it is patented. Nevertheless, it is encouraging that 88 percent of inventions are imple-mented, 37 percent of the ideas are codified and only 12 percent of the ideas remain in tacit form.

The results related to knowledge codification show that the Serbian ICT sector mainly includes the work process codification (57 percent), spe-cific experiences (54 percent) and the way employees work (43 percent). The experience of employees is thus codified. In 23.5 percent of cases, the employees codify new ideas for work process improvements, which is a relatively satisfactory percentage of process improvement codification. Considering the knowledge base, the results reveal that ICT companies are not oriented toward creating and updating the knowledge base, because most companies have information on education and personal data in their employee databases. For these companies, even data on work experience are not among the most relevant.

According to their relevance to an ICT company's success, the ranking (in decreasing order) of defined SC value drivers is as follows: (1) ICT, (2) employees' communication and interaction, (3) managerial processes, (4) process and procedural innovation, (5) databases, (6) brands and trade-marks, (7) R&D, (8) technological opportunities for knowledge transfer and acquisition, (9) corporate culture and (10) product innovation develop-ment. *The key SC value drivers in the Serbian ICT industry are ICT and employees' communication and interaction.* The result in which technol-ogy is the most important driver of SC for ICT companies is logical and expected. However, that managers determine innovative products to be the least influential for business performance and success of their organizations is really surprising.

The key stakeholders for ICT companies in Serbia are business partners, banks and local authorities, in that order of importance. The fact that business partners have the highest ranking is a logical result, because ICT companies must have strong partners in order to be competitive. Banks are an important source of funding, and the importance of local govern-ments may be either a consequence of a larger number of respondents from public companies, or an indication of the orientation of the local market. According to the managers, the key sources of competitiveness are product/service quality and reliability. Less important sources of competitiveness are the long tradition and innovation, and the least important is the image. That innovation is considered a less important source is absolutely unjustifiable and reveals a lack of understanding of the importance of product innovation and customer needs. The ICT companies in Serbia mostly acquire knowledge through training and education, cooperation with customers, hiring people with the appropriate competences and learning from the experiences of more successful organizations. The least important sources of knowledge acquisition are faculties and research institutes.

The following is the ranking of RC value drivers: (1) customer relationship, (2) perceived image, (3) relationship with media, (4) supplier relationship, (5) relationship with local community, (6) relationship with financial institutions (7) integration of external knowledge, (8) relationship with competitors, (9) relationship with shareholders and investors and (10) social involvement. *The key RC value drivers in Serbian ICT companies are customer relationship and image.*

Based on the key value drivers of human, structural and relational capital, the key IC value drivers of Serbian ICT companies can be established (see Table 6.4).

The questionnaire is adequate for investigating phenomena of IC in ICT companies, because Cronbach's alpha is 0.8587 (see Table 6.3). IC of organizations in the telecommunications and IT industry is most relevantly described by the following: the impact of satisfaction and motivation of employees to innovate processes and procedures, empathy of employees (HC and RC), the importance of customer relations, image, acquiring new knowledge about the needs of the users, the business dependence on key users (RC) and the impact of IT on communication and cooperation between employees and business results, as well as the influence of informal relations on employee effectiveness (SC). Innovation is more the result of employee job satisfaction and a stimulating atmosphere than of rewards. The observed organizations should increase direct stimulation of employee innovativeness, which is crucial for their development. Employee social skills are also important, followed by cooperation with the aim of knowledge sharing. Although employees from different parts of the organization collaborate to some extent, teamwork is not sufficiently represented. Regarding the process of knowledge sharing within these organizations, the problem is in HC because the employees are not ready to share their knowledge, and in an organizational culture, confidence among employees is crucial for knowledge sharing.

Analysis of Intellectual Capital in the Serbian Banks

Fifty managers from seven Serbian banks participated in the survey (see Table 6.1). The majority of the respondents from the banking sector were from large organizations (41 percent), a slightly lower percentage (37 percent) was from small organizations and 22 percent of respondents were from medium-sized organizations (see Table 6.2). The largest percentage of respondents (41 percent) were aged 26 to 35 years, had a college education (61 percent) and 11 to 20 years of service (33 percent).

Regarding the professional development of managers in the banking sector, 55 percent of managers attend professional training events once or twice a year (43 percent of them attended a training less than six months ago), whereas 45 percent of managers improve themselves less frequently (12 percent of managers have never attended training after completing formal education). The managers in the banking industry appreciate the most the following about their employees: expertise, dedication and cooperation. On the other hand, the least important qualities are innovation and continuous improvement of employees, which is absolutely inconsistent with the requirements for modern banks set by the knowledge economy. According to the managers, employees in the banking sector are mostly motivated by money, much less so by public praise and promotion and the least by a quality work environment and nonmonetary benefits.

The ranking of HC value drivers according to their relevance for Serbian banks is as follows: (1) efficiency, (2) motivation, (3) experience, (4) education and knowledge sharing, (5) managing competence and leadership, (6) expertise, (7) strategic alignment, (8) innovativeness and (9) social skills. *The key HC value drivers are efficiency, motivation, experience, and education and knowledge sharing.*

The analysis of managers' attitudes toward transforming knowledge into innovation show that ideas are mostly spontaneously applied (32 percent), 30 percent of new ideas are continually implemented and 22 percent of them are implemented according to defined procedures. Approximately 45 percent of inventions are codified, 22 percent remain in tacit form, and 8 percent are patented. Almost all of the observed banks have private information about employees, details of work experience and their education in their employee databases. They are significantly less oriented to the creation of a knowledge base that could include more realistic knowledge, skills and experience of employees. Considering the codification of knowledge, the results show that employees in the banking sector document the most their work processes (61 percent), their specific experience (43 percent) and the way they work (35 percent), whereas they document new ideas for improving work processes the least (12 percent).

According to the assessment of the importance of SC value drivers in Serbian banks, the following ranking (in decreasing order) is observed: (1) corporate culture, (2) process and procedural innovation, (3) ICT, (4) employees' communication and interaction, (5) product innovation development, (6) managerial processes, (7) brands and trademarks, (8) databases, (9) R&D and (10) technological opportunities for knowledge transfer and acquisition. *The key SC value drivers are corporate culture, process and procedural innovation, and ICT.*

According to the previous results, it can be noted that banks in Serbia are not significantly focused on R&D activities, because all the drivers related to R&D—for example, innovativeness in HC as well as R&D, opportunities for knowledge transfer and acquisition in SC—are not seen as relevant value drivers in Serbian banks. In addition, there is no cooperation between banks and sources of knowledge and innovation, for example, faculties, institutes, etc. One explanation may be that the observed banks receive the final products, services, processes and procedures from their (foreign) headquarters and only customize them for the Serbian market.

The analysis of RC shows that in Serbia, according to the managers' opinions, banks mostly cooperate with business partners, banks and government institutions, which is logical because the banking sector is oriented toward state institutions (for example, National Bank of Serbia, National Mortgage Insurance Corporation of Serbia) and other banks. On the other hand, they cooperate with universities and research institutes the least. In addition, the key sources of competitiveness are quality of service and reliability. The next most important sources are image and innovation, and the least important source of their competitiveness is a long tradition. The managers think that a long tradition in the banking sector is not crucial for the users because they choose the appropriate bank based on quality of service, reliability and sometimes the image. Knowledge in banking organizations is generally acquired through employee trainings and education and by employing people with competence, much less so through cooperation with customers and learning from more successful organizations, whereas universities and research institutes are insignificant for banks in terms of new knowledge acquisition.

Finally, the results related to the importance of RC value drivers show the following ranking (in decreasing order): (1) customer relationship, (2) perceived image, (3) relationship with media, (4) relationship with shareholders and investors, (5) integration of external knowledge, (6) relationship with local community, (7) relationship with financial institutions, (8) relationship with competitors, (9) supplier relationship and (10) social involvement. *The key RC value drivers in Serbian banks are customer relationship and perceived image.*

Setting aside HC, SC and RC value drivers, IC value drivers for the Serbian banking sector can be established (see Table 6.4).

The questionnaire is adequate for investigating phenomena of IC in banks, because Cronbach's alpha is 0.8612 (see Table 6.3). Within the IC of the observed organizations, the synergy between the structural and relational capital is dominant, which is a function of generating new knowledge, as well as HC management, by identifying and encouraging value-creation sources. Systematic innovation and rewarding initiative, as well as considering continual professional development in the analyzed banks, encourage innovation, responsibility and entrepreneurial attitudes of employees. The consequence of such management is employee satisfaction and motivation, which in turn stimulate the process of value creation within the surveyed organizations. It is important that these organizations increasingly identify both existing and missing knowledge, because this process is the basis for the generation of new knowledge. Branding is largely represented, whereas IT greatly influences the communication and cooperation of employees, as well as the business results. The shared values and beliefs exist to some extent within these organizations, but this is not the result of leadership in the banking sector, because leadership is not dominant in the analyzed organizations.

5. IC REPORTING MODELS WITHIN DIFFERENT SERBIAN INDUSTRIES

Basic assumptions are that dominant characteristics of IC, as well as key IC value drivers, largely select the group of relevant IC indicators (Arbeitskreis Wissensbilanz 2004; Cabrilo et al. 2009, Cabrilo and Grubic-Nesic 2010). Therefore, based on the key IC value drivers identified by Pareto analysis, as well as additional specific features of IC identified by factor analysis, groups of relevant IC indicators (IC reporting models) for observed industries are defined. These models are presented in Table 6.4.

The key IC value drivers identified within Serbian industries (see Table 6.4) are dominant in defining the group of relevant IC indicators. For each key IC value driver, there are many indicators by which it can be appropriately highlighted and measured. However, since the number of relevant indicators measuring a particular IC value driver should be reduced to three to five indicators, the specific IC features and knowledge flows within observed industries affect the choice of the final group of relevant IC indicators.

The groups of the relevant IC indicators present general IC reporting models adapted to the particular Serbian industries. The general model is suitable for comparison within the industry, as it is necessary to apply the same IC indicators to all analyzed companies. The comparison is only possible when the same IC indicators are applied. However, considering that IC is a context-specific resource, it is possible to conclude that there is no set of indicators that is general enough to encompass the needs of various organizations, industries and national economies, and include all the necessary specificities of the organization or environment. Therefore, if the proposed models are not used to compare companies in the same sector, but for managerial purposes, the company can select indicators from the proposed group or define some new indicators, in accordance with its specificities, defined objectives and available data, that are necessary to calculate each of the selected indicators.

Table 6.4 Overview of key IC value drivers, the most relevant statistical factors and IC indicators in different Serbian industries

Industry	The key IC value drivers	The most relevant statistical factors	The IC indicators
Utility services	eficiency experience motivation managerial processes employees' interaction ICT process and procedural innovation customer relationship relationship with local community	F1—Rewarding and encouraging employee innovativeness F2—External knowledge acquisition (suppliers, competitors) F3—Employee experience (professional + seniority) F4—The IT impact on communication, collaboration and business performance F5—The impact of informal communication on the employee efficiency	Value added per employee, Percent of employees who realize goals before deadline, Average seniority of employees. Rookie ratio, Average professional experience, Employee satisfaction index (survey). Average number of absence days per employee. Percentage of employees with a large number of working hours. Employee satisfaction with the administration and management; number of managerial meetings; average time spent on vocational training (managers); number of different sector staff meetings; number of internal document exchange (mail, e-mails); quality of internal collaboration in the survey; cost of IT education/ total IT costs: number of intranet and internet users; number of database file accesses; number of employee suggestions for improving processes and procedures; proportion of implemented ideas (number of implemented ideas/total number of ideas); number of newly implemented processes and procedures per employee; average user satisfaction; number of appeals/index of the local community satisfaction; number of the local community visits

Industry	employee efficiency	F1—Motivation, rewarding, training	Value added per employee, Percent of employees who realize goals before deadline, Number of employees rewarded for outstanding results, Average seniority of employees, Growth in professional experience, Rookie ratio, Employee satisfaction index (survey). Average number of absence days per employee, Staff turnover, Interdisciplinary projects, Experience exchange meetings, Number of meetings with knowledge transfer, Average age of managers, Quality of managing activities (employees' survey), Education days per manager, Shared knowledge documents on the intranet, Product innovation rate, Customer structure, Customer satisfaction index. Percent of total revenues of 5 largest customers. Percent of suppliers enhancing product quality. Proportion of turnover with 5 largest suppliers Supplier quality index (1–5 scale)
	employee experience	F2—Knowledge sharing and acquisition (cutomers, suppliers)	
	employee motivation	F3—Employee experience (professional + seniority)	
	employees' interaction	F4—Business dependence on the key experts	
	managerial processes		
	customer relationship	F5—Employee lack of commitment	
	supplier relationship		
Mining and energy	employee efficiency	F1—R&D activities in new knowledge generation	Percentage of experts, Value-added margin, Sales per employee. Employee Satisfaction Index, Absenteeism, Percentage of employees with a large number of working hours. Average seniority, Average professional experience, Rookie ratio, Number of projects based on collaboration of departments, Number of process teams. Internal cooperation quality and knowledge transfer (survey). Number of organizational units,
	employee motivation	F2—Trust, openness, satisfaction	
	employee experience	F3—The IT impact on communication, business performance and collaboration	
	employees' interaction		

(Continued)

Table 6.4 (Continued)

Industry	The key IC value drivers	The most relevant statistical factors	The IC indicators
	managerial processes	F4—Business dependence on the key experts	Employee Entitlement Level (Survey), Percentage of key processes that are tracked manually, Number of jobs based on computer work. Percentage of employees who are excellent IT users. Consumer Satisfaction Index. 50% of revenue—the number of customers, Number of complaints. Number of proposals and suggestions of suppliers, Longevity of cooperation with the top 5 suppliers, Percentage of reputable suppliers
	ICT		
	employees' interaction	F5—Creativity and knowledge sharing (intra-transfer)	
	managerial processes		
Services	employee efficiency	F1—The organizational culture supports knowledge sharing	Value added per employee, Employees with part of the salary based on performance (proportion), Number of employees rewarded for outstanding results, Employee turnover. Employee satisfaction index (survey), Absenteeism. Average seniority of employees. Growth in professional experience. Rookie ratio. Average competence index. Professional development per employee (days), Versatility and creativity index, Number of internal meetings, Number of informal meetings and social events, Number of conflict situations, Average managerial experience of managers, Quality of managing activities (employees' survey), Training days per manager. Proportion of new customers. Share of marketing and PR costs in turnover. Presence in media. Reputation index (survey)
	employee motivation	F2—External knowledge acquisition and conquering new markets easily	
	employee experience	F3—IT impact on cooperation and business results	
	employee expertise		
	employees' interaction	F4—Rewarding (for result contribution, initiative and innovativeness)	
	managerial processes	F5—Level of expertise and employee experience	
	customer relationship		
	image		

Sector	Factors		Indicators
Media	employee efficiency	F1—The impacts of IT and organizational culture on cooperation, tracking of customers, suppliers and competition	Average level of daily plan achievement; average number of items per employee; percentage of part-time workers; average employee experience, percentage of Rookies expert team; positions in the media at an average salary: percentage of employees participating in surveys; employee satisfaction index (wages, conditions, available equipment-technology); average competency index; number of training days per employee; average cost of development activities per employee; IT competence at the organizational level; percentage of competent IT users; size and availability of databases; proportion of multiple team members; quality of internal collaboration and knowledge transfer (poll); rank in the ratings; loyalty index of viewers; number/quality of the advertising contracts
	employee experience	F2—The impact of quality on business performance	
	employee motivation	F3—Significance of employee creativity	
	employee expertise	F4—Employee experience (professional + seniority)	
	ICT		
	employees' interaction	F5—Employee lack of commitment	
	customer relationship		
	image		
ICT	employee efficiency	F1—The impact of employee satisfaction and motivation on innovation processes and procedures	Value added per employee; percentage of employees who accomplish the tasks within the stipulated time; average employee age: training days per employee; percentage of employees in R&D, Creativity Index; average professional experience; average seniority; proportion of Rockies in the expert team; proportion of employees with a large number of jobs hours; average employee satisfaction with the individual competency development; sector position by the average salary; average satisfaction with the leadership
	employee expertise	F2—Image and market research for better knowledge acquisition	
	employee experience	F3—The impact of IT on communication, business performance and collaboration	
	employee motivation		

(*Continued*)

Table 6.4 (Continued)

Industry	The key IC value drivers	The most relevant statistical factors	The IC indicators
	manag. competence and leadership ICT employees' interaction customer relationship image	F4—The impact of informal communication on the employee efficiency F5—Employee social skills	(survey), days of training and training costs of managers; annual plan and objective achievements; development costs of IT/total IT costs; number of new entries in the database; number of discussion groups in the organization; number of process teams; number of annual informal occasions; frequency of repeated orders; number of client appeals/complaints. Website visitation; company image (survey); presence in the media
Banking	employee efficiency employee motivation employee experience education and knowledge-sharing	F1—HC management—identifying and encouraging the source of value creation F2—Structural and human capital synergy F3—The importance of employee social skills and training	Number of account per employee; average time of requirement processing; average number of daily pay-ins and pay-outs per employee; Bank position (in the sector) per an average net salary; proportion of employees with a large number of working hours; number of days of absence from work; average professional experience; average seniority; number of new employees with mentors; number of training days per employee; average employee satisfaction;

corporate culture		development of individual competencies; measures employee values and attitudes; number of days of social activities per year; organization image among the employees; number of employee suggestions for improving processes and procedures, proportion of implemented ideas; IT costs as the percentage of total costs: IT training at the organizational level, market share (growth percentage); number of newly opened and closed accounts
process and procedural innovation		
ICT		
customer relationship	F4—Dependence on the key clients	
image	F5—Branding	

6. THE MOST IMPORTANT OBSERVATIONS

The results for the reliability test (Cronbach's alpha) indicate a very high degree of consistency in each industry (see Table 6.3), pointing to the fact that the questionnaire is adequate for IC analysis within different industries.

The comparative IC analysis in seven different Serbian industries has indicated the existence of interindustry variety from the perspective of IC (Cabrilo 2009), as there are no two industries with the same groups of the key IC value drivers (see Table 6.4). Different groups of IC indicators for particular industries are mostly the consequence of the differences in groups of the key IC value drivers. On the other hand, certain similarities have been observed among particular industries (Cabrilo 2009). For example, employee efficiency, experience and motivation, as well as customer relationship, are considered key IC value drivers in all observed industries. Employee communication and interaction is the key IC value driver in six out of seven observed industries, ICT in five out of seven industries, and managerial processes and image are considered key IC value drivers in four out of seven industries. These and other similar IC characteristics disclosed within different industries present the basis of the general IC reporting model in Serbia (Cabrilo et al. 2009). The general IC reporting model presents an opportunity to compare companies from different industries. In the study conducted on a mixed sample of Serbian companies from different industries (Cabrilo et al. 2009), Cronbach's alpha is 0.5885, which is low compared with a very high degree of consistency identified in each industry (see Table 6.3). It indicates that the IC specificities within industries are observed more accurately. Therefore, it is possible to conclude that area reduction in which the questionnaire is applied, the IC measures are determined more precisely.

Results show that certain IC value drivers crucial to innovation (such as employee innovativeness, expertise, education and knowledge sharing, product innovation development, process and procedural innovation, and R&D) are overlooked as the key ones for business success and competitiveness in the most of the observed industries. Innovativeness, R&D and product innovation development are not in the group of relevant IC value drivers in any of the industries. Education and knowledge sharing are seen as relevant only in banking, process and procedural innovation only in utility services and banking, and employee expertise in media, ICT and services.

These results illustrate that managers are not sufficiently aware of the fact that innovation and lifelong learning are the ultimate tools for business success in the modern economy. The failure to attach adequate importance to innovation causes insufficient innovativeness stimulation and a lack of managerial initiatives oriented to innovation. Because innovation is the key driver of corporate value and competitiveness (Aramburu et al. 2006; Castellacci 2008; Cefis and Marsilli 2005), these managers' attitudes toward innovation result in low competitiveness of Serbian companies in the markets and low competitiveness of the Serbian economy. According to the World Economic Forum (WEF) Report on the Global Competitiveness Index 2013–2014, Serbia is in the efficiency-driven stage of development, which is between the factor-driven and innovation-driven stages of development. For the next innovation-driven stage of development, Serbian companies should be able to compete in the global market with new and unique products, so it is necessary to improve IC value drivers crucial to innovation. In the context of the efficiency-driven economy in Serbia, the research results presented in this chapter—efficiency being on top of the list of HC value drivers and innovativeness close to the last position in all observed industries, as well as all SC value drivers related to innovation being overlooked as the key ones—are logical and unsurprising.

However, perhaps the biggest surprise is that the innovative product development has the least impact on business results and organization success in the ICT sector. In this industry, which is very knowledge intensive and largely subjected to rapid technological change, the development of innovative products is a prerequisite for survival in the market, whereas R&D is the foundation of organization competitiveness in the sector.

7. THEORETICAL AND PRACTICAL IMPLICATIONS

The awareness of IC specificities has initiated number of studies aimed at adjusting IC measuring and reporting to national IC (Stam and Andriessen 2009; Bontis 2004; Pulic 2002; Pasher 1999, Lin and Edvinsson 2011), regional clusters (EC 2006) and even towns (Bounfour and Edvinsson 2005). Thus, *theoretical implications* of this research are the fine-tuning of IC reporting to environmental and industrial features and the contribution to the existing knowledge and experience related to the IC measuring, reporting and managing.

Considering *practical implications,* the defined groups of the relevant IC indicators, adjusted according to the specificities of the industries, simplify and facilitate the application of the IC reporting and enable more precise insight into the IC, which is the basis for effective strategic decision making and IC mobilization within different Serbian industries. This can positively influence the performance and competitiveness of Serbian companies, as well as the competitiveness of the entire economy. The groups of the proposed indicators should not be seen as the final sets of indicators, but as a starting point for IC reporting within Serbian industries. In addition, based on the IC analysis within different industries, numerous managerial initiatives are proposed, aimed at developing the existing IC. It is also possible to compare companies within particular industries, which may contribute to their further development.

No scientific endeavor is without limitations (Serenko and Bontis 2013), and this research is not an exception. The research is concerned with Serbian companies; hence, the results are not intended to be generalized directly to other economic environments. The relevance of IC value drivers, which has strongly influenced the defined IC reporting models, has been assessed by Serbian managers. Another limitation arises due to the lack of implementation of presented IC reporting models in Serbian companies and further improvements based on company experiences. It is fully compliant with the findings of Dumay (2009a, 2009b, 2012), Lönnqvist et al. (2009) and Chiucchi (2013) related to the asymmetry between the interests shown by researchers and practitioners for IC frameworks and implementation of these frameworks in practice. Finally, the group of relevant IC indicators within the observed industry does not include indicators on employee innovativeness, innovative product development and R&D activities, because the managers in the surveyed Serbian industries did not identify them as key IC value drivers for business success. However, in the baseline methods (IAM, Danish Guidelines, MERITUM Guidelines, Wissensbilanz), IC measures mainly include competence development, innovativeness and innovative activities such as R&D. These methods thus respect the significance of these IC drivers and recognize them as the key to competence and business success. This further indicates that the specifics of the economic environment may in some way affect the group of the key IC value drivers, and thus, the appropriate IC reporting model.

8.   CONCLUDING REMARKS

The power of the existing IC frameworks is that they can be changed to suit individual organizations (Dumay and Rooney 2011). According to the previous sections, this chapter has demonstrated that it is possible to take popular IC reporting models such as the IAM (Sveiby 1997a, 1997b), Danish Guidelines (DATI 2000), MERITUM Guidelines (MERITUM 2002) and Wissensbilanz (Arbeitskreis Wissensbilanz 2004) and change, mix and integrate them to suit the particular industry's needs, rather than try to adopt them verbatim. IC knowledge for seven different Serbian industries is synthesized into separate IC overviews of a particular industry. Based on this wide-range IC analysis, IC reporting models adapted to the particular facets of the industries are defined. By refining IC reporting with respect to particular industrial features, it is possible to capture and picture IC more precisely, which makes IC measuring and reporting more accurate and easier to implement in different industries (Cabrilo 2009).

The IC measures proposed in this chapter are not concerned merely with metrics, but also with strategic decision making, change and learning activities. It is fully compliant with Edvinsson's (2013, 166) conclusion that "too much focus on metrics and measurements means that there is not enough focus on the real strategy process".

Although the IC community has made significant advances in assessing and reporting methods (Edvinsson and Malone 1997; Sveiby 1997a; Roos et al. 1997; Stewart 1997; Bontis 1999; Sanchez et al. 2000; Andriessen 2004; Chiucchi 2013), there is not one only IC reporting model universally accepted. Standardization (Cabrilo 2009) and a legislative framework for IC reporting (Burgman and Roos 2007) are absolutely necessary conditions for moving forward. Therefore, research projects that are tailored to specific environments while utilizing large data sets such as the present one can contribute to the convergence of existing IC measuring and reporting models.

Finally, as there is a need to go beyond IC reporting in order to increase the IC consciousness (Edvinsson 2013), the author's research efforts are aimed at linking IC and innovation and using IC reporting for a more comprehensive assessment of innovation performance, as well as creating more effective innovation strategies (Cabrilo and Grubic-Nesic 2012a; Cabrilo et al. 2013).

REFERENCES

Andriessen, D. 2004. *Making Sense of Intellectual Capital: Designing a Method for the Valuation of Intangibles.* Burlington: Elsevier Butterworth-Heinemann.

Andriessen, D. and Stam C. 2004. *Intellectual Capital of the European Union, Measuring the Lisbon Agenda.* Diemen: Center for Research of Intellectual Capital.

Aramburu, N., Sáenz J. and Rivera O. 2006. "Fostering innovation and knowledge creation: The role of management context". *Journal of Knowledge Management,* 10 (3), 157–168.

Arbeitskreis Wissensbilanz. 2004. "Intellectual capital statement—Made in Germany." Berlin: *Federal Ministry of Economics and Labour.* http://www.akwis sensbilanz.org/Infoservice/infomaterial.htm. Accessed June 18, 2007.

Ax, C. and Marton J. 2008. "Human capital disclosures and management practices". *Journal of Intellectual Capital,* 9 (3), 433–455.

Bontis, N. 1998. "Intellectual capital: An exploratory study that develops measures and models". *Management Decision,* 36 (2), 63–76.

Bontis, N. 1999. "Managing organizational knowledge by diagnosing intellectual capital: Framing and advancing the state of the field". *International Journal of Technology Management,* 18 (5–8), 433–462.

Bontis, N. 2002. "Managing organisational knowledge by diagnosing intellectual capital: Framing and advancing the state of the field." In Choo, C. and Bontis, N. (Eds), *The Strategic Management of Intellectual Capital and Organisational Knowledge.* Oxford: Oxford University Press, 621–642.

Bontis, N., Crossan M. and Hulland J. 2002. "Managing an organizational learning system by aligning stocks and flows". *Journal of Management Studies,* 39 (4), 437–470.

Bontis, N. 2004. "National Intellectual Capital Index: A United Nations initiative for the Arab region". *Journal of Intellectual Capital,* 5 (1), 13–39.

Bontis, N., Janosevic S. and Dzenopoljac V. 2013. "Intellectual capital and the corporate performance of Serbian banks". *Actual Problems of Economics,* 4 (April), 287–299.

Bontis, N., Keow W. and Richardson S. 2000. "Intellectual capital and business performance in Malaysian industries". *Journal of Intellectual Capital,* 1 (1), 85–100.

Bounfour, Ahmed, and Edvinsson Leif. 2005. *Intellectual Capital for Communities: Nations, Regions and Cities,* Boston: Elsevier Butterworth-Heinemann.

Bozbura, F. TuncT. 2004. "Measurement and application of intellectual capital in Turkey". *The Learning Organization,* 11 (4/5), 357–367.

Burgman, R. and Roos G. 2007. "The importance of intellectual capital reporting: Evidence and implications". *Journal of Intellectual Capital,* 8 (1), 7–51.

Cabrilo, S. 2005. "The first IC reports in Serbia and Montenegro". *INFO M,* 15–16, 15–21.

Cabrilo, S. 2009. "IC-based inter-industry variety in Serbia." *Electronic Journal of Knowledge Management,* 7 (4), 425–436.

Cabrilo, S., Grubic-Nesic L. and Mitrovic S. 2013. "Study on human capital gaps for effective innovation strategies in the knowledge era". Paper Presented at the 8th International Forum on Knowledge Assets Dynamics (IFKAD)—Smart Growth: Organizations, Cities and Communities, Zagreb, Croatia, June 12–14.

Cabrilo, S. and Grubic-Nesic L. 2010. "A strategic model for intellectual capital reporting: Study of service industry in Serbia". Paper Presented at the 2nd European Conference on Intellectual Capital, Lisbon, Portugal, March 29–30.

Cabrilo, S. and Grubic-Nesic L. 2012a. "IC-based innovation gap assessment: A support tool for the creation of effective innovation strategies in the knowledge era". Paper Presented at the 4th European Conference on Intellectual Capital, Helsinki, Finland, April 23–24.

Cabrilo, S. and Grubic-Nesic L. 2012b. "The role of creativity, innovation and invention in knowledge management". In Suckley, S. and Jakovljevic, M. (Eds.) *Knowledge Management Innovations for Interdisciplinary Education: Organizational Applications.* Hershey PA: IGI Global, 207–233.

Cabrilo, S., Uzelac Z. and Cosic I. 2009. "Researching indicators of organizational intellectual capital in Serbia". *Journal of Intellectual Capital,* 10 (4), 573–587.

Carlucci, D., Marr B. and Schiuma G. 2004. "The knowledge value chain—how intellectual capital impacts business performance". *International Journal of Technology Management,* 27 (6–7), 575–590.

Castellacci, F. 2008. "Innovation and the competitiveness of industries: Comparing the mainstream and the evolutionary approaches". *Technological Forecasting and Social Change,* 75 (7), 984–1006.

Cefis, E. and Marsili O. 2005. "A matter of life and death: Innovation and firm survival". *Industrial and Corporate Change,* 14 (6), 1167–1192.

Chiucchi, Maria Serena. 2008. "Exploring the benefits of measuring intellectual capital: The Aimag case study." *Human Systems Management,* 27 (3), 217–30.

Chiucchi, M.S. 2013. "Measuring and reporting intellectual capital: Lessons learnt from some interventionist research projects". *Journal of Intellectual Capital,* 14 (3), 395–413.

Choo, C.W. and Bontis N. 2002. *The Strategic Management of Intellectual Capital and Organizational Knowledge.* New York: Oxford University Press.

Clark, A. 2003. "Returns to human capital investment in a transition economy: The case of Russia, 1994–1998". *International Journal of Manpower,* 24 (1), 11–30.

DATI. 2000. *A Guideline for Intellectual Capital Statements: A Key to Knowledge Management,* Copenhagen: Danish Agency for Trade and Industry.

Daum, H.J. 2003. "Intellectual capital statements." *Controlling,* 15 (3/4), 143–54.

Deol, H.S. 2009. "Strategic environment and intellectual capital of Indian banks". *Journal of Intellectual Capital,* 10 (1), 109–120.

Drucker, P.F. 1993. "The rise of the knowledge society". *Wilson Quarterly,* 17 (2), 52–70.

Dumay, J. 2009a. "Reflective discourse about intellectual capital: Research and practice". *Journal of Intellectual Capital,* 10 (4), 489–503.

Dumay, J. and Rooney J. 2011. "Measuring for managing? An IC practice case study". *Journal of Intellectual Capital,* 12 (3), 344–355.

Dumay, J. 2009b. "Intellectual capital-measurement: A critical approach". *Journal of Intellectual Capital,* 10 (2), 190–210.

Dumay, J. 2012. "Grand theories as barriers to using IC concepts". *Journal of Intellectual Capital,* 13 (1), 4–15.

Ederer, P., Schuler P. and Willms S. 2007. *The European Human Capital Index: The Challenge of Central and Eastern Europe.* Brussels: The Lisbon Council.

Edvinsson, L. 2013. "IC 21: Reflections from 21 years of IC practice and theory". *Journal of Intellectual Capital,* 14 (1), 163–172.

Edvinsson, L. and Malone M.S. 1997. *Intellectual Capital: Realising Your Company's True Value by Finding Its Hidden Brainpower,* New York: Harper Collins.

European Commission. 2006. *RICARDIS—Reporting on Intellectual Capital to Augment Research, Development and Innovation in SMEs,* High Level Expert Group & European Commission, Luxembourg: Directorate-General for Research Office for Official Publications of the European Communities Distributor.

Fletcher, A., Guthrie J., Steane P., Roos G. and Pike S. 2003. "Mapping stakeholder perceptions for a third sector organization". *Journal of Intellectual Capital,* 4 (4), 505–527.

Grant, R.M. 1996. "Toward a knowledge-based theory of the firm". *Strategic Management Journal,* 17, 109–122.

Guthrie, J., Petty R. and Ricceri F. 2006. "The voluntary reporting of intellectual capital: Comparing evidence from Hong Kong and Australia". *Journal of Intellectual Capital,* 7 (2), 254–271.

Guthrie, J., Ricceri F. and Dumay J. 2012. "Reflections and projections: A decade of intellectual capital accounting research". *British Accounting Review,* 44 (2), 68–82.

Janosevic, S., Dzenopoljac V. and Bontis N. 2013a. "Intellectual capital and financial performance in Serbia". *Knowledge and Process Management,* 20 (1), 1–11.

Janosevic, S., Dzenopoljac V. and Dimitrijevic S. 2013b. "Analysis of intellectual capital practices in Serbia". *Actual Problems of Economics,* 6 (June), 548–562.

Kamath, G.B. 2007. "The intellectual capital performance of the Indian banking sector". *Journal of Intellectual Capital,* 8 (1), 96–123.

Kaplan, R.S. and Norton D.P. 1996. *The Balanced Scorecard: Translating Strategy into Action,* Boston: Harvard Business School Press.

Karagiannis, D., Nemetz M. and Bayer F. 2009. "A method for comprehensive intellectual capital management and reporting: The case of BOC Information Systems". *Journal of Intellectual Capital,* 10 (1), 93–108.

Kaufmann, L. and Schneider Y. 2004. "Intangibles: A synthesis of current research". *Journal of Intellectual Capital,* 5 (3), 366–388.

Kianto, A., Hurmelinna-Laukkanen P. and Ritala P. 2010. "Intellectual capital in service- and product-oriented companies". *Journal of Intellectual Capital,* 11 (3), 305–325.

Kong, E. 2008. "The development of strategic management in the nonprofit context: Intellectual capital in social service nonprofit organizations". *International Journal of Management Reviews,* 10 (3), 281–299.

Kontic, L. and Cabrilo S. 2009. "A strategic model for measuring intellectual capital in Serbian industrial enterprises". *Economic Annals,* LIV (183), 89–118.

Kovach, K.A. 1987. "What motivates employees? Workers and supervisors give different answers". *Business Horizons,* 30 (5), 58–65.

Lerro, A. and Schiuma G. 2013. "Intellectual capital assessment practices: Overview and managerial implications". *Journal of Intellectual Capital,* 14 (3), 352–359.

Lin, C.Y-J and Edvinsson L. 2008. "National intellectual capital: Comparison of the Nordic countries". *Journal of Intellectual Capital,* 9 (4), 525–545.

Lin, C.Y-J and Edvinsson L. 2011. *National Intellectual Capital: A Comparison of 40 Countries,* New York: Springer.

Lönnqvist, A., Kianto A. and Sillanpää V. 2009. "Using intellectual capital management for facilitating organizational change". *Journal of Intellectual Capital,* 10 (4), 559–572.

Low, J. 2000. "The value creation index". *Journal of Intellectual Capital,* 1 (3), 252–262.

Marr, B. 2004. "Strategic management of intangible value drivers". In Coate, P. (Ed.) *Handbook of Business Strategy 2005.* Bradford, GBR: Emerald Group Publishing Limited, 147–154.

Marr, B., Gray D. and Neely A. 2003. "Why do firms measure their intellectual capital?" *Journal of Intellectual Capital,* 4 (4), 441–464.

Marr, B. and Roos G. 2005. "A strategy perspective on intellectual capital". In Marr, B. (Ed.), *Perspectives on Intellectual Capital: Multi-Disciplinary Insights into Management, Measurement, and Reporting.* Amsterdam: Elsevier Butterworth-Heinemann, 28–41.

Marr, B., Schiuma G. and Neely A. 2004. "Intellectual capital—defining key performance indicators for organizational knowledge assets". *Journal of Intellectual Capital,* 10 (5), 551–566.

MERITUM. 2002. *Proyecto MERITUM: Guidelines for Managing and Reporting Intangibles,* Madrid: MERITUM.

Mouritsen, J. 2006. "Problematising intellectual capital research: Ostensive versus performative IC". *Journal of Intellectual Capital,* 19 (6), 820–841.

Mouritsen, J. 2009. "Classification, measurement and the ontology of intellectual capital entities". *Journal of Human Resource Costing and Accounting,* 13 (2), 154–172.

Mouritsen, J. and Roslender R. 2009. "Critical intellectual capital". *Critical Perspectives on Accounting,* 20 (7), 801–803.

Nahapiet, J. and Ghoshal S. 1998. "Social capital, intellectual capital and the organizational advantage." *Academy of Management Review,* 23 (2), 242–266.

Opsahl, R.L. and Dunnette M.D. 1966. "The role of financial compensation in industrial motivation". *Psychological Bulletin,* 66 (2), 94–118.

Pasher, E. 1999. *The Intellectual Capital of the State of Israel,* Herzlia Pituach: Edna Pasher PhD & Associates.

Pike, S. and Roos G. 2004. "Mathematics and modern business management". *Journal of Intellectual Capital,* 5 (2), 243–256.

Pike, S., Rylander A. and Roos G. 2002. "Intellectual capital management and disclosure". Paper Presented at the 5th World Congress on Intellectual Capital, Hamilton, Ontario, Canada, January 10–12.

Prieto, I.M. and Revilla E. 2006. "Assessing the impact of learning capability on business performance: Empirical evidence from Spain." *Management Learning,* 37 (4), 499–522.

Pulic, A. 2002. *Intellectual Capital: Efficiency in Croatia Economy,* Zagreb: International Business Efficiency Consulting LLC.

Roos G. 2004. "Intellectual capital and strategy: A primer for today's manager". In Coate, P. (Ed.), *Handbook of Business Strategy 2005.* Bradford, GBR: Emerald Group Publishing Limited, 123–131.

Roos, J., Roos G., Edvinsson L. and Dragonetti N.C. 1997. *Intellectual Capital: Navigating in the New Business Landscape.* London: Macmillan.

Saint-Onge, H. 1996. "Tacit knowledge: The key to the strategic alignment of intellectual capital". *Strategy and Leadership,* 24 (2), 10–16.

Sanchez, P., Chaminade C. and Olea M. 2000. "Management of intangibles: An attempt to build a theory". *Journal of Intellectual Capital,* 1 (4), 312–327.

Schiemann, W.A. 2008. "From crunching numbers to counting human capital". *Financial Executive,* 24 (4), 53–55.

Schiuma, G., Lerro A. and Sanitate D. 2008. "Intellectual capital dimensions of Ducati's turnaround—exploring knowledge assets grounding a change management program". *International Journal of Innovation Management,* 12 (2), 161–193.

Senge, P. 1990. *The Fifth Discipline,* New York: Doubleday.

Serenko, A. and Bontis N. 2013. "Investigating the current state and impact of the intellectual capital academic discipline". *Journal of Intellectual Capital,* 14 (4), 476–500.

Sharma, R.S., Hui P. and Tan M-W. 2007. "Value-added knowledge management for financial performance: The case of an East Asian conglomerate". *VINE,* 37 (4), 484–501.

Stam, C. and Andriessen D. 2009. "Intellectual capital of the European Union 2008: Measuring the Lisbon strategy for growth and jobs". *Electronic Journal of Knowledge Management,* 7 (4), 489–500.

Stewart, T.A. 1997. *Intellectual Capital: The New Wealth of Organizations,* New York: Doubleday.

Sullivan, P.H. 1998. "Introduction to intellectual capital management". In Sullivan, P.H. (Ed.), *Profiting from Intellectual Capital: Extracting Value from Innovation.* New York: John Wiley & Sons, 3–18.

Sveiby, K-E. 1997a. *The New Organizational Wealth: Managing and Measuring Knowledge-Based Assets.* San Francisco: Berret-Koehler.

Sveiby, K-E. 1997b. "The intangible assets monitor". *Journal of Human Resource Costing and Accounting,* 2 (1), 73–97.

Tovstiga, G. and Tulugurova E. 2009. "Intellectual capital practices: A four-region comparative study". *Journal of Intellectual Capital,* 10 (1), 70–80.

Whyte, W.F. 1955. *Money and Motivation—An Analysis of Incentives in Industry.* New York: Harper and Row.

Xiao, J. and Lo L.N.K. 2003. "Human capital development in Shanghai: Lessons and prospects". *International Journal of Educational Development,* 23 (4), 411–427.

Yi, A. and Davey H. 2010. "Intellectual capital disclosure in Chinese (mainland) companies". *Journal of Intellectual Capital,* 11 (3), 326–347.

Yu, A. and Humphreys P. 2013. "From measuring to learning?—Probing the evolutionary path of IC research and practice". *Journal of Intellectual Capital,* 14 (1), 26–47.

7 Shaping New Managerial Models for European Universities
The Impact of Reporting and Managing IC

Susana Elena-Perez*, Karl Heinz Leitner, Giustina Secundo and Žilvinas Martinaitis

1. INTRODUCTION

Globalization, scientific and technological processes and, in Europe, the Bologna process, are creating an increasingly competitive environment for universities (Weber 2006). Universities are key players in the national innovation systems and in the promotion of regional development, in synergy with business and local governments (Etzkowitz 2004). Like many other organizations, they also have to demonstrate adequate resource management and accountability in support of clearly defined and feasible goals, which are crucial during periods of financial crisis and budget cuts. In this context, the conceptualization and functioning of universities are changing toward more autonomous, efficient and competitive institutions.

The more autonomous a university is, the more it should, in principle, be able to better manage its financial and other internal affairs, which could make it more efficient, less dependent on external shocks and thus more able to adapt to a rapidly changing environment.

However, to cope with these challenges—and despite the general policy recommendations toward the implementation of new management tools and governance modes (European Commission 2006, 2013)—most universities are not implementing significant changes in the way they are managed (Elena and Sanchez 2013; Ramirez Corcoles et al. 2011). Management of universities has become, at the same time, the main solution and barrier to tackling the emerging challenges.

The key issue is the effective management of intangible assets and intellectual capital (IC) that constitutes the largest proportion of

* The views expressed are purely those of the author and may not in any circumstances be regarded as stating an official position of the European Commission.

universities' assets. In this context, IC approaches seem to be of prime importance. In practical terms, IC strategic management focuses on the ways to visualize and use individual and organizational resources and capacities in a holistic manner, with a focus on intangible assets, and on how to develop in a sustainable manner such resources and activities (Secundo et al. 2014).

From a conceptual perspective, IC management and reporting are deeply embedded within the new public management (NPM) ideas and trends in the reform of the public sector. Both face the same challenges in terms of the difficulties in implementing managerial instruments borrowed from the private sector in a public organization with a strong academic culture. Both advocate the introduction of strategic plans and measuring of objectives. Despite their commonalities, there are also contradictions and tension between both approaches. The post-NPM movement that emerged some years later seems to be more compatible with IC approaches because they conceptualize the organization in a holistic way and focus on capacities and intangible assets.

Beyond the general NPM and post-NPM doctrine for the public sector, the modernization of the university is still a priority today (European Commission 2006, 2013). As part of this modernization process, it is clear that universities should incorporate new managerial tools to better govern their internal affairs. In this context, we believe an IC framework could be a valuable tool to help universities be sustainable and more competitive.

Recently, the project "Quality Assurance in Higher Education through Habilitation and Auditing"[1] has been carried out, with the ultimate goal of preparing a guideline for applying IC reporting in higher education (HE) institutions (Leitner et al. 2014). Based on the experiences and good practices with IC management and reporting in universities at the international level, the project addressed some of the key issues and lessons when developing IC guidelines for European universities. This chapter is based on the work done within this project.

The primary objective of this chapter is to reflect on the IC concept from the (post)-NPM perspective, analyzing the extent to which there are complementarities or contradictions between both approaches in the specific case of European universities. Furthermore, the chapter studies the strategic impacts of measuring and reporting on IC in universities, following a three-level pyramid approach: department, university, region/society.

The remainder of the chapter is structured as follows: Section 2 explains IC management in the context of new (and post) public management; Section 3 addresses the concept of managerial and entrepreneurial universities; Section 4 focuses on the impacts of measuring and reporting IC in universities at the three mentioned levels; and finally, Section 5 draws the lessons learned and the ways forward.

2. INTELLECTUAL CAPITAL MANAGEMENT IN THE
CONTEXT OF (POST) NEW PUBLIC MANAGEMENT

IC management and reporting are deeply embedded within a wide set of ideas and trends in the reform of the public sector, coined new public management (NPM). Under this heading, we find the changes that occurred in the public sector in most Organization for Economic Cooperation and Development (OECD) countries[2] during the 1980s and 1990s mainly concerned with public accountability and intended to guide public administrations toward a more efficient model in response to a perceived lack of focus on outcomes, efficiency and transparency in national bureaucracies (Hood 1991, 1995; McLaughlin et al. 2002). The solution suggested by the NPM was to introduce managerial instruments and techniques borrowed from private enterprises to the public sector. This typically included delegation, decentralization and deregulation, results-based funding formulas, accountability, strategic management and planning, adoption of contract-based relationships, measuring performance, punishing (or rewarding) organizations based on achieved results, output control, and strengthening of managerial culture (OECD 1997; Hood 1991, 1995; Aucoin 1990). Despite these general aspects, it is important to note that NPM is not, in the realm of practice, a unified set of features and practices that are unified, but ones that vary depending on the sector (health, education, research or social services), and even within it (Dent et al. 2004).

NPM-style reforms had a profound effect on the governance of European HE institutions. They have been granted more institutional autonomy to manage their financial and human resources, deciding on course content, research programs and size of student enrolment (Elena and Sanchez 2013; De Dominic et al. 2011; European University Association 2005 and 2007).

To what extent are there complementarities or contradictions between NPM and IC management? One could argue that from a conceptual standpoint, both are the same. First, conceptually, both emphasize that production and dissemination of knowledge could and should be "managed". This stands in sharp contrast to traditional European university structures that are based on the principle of self-governance (as opposed to management by objectives), collegial decision making (as opposed to wide discretion of the chief executive officer [CEO]) and reliance on academic ethics and values (as opposed to systems of incentives). This suggests that the introduction of the principles of NPM and IC management face similar challenges in terms of clashes between academic and managerial cultures, as well as incompatibility with governance institutions. Second, both NPM and IC management advocate introducing similar managerial techniques: development of strategic plans with a strong focus on objectives, introduction of measurement and monitoring systems, annual reporting, etc. Finally, reforms carried out in Austria during the last decade exemplify that IC management could be used as an instrument in implementing NPM principles.

On the other hand, there are substantial tensions and contradictions between NPM and IC management. NPM's focus on results-based funding implies that objectives for universities are set by political principles. Failure to meet targets is likely to have negative fiscal consequences. This stands in sharp contrast to IC management that aims to facilitate self-discovery with the view of assessing one's own strengths and redefining a university's mission and objectives (Elena et al. 2011; Sanchez et al. 2009; OEU 2006). As a result, if objectives and targets are set externally and linked with financial sanctions, this undercuts the rationale for introducing IC management.

The NPM doctrine strongly emphasizes the need to move the focus from inputs and processes to outputs and outcomes. In contrast, IC management focuses on intangible resources and activities that are interpreted as inputs. Finally, most of the branches of the NPM doctrine suggest that organizations with a focus on multiple stakeholders lose focus and underperform. Hence, organizations should be accountable either to a limited set of political principles or the end beneficiary of the service. In contrast, the IC framework addresses different stakeholders simultaneously, providing a better view of how collaboration and networking are key drivers in the value-creating process of a public organization (Almqvist and Skoog 2007).

The post-NPM movement in the late 1990s emerged as a response to the perceived weaknesses of the NPM doctrine—that is, focus on efficiency came at the costs of quality and diminished structural capacities, and the emphasis on several measurable outcome indicators led to the emergence of single-purpose agencies that ignored the "unmeasurable" and broader societal needs (Gregory 2003). Hence, post-NPM appeared as a group of loosely coupled efforts aimed at (1) building the structural capacities of public organizations, which shifted the focus from outcomes to inputs; (2) better coordination of efforts with an emphasis on networks and cooperation; and (3) building "common values and ethics" instead of fostering NPM-style competition (Christensen and Lægreid 2007).

The principles of the post-NPM doctrine seem to be highly compatible with the logic of IC management. Both emphasize a holistic and multidimensional approach to assess performance, strengths and weaknesses. Both understand the importance of networks and cooperation with other organizations and society at large, instead of treating external actors merely as clients. Furthermore, post-NPM and IC management focus on capacities and assets of organizations rather than solely on outputs.

3. TOWARD MORE MANAGERIAL AND ENTREPRENEURIAL UNIVERSITIES

Since the mid-1980s, reforming HE systems has been a priority on the political agenda of Western countries. In addition to the traditional academic functions of universities—knowledge dissemination (teaching) and creation (research)—the enhanced role of the "third mission"[3] activities is crucial for the transformation of universities and their consolidation as critical players in socioeconomic development (Foray et al. 2012; Kempton et al. 2013). To a large extent, this could be considered the effect of stronger government policies to strengthen the links between universities and the region where they are located, especially with the business sector, and also an effect of firms' tendency to use universities' research infrastructure for their research and development (R&D) objectives, thus indirectly transferring part of their costs to the state, which provides a large part of university funding (Slaughter and Leslie 1997).

Today, universities are required to operate in a more entrepreneurial way, being able to exploit and commercialize better their research results and spinning out knowledge-based enterprises (Kirby 2006). This process leads to a new configuration of a university called an "entrepreneurial university" in which new dynamics and virtuous collaboration with industrial communities and social institutions are facilitated (Clark 1998; Etzkowitz 2004; Gibb and Hannon 2006; Ropke 1998). Accordingly, and because of government budget cutbacks, universities should set up a more diversified funding portfolio with third-stream income sources, such as donations, royalties, contracts with private companies or campus services (De Dominic et al. 2011; Clark 1998).

In this context, it seems that the need to engage with multiple stakeholders to achieve the third mission is more pressing today than in the past. Moreover, the main driving forces—economic (decrease of public funds for research), social (growing importance of accountability) and cultural (Mode 2 of knowledge production [Gibbons et al. 1994])—produce a complex context and have forced intense debate about how these institutions should be managed (Deem 2001). Becoming an entrepreneurial university requires radical changes in traditional managerial styles as well as in the governing modes (Rappert and Webster 1997). As part of the changes in the orientation of contemporary universities, a new trend called "new managerialism" appeared.

The discussion of new managerialism in universities should be set in the broader context of NPM mentioned in the previous section. Under this approach, traditional university governance modes are not considered fully capable of running these organizations according to the effectiveness and efficiency criteria demanded by the new socioeconomic context and, as a result, new managerial skills and practices are required (Amaral et al. 2003).

In the specialized literature, it is difficult to find a clear definition or a complete set of characteristics forming the notion of new managerialism. Nonetheless, it is used to refer to the application of values and techniques used in the private sector to universities in order to provide them with the necessary tools to improve internal management (Clark 1998; Ferlie et al. 1996; Meek 2003).

In sum, current university internal structures and decision-making processes are being questioned because they seem somewhat inappropriate for managing contemporary universities. Accordingly, efficiency and effectiveness, accountability, development of strategic plans, total quality management, and teaching and research auditing procedures have become important tools to govern these institutions. In this context, the introduction of IC approaches could be a suitable solution to deal with the new management requirements.

4. THE IMPACT OF MEASURING AND REPORTING IC IN UNIVERSITIES

The systematic identification, management and reporting of IC indicators is of strategic importance in today's universities and can help them make the best use of available resources.

However, the implementation phase is not easy. The distinguishing features of the university raise the problem of identifying proper frameworks to analyze success, performance and strategic impact (Secundo et al. 2010), particularly in terms of intangible and knowledge assets generated. In the realm of practice, an increasing number of universities and research centers in Europe have developed IC management and reporting models. However, so far, their application has been mainly based on a voluntary basis. An important effort to provide a homogenous and comprehensive framework for managing and reporting IC in universities was developed by the Observatory of European Universities (Sánchez et al. 2009; OEU 2006). The Austrian case is a remarkable example because it is the only one where there is a law that includes the compulsory delivery of an IC report ("Wissensbilanz") by its publically funded universities since 2006 (Altenburger and Schaffhauser-Linzatti 2006).

Despite practical experiences and the consistent body of knowledge, there is still a lack of systematic studies of the links between IC and value creation in universities, especially for the evolving organizational model and trends in which universities and HE systems in general are immersed. The investigation of how IC sustains and drives value-creation dynamics is thus a key issue to be addressed.

To address this sensitive issue, it is necessary to identify suitable indicators for assessing the performance of universities and for evaluating the strategic impact of the IC measurement and reporting. We propose to do it at three different levels: (1) course or department level, (2) university-wide level and (3) society and regional development level. There is an increasing difficulty in measuring and reporting the strategic impact of IC when we move from the course or department level to the society and region level (see Figure 7.1).

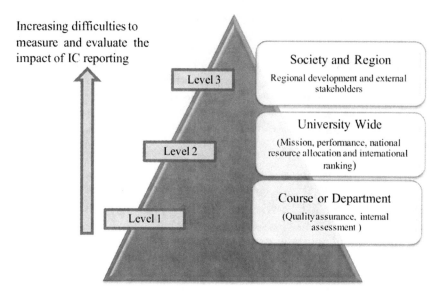

Increasing difficulties to measure and evaluate the impact of IC reporting

Level 3

Level 2

Level 1

Society and Region

Regional development and external stakeholders

University Wide

(Mission, performance, national resource allocation and international ranking)

Course or Department

(Quality assurance, internal assessment)

Figure 7.1   The strategic impact of measuring and reporting IC in universities

Source: Leitner, K-H., Curaj, A., Elena-Perez, S., Fazlagic, J., Kalemis, K., Martinaitis, Z., Secundo, G., Sicilia, M-A. and Zaksa, K. 2014. "A strategic approach for intellectual capital management in European universities. Guidelines for implementation". UEFISCDI Blueprint Series, Bucharest.

The Impact of Measuring and Reporting IC at Course or Department Level: Quality Assurance and Internal Assessment Report

Quality assurance is a comprehensive term referring to how HE institutions and universities manage research projects, teaching and learning opportunities to help students progress and achieve success. IC reporting can support the investigation of concerns about the standards and quality of HE provision, and the accuracy and completeness of the information institutions publish about their internal assessment report. Where some IC indicators evidence some weaknesses and where the evidence suggests broader failings, the university governance should be able to identify the strategic impact on quality management and standards at a course or department level (or faculty level when necessary), introducing the necessary revisions and changes. IC management at this level is related more to internal assessment for improving the quality assurance process. These concerns should be managed by the university governance board at a faculty or department level, including the rector, the faculty dean, the director of the department and eventually the main stakeholders at the ministry level.

The Impact of Measuring and Reporting IC at the University Level: Mission, Performance, Resource Allocation and International Rankings

The increasing national and international competition to attract students, scientists, research funds and other sources of income, as well as ranking and reputation, is a continual challenge for European universities. This competition allows IC development to be considered at first as a mission for universities and HE institutions as they are created and funded, with the purpose of building the workforce of tomorrow, stimulating organizational and technological innovation, and enhancing the network of relationships that cross-fertilize industrial and academic expertise. Second, IC is a metric of performance, and the intangible report may well represent for HE and research organizations what the balance sheet and the income statement are for business companies. Third, IC reporting results could influence the financing of universities by national ministries through the different funding formulas and, hence, resource allocation by universities to their faculties and departments. Finally, IC reporting for universities can impact visibility at national and international levels. The analysis derived from some targeted indicators would allow the university governance to set up strategic directions to improve resource allocation and position in international ranking.

The Impact of Measuring and Reporting IC at a Regional Level and Overall: External Steering Process with Stakeholders, Regional Development and Monitoring Partnerships between University and Local Government

The mentioned changes at the university level demand from universities an entrepreneurial orientation with increasing market relations and a stronger self-reliance, which will be associated with considerable opportunities, but also risks. The strategic impact of IC reporting at societal and regional levels allows universities to implement the general recommendation defined in the European Union (EU) Guide "Connecting Universities to Regional Growth" (Goddard 2011), that is, the active engagement of universities and other HE institutions in regional innovation strategies for smart specialization, in cooperation with research centers, businesses and other partners in the civil society. Universities have a potentially pivotal role to play in the social and economic development of their regions because they are a critical "asset" of the region. The universities are called to strengthen a steering core with a clear mission and vision, to interact with external stakeholders in the "outside" world, to identify a diversified funding base (less state funding) and to adopt an interdisciplinary activity for developing an integrated entrepreneurial culture. Successful measurement and reporting of IC resources of the university can have a positive effect on their regional economies and achievement of comprehensive regional strategies. At first, this could allow public authorities and other stakeholders to understand the principles underlying why universities can be important agents in regional development. Second, IC reporting could support the strategic debate between universities and regional authorities understanding each other's drivers. Finally, IC reporting is at the basis of the strategic coordination of the universities within a wider national or regional policies context. Of course, the strategic impact of measuring IC at societal and regional levels is not free of risks. Universities that are more involved in these transformations processes distinguish themselves through market performance orientation, as well as a clearly recognizable profile based on their scientific strengths. Under these circumstances, many universities will find themselves in a situation of conflict between the growing pressure of commercialization and gain orientation on one side and the wish to fulfil their claim for academic quality on the other. Realizing the right balance requires responsible and competent leadership, the mobilization of all members of the institution toward the common goal and the bonding of all the stakeholders in the regional context.

5. FINAL REMARKS: LESSONS LEARNED AND WAYS FORWARD

Based on the specialized literature and the work carried out in the project "Quality Assurance in Higher Education through Habilitation and Auditing," this chapter presents the key lessons learned when analyzing the strategic impact of IC measuring and reporting in universities. These lessons are clustered into five groups: (1) IC management, (2) harmonization of indicators, (3) integration of IC management with other managerial tools, (4) IC reporting and potential users and (5) conditions for implementation.

I.   Impacts of IC Management:

- The impact of IC management on universities' performance depends heavily on the universities' managerial capacities, resources and legal-administrative framework. Highly autonomous universities with strong managerial capacities are more likely to successfully exploit the potential of IC management in identifying and implementing strategic objectives. On the other hand, the top-down imposition of IC reporting on universities with low managerial capacities could lead to higher administrative burden without actual effects on performance.
- IC systems provide information that is also of high interest for policy makers. They get useful information for the strategic formulation of national and regional research programs, evaluation of research proposals submitted by research organizations and universities, and the strategic development of the research sector in general.
- IC management and reporting enhance and foster a culture favoring a balanced qualitative and quantitative assessment of research and education.

II. Harmonization of IC Management Systems and Indicators

- A certain level of harmonization and standardization is important to assure comparability between universities. Currently, there exist a number of initiatives at the European level to standardize some common indicators relevant for the management and governance of universities, such as the Multiranking Project.[4] Although these initiatives do not focus on IC as such, the aim is to enable universities to assess themself vis-à-vis other institutions. However, there is also a trade-off between a high standardization of indicators and leaving scope for using highly university-specific indicators. In Austria, for instance, a long list of IC indicators has been defined by law, which probably crowded out the motivation of universities to report on more specific and unique indicators.
- In general, indicators that are related to funding can be expected to have the greatest impact (e.g., scientific publications or percentage of competitive funds of the total university budget) and deserve more management attention. In order to use IC reports for resource allocation and strategic control, managers are often focusing on a smaller set of indicators and partly define their own specific indicators.

III. Integration of IC Management and Other Managerial Techniques

- IC management and reporting systems often overlap with other reporting and management systems (such as performance contract, quality management or traditional annual account), and hence, it is important to define the scope, goals and relation to other management and reporting systems and, when possible, to integrate IC reporting into already existing schemes (or vice versa: integrate existing schemes into IC reporting).
- One of the biggest dangers when developing an IC report is to define too many goals and indicators. Kaplan and Norton, the authors of *The Balanced Scorecard* (1996), postulated twenty to twenty-five indicators at the most, but the human capacity to process information is "5 plus minus 2". If neither the picture of the company's future development nor the important intangible resources required are clear, people or organizations tend to want "everything". In the Austrian case, fifty-three indicators (for which additional subcategories were defined) are too difficult to be controlled deliberately, and thus, universities need to define the most relevant measures for their specific goals and strategies and to have the strongest possible impact on the output.

IV. IC Reporting and Potential Users

- Different stakeholders have different information needs in terms of intangibles and IC. For instance, public administrators and university governors demand more information on the university's relationship with the business sector and on graduate employability, whereas students need better information on the quality of teaching and satisfaction among graduates. Administration staff is basically interested in information related to human capital and the university's social and cultural commitment, and teaching and research personnel is more focused on information related to the institution's research capabilities and competences and relations with other universities (Ramirez et al. 2011).

• In contrast to performance measurement systems, quality management instruments and evaluations frequently proposed for this type of public organization, IC reports explicitly focus on the IC and, hence, enlarge the existing input and output categories. In this context, for instance, structural capital has to be considered a blind spot within large research organizations or universities.

V.   Conditions for Effective Use of IC Management

• IC reports can only help to formulate more clearly university goals and strategies in specific contexts. Strong links between IC indicators and funding create pressures for "window dressing" rather than facilitating a learning process.

• Generally, the valuation of IC indicators is dependent on the specific goals and the regional, national and cultural context of the university or organizational unit. Hence, the description of the specific aims and contexts is necessary.

• Universities are not likely to reveal sensitive information that could show their failures or weaknesses because it could be interpreted as a lack of managerial competences; it could discourage external stakeholders from future partnerships and weaken their competitive position.

• International experiences reveal that there is excessive concentration on "knowledge stocks" instead of on "knowledge flows". That is, IC reports still fail to capture the dynamics of knowledge that create value and mainly focus on static resources. Measurement of processes and synergies (what the university is doing) is more valuable than the measurement of resources or stocks (what the university possesses).

• The quality and alignment of the information system and associated IT infrastructure supporting IC reporting becomes a limiting or enabling factor to IC reporting, as it directly affects availability and cost for its effective implementation. This standardization and interoperability of the information system supporting IC reporting is the key enabling factor for integrating IC reporting systems into levels higher than the institution, that is, regional, national or even global.

- There is also the danger that IC measurement programs may be used in internal politics and, consequently, an IC project becomes a means of division, not unification, of employees around the common goal.

Taking the aforementioned points into consideration, further research should be done on the real implementation of IC models in universities. Given the strong academic culture of European universities, it is still controversial to introduce "business" thinking to steer these institutions, and only a few universities are in the process of changing radically their managerial principles. However, the higher level of autonomy that European universities have today leave room for further investigation. The potential benefits and limitations of IC approaches, as well as further empirical evidence on the value-creation chain of universities, can only be achieved by working directly with and for universities.

NOTES

1. Project run by the Executive Agency for Higher Education and Research Funding of Romania (EUFISCDI) and cofunded by the European Social Funds (Sectoral Operation Programme Human Resources Development 2007–2013).
2. Although the NPM doctrine has been applied to different OECD and non-OECD countries, the United Kingdom had an essential role in the development of this notion and can claim to be its "birth place" (McLaughlin et al. 2002). However, it is important to note that there were significant variations in the degree to which NPM principles were taken up by different countries in the 1980s (Hood 1995).
3. It refers to all activities whereby universities can directly address social welfare and private or public economic objectives. It is also conceptualized as a "third stream" (Molas-Gallart 2005).
4. For more information on the project, see http://www.u-multirank.eu.

REFERENCES

Almqvist, R. and Skoog, M. 2007. "Colliding discourses?: New public management from an intellectual capital perspective". In Chaminade, C., Catasus, B. (Eds.). *Intellectual Capital Revisited: Paradoxes in the Knowledge Intensive Organization.* Cheltenham: Elgar, 100–123.

Altenburger, O. and Schaffhauser-Linzatti, M. 2006. "Controlling universities' intellectual capital: Are the recently implemented Austrian instruments adequate?" Paper presented at the EIASM Workshop on Visualising, Measuring, and Managing Intangibles and Intellectual Capital, Maastricht, October 25–27.

Amaral, A., Meek, L.V. and Larsen, I.M., Eds. 2003. *The Higher Education Managerial Revolution.* The Netherlands: Kluwer Academic Publishers.

Aucoin, P. 1990. "Administrative reform in public management: Paradigms, principles, paradoxes and pendulums". *Governance* 3 (2), 115–137.

Christensen, T. and Lægreid, P. 2007. *Transcending New Public Management.* Aldershot: Ashgate.

162   *Susana Elena-Perez et al.*

Clark, B.R. 1998. *Creating Entrepreneurial Universities. Organizational Pathways of Transformation.* Oxford: IAU Press Pergamon.

De Dominicis, L., Pérez, S.E. and Fernández-Zubieta, A. 2011. "European university funding and financial autonomy: A study on the degree of diversification of university budget and the share of competitive funding". Luxemburg: European Commission, Joint Research Centre, Institute for Prospective Technological Studies. EUR 24761 EN.

Deem, R. 2001. "Globalisation, new managerialism, academic capitalism and entrepreneurialism in universities: Is the local dimension still important?" *Comparative Education,* 37 (1), 7–20.

Dent, M., Chandler, J. and Barry, J. 2004. *Questioning the New Public Management.* Aldershot and Burlington: Ashgate Publishing Limited.

Elena-Pérez, S., Saritas, O., Pook, K. and Warden, C. 2011. "Ready for the future? Universities' capabilities to strategically manage their intellectual capital". *Foresight,* 13 (2), 31–48.

Elena, S. and Sánchez, P.M. 2013. "Autonomy and governance models: Emerging paradoxes in Spanish universities". *Perspectives: Policy and Practice in Higher Education,* 17 (2), 48–56.

Etzkowitz, H. 2004. "The evolution of the entrepreneurial university". *International Journal of Technology and Globalization,* I (1), 64–77.

European Commission. 2006. "Delivering on the modernisation agenda for universities: education, research and innovation". COM (2006) 2008 final. Brussels.

European Commission. 2013. "Report to the European Commission: Improving the quality of teaching and learning in Europe's higher education institutions". High Level Group on the Modernisation of Higher Education. Luxemburg: European Commission. http://ec.europa.eu/education/library/reports/modernisation_en.pdf. Accessed April 14, 2014.

European University Association (EUA). 2005. "Glasgow Declaration: Strong universities for a strong Europe." Brussels: European University Association. http://www.eua.be/eua/jsp/en/upload/Glasgow_Declaration.1114612714258.pdf. Accessed April 14, 2014.

European University Association (EUA). 2007. "Lisbon Declaration: Europe's universities beyond 2010: Diversity with a common purpose". Brussels: European University Association. http://www.eua.be/fileadmin/user_upload/files/newsletter/Lisbon_declaration.pdf. Accessed April 14, 2014.

Ferli, E., Ashburner, L., Fitzgerald, L. and Pettigrew, A. 1996. *The New Public Management in Action.* Oxford: Oxford University Press.

Foray, D., Goddard, J., Goenaga, X., Landabaso, M., McCann, P., Morgan, K., Nauwelaers, C. and Ortega-Argilés, R. 2012. "Guide to research and innovation strategies for smart specialisation (RIS3)." Brussels: European Union, Regional Policy Brussels. http://s3platform.jrc.ec.europa.eu/s3pguide. Accessed May 10, 2013.

Gibb, A. and Hannon, P. 2006. "Towards the entrepreneurial university?" *International Journal of Entrepreneurship Education,* 4, 73–110.

Gibbons, M., Limonges, C., Nowotny, H., Schwartzman, S., Scott, P. and Trow, M. 1994. *The New Production of Knowledge: The Dynamics of Science and Research in Contemporary Societies.* London: Sage Publications.

Goddard, J. 2011. "Connecting universities to regional growth: A practical guide, Brussels." European Union, Regional Policy Brussels. http://ec.europa.eu/regional_policy/sources/docgener/presenta/universities2011/universities2011_en.pdf. Accessed May 10, 2013.

Gregory, R. 2003. "All the king's horses and all the king's men: Putting New Zealand's public sector back together again". *International Public Management Review,* 4 (2), 41–58.

Hood, C. 1991. "New public management for all seasons". *Public Administration*, 69, 3–19.

Hood, C. 1995. "The new public management in the 1980s: Variations on a theme". *Accounting, Organisations and Society*, 20 (2/3), 93–109.

Kaplan, R.S. and Norton, D.P. 1996. *The Balanced Scorecard: Translating Strategy into Action*. Boston: Harvard Business School Press.

Kempton, L., Goddard, J., Edwards, J., Hegyi, F.B. and Elena-Pérez, S. 2013. "Universities and smart specialisation". JRC Technical Report, S3 Policy Brief Series, No. 03/2013, European Commission Joint Research Centre, Institute for Prospective Technological Studies.

Kirby, D. 2006. "Creating Entrepreneurial Universities in the UK: Applying Entrepreneurship Theory to Practice', *Journal of Technology Transfer*, 31, 599–603.

Leitner, K-H., Curaj, A., Elena-Perez, S., Fazlagic, J., Kalemis, K., Martinaitis, Z., Secundo, G., Sicilia, M-A. and Zaksa, K. 2014. "A strategic approach for intellectual capital management in European universities. Guidelines for implementation". UEFISCDI Blueprint Series, Bucharest.

McLaughlin, K., Osborne, S.P. and Ferli, E. 2002. *New Public Management. Current Trends and Future Prospects*. London and New York: Routledge,

Meek, V.L. 2003. "Governance and management of Australian universities enemies within and without". In Amaral, A., Meek, V.L., Larsen, I.M. (Eds.), *The Higher Education Managerial Revolution*. The Netherlands: Kluwer Academic Publishers, 179–202.

Molas-Gallart, J. 2005. "Defining, measuring and funding the third mission: A debate on the future of the university". *Coneixement i Societat* 7, 6–27.

Observatory of the European University (OEU). 2006. "Methodological guide, final report of the Observatory of the European University". PRIME Project. www.prime-noe.org. Accessed December 18, 2013.

OECD. 1997. *In Search of Results: Performance Management Practices in Ten OECD Countries*. Paris: Public Management Committee, OECD.

Ramírez Córcoles, Y., Santos Peñalver, J.F. and Ponce, A.T. 2011. "Intellectual capital in Spanish public universities: Stakeholders' information need". *Journal of Intellectual Capital*, 2 (3), 356—376.

Rappert, B. and Webster, A. 1997. "Regimes of ordering: The commercialisation of intellectual property in industrial-academic collaborations". *Technology Analysis and Strategic Management*, 9 (2), 115–130.

Ropke, J. 1998. "The entrepreneurial university: Innovation, academic knowledge creation and regional development in a globalized economy". Working Paper, Philipps-Universitat Marburg, Germany.

Sánchez, M.P., Elena, S. and Castrillo, R. 2009. "Intellectual capital dynamics in universities: A reporting model". *Journal of Intellectual Capital*, 10 (2), 307–324.

Secundo, G., Elena, S., Martinaitis, Z. and Leitner, K-H. 2014. "Intellectual capital management in European universities in times of changes: An IC maturity model". Submitted to the IFKAD (International Forum on Knowledge assets Dynamics) Conference, July 24–25, 2014 *(Forthcoming)*.

Secundo, G., Margherita, A., Elia, G. and Passiante, G. 2010. "Intangible assets in higher education and research: Mission, performance or both?" *Journal of Intellectual Capital*, 11 (2), 140–157.

Slaughter, S. and Leslie, L. 1997. *Academic Capitalism: Politics, Policies, and the Entrepreneurial University*. Baltimore, MD: Johns Hopkins University Press.

Weber, L.E. 2006. "University governance, leadership and management in a rapidly changing environment". In Fromec, E., Kohler, J., Purser, L. and Wilson, L. (Eds.), *EUA Bologna Handbook: Making Bologna Work*. Brussels & Berlin: European University Association and Raabe Academic Publishers (EUA-RAABE), 107–126.

Part IV

Intellectual Capital Reports in Asian Institutions

8 A Knowledge Management Approach to Intellectual Capital Reporting in Hong Kong

Rongbin W.B. Lee and Jessica Y.T. Yip

1. INTRODUCTION TO THE WORK OF THE KNOWLEDGE MANAGEMENT AND INNOVATION RESEARCH CENTER

The Knowledge Management and Innovation Research Center (KMIRC) of The Hong Kong Polytechnic University was set up in 2007 for the promotion of practice and research of knowledge management (KM) and intellectual capital (IC) management in Hong Kong and the neighboring regions. Most of our research is company and industry based. The capabilities and competences of the KMIRC are further strengthened by the international alliances it has formed with leading practitioners, many of whom are regarded as "Hall of Famers" of knowledge management, and with renowned research centers worldwide. The KMIRC is actively engaged in research and scholarly activities in both the technological aspects and the human and organizational aspects of KM. It has pioneered research and practice in KM in various industrial sectors. Currently, there are three focuses of research in the center:

- Intellectual capital management
- Knowledge systems technologies
- Organizational learning

The research activities of the three domains cover the full spectrum of KM, and they support one another. Knowledge system technologies deal mainly with knowledge that has been elicited and codified, whereas organizational learning concerns how the tacit and implicit organizational knowledge can be shared inside and outside an organization. Thus, an important function of KM is to convert the human capital of an organization into its structural and relational capital through the deployment of appropriate information technology and organizational learning techniques. The KMIRC has firmly established itself as the major KM and IC consultancy and training service provider in Hong Kong. With a growing demand for KM training and consultancy services, the KMIRC is involved in many KM projects offered by the private sector, public organizations and government departments. The work of KMIRC has encouraged many organizations/companies to launch various KM projects and to recruit our students as interns to work for their final-year projects. Over the years, more than 100 company-based undergraduate final-year projects have been solicited. KMIRC's consultancy projects span all stages of an enterprise's KM journey. Through these high-level consultancy services, KMIRC has helped various sectors, ranging from public utilities, aviation, government, manufacturing, social work, printing and publishing, health care and more, to kick-start and fine-tune their KM journey, yielding productivity enhancements, cost savings and innovations, as well as enhanced trust for knowledge sharing. So far, we have collected more than 100 cases on lessons learned, which serve as an invaluable knowledge repository for KM research study. The research work of the center thus greatly supports the teaching of the unique master of science program in KM.

The center has also organized the prestigious Global MAKE (Most Admired Knowledge Enterprise Award) for organizations and enterprises in Hong Kong and mainland China in order to promote KM to a wider sector. Through the launch of the award, it also helps in nominating local enterprises to be listed alongside the world's most successful organizations in KM. Awardees include government departments and large public utility companies, as well as a number of big companies in the private sector. Many of the MAKE award criteria are related to the creation and utilization of IC and its implementation in practice to help an organization achieve its business objectives. Following are our views on the relationship between KM and IC, and the methods we developed to chart IC and audit knowledge assets in Hong Kong.

2.   RELATIONSHIP BETWEEN KNOWLEDGE MANAGEMENT AND INTELLECTUAL CAPITAL

Since the early 1990s, the importance of KM in creating an organization's competitive advantage has been widely recognized worldwide in the government, public and private sectors for the codification of information and knowledge, the processing of knowledge (the creation, capture, classification, storage and conversion from implicit to explicit), the reporting and management of IC, innovation and learning capability in firms and organizations. KM is an application-oriented discipline that deals with an interdisciplinary and complex area of study by integrating technology-centered and human-centered approaches from the perspective of knowledge and systems science.

KM is about knowledge preservation, knowledge creation and knowledge diffusion, whereas IC is concerned with managing and reporting the organizational knowledge assets. They are closely related. Different perspectives have different definitions of what KM is. One of the practical definitions is to see KM as a systematic way of evaluating and managing knowledge assets and its creation and utilization in an organization. The link between these two activities is shown in Figure 8.1.

An integrated approach to KM and IC is adopted by the KMIRC (Lee et al. 2013). By adopting the latest information technology to preserve knowledge, the structural capital of an organization is created—that is, the capital that will stay in the company and remain assets of it. The flow of knowledge among individuals, teams, the organization, its strategic networks, clients and users creates valuable relational capital in order to gain the support and trust of its employees and business partners, as well as its customers. On the other hand, the knowledge-creating process depends greatly on the human capital of an organization, which determines its innovative capability.

Thus, an important business objective of KM is to help create the IC of a company. An intellectual asset is a part of the IC that is recorded, whereas intellectual property is only a small part of the intellectual assets that has been legally protected (see Figure 8.2). It must be realized that a substantial part of the IC in an organization is still implicit and resides in the heads of its employees.

An IC audit will help make the hidden part of an intangible asset explicit and will identify and assess risk factors and potential loss so as to meet the business goals of the company or organization.

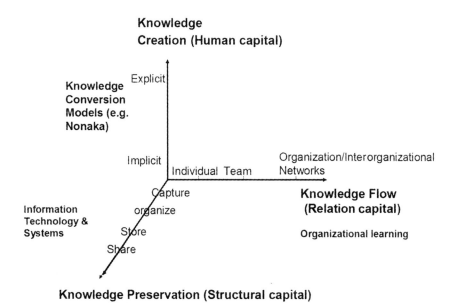

Figure 8.1 Relationship between KM and IC

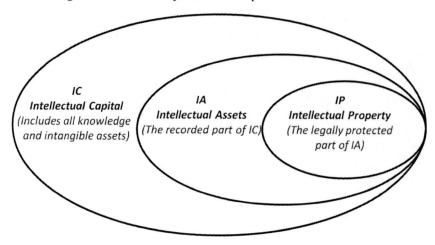

Figure 8.2   Relationship between intellectual capital, intellectual asset and intellectual property

3.   INTELLECTUAL CAPITAL MANAGEMENT (ICM)

Currently, there are many well-known IC reporting models and management frameworks, such as IC Rating, Value Creation Efficiency Analysis (VAIC), Intangible Assets Monitor, The Danish Guidelines on Intellectual Capital Reporting and The Intellectual Capital Statement (InCas). These models are well structured and well designed by the owners of the tool and use either a standard template a predesigned questionnaire through which input is gathered. Due to the predefined components under the IC taxonomy, some aspects of the operations that are specific to the company may be overlooked. This may result in a lower level of involvement and commitment of the frontline staff of an organization.

A bottom-up IC assessment framework called the Intellectual Capital Charting (ICC) has been developed by KMIRC (Durst et al. 2014). This approach has been evaluated continually and implemented in various industries and organizations in Hong Kong. The ICC tool is an IC audit tool that yields a list of IC elements (constituents of IC) of a firm. The ICC also helps develop a strategic view of an organization in terms of the health of its intangible assets and its risk of knowledge loss.

IC elements can vary across companies. These elements are not only industry specific, but very often also company specific. The investigator would first study the background of the company using relevant documents, be familiar with its operation and staff, and collect stories from both the frontline and managerial staff about their daily work. From the data collected, the key points are coded, extracted and then clustered to become IC elements, which are then grouped under the category of human capital (HC), structural capital (SC) and relational capital (RC), respectively. The process and steps are similar to the data collection phase of the grounded theory (Glaser et al. 1967). A workshop among the staff representatives is then held to arbitrate on the appropriateness of the IC elements chosen and then determine collectively their relative weightings in terms of their importance (Figure 8.3). An IC value tree (Figure 8.4) showing the list of IC elements under the three main categories of IC is then constructed. The corresponding IC indicators are then identified among the staff. These indicators are intended to give a quantitative measurement of the goals to be achieved in each of the IC elements identified.

Weighting of IC Elements

Each participant in the workshop gives an importance weighting to each identified IC element on a scale of 1–10 (1 represents the score of least importance, and 10 represents the score of highest importance). These

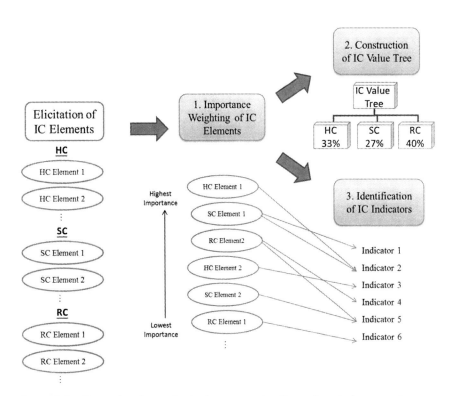

Figure 8.3 Operational steps in the bottom-up intellectual capital approach

relative weightings are normalized as percentages of the overall IC of the company, which is figured as 100. The higher the percentage, the higher is its importance. The values obtained from each staff member are then averaged.

Construction of IC Value Tree

The average importance weighting of each IC element is computed and listed under the three main IC categories, HC, SC and RC, in the form of an IC value tree. Figure 8.4 shows an IC value tree from a marketing department in a public utility company. It lists the top five most important HC, SC and RC elements, which can then be used later in formulating the business strategy of the particular business unit. The overall weightings of the HC, SC and RC help determine whether equal emphasis has been placed on the building of these elements. For example, the weighting of the three IC capitals in the IC value tree is 34 percent, 33 percent and 33 percent, respectively. This represents a mature type of intangible assets management, as equal effort of emphasis has been placed on each capital item. If the weighting of HC is too high, it means there should be more effort to convert some of these into the SC of the company, and this is the essence IC management.

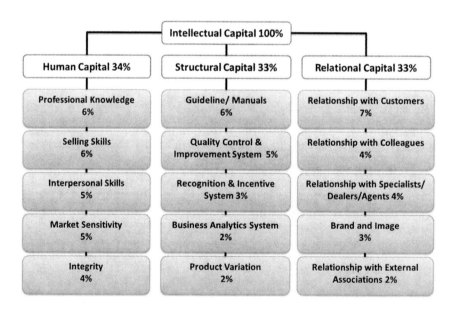

Figure 8.4   IC value tree

Identification of IC Indicators

To measure the effectiveness of IC management, IC indicators are identified through iterative discussion with participants in the workshop (Table 8.1). Colleagues come to a consensus on which indicators should be measured. The major differentiation between the bottom-up and traditional top-down indicators is that colleagues will have a higher sense of engagement in improving the indicators because they are the ones who proposed them.

An IC report is needed to explain the hidden values and assets of an organization (Edvinsson and Malone 1997). The ICC introduced earlier is a useful tool for the provision of transparency to various stakeholder assets during the compilation of the IC report. The bottom-up approach helps in developing a collective and consensus view on the strengths and weaknesses of a firm in terms of its intangible assets. This methodology has been successfully applied in various sectors in Hong Kong, ranging from government, manufacturing, education, public utilities and nongovernmental organizations (NGOs).

Table 8.1 Examples of IC indicators

IC Elements	Relevant Tacit Knowledge
Professional Knowledge	Understand the Project Plan
	Understand the Project Design & Rationale
	Understand the Client and Design Preference
	Understand the Consultant
	Product/ New Product Knowledge
	Realize the Product Inventory
	Knowledge of Design System
	Knowledge of Ordinance
	Estimate of Running Cost
	Knowledge of Product Maintenance and Installation
	Understand the Product Offer
Selling Skills	Collaboration with External Parties
	Seek Help from Customer
	Communication with Consultants/ Customers
Interpersonal Skills	Emotional Intelligence
Market Sensitivity	Degree of feasibility of an Opportunity
	Understand the Market Competition
	Understand the Product Adoption Feedback

4.   STRUCTURED KNOWLEDGE AUDIT

The knowledge associated with HC and RC is mostly implicit (known but not recorded) or tacit (unknown if not properly elicited from the owner and not recorded), whereas the knowledge associated with SC is often explicit (recorded in a database or document). To reduce the risk of losing these important intangible assets, they should be studied in detail with a proper knowledge audit (Shek et al. 2009) to determine the critical knowledge assets that are most important to the operation of the company and to record these to become the intellectual assets (in explicit form) of the company. A knowledge audit offers a detailed record and assessment of the knowledge assets, such as its owners, users, risk of loss, etc. This helps to determine the critical knowledge assets of a company and minimize any losses.

A structured knowledge audit methodology called STOCKS (Strategic TOols to Capture Critical Knowledge and Skill) has been developed by the KMIRC of The Hong Kong Polytechnic University to reveal the documents, tacit knowledge assets and critical IT tools, as well as critical stakeholders related to a key business process. The data are obtained from respondents through structured questionnaires and a series of interactive workshops with representatives of the company. The STOCKS questionnaire consists of various forms to be filled in, inquiring about the use of the technical platform, tacit knowledge flow and document flow in a firm (see Figure 8.5 for an example). These data collected from the questionnaire can be mapped with the IC elements elicited from the ICC methodology.

After receiving the STOCKS questionnaires, a representative sample of colleagues in the company (around 20 percent at least) will be invited to a STOCKS workshop. Colleagues with similar job tasks are clustered in the same group. Before the workshop, the data collected by the STOCKS questionnaires are consolidated and summarized in a STOCKS schema (see Figure 8.6). Information regarding the business process, the supporting IC elements, documents and tacit knowledge are listed in the first five rows of the STOCKS schema, using Post-its. Then, the workshop participants are required to match the relevant documents, tacit knowledge and IC elements with each of the operational steps of the business process being audited. Very often, the terminology used to describe the entries needs to be agreed to among the different parties. The use of Post-its facilitates group discussion, as they can be changed and moved around easily to any position in the STOCKS schema.

After the STOCKS workshop, the relationship between tacit knowledge assets belonging to each IC element identified from the IC value tree can be visualized as an inventory list (see Table 8.2), enabling management to devise plans on what specific kind of knowledge assets need to be strengthened or retained if they carry a high importance weighting. For example, to enhance the professional knowledge of colleagues, efforts should be made to help colleagues understand project plans, design rationales, client requirements, etc.

Document Sent / Submitted / Forwarded / Uploaded / Produced

Please list the document(s) (including online reports) and associated information you send/submit/forward/upload/produce when you carry out the tasks.

Document Sent / Submitted / Forwarded / Uploaded / Produced	Task(s) No.	Rating on the frequency of use *	Rating on the ease of uploading the document**	Rating on the importance of the document to the process***	Document Format						Destination of Document						
					Hardcopy			Softcopy						People			
					Printed	Fax	Handwritten	Format (e.g. word, PPT, excel, pdf, etc.)	Multi-media file (e.g. movie, voice file)	Within Your Dept.	Other Dept. (Please specify)	External to Towngas	(Write down the name of the person / dept. who you pass the document)	Self-use only	IT Tools/Platforms No. (Refer to Form 1)	Others (Please specify):
1.																
2.																
3.																
4.																
5.																
6.																
7.																
8.																
9.																

Figure 8.5 STOCKS questionnaire

* Rating on Frequency of use 1—Never; 2—Less than once a month; 3—Less than once a week; 4—Several times a week; 5—Everyday
** Rating on the ease of uploading the document: 1—Very difficult; 2—Somewhat difficult; 3—About right; 4—Relatively easy; 5—Easy
*** Rating on the importance of the document to the process: 1—Not important; 2—Least important; 3—Somewhat important; 4—Important; 5—Very important

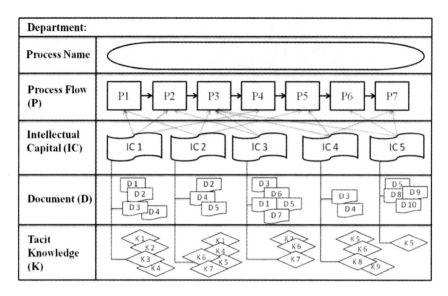

Department:	
Process Name	(oval)
Process Flow (P)	P1 → P2 → P3 → P4 → P5 → P6 → P7
Intellectual Capital (IC)	IC 1 · IC 2 · IC 3 · IC 4 · IC 5
Document (D)	D1 D2 D3 D4 / D2 D4 D5 / D3 D6 D1 D5 D7 / D3 D4 / D5 D8 D9 D10
Tacit Knowledge (K)	K1 K2 K3 K4 / K1 K4 K6 K5 K7 / K2 K6 K7 / K5 K6 K8 K9 / K5

Figure 8.6   STOCKS schema

Table 8.2   Relationship between tacit knowledge assets and IC elements

	Human Capital
Interpersonal Skills	% of staff feeling comfortable at work
	Average duration to close a deal
	No. of collaborative projects per year
	No. of complaints per year
	Success rate per person
	Years of work experience
Market Sensitivity	Additional sales
	Amount of info in newspaper clipping database and other media clippings database
	Customer surveys
	No. of exhibition/seminars attended
	No. of market information updates sharing
	No. of Product Briefings or hands-on practice workshop
	No. of suggestions reported to Market Intelligence Programme

(*Continued*)

Table 8.2   (Continued)

Human Capital	
Professional knowledge	Hours of professional training CPD
	No / % of professional qualifications achieved
	No. of staff having engineering-related Bachelor Degrees
	No. of staff having Master Degrees
	Years of work experience
Work Attitude	% of participation
	% of staff feeling colleagues' support
	% of staff feeling self-leaming atmosphere at work
	Completeness of report/quotation (i.e. on time)
	Punctuality rate

Structural Capital	
Corporate Culture	% of staff feeling happy about work environment
	Frequency of ambassador program meeting/monthly meeting
	No. of leaflets, newsletters, SMS
	No. of safety functions
	No. of safety relations
Customer Relationship Management (CRM)	% of customers whose information is stored in Excel database
	Amount of quotations sent/accepted
	Amount of sponsorship to customers per year
	No. of visit to customer
	No. of clients handled by each engineer
	No. of quotations accepted
	No. of quotations sent
	No. of sponsorships to customers per year
	No. of updates in Excel database
	No. of updates in PMS
	No. of updates in Siebel
Product Variation	No. of countries from which products are imported from
	No. of new products released per year
	Range of product prices
	Update frequency of products

(*Continued*)

Table 8.2   (Continued)

Structural Capital	
Recognition & Incentives Scheme	Amount of commission claimed
Work Manuals/ Guideline	No. of work manuals
	% of staff findings the work manual useful

Relational Capital	
Brand & Image	Maintenance rate of product
	Market share
	No. of equipment sales
	No. of renewed contracts
	Product/tariff discounts
Relationship with consultants	No. of meeting/site-visits to consultants
	No. of referrals/enquiries from consultants
Relationship with customers	Contracts renewal rate
	Market share
	No. of association functions participate in sponsorship
	No. of customer visits
	No. of quotations issued
	No. of survey orders
	Ratio of sales contactsto sales closed
Relationship with Developers	Avg. duration of developer relationship
	No. of deals with developers
Relationship with government	Participation frequency with trade associations
	Success rate in attaining letter of approval (EMSD/EPD)

The knowledge audit workshop serves to explore the knowledge representation of IC elements identified in the IC value tree in the form of a three-level taxonomy. For example, Figure 8.7 shows a taxonomy of the "guidelines/manuals" of certain business steps as layers of knowledge items, which are not normally included in an IC report.

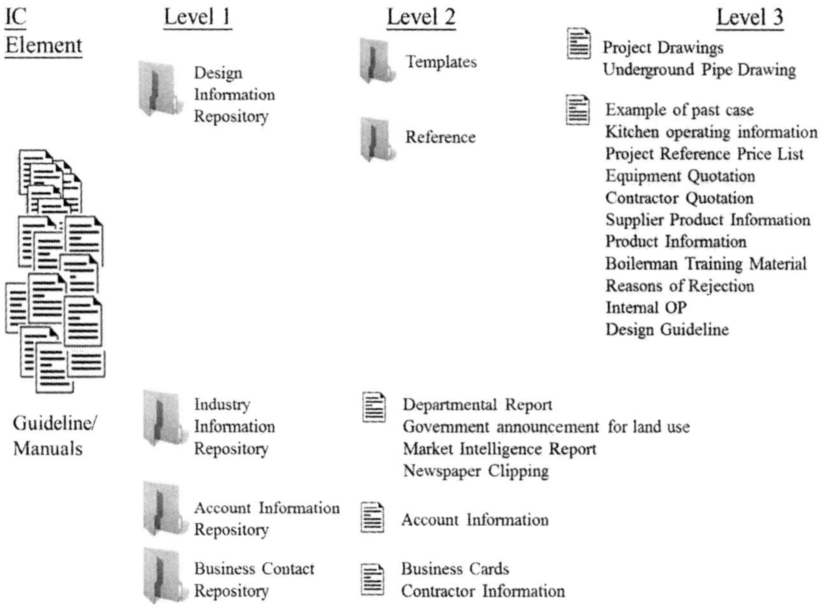

IC Element	Level 1	Level 2	Level 3

Design Information Repository → Templates → Project Drawings / Underground Pipe Drawing

Reference → Example of past case / Kitchen operating information / Project Reference Price List / Equipment Quotation / Contractor Quotation / Supplier Product Information / Product Information / Boilerman Training Material / Reasons of Rejection / Internal OP / Design Guideline

Guideline/Manuals → Industry Information Repository → Departmental Report / Government announcement for land use / Market Intelligence Report / Newspaper Clipping

Account Information Repository → Account Information

Business Contact Repository → Business Cards / Contractor Information

Figure 8.7   A three-level document taxonomy related to the IC element of guidelines/manuals

5.   INTELLECTUAL CAPITAL MANAGEMENT PROGRAM (IC LITE) FOR SMEs

Small and medium enterprises (SMEs)—manufacturing companies employing fewer than one hundred employees and nonmanufacturing companies employing fewer than fifty employees—provide job opportunities to more than one million workers, and in 2013, there were about 310,000 SMEs in Hong Kong. SMEs account for over 98 percent of the total business units in Hong Kong and contribute an indispensable part of the local economies. However, unlike the large corporations, they lack the resources to innovate on their own. Many of the SMEs' problems are rooted in their lack of appreciation of the knowledge assets they need to protect, inadequate training of HC, unwillingness to invest in management support issues and lack of understanding of risk mitigation measures. Overall, there is a lack of a strategic management framework to manage and expand their knowledge capital. In view of these inadequacies, the Intellectual Property Department (IPD) of the Hong Kong Special Administrative Region (SAR) Government launched an IC Lite program to enhance the strategic thinking of SMEs in the managing and protecting of their intellectual assets. The objectives of the program are to help SMEs to:

- Find the hidden assets inside their enterprise, list and analyze them scientifically
- Identify and minimize the risks in their hidden assets

The program was launched in 2009, and the service was free for SMEs. Participating organizations receive a free set of intellectual capital management (ICM) training materials. A pool of ICM consultants received a three-week training course with a practicum conducted by the KMIRC of The Hong Kong Polytechnic University. They were then deployed at SME worksites two times (up to three hours per visit), assisting in writing up a simple IC report for internal reference and an IC statement for the client's stakeholders with the guide of a standard worksheet. The IC reports help to identify the crucial IC elements and the IC value tree, which are important to the success of the company. The consultants work with the SMEs' staff to assess their weightings and their risk factors, as well as finding ways to mitigate their risks. More than 30,000 SMEs were contacted, and within four months after the roll-put phase, more than 120 SMEs were selected and joined the program. The business of these companies includes manufacturing, design, biotech, retailing, financing, education, hotels and various business services. A certificate is issued by the IPD to those SMEs who successfully completed the program by producing an IC report to recognize their participation. Although this limited program only covered one year, it has helped to spread the practice of IC reports to SMEs, who would otherwise not be aware of the importance of managing their intangible assets.

Recently, a modified schema based on the three dimensions of managing IC for SMEs through knowledge preservation, knowledge flow and knowledge creation (Figure 8.1) has been designed for SMEs applying for the Hong Kong MAKE award.

ACKNOWLEDGMENTS

Part of this chapter was presented at the 2013 Annual Meeting of the Japanese Intellectual Asset Management Association in Tokyo. The authors also wish to thank the Research Committee of The Hong Kong Polytechnic University and The Hong Kong and China Gas Company Limited (Towngas) for the provision of a Teaching Company Scheme (project code: H-ZW0U) to one of the authors, Jessica Yip, to conduct IC research in Hong Kong.

REFERENCES

Durst, S. Yip, J.Y. and Lee, W.B. 2014, "SME succession planning and knowledge loss assessment". In Ordoñez de Pablos, P., Jovell Turró, L., Tennyson, R.D. and Zhao, J. (Eds.), *Knowledge Management for Competitive Advantage During Economic Crisis*. Hershey, PA: IGI Global.

Edvinsson, L. and Malone, M.S. 1997. *Intellectual Capital: Realizing Your Company's True Value by Finding Its Hidden Brainpower.* New York: HarperBusiness.

Glaser, B.G. and Anselm Strauss, L. 1967. *The Discovery Of Grounded Theory: Strategies for Qualitative Research* Chicago: Aldine.

Lee, W.B., Lui, C.C., Yip, J.Y., and Tsui, E.Y. 2013. "Exploration in intellectual capital practice: A knowledge management perspective". In Ordóñez de Pablos, P., Tennyson, R. and Zhao J. (Eds.), *Intellectual Capital Strategy Management for Knowledge-Based Organizations*. Hershey, PA: Business Science Reference, 225–238. doi:10.4018/978-1-4666-3655-2.ch013.

Shek, W.Y, Lee, W.B. and Cheung, C.F. 2009. "Mapping and auditing organizational knowledge assets using the interactive STOCKS methodology", *International Journal of Learning and Intellectual Capital*, 6 (1/2), 71–101.

9 Reporting on Intangibles
A Recent Survey from Japan

Tadanori Yosano

1. INTRODUCTION

This chapter strives to explain why the Japanese Intellectual Asset-based Management (IAbM) report is more suitable for the small and medium enterprise (SME)–financial institution relationship with a detailed Japanese historical socioeconomic background. The Japanese Ministry of Economy, Trade and Industry (METI) first focused on the listed company–market actor relationship; however, the overlap between the intellectual capital (IC) information demand and supply was smaller than expected. This chapter explains why there was a mismatch with IC information and addresses why nonlisted SME IC information for financial institutions has been effective in IC disclosures with the previously shown empirical evidence. This chapter also addresses why nonlisted SME IC information for financial institutions has created some movement in the IC field by capturing main actors, such as METI, Organization for Small & Medium Enterprises and Regional Innovation, Japan (OSMERI) and other key IAbM supporters.

2. WHAT IS LACKING IN JAPANESE LISTED COMPANIES FOR NONFINANCIAL INFORMATION DISCLOSURE?

The IAbM Report and Disclosure Practice of Listed Japanese Companies

The Japanese METI (2005) published the "Guideline for Disclosure of Intellectual Assets-based Management" in October 2005. The preceding Danish "Guideline for Intellectual Capital Statements" (DMTI 2000; DMSTI 2003) and MERITUM Guidelines (MEasuRing Intangibles To Understand and improve innovation Management) (MERITUM 2000) served as frequent references during the deliberation of this new guideline. The METI guideline's purpose is to be a communication tool between large firms and stakeholders in the securities market, with investors as central actors (Figure 9.1):

> [T]he value of the corporation realized in the market will increase (such as an increase in the aggregate market value), financing of the corporation will become easier; efforts for and investment in the creation and utilization of intellectual assets will increase; corporate value will further increase and intellectual assets based management will be further strengthened; and it leads to the next disclosure. (SMIA 2005, p. 27)

The IAbM report needs the value-creation perspective from a managerial viewpoint, which is typically represented in a style shown in Table 9.1. First, the IAbM needs the value-creation perspective of how the company has accumulated IC resources in the organization and how they have utilized these resources in accordance with their strategy up until now. Second, the IAbM needs the strategic view of how companies plan their investments in order to acquire prospective resources that can be used to execute their future business plan. It is an essential and vital task to manage corporate resources, such as tangible and IC, into mobilized vectors along the direction indicated by corporate management strategies (Yosano 2011, 8).

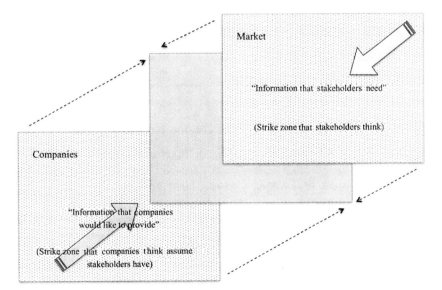

Figure 9.1 Stakeholders whose central actors are investors

Source: Interim report by the Management and Intellectual Assets Subcommittee, New Growth Policy Committee, Industrial Structure Council, 2007, p. 37.

Table 9.1 Typical style of Intellectual Assets-based Management report by "Guidelines for Disclosure of Intellectual Assets-Based Management"

[Main body]

(General) Basic management philosophy
          Outline of business characteristics

(From Past to Present)

A: Management policy in the past

B: Investment (based on A) (performance figures included)

C: Unique intellectual assets accumulated in the company, strengths based on them, and value creation method (based on A and B) (supporting intellectual assets indicators included)

D: Actual performance in the past, such as profits (as a result of value creation C) (figures included)

(From Present to Future)

E: (Based on C and the assessment of the past to the present) Intellectual assets that rooted in the company and will be effective in the future, and future value creation method based on them (supporting intellectual assets indicators included)

F: Identification of future uncertainty/risk, how to deal with them, and the future management policy including those elements

G: New/Additional investment for maintenance and development of intellectual assets needed (in line with the management policy F) (figures included)

H: Expected future profits, etc. (based on E to G) (numerical targets included)

[Attachment]

Other intellectual assets indicators (optional)

Source: Koga and Yosano, 2008, p. 25

Mismatch between IC Information Demander and Supplier

The overlapping IC information between stakeholders need and company supply, shown in Figure 9.1, has been narrower than ever expected. The disclosure practices of listed companies have not prevailed yet in 2013 (Table 9.2). Japanese listed companies currently disclose a lot of nonfinancial information via multimedia, such as the corporate social responsibility (CSR) report, business philosophy and vision, intellectual property report, and midterm business plan (Figure 9.2). All of these reports are voluntary, especially the CSR report; 439 listed companies disclosed this information in 2006. Why have IC reporting practices not prevailed or acquired legitimacy (Yosano 2011) within the Japanese stock market actors? In regard to information suppliers, Sumita (2008) "guess[ed] this is because it is difficult to summarize an IAbM report in an existing specific section of a company, whereas intellectual property (IP) reports can be handled by the IP section,

Table 9.2 Japanese disclosure practices of intellectual capital report

year	Listed Companies				Non-listed companies			
	Intellectual Capital Report	Intellectual Property Report	Part of Annual Report	Other Media	Intellectual Capital Report	Intellectual Property Report	Part Annual Report	Other Media
2004	-	12	18	-	-	-	-	-
2005	1	19	28	-	2	0	0	-
2006	2	21	32	-	8	2	0	0
2007	1	-	2	-	14	-	-	2
2008	6	-	1	-	26	-	-	-
2009	-	-	-	-	40	-	-	-
2010	-	-	-	-	73	-	-	-
2011	-	-	-	-	88	1	-	-
2012	-	-	-	-	74	-	-	-
2013	-	-	-	-	33	-	-	-

Source: Foundation of Intellectual Asset Management Center, Available at http://www.jiam.or.jp/CCP013.html, http://www.jiam.or.jp/CCP014.html (accessed 31 March 2014).

and CSR reports by the CSR section. This indicates that an IAbM report describing the total picture of the management requires a corporate manager to grasp the total shape of the organization and establish a clear vision, and also suggests that the IAbM is more easily achieved in SMEs, where there is some room for modification in the management system than in big business (ibid., 218)." We can also guess that the companies, especially large listed ones, disclose a lot through multimedia, and they would feel a slight burden if they were required to disclose an additional IAbM report.

When we turn our attention to information demanders that the central corporate disclosure uses, Japanese analysts, on average, have a short-term viewpoint for corporate evaluations, especially for sell-side analysts. The METI (2007) questionnaire/survey showed that 64.7 percent of sell-side analysts have a short-term, almost one-year, perspective, when they evaluate a company (Panel A of Table 9.3). The main reasons for their short-term view are (1) they are responsible for a short-term evaluation in their company, and (2) their performance is judged within a short period (Panel B of Table 9.3). They also attached great importance to the "Ease of understanding", "Comparability" and "Linkage to the corporate value" (Panel C of Table 9.3). These results show that central information users—financial analysts—are inclined to short-term viewpoints and place great importance on the ease of handling and controlling information from a distance (Robson 1992). Japanese analysts' short-term viewpoint implies that the financial analyst

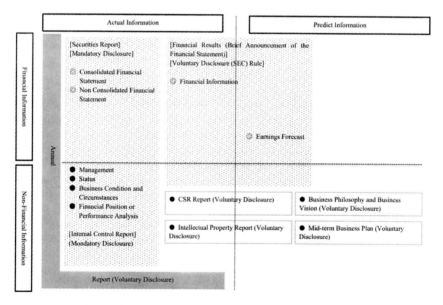

Figure 9.2 Current mandatory, timely and voluntary disclosure practices of Japanese listed companies

Source: Survey and Research Report on Corporate Disclosure of Non-Financial Information, 2012, p. 3, *in Japanese.*

is not greatly interested in the nonfinancial information which has the difficulties in handling and contro Another questionnaire/survey (Sakakibara et al.
2005; Sakakibara et al. 2010), which used 324 Japanese financial analysts in
2005, showed the clear difference between large and SME listed companies.
Japanese financial analysts utilize five of fifteen IC items (corporate strategy,
growth opportunities, market share, brand power and research and development [R&D] investments) to a high degree (mean score over 4 on the 5 Likert
scale) when evaluating large listed companies. They also utilize five of fifteen
IC items (top management quality, corporate strategy, growth opportunities,
R&D investments and market share) to a high degree when evaluating SME
listed companies (Table 9.4). The highly utilized four items (corporate strategy,
market share, brand power and R&D investments) can be gathered from other
disclose-media. The IC items which have the difficulties in gathering from other
disclose-media are all below 4 on average. This result suggests that difficulties in
accessing IC hamper the use of IC. This is why the IAbM guidelines were introduced in 2005. However, the IAbM disclosure practice has not prevailed yet.
One of the main reasons for this is the difficulty in developing the key performance indicator (KPI). Actually, the IAbM guidelines place great importance on
the disclosure of the KPI, and they provide details, not only for KPI sample categories, but also some sample KPI measures, whose representatives are shown
in Table 9.5. However, it may still be difficult to develop exact KPI measures
within an individual company. It is much more difficult to have common KPI
measures that are easy to understand and to compare within the same sector.

Table 9.3 Questionnaire analysis for the Japanese financial analysts. Panel A. The time
frame of corporate evaluation by each type of analyst. Panel B. Why do financial analysts
evaluate companies for a short period? (Multiple responses). Panel C. Desirable IR attributes for the disclosure of intellectual assets-based management by each type of analyst.

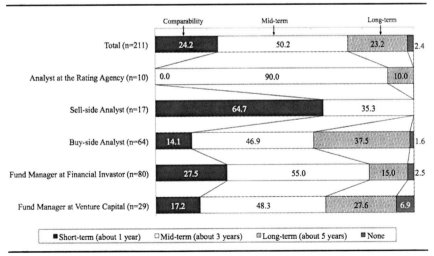

Source: METI, 2007, p. 19.

(*Continued*)

Table 9.3   (Continued)

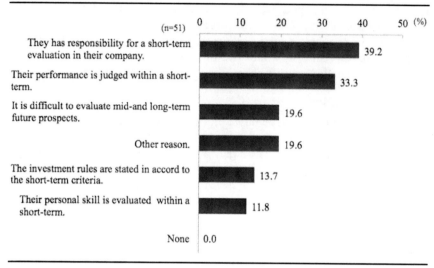

Source: METI, 2007, p. 20.

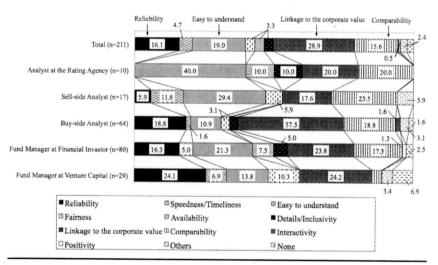

Source: METI, 2007, p. 20.

Table 9.4 Financial analyst survey: Degree of use for corporate evaluation

Japanese Large listed companies			
Intellectual capital measures	Category	Mean	Standard deviation
Corporate strategy	SC	4.44	0.804
Growth opportunities	RC	4.32	0.782
Market share	RC	4.22	0.803
Brand power	RC	4.11	0.832
R&D investments	SC	4.11	0.801
Top management quality	HC	3.97	0.811
Business alliances	RC	3.81	0.799
Customer satisfaction	RC	3.77	0.904
Top executive succession policy	SC	3.34	0.945
Employee training	HC	3.23	0.885
Corporate governance structure	SC	3.08	1.013
Employee participation	HC	3.04	1.010
Personnel turnover	HC	2.91	0.941
Quality assurance systems	SC	2.89	1.066
Employee satisfaction	HC	2.85	0.953
SME listed companies			
Top management quality	HC	4.66	0.771
Corporate strategy	SC	4.61	0.799
Growth opportunities	RC	4.47	0.894
R&D investments	SC	4.10	0.828
Market share	RC	4.00	0.997
Business alliances	RC	3.95	0.882
Brand power	RC	3.86	0.912
Top executive succession policy	SC	3.86	1.036
Customer satisfaction	RC	3.82	0.933
Employee training	HC	3.49	0.999
Employee participation	HC	3.42	1.118
Personnel turnover	HC	3.35	1.085
Employee satisfaction	HC	3.20	1.064
Corporate governance structure	SC	2.95	1.013
Quality assurance systems	SC	2.90	1.091

Source: sakakibara et. al., 2005, p. 8.

Table 9.5 Intellectual assets categories and indicators according to the IAbM guidelines

Intellectual Assets Categories	Examples of KPI (Key Performance Indicator)s
Management stance/leadership	Degree of internal penetration of management principles External transmission of information by top manager (external PR activities) Development of future leaders (average age of subsidiary presidents)
Selection and concentration	Competitiveness of major business (sales, profit, profit rate) — Proportion of major business to the entire sales (sales) — Proportion of major business to the operating profit — Operating profit margin of major business Weighted average of the numbers of companies providing the same products/services Review performance of unprofitable department Degree of R&D concentration Differentiation of market Employee assessment
External negotiating power/relationships	Weighted average of market share of main products/services in the main business Degree of customer satisfaction Changes in customer unit price New customer sales ratio (in B to B business) or growth rate of new customers or members (in B to C business), compared to those in the previous year Price elasticity value of product sales as compared to changes in the cost of goods purchased (price pass-through capability) Price elasticity value of the goods purchased as compared to changes in material market conditions (negotiation power) Financing capacity
Knowledge creation/innovation/speed	R&D expenditure (or ability development costs) vs. sales Outsourced R&D cost ratio Number of intellectual property owned economically meaningful term Employees' average age and increase/decrease from the previous year New products rate

(Continued)

Table 9.5 (Continued)

Intellectual Assets Categories	Examples of KPI (Key Performance Indicator)s
Teamwork/ organizational knowledge	In-house improvement proposal for quality control system, number of proposals and improvements achieved
	Number of lateral projects
	Degree of employees' satisfaction
	Incentive system (including yearly contract system)
	Job leaving ratio
Risk management/ governance	Compliance system
	Number of public announcements regarding risk Information and speed of public announcement of problems
	Diversification of risks
	Risk of being an acquisition target
	Compensation claims in pending lawsuits
	Risk of information leakage (number of trade secrets and ratio of core employees who deals with them)
Coexistence in society	Amount of environment-related investment
	Number of SRI funds which adopted the corporation
	Corporate-image survey and ranking results

Source: Guideline for Disclosure of Intellectual Assets-based Management, 2008, pp. 14–16.

3. THE SHIFT FROM LISTED COMPANY–INVESTOR COMMUNICATIONS TO NONLISTED SME–FINANCIAL INSTITUTION COMMUNICATIONS

The Movement from the Organization for Small and Medium Enterprises and Regional Innovation in Japan

The Japanese government shifted their IC disclosure target from listed company–investor communications to nonlisted SME–financial institution communications. The OSMERI, which is affiliated with METI, set up a "research group of Intellectual Asset-based Management for SMEs" in January 2006, deliberated the expansion of IAbM support measures for SMEs, and, in March 2007, issued the IAbM guideline for SMEs (Intellectual Asset-Based Management Manual for Small and Medium Enterprises) (OSMERI 2007). SMEs have the advantage of establishing a clear total picture of the management strategy and the shape of the organization (Sumita 2008, 218) mentioned. However, they often lack long-term strategic management views and a well-designed organizational structure that moves their strategies forward, especially nonlisted SMEs. Therefore, the main difference between the IAbM Manual for SMEs, compared with the IAbM guidelines, is the former focuses on the strengths, weaknesses, opportunities, and threats (SWOT) analysis to capture SME strengths and weaknesses and encourages the redevelopment of their long-term strategic management view considering their strong and weak attributes (Table 9.6). The second difference is a reduction in detailed stakeholder communication aspects, such as the number of socially responsible investing (SRI) funds and corporate ranking results. The third difference is that the manual has four concrete SME examples. These examples include an actual IAbM report for these firms. One of them is Showa Deniki, the pilot program company from Japan for the International Integrated Reporting Council, started in August 2010, who strives to introduce a new approach to corporate reporting.[1]

This shift has been successful thus far. Many nonlisted companies started disclosing their IAbM report soon after the publication of the IAbM Manual for SMEs. Table 9.2 shows that at least 297 companies disclosed an IAbM report between 2007 and 2013. However, it is difficult for METI to detect all the practices of nonlisted companies. Many SMEs have been disclosing an IAbM report with the help of the OSMERI, SME management consultants, administrative scriveners and sometimes local lenders, which this chapter will discuss in the next section.

Soon after publishing the IAbM Manual for SMEs, the OSMERI initiated the research, focusing on the perception of financial institutions for IC when they lend to the SMEs. Why did they focus on SME lending? One reason is that Japanese SMEs still rely heavily on loans from financial institutions, contrary to large companies in Japan. The SME equity ratio has slightly increased from 25.1 percent in 2007 to 30.7 percent in 2009 (JSBRI 2011, 423). However, a long-term loan from financial institutions holds a great amount, 32.2 percent, of total liabilities (ibid., 421). On the other hand, large company equity ratios have greatly increased from 31.9 percent in 2007 to 30.6 percent in 2009 (ibid, 423). The decrease in loans from financial institutions for large companies has been the long-term tendency in Japan (Table 9.7).

At the same time, local Japanese lenders were under the "Action Program Concerning Enhancement of Relationship Banking Functions" (FSA 2003), which was introduced by the Japanese Financial Service Agencies (FSA) in March 2003. This program encouraged regional banks and cooperative financial institutions to move away from transaction lending and move toward relationship lending.[2] "Relationship" in the banking context implies close lender–borrower connections. Therefore, we define "relationship lending" as mutually beneficial banking transactions that occur through the accumulation of nonfinancial information from closer lender–borrower connections (Yosano and Nakaoka 2011a, 5). Several IC measures are considered nonfinancial information, and therefore, introducing the IAbM to SMEs was appropriate within the FSA's Action Program.

Table 9.6 The standard procedure of intellectual asset-based management

<<Procedure of intellectual assets-based management>>

[Recognizing own company's strengths (stocktake of intellectual assets)]

Firstly, write out the strengths of your own company. SWOT analysis may be effective in this process. This is a stocktake of the sources of your company's strengths and other elements that are important for the company. ※SWOT analysis: Analysis method that examines a company's strengths, weaknesses, opportunities, and threats with the aim of summarizing overall assessment.

[Summarizing how the company's strengths lead to profits (scenario making)]

Examine past achievements to document the management policy on how the company's strengths have generated and will generate profits. In the process, associate fiscal figures with intellectual assets and other non-financial elements.

[Clarifying the management policy and identifying management indicators (visualization technique)]

I order to achieve the above management policy, identify management indicators that serve as internal guide for the core part of the policy.

[Compiling a report (visualization technique)]	[Implementing an Intellectual Asset-based Management]
Draw up an Intellectual Asset-based Management Report. Of the above management indicators, present those that can be disclosed in the context of the management policies, so that it form part of information with a high level of profit achievability. This visualizes the company's latent potential, enhances common mentality between management and employees, and generates strong commitment.	Enforcing the above management policies and management indicators within the company. It is also important to measure management indicators and conduct regular check/improvement actions (PDCA management cycle) to enhance business performance.

—————— Internal management ——————

—————— External communication ——————

[Disclosure to stakeholders: Utilizing and collaborating with external resources]

Present the Intellectual Asser-based Management Report, together with financial statements, to employees, job applicants (human resources), business associates, financial institutions, local communities, investors, and others, Provide a highly credible report so that they can correctly assess the company's future potential, which leads to the company's appeal. This is expected to generate effects such as expanding business associates.

Source: Intellectual Asset-based Management Manual, OSMERI, 2007, p. 10.

Table 9.7   Ratio of loans from financial institutions to total assets for Large Japanese companies

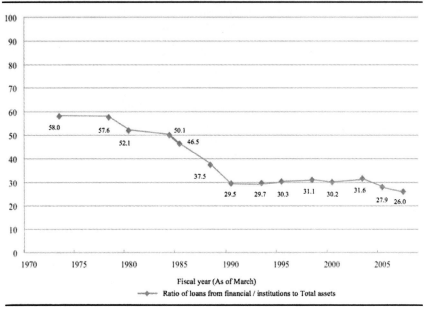

Fiscal year (As of March)

———◆——— Ratio of loans from financial / institutions to Total assets

Source: Hirota, 2009, p. 29.

In February 2008, OSMERI set up a working group to strengthen financing based on SME IC information and published two types of research reports (OSMERI 2008a, 2008b). One is the "Guideline to Practice the Intellectual Asset-based Management for SMEs." This guideline recommends that SMEs disclose a two-page IAbM report in order to achieve two main purposes. First, the company can easily grasp the summary of their IAbM. Second, IAbM supporters, such as enterprise management consultants and administrative scriveners, would have a manual. The ultimate goal was to make this IAbM practice more popular among SMEs. The second research report established was "Surveys and Research Pertaining to Intellectual Asset-Based Finance". This report involves questionnaires/surveys conducted with all Japanese financial institutions and analyzes in detail their perception of IC information usage and the manner of utilization toward judging a lending decision and supporting SME businesses (Koga and Yosano 2008).

This report shows that 28 percent of financial institutions utilize IC information when they evaluate borrowers in the lending decision. The usage ratio of 28 percent of nonfinancial information is less than the usage ratio (35 percent) for nonfinancial information in stock investment decisions reported in the survey analysis of institutional investors in the European Union (EU) and U.S. (Mavrinac and Siesfeld 1995, 13). Taking into consideration the fact that the reward of financing is constant (interest income) and, therefore, the risk that financial institutions can undertake is limited, as opposed to the volatile reward of investor investment, the usage ratio of 28 percent in a "conservative" credit risk rating is considerably high (Koga and Yosano 2008, 2). However, as with Japanese financial analysts, their utilization of IC information is inclined toward management, management strategy and management policies (Table 9.8). They usually do not use many accumulated IC resources and the IC creation process till now and into the future (categories such as customers/suppliers, employees, basic of organization and risk management/governance). IC resources and the IC creation process are the core components that realize the company's management and strategy. However, lenders also think that it is difficult to access IC information. When Yosano and Nakaoka (2011b) analyzed the same questionnaire sample in detail, they found that the lenders who utilized IC information in regard to management and business significantly, record higher profitability than lenders who do not. We also found that the lenders, who utilize IC information in regards to network information, such as customers and suppliers, also record a higher profitability than lenders who do not. They also confirmed that utilization of network information is more effective when they are in a highly competitive region (p. 34).

Current Action from the OSMERI and Other Related SMEs–Local Lender Relationships

The previous section showed some evidence that supports the movement from SMEs–local lender relationships in regard to the IAbM. The IAbM disclosure practice for SMEs is effective for communicating with lenders, and this OSMERI involvement is ongoing. The OSMERI revised the IAbM Manual Guideline for SMEs (OSMERI 2008b) in 2012 (OSMERI 2012). The revised version provided six different manuals in accordance with the purposes of IAbM disclosure: (1) Venture, (2) Relationship banking, (3) Business succession,

Table 9.8 Lender's evaluation level of non-financial items when in financing decisions

OSMERI Categories	non-financial items	evaluation level* average
manager	personal assets of management	3.99
	successor's presence	3.95
	capability of management	3.93
	character of management	3.78
	health condition of top management	3.61
	leadership	3.49
	age of top management	3.47
	career of management	3.41

(Continued)

Table 9.8 (Continued)

OSMERI Categories	non-financial items	evaluation level* average
	concentrative level of the business	3.37
	the ability of make a plan/idea	3.36
	career in the sector	3.35
	networks of management	3.25
	publicity activities	3.08
internal/external business environment	business climate/sensitivity	3.80
	status of competitors	3.73
	market share/position of the sector	3.53
business contents	history and track record of business	3.85
	superiority of technologies	3.85
	superiority of the main business	3.84
	superiority of products/services	3.81
	superiority and brand of products/services	3.68
	intellectual property (rights)	3.44
customers/ suppliers	financing affordable	4.01
	financing from another main financial institution	3.96
	presence of main financial institution	3.86
	customers and their status	3.63
	suppliers and their status	3.42
	relationship with customers	3.41
	customer satisfaction	3.32
	relationship with suppliers	3.30
	sales promotion/advertising campaign activities	3.12
employees	holders of qualifications/ technologies	3.24
	know-how	3.23

(*Continued*)

Table 9.8   (Continued)

OSMERI Categories	non-financial items	evaluation level* average
	the number of employees	3.13
	turnover ratio	3.04
	average age of employees (year to year)	2.95
	incentive system	2.77
basic of organization	business schedules	3.95
	affiliates	3.88
	support system of parent company	3.66
	management philosophy	3.45
	business model	3.43
	corporate brand	3.32
	In-house mechanism	3.28
	status of research and development	3.26
	smoothness of management-labor relations	3.09
	situations of introduction of the IT system	3.06
	enhancement level of corporate education	303
	the number of branches	2.99
	in-house improvement proposal system/the number of improvement executions	2.87
	personal evaluation system	2.81
risk management/ governance	compliance system	3.64
	legal risk management	3.60
	risk management of information leakage	3.34

*Evaluation level is measured by using five likert scales.
Source: Koga and Yosano, 2008, p. 15.

(4) Intellectual property, (5) Marketing and (6) Human resource develop-ment and recruiting (Table 9.9). Relationship lending is still the key pur-pose for IAbM disclosure, and the main characteristic in the revision is that it places great importance on the relationship between IC measures and the financial result. IAbM disclosure makes it difficult for companies to transmit IC resources and information about the IC creation process to stakeholders. Hence, the challenge for this revision was to allow readers to understand current financial results more clearly by requiring the com-pany to disclose the relationship between how current IC resources have been accumulated and how they have been created. In addition, the revision requires the company to disclose the relationship between how it will create new IC resources and their plan to process this creation in the future and the future financial results (Figure 9.3). It would also be beneficial for readers to understand more clearly whether the company transfers in information with a value-creation viewpoint. If the revised version is successful, then it might lead to a reliable enhancement and comparability of IC measures.

Another prominent action was from the Hyogo Industry Enhancement Center and their local lender membership. Tanyou credit bank has initiated the use of the IAbM to support SME businesses since 2008 in conjunc-tion with the Hyogo Industry Enhancement Center. Tanyou credit bank has supported SMEs to disclose the IAbM report: nine SMEs in 2009, eleven in 2010 and twenty-two in September 2011 (JSBRI 2012, 43). The Japan Small Business Research Institute (JSBRI), Osaka branch (2012) also intro-duced four cases where the Tanyou credit bank supported creating an IAbM report, and some of them have been financed because the IAbM reduced the IC information barrier (Holland and Johanson 2003). Tanyou credit bank can have confidence in future business prospects that jointly produce the IAbM. JSBRI, Osaka branch, also introduced other membership lender cases, such as the Tajima credit bank, Hyogo West credit bank and Amaga-saki credit bank, which started supporting the IAbM in 2009.

4.   CONCLUDING REMARKS

This chapter strives to explain why the Japanese IAbM report practices are more inclined towards SMEs and why financial institutions are one of the most important stakeholders by looking at it from a detailed historical socioeconomic background. For the information supply side, it is difficult for large firms to grasp their long-term value-creation viewpoint, and dis-closing a lot of information through multimedia becomes a slight burden for them. The demand-side market actors also have a short-term evaluation viewpoint and face difficulties in accessing IC information. On the other hand, it is much easier for SMEs to establish a clear total picture of the management strategy and the shape of the organization if they discuss and map the strengths and weaknesses in their organizations. In addition, one of

Table 9.9 Utilization and implementation of report

Target Reader	Purpose	Sample of the guidance
Customers and Suppliers	Company Information to the New business clients	How to describe the multiple businesses
	Business Explanation about the New Product and Service	Focused description of their businesses
	Collaboration with Suppliers and Partners	Relationship with Suppliers and Partners
	Technologies, Know-how and their Management	refer to the theme: Intellectual Property
Financial Institutions	Financial Report	refer to the theme: Relationship Banking
	Technologies and Business Model	• • • • •
	New Business	Explanation in the Report and the Financial Report
	Business Succession	Explanation in the Report and the Financial Report
Recruitment	Informally Promised Employment for New Graduates and Mid-Career Recruiting	refer to the theme: Human Resource Development
Employee	Business Succession	refer to the theme: Business Succession
	Business Operation Improvement	• • • • •
	New Employee Training	refer to the theme: Human Resource Development refer to the theme: Marketing refer to the theme: Venture

Source: OSMERI, The revised "Intellectual Asset-based Management Manual for Small and Medium Enterprises," 2012, p. 31.

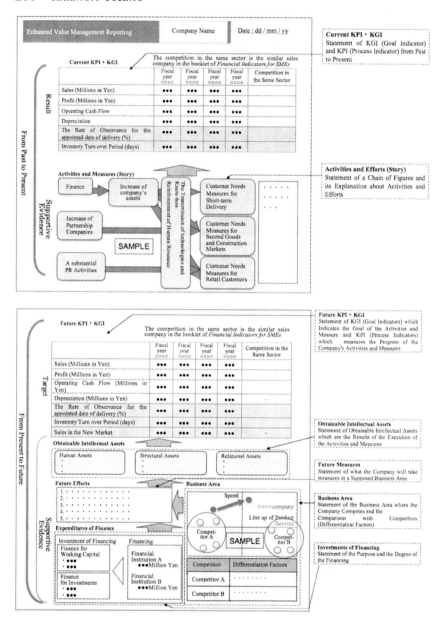

Figure 9.3   Sample guideline: The theme of the relationship banking

Source: The revised "Intellectual Asset-Based Management Manual for Small and Medium Enterprises," 2012, p. 34.

the important stakeholders, financial institutions, places a certain amount of importance on IC measures when making their loan decisions. The lenders who pay attention to networks, such as customers, suppliers, management and business, actually gain a higher profit on average.

Since the 2000s, the explanation power of financial information has become weaker (Kagaya 2012; IIRC 2011), and earnings volatility has become dramatically broader (Yosano 2014, forthcoming). Therefore, the surrounding risk circumstances of companies have expanded greatly. It is clear that an adequate evaluation of default risk and growth opportunities requires other information than financial measures. IC measures are still prominent candidates. In Japan, the main companies targeted for IAbM practices are SMEs. Communication has been ongoing between nonlisted SMEs and financial institutions, and there's hope that large listed companies will conquer two main obstacles in the near future. First is a grasp on the long-term management viewpoints and allocating IC resources in the proper strategic business plan. Second is to establish adequate KPIs for stakeholders to understand and compare with competitors in the same section. These actions would enhance the spread of IAbM disclosure practices and revive the engine of the Japanese economy.

NOTES

1. Their report demonstrates the links between an organization's strategy; governance and financial performance; and the social, environmental and economic context where it operates.
2. The increase in interbank and market-driven competition threatens the survival of regional banks and credit unions. After the 1998 deregulation, bank infrastructures were further reduced, and the occurrence of mergers and acquisitions increased. Therefore, in March 2003, the FSA introduced an action program to prevent bankruptcy (Yosano and Nakaoka 2011a, 5).

REFERENCES

Danish Ministry of Trade and Industry (DMTI). 2000. *A Guideline for Intellectual Capital Statements—A Key to Knowledge Management*. Copenhagen.
Danish Ministry of Science, Technology and Innovation (DMSTI). 2003. *Intellectual Capital Statements—The New Guideline*. Copenhagen.
Hirota, S. 2009. "Main Bank Relationships in Japan: From monitoring to risk hedging." RIETI Discussion Paper Series, 1–40.
Holland, J. and Johanson, U. 2003. "Value-relevant information on corporate intangibles—Creation, use, and barriers in capital markets—'Between a rock and a hard place'". *Journal of Intellectual Capital*, 4 (4), 465–486.
International Integrated Reporting Council (IIRC). 2011. *Towards Integrated Reporting -Communicating Value in the 21st Century*.
Japanese Financial Service Agency (FSA). 2003. "Action program concerning enhancement of relationship banking functions".
Japan Small Business Research Institute (JSBRI). 2011. *White Paper on Small and Medium Enterprises, in Japanese*.
Japan Small Business Research Institute (JSBRI), Osaka Branch. 2012. *The Actual View of Intellectual Assets-based Management Support for SMEs with Financial Institutions*.
Kagaya, T. 2012. "Management disclosures in emergency situations? Evidence from the great east Japan earthquake". *Proceedings of 35th EAA Annual Congress*. Ljubljana, Slovenia. May 9–11, 2011.

Koga, C. and Yosano, T. 2008. "Influence of Intellectual capital information on credit risk rating process/criterion and credit conditions—Survey analysis to Japanese financial institutions". *Discussion Paper No.2008–52, Graduate School of Business Administration, Kobe University,* 1–25.

Mavrinac, S. and Siesfeld, T. 1998. "Measures that matter: An explanatory investigation of investors' information needs and value priorities". Paris: OECD.

MEasuRing Intangibles To Understand and improve innovation Management (MERITUM). 2000. *MERITUM Guidelines.*

Ministry of Economy, Trade and Industry (METI). 2005. *Guidelines for Disclosure of Intellectual Assets Based Management,* 1–54.

Ministry of Economy, Trade and Industry (METI). 2007. *The Empirical Analysis Survey for a Viewpoint and Disclosure of Intellectual Assets-based Management Report, in Japanese.*

Organization for Small & Medium Enterprises and Regional Innovation, Japan (OSMERI). 2007. *Intellectual Asset-based Management Manual for Small and Medium Enterprises,* Organization for Small & Medium Enterprises and Regional Innovation, *in Japanese.*

Organization for Small & Medium Enterprises and Regional Innovation, Japan (OSMERI). 2008a. *Guidelines for Survey and Research Report on Intellectual Asset-Based Finance.*

Organization for Small & Medium Enterprises and Regional Innovation, Japan (OSMERI). 2008b. *Guidelines to Practice the Intellectual Asset-based Management for SMEs.*

Organization for Small & Medium Enterprises and Regional Innovation, Japan (OSMERI). 2012. *The Revised Intellectual Asset-based Management Manual for Small and Medium Enterprises,* Organization for Small & Medium Enterprises and Regional Innovation, *in Japanese.*

Robson, K. 1992. "Accounting numbers as inscription—Action at a distance and the development of accounting". *Accounting Organizations and Society,* 17 (7), 685–708.

Sakakibara, S., Hansson B. and Yosano, T. 2005. "The value relevance of the intellectual capital information in corporate stock valuation: A perception of the analysts". *Journal of Economics & Business Administration,* 191 (5), 1–19, *in Japanese.*

Sakakibara, S., Hansson, B., Yosano, T. and Kozumi, H. 2010. "Analysts' perceptions of intellectual capital information". *Australian Accounting Review,* 20 (3), 274–285.

Subcommittee on Management & Intellectual Assets (SMIA), New Growth Policy Committee, Industrial Structure Council. 2005. Interim Report by Subcommittee on Management & Intellectual Assets, 1–83.

Sumita, T. 2008. "Intellectual assets-based management for innovation: Lessons from experiences in Japan". *Journal of Intellectual Capital,* 9 (2), 206–227.

Yosano, T. 2011. "Exploring to acquire the legitimacy management and disclosure of intellectual capital information practice". *Discussion Paper No. 2011–47, Graduate School of Business Administration, Kobe University,* 1–17.

Yosano, T. 2014. "The challenge of the global risk exposure to the financial report". *Discussion Paper, Graduate School of Business Administration, Kobe University, forthcoming,* 2014.

Yosano, T. and Nakaoka, T. 2011a. "Soft information management effects on lending credit terms in Japan". *Discussion Paper No. 2011–34, Graduate School of Business Administration, Kobe University,* 1–24.

Yosano, T. and Nakaoka, T. 2011b. "The roles of relationship lending and utilization of soft information on bank performance in competitive local markets". *Discussion Paper No. 2011–41, Graduate School of Business Administration, Kobe University,* 1–36.

10 IC in Japan

Governmental Guidelines, Financial Market Perceptions and Company Practice

Ulf Johanson and Chitoshi Koga

1. INTRODUCTION

At the beginning of the millennium, the Japanese government urged that "in the 21st century, Japan needs to discover new economic opportunities by attaching further importance to intellectual property" (METI 2002). In response to the stagnation in the Japanese economy, as well as the increasing international competitiveness in business activities, it became necessary to seek a new model for growth, such as the creation of high-value-added intangibles assets or intellectual capital/intellectual property (IC/IP). The interest in IC was expressed by the Ministry of Trade and Industry in 2004 (METI 2004, 94–98) and summarized by Johanson et al. 2006:

1. Becoming a nation that quests for sustained growth of its economy and society through vigorous promotion of creation, protection and exploitation of intellectual property, namely, a "nation built on intellectual property", is an urgent goal for Japan to strengthen its industrial competitiveness.
2. There is a need to enhance dramatically the exploitation of intellectual property, as well as its creation and protection. It is important to recognize the intellectual property strategy as the center of the management strategy, called "intellectual property-backed management", in the trinity of business strategy, R&D strategy, and intellectual property strategy.
3. It is important that an environment is constructed that permits companies that practice "intellectual property-backed management" to receive fair valuation in the capital market while they strive to achieve sustained growth.
4. For the mutual understanding between companies and capital markets about the information disclosure of companies' "intellectual property-backed management", especially about the information of patent and R&D, intellectual property information disclosure will be required[; the] *Guideline for Intellectual Property Information Disclosure* (GIPID) is [the] basic guideline. (p. 475)

Since 2002, a number of reports addressing IC or IC property have been issued. These include *Intellectual Property Policy Outline* (2002); *Guideline for Intellectual Property Information Disclosure* (GIPID) (METI 2004); *Guidelines for Disclosure of Intellectual Assets-based Management* (IAbM) (METI 2005); *Intellectual Asset-based Management Manual for Small & Medium Enterprises* (SMRJ 2008) (See Table 10.1).

SMRJ refers to the Organization for Small & Medium Enterprises and Regional Innovation. It is an independent agency supporting start-ups and new business development. In addition, it supports small and medium enterprises' (SME) growth and development of SME infrastructure. SMRJ was established in 2004 under jurisdiction of the Ministry of Economy, Trade and Industry (METI).

Table 10.1   Historical development of Japanese governmental guidelines for Intellectual Property and IC reports

Issue date	Issue organization	Name of report/guideline
June 5, 2002	METI and Japan Patent Office	*Task Force on Industrial Competitiveness and Intellectual Property Policy*
July 3, 2002	Government of Japan, Strategic	*Intellectual Property Policy Outline*
January 2004	METI	*Guideline for Intellectual Property Information Disclosure (GIPID)*
August 12, 2005	METI, Subcommittee on Management & Intellectual Assets Growth Policy Committee, Industrial Structure Council	*Inteirm Report by Subcomittee on Management and Intilectual Assets*
October 2005	METI	*Guideline for Disclosure of Intellectual Assets Based Management (IAbM)*
March 2007	Organization for Small & Medium Enterprises and Regional Innovation (SMRJ)	*Intellectual Asset-Based Management Manual for SMEs*
October 2008	SMRJ	*Guidelines for Practices of Intellectual Asset-Based Management for SMEs (SMRJ)*

In this chapter, experience of IC in Japan is described, analyzed and discussed. With regard to terminology, the Japanese guidelines use either "intellectual property" or "intellectual assets". In the chapter, these concepts will be used when the actual guideline is addressed. However, when discussing experience with the guidelines, we will use "intellectual capital". The reason for this is that in the Japanese practice, as well as for our present purposes, IC is more or less equal to intellectual assets.

The chapter starts with a description of the content of the three most important guidelines: GIPID, IAbM and SMRJ. This section is followed by a summary of findings from eight different Japanese studies that have been performed by our two research groups, that is, Professor Chitoshi Koga's group in Japan and Professor Ulf Johanson's group in Sweden. The research teams will later be named the Koga group, the Johanson group or the Koga-Johanson group in the text. The investigations are presented in Sections 3 and 4. The first of these sections contains findings from five firm studies, and the second findings from three different investigations of IC from a financial market perspective. Five of the studies have been published earlier, whereas three are more recent and have not been published elsewhere. The three most recent studies will be given more space than the others. A summary and a comparison between the studies are provided in Section 5. Concluding comments are provided in the last section.

The eight studies were performed for different reasons. Various methodologies were also used. In spite of this, we will use the opportunity to compare the results in order to raise some important questions from a decades-long experience with IC guidelines in Japan. This will be obtained in the concluding section.

2. THE GOVERNMENTAL GUIDELINES

In this section, the three guidelines—GIPID, IAbM and SMRJ—are described and compared. All of the guidelines were developed by government policy makers, even if the preliminary proposals were discussed with firms, academics and financial market representatives.

The primary purpose of these guidelines is to help corporations prepare IC reports. Whereas the GIPID primarily focuses on the report, the IAbM's ambition reaches much further. It is also intended to facilitate and improve management, decision making and learning with respect to the best use of companies' abilities. The report is intended to influence stakeholders' learning about firms' capabilities. The role of the IAbM is defined by METI (2005, P1) as follows:

> Intellectual assets-based management is a management itself rather than an aspect of management. It is a management method to enhance corporate value with an eye to many stakeholders. Based on the

pursuit of interest, this method intends to make sustainable profits and growth through making the best use of the corporation's own ability.

Both GIPID and IAbM share the insight that companies need to develop their knowledge resources, especially processes and technologies. In contrast to the IAbM, the GIPID does not focus on human capital (HC), even if some sample companies demonstrate that addressing HC is unavoidable. Thus, both of the guidelines either explicitly or implicitly raise a demand for firms to manage the part of their resources that deals with knowledge in a broad way and to employ the best tools and methods to support knowledge management (Johanson et al. 2006, 482).

The GIPID does not include any suggestions with respect to key performance indicators (KPIs), whereas the IAbM guidelines show detailed examples of indicators with explanations and implications. The latter includes such indicators as business competitiveness, degree of research and development (R&D) concentration, differentiation of market and degree of customer satisfaction.

The fundamental objectives of IAbM are expressed as follows:

1. "Top managers inform business activities to produce sustainable profits and enhance corporate value to stakeholders in a story [that is] easy to understand, and
2. Share a sense of value with stakeholders". (p. 2)

This is to say that the IAbM is important for both internal and external reasons. In the management process that supports the IAbM report, developing management targets, as well as visualizing the measurement system, are necessary conditions, but the most significant part of the IAbM report is the value-creation story supported by various indicators. This demonstrates corporate awareness of future uncertainties, as stated in the *Interim Report* (New Growth Policy Committee, Industrial Structure Council 2005, 58). In the management process, the Balanced Scorecard (BSC) could serve as a useful tool, but the BSC is not sufficient for the development of all firm strategies. It is further suggested that the story about future value creation could be developed by using, for example, the report on IP rights, that is, the GIPID report, or if no IP report has been performed, by doing a strengths, weaknesses, opportunities and threats (SWOT) analysis of the business (ibid., 53).

In short, an IAbM report should contain the following building blocks:

• Management philosophy

  • Characteristic of business and basic vision

- Past to present, that is, how have we reached today's:

  - Management policy
  - Investment performance
  - Intellectual assets and value chain
  - Financial performance

- Present to future, that is, how will we look in the future regarding:

  - Vision
  - Investment plans
  - Sustainability

- Intellectual assets indicators

The indicators are proposed to cover the following areas, shown in Table 10.2 (ibid, 14):

Table 10.2 Indicator groups and indicators according to the IAbM guideline

Indicator group	Type of indicators (examples)
Management stance/Leadership	• Degree of internal penetration of management principles assessment of business model • Development of future leaders (average age of subsidiary presidents)
Selection and concentration	• Proportion of major business to the entire sales • Degree of R&D concentration
External negotiation power/relationships	• Degree of customer satisfaction • New customer sales ratio
Knowledge creation/innovation/speed	• R&D expenditure • Employees average age in relation to previous year
Teamwork/organizational knowledge	• Degree of employees satisfaction • Number of lateral projects
Risk management /governance	• Compliance system • Compensation claims in pending lawsuits
Coexistence in society	• Amount of environment–related investment • Corporate image survey and ranking results

3.   FINDINGS FROM FOUR FIRM STUDIES

The present section contains five studies. The first of these is a content analysis of Japanese firms that, after the launch of the GIPID, had followed the guideline and disclosed an IP report. The second study, which was performed a couple of years later, was an explorative case study of how four firms had exploited the IAbM guideline. Some years later, the status of IAbM disclosure in Japan was achieved using survey responses from corporate managers. This is followed by a recent investigation of three SMEs that have published an IAbM report. Finally, the last study addresses a major bank that also has produced a report.

Study No. 1: Content Analysis of Twelve Firms in 2005

One year after the GIPID was released, twelve Japanese firms disclosed an IP report as a supplement to the annual report. A content analysis of these reports was performed by the Koga group. Parts of the content analysis were published in 2006 by Johanson et al. in the *Journal of Intellectual Capital*. The text in this section originates from that article.

The content analysis revealed significant differences even if the structure and headlines proposed by the GIPID were used. When the published items were classified into structural, relational and human capital (MERITUM, 2002), it was surprising to recognize that 52 percent of all items referred to structural capital (SC), whereas the relational capital (RC) items amounted to 42 percent, and HC only to 6 percent of all IC items. This frequency deviates substantially from other investigations, for example, from Australia (Guthrie and Petty 2000) and Ireland (Brennan 2001). In our study, the frequency of reporting SC was significantly higher, RC about equal and HC significantly lower. The Japanese findings may not be surprising because the GIPID prominently addresses structural and relational issues. Consequently, all sample companies disclose patents, management processes, business alliances and license contracts. With respect to patents, it is interesting to note that Hitachi reports that they aim to acquire five patents to protect against future risk. This was called the "Five Fighting Patents Action (FFPA)" (Hitachi 2004, 15). The "patent strategy action" is classified into three stages— "gold", "silver" and "copper"—based on its competitive strength to appeal the companies' positive attitude toward IP disclosure. (Hitachi was the company that prepared the most refined IP statement.)

According to the GIPID, it is desirable to supply specific business purposes or strategies. All sample companies except one did so when they disclosed management strategies in some way. The management process includes the system and the policy concerning the acquisition and management of IP rights and the treatment of secret information. The extent and style of the disclosure varied. Some companies published an abstract management philosophy, whereas others preferred more specific company purposes and goals. Most of the companies disclosed some sort of policy (such as an "IP Management Policy" or a "Policy on Company Ethics and Behavior"), but it was not apparent how the companies dealt with the policies.

Regarding RC, the core items were the business alliances and the license contracts. The guideline recommends that companies disclose the license incomes and expenditures on the basis of different critical segments or fields, as well as the content of the license strategy. Most companies seemed to realize "licensing activity as the tool to secure the competitive advantage, and the distinction from the other companies' products rather than to obtain the licensing income" (Olympus 2004).

Study No. 2: Case Studies of Four Firms in 2006

In 2006, another kind of follow-up was performed by the Koga-Johanson group. This time, the target was to understand how the IAbM was received by firms. A number of large, medium-sized and small firms were approached. At the end, out of twenty firms that had disclosed an IAbM report in 2006 or 2007, four SMEs were interviewed (Sumita 2007). The results and the elaboration around the findings were published (Johanson et al. 2009). The following text emanates from that article.

Generally, the IAbM reports of the four case organizations followed the IAbM guidelines. This was not surprising because all of the four case firms had been approached by and were assisted in some way by METI. The value-creation story was the most important part of the report, and superior technology was regarded as the most important IC category. The second most important IC categories relate to RC, such as alliances and well-recognized people.

In the IAbM guidelines, the internal management perspective is strongly underlined. But the internal management perspective was not the most prominent interest of the four case firms. The motives had to do with creating images, describing possibilities, creating holistic pictures, improving management and creating long-term relationships. The objectives concerned challenging traditions and relations to be able to expand on the market. According to our theoretical analysis, the motives were about creating new spaces for knowledge creation, or new *ba*'s as Nonaka and Nishiguchi (2001) suggest, by challenging formal rules, values, norms and routines that act as barriers to business improvement.

By referring to the work performed by the government concerning IAbM reports, as well as indicating the close cooperation with METI in creating the report, the firms gained credibility. This credibility was supposed to have a spillover effect even on the products and was thereby regarded to be beneficial even in relation to the customer communication.

Financial profit was not regarded as the only corporate target by the case firms. The management vision and the value system were largely based on some kind of a passion. All of the chief executive officers (CEOs) expressed the ambition to expand their enterprises in order to increase the potential of demonstrating the superiority of their products. They were dynamic firms actively interacting with the environment through the process of knowledge creation (Nonaka and Nishiguchi 2001). The IAbM report was a tool for the CEO to externalize his subjective tacit knowledge into objective explicit knowledge to be shared. The latter is supposed to affect, that is, internalize, the other person's tacit knowledge and then again expand explicit knowledge.

However, as Nonaka and Toyama (2005) suggest, the management philosophy and the management policy, or as the authors referred to it, knowledge vision, would be hardly anything more than empty words if there were no concrete concept, goal or action standard (in the IAbM reports, equal to business contents performance, intellectual assets and strategy) to connect the vision with the knowledge creating process of dialogues and practice. By using the IAbM report as a communication device, the dialogue with mostly banks and customers was supposed to be affected. The report was supposed to address and change the knowledge context.

All four firms investigated in the present study focused on their uniqueness. At a general level, they followed the structure of the IAbM, but at a detailed level; for instance, regarding measures, they were very different from the guideline.

Study No. 3: Analysis of IABM Reports in 2010

In 2010, it was time for the next follow-up of experiences with the IAbM guideline. It was suggested that exploring developments in reports for IC disclosure required further clarification, not only of recent trends for such disclosure, including theoretical comparisons, but also of the companies' awareness regarding IC disclosure. The status of IC disclosure was investigated by METI using a questionnaire that was sent to firms that had prepared an IAbM report in March 2010. Therefore, the companies in the sample were those that place relatively high importance on IC. The questionnaire was sent to 116 companies, of which 71 responded—a response rate of 61.2 percent. Furthermore, five of the seventy-one responses were incomplete. These were excluded from the analysis, leaving sixty-six companies in the survey sample. Because the findings shown here are rather recent and have not been published outside Japan, more text is devoted to this section (Koga et al.2011, 162–171).

When the Koga group analyzed the responses, topics like purpose, content, effectiveness and credibility of the IAbM report were considered to be of primary interest. The following questions were formulated and will be answered next:

1. Who is preparing and disseminating the IAbM report? (preparer)
2. Who represents the target audience for this report? (objectives, audience)

3. Did the report's release have any effect? (effectiveness)
4. What disclosure items were considered important to achieving the report's objectives? (content)
5. Which data items and viewpoints contributed most to assuring the report's credibility? (assurance of credibility)
6. What major steps were taken to assure credibility? (assurance of credibility)

Who Is Preparing and Disseminating the IAbM Report?

Of the sixty-six participating companies, more than half (thirty-seven) were manufacturing businesses, and the remaining twenty-nine were nonmanufacturing businesses. In terms of the number of employees, twenty-eight (approximately 40 percent) of the companies were very small businesses of ten or fewer employees, whereas only twelve companies had more than one hundred employees. We can, therefore, infer that small businesses, that is, companies with one hundred or fewer employees, are more likely to prepare and disseminate IAbM reports than are companies with more than one hundred employees. Hereafter, we refer to companies with ten or fewer employees as small-scale businesses and those with more than one hundred employees as medium-scale businesses.

Who Represents the Target Audience for This Report?

Table 10.3 shows the survey responses from the target audience by type of industry and number of employees. Respondents ranked target audiences by five degrees of importance. Employees were considered most important, followed by new clients and then by financial institutions and existing clients/ trading partners, respectively.

Significant statistical differences existed between manufacturing businesses and nonmanufacturing businesses as to whether the target audiences for these reports are local residents, new clients, investors (shareholders), consumers or students and job applicants. For these five categories, manufacturing businesses tended to regard them as more important than did nonmanufacturing businesses. Also, we observed very small statistical differences in the target audience by company size. The only small difference was that medium-scale businesses were more focused on students and job applicants than were small-scale businesses.

Did the Report's Release Have Any Effect?

The effectiveness of IAbM reports was highest for employees, followed by financial institutions, existing clients and trading partners, and new clients (see Table 10.4). Interestingly, there were two instances where effectiveness was lower than the degree of importance: employees (−0.115

Table 10.3 Target audience for IAbM reports

	Total (N = 66)	Mfg. businesses (N = 37)	Non-mfg. businesses (N = 29)	Difference	z-value	p-value
New clients	3.525	3.765	3.222	0.542	2.452	0.014 **
Local residents	2.066	2.294	1.778	0.516	2.932	0.003 ***
Investors (shareholders)	2.164	2.353	1.926	0.427	2.049	0.041 **
Students and job applicants	2.967	3.147	2.741	0.406	1.766	0.077 *
Corporate succession (future management)	2.295	2.471	2.074	0.397	1.200	0.230
Consumers (individuals)	2.295	2.441	2.111	0.330	1.844	0.065 *
Employees	3.656	3.765	3.519	0.246	1.110	0.267
Existing clients and trading partners	3.230	3.324	3.111	0.212	1.284	0.199
Financial institutions	3.279	3.088	3.519	-0.431	-1.078	0.281

	Total (N = 66)	Medium-Scale businesses (N = 12)	Small-Scale businesses (N = 28)	Difference	z-value	p-value
Investors (shareholders)	2.164	2.727	2.240	0.487	0.685	0.493
Students and job applicants	2.967	3.182	2.760	0.422	2.231	0.026**
Employees	3.656	3.727	3.440	0.287	0.926	0.354
Local residents	2.066	2.091	1.840	0.251	0.219	0.827
Corporate Succession (future management)	2.295	2.000	2.120	-0.120	0.418	0.676
New clients	3.561	3.583	3.750	-0.167	-0.632	0.528
Financial institutions	3.279	3.091	3.320	-0.229	0.274	0.784
Existing clients and trading partners	3.230	3.000	3.360	-0.360	0.124	0.902
Consumers (individuals)	3.525	3.273	3.840	-0.567	-0.503	0.615

Table 10.4 Degree of importance and effectivenes

	Degree of importance (N = 66)	Effectiveness (N = 66)	Difference	z-value	*p-value*
Local residents	2.066	2.475	0.410	2.513	0.012**
Investors (Shareholders)	2.164	2.557	0.393	2.036	0.042**
Corporate Succession (future management)	2.295	2.623	0.328	1.515	0.130
Consumers (individuals)	2.295	2.541	0.246	1.230	0.219
Existing clients and trading partners	3.230	3.328	0.098	0.458	0.647
Financial institutions	3.279	3.361	0.082	0.139	0.890
Students and job applicants	2.967	3.000	0.033	0.192	0.848
Employees	3.656	3.541	−0.115	−1.016	0.310
New clients	3.525	3.279	−0.246	−1.802	0.072*

***,** and * denote statistical significance at the 1%, 5% and 10% levels respectively

points) and new clients (–0.246 points). The relationship between the degree of importance and effectiveness was statistically significant at the 5 percent level for local residents and investors and at the 10 percent level for new clients.

What Disclosure Items Were Considered Important to Achieving the Report's Objectives?

The results regarding this question illustrate that companies most frequently use these reports to promote their strengths. Among the ten possible choices, companies placed the greatest importance on "illustrating the company's strengths", followed by "competitive advantage and marketability of strengths". Ranking fourth in importance was "business plan that exploits company strengths".

The third and fifth most important were "management philosophy and company policy" and "comprehensibility/does it tell a story?", respectively. We interpret this as a corporate stance of telling the company's story to stakeholders in an understandable way, thus promoting the company's values, which is consistent with the primary objective of the IAbM report as set forth by the METI.

We also observed that manufacturing businesses placed more importance on the "relationship between business results and key performance indicators" and on the "relationship between business plans and key per-formance indicators" than did nonmanufacturing businesses. Still, neither of these items was viewed as being of major importance, and we saw no differences in terms of the size of a company.

Differences were statistically significant between small-scale businesses and medium-scale businesses for two responses: "likelihood of achieving the business plan" and "management philosophy and company policy". In these instances, we observed that medium-scale businesses placed more importance on these points.

Which Data Items and Viewpoints Contributed Most to Assuring the Report's Credibility?

The top three responses regarding assuring the credibility of IAbM reports were "illustrating the company's strengths from its business results", "com-petitive advantage and marketability of strength" and "business plan that exploits company strengths". These responses conformed with those that ranked the objectives of IAbM reports. However, we did not find any sig-nificant statistical differences in the responses by type of industry. The two responses that indicated statistically significant differences by type of industry were "relationship between business results and key performance indicators" and "relationship between business plans and key performance indicators". We found that the degree of importance placed on these items was higher among manufacturing businesses than among nonmanufacturing businesses.

Statistically significant differences by size of business were observed for three items: "relationship between business results and key performance indicators", "management philosophy and company policy" and "competi-tive advantage and marketability of strengths".

The differences between small- and medium-scale businesses were most pronounced for "relationship between business results and key performance indicators". We refer to the difference in degree of importance and scores (the average value) for assuring credibility as the "credibility gap". For medium-scale businesses, the degree of importance was 3.250 and the credibility assur-ance score was 3.500, indicating that IAbM reports likely play an important role in assuring credibility. For small-scale businesses, the degree of impor-tance was 3.143 and the credibility assurance score was 2.964, indicating less correlation between the importance attributed to "relationship between busi-ness results and key performance indicators" and assuring credibility.

What Major Steps Were Taken to Assure Credibility?

The three items considered the most important for assuring credibility were "ensuring consistency with management philosophy in developing the story of value creation", "assessing the correlation among data" (company strengths, business plan, etc.) and "obtaining support team cooperation and participation". No items exhibited differences of statistical significance when classified by type of industry. However, compared with nonmanufacturing businesses, manufacturing businesses appear to be geared more toward key performance indicators, as indicated by the degree of importance they place on "linking the company's intellectual asset strengths with key performance indicators" and "setting initial key performance indicators and their measurement". Meanwhile, nonmanufacturing businesses gave higher marks to "assessing the correlation among data" (the company's strengths, business plan, etc.) and "ensuring consistency with management philosophy in developing the story of value creation", indicating that they tend to consider overall business activity as a "story" of intellectual assets that increase the values of the corporation and solidify correlations between business activities and their own strengths in the form of intellectual assets.

Comparing companies by size, we verified statistical differences between two items: "maintaining correlation between business results and financial indicators" and "ensuring consistency with management philosophy in developing the story of value creation".

Study No. 4: SME Case Study in 2014

Representing well-managed SMEs that have prepared an IAbM report at least once during the last five years, three firms were selected for interviews in spring 2014 by the Koga group. The companies were Nakano Manufacturing Corporation, Cozy Corporation and Nimbari Corporation. Written responses were collected with the assistance of the Osaka Prefecture Chief Researcher. The results from these interviews have not been published earlier. Their profiles are briefly shown in Table 10.5.

Table 10.5   Three SME profiles

	Nakano Manfacturing Co.	Cozy Corporation Co.	Nimbari
Founded	1949 (1957incorporated)	1985	1954
Capital	12 million	25 million	10 million yen
Number of Employees	50	515	97
	Production of automatic converter clutches, Power conserves, ship reduction	Sales of print T-shirts	Production custom-made steel furniture, fixture and various precision sheet metal

(*Source:* Nakano IAbM 2011; Cozy IAbM 2010; Nimbari IAbM 2008)

The responses address motivation, frequency, effect and difficulties in preparing the IAbM report.

Motivation and expected effect: The firms have various motivations and expectations for preparing the IAbM report. Both Nakano and Nimbari were motivated to prepare the report by the recommendation of a business data management company. The president of Nakano, who had decided to prepare it with the assistance of an independent SME consultant, said:

> I have decided to introduce the IAbM report to review our value of the company thoroughly, and to encourage our company to continually grow even under the severe economic circumstance. That was just the period when our sales amount has dropped to the half of our normal one due to the severe Lehman Brothers shock.

Nakano assumed several effects of this kind of innovative challenge, such as sharing their business strength, business succession, development of new customers and improvement of the broken networks. Nimbari was also motivated by the same data management company, because "we had no idea of what an IAbM report was".

On the other hand, Cozy Corporation, which intended to implement an Initial Public Offering (IPO), was primarily motivated to take advantage of the IAbM report as a communication and advertisement tool. This company issued the IAbM report in 2010, but never again after that.

IC management and reporting effects: In order to ensure ongoing prosperity and growth, all companies suggested that they must increase the differentiation of their products and services. They identify their sources of competitiveness as IC. Nakano recognized its precision cutting technology, total coordination ability, prompt production system and high-quality management system as essential IC. Nakano issued the first IAbM report in 2009 and revised it in 2011. The report is comprehensive and visually well refined with many pictures. It presents the interrelationship between various IC and the value chain. Further, Nakano acknowledges some favorable effects, including clarification of the company's business strategy, increase in the employees' motivation, acceleration of the business transactions with new customers and penetration of the company philosophy.

By contrast, the IAbM reports of Nimbari and Cozy are relatively simpler and more descriptive. Nimbori's report appears to follow the METI guideline in discussing "the past-present-future business developments". This company also emphasizes their precision sheet-metal technology and high-quality production system. The company used the work with the IAbM report to review and analyze their business performance. Cozy, a high-growth sales company, was more concerned with its brand equity as IC and assumed that the report should be a successful tool in raising funds.

Difficulties and future challenges: In spite of a positive experience, or at least future high expectations, some difficulties were also mentioned by the respondents. Some of these were as follows: "it took a lot of time to pre-pare the IAbM report—approximately 2,700 hours in total"; "we need a repeated discussion to construct the value-chain map"; "certain devices and skills are needed to select, summarize the data and present it in an under-standable manner" President of Nakano Co. "we must be careful so that the future plan will be just the rice cake in the picture" (President of Nimbari co.).

Study No. 5: Development Bank Case Study in 2014

In 2014, a large policy-based financing institution, the Development Bank of Japan, Inc. (DBJ), was approached and analyzed by the Koga group. The basic idea was to increase understanding of how important IC management is for them, how they deploy IC and how they look upon the relationship between IC and corporate social responsibility (CSR). The major source of IC information is the *Annual Report & CSR Report 2013*. A large company providing an IC report is rare in Japan. Therefore, the DBJ's case is valuable as one of the best-practice cases among leading Japanese companies.

DBJ was originally established in 1951 for the purpose of lending loans for the rationalization, modernization and cultivation of such important industries as coal and steel in response to the demand to grow the national economy and industry. Thereafter, DBJ's focus was significantly expanded, including development of power supply, improvement of energy and export capacity, as well as technological development. In 2008, DBJ was estab-lished as part of the government's promotion of administrative reform. The new DBJ has taken over all assets of DBJ through privatization. Some of the basic profile data as of July 1, 2013 (*Annual Report and CSR Report 2013*) are:

- Capital: ¥1,206,953 million (100 percent owned by Japanese government)
- Total assets: ¥16,183.8 billion
- Loans: ¥14,015.4 billion
- Number of employees: 1,168

At glance, the DBJ Intellectual Asset Report is unique in terms of com-prehensiveness and integration of the reporting elements, for example, cor-porate philosophy, management strategy, business model, IC and corporate data. The IAbM report constitutes one essential element of the *Annual Report and CSR Report,* which makes it more similar to an integrated report (Recently major listed companies in Japan are more likely to prepare an integrated report rather than a separate report.)

The IAbM report was analyzed with an eye to why the report was pro-duced, what it contains and how it was performed.

The why issue: DBJ assumes the IAbM to be essential to enhancing cor-porate value. In order to ensure ongoing prosperity and profit, companies should differentiate themselves for competitive reasons (DBJ 2013, 94). Specific technologies, expertise, human resources and business models are some factors that lead to such differentiation. DBJ defines these sources of differentiation or competitiveness as IC. In other words, IC is a "core component of corporate value", and managing IC effectively creates opportunities to increase corporate value.

> Determining an entity's true corporate value requires the evaluation of these company-specific strengths. DBJ's activities related to intellectual assets are designed to foster the application of these intangible sources of corporate value that underpin a company's future economic performance. (p. 94)

After privatization, DBJ set out the new corporate philosophy of "applying financial expertise to design the future" and established new a mission as "building customer trust and [realizing] an affluent society by problem-solving through creative financial activities" (http://www.dbj.p/en/co/info/privatization.html). From the standpoint of maintaining customer trust, DBJ has created a wide variety of networks covering both the public and private sectors.

With respect to IC, DBJ recognizes an accumulated expertise in screening and evaluating long-term projects and in resolving issues, as well as the widespread use of their financial platform (DBJ Report, 94). These IC categories form the basis for developing the financial methods. In addition, they enable DBJ to respond quickly to changing policy requirements and play a major role in DBJ's ability to continuously add economic and social value. Figure 10.1 shows the relationships between DBJ's corporate philosophy, management strategy and IC. Figure 10.2 indicates the relationships between IC, business models and corporate value.

What and how issues: DBJ identifies three types of IC: SC, HC and RC. RC includes cooperation with central governmental agencies and regional government bodies (ibid., 95). The company takes advantage of these networks to disseminate information about their interest rate subsidy system based on environmental ratings, as well as other interest subsidiary systems put in place by national and regional government bodies. DBJ also works to create and develop financial platforms by collaborating with public- and private-sector financial institutions, maximizing their multifaceted combination of networks consisting of various professionals (ibid, 95).

Regarding HC, DBJ's ability to provide an appropriate solution for shareholders depends on the ability of their executives and other employees. All DBJ members work and maintain a long-term and neutral perspective, approaching new business with a spirit of innovation and challenge (ibid., 95). The corporate finance training program for all employees helps develop screening expertise. These menus, combined with on-the-job training, raise

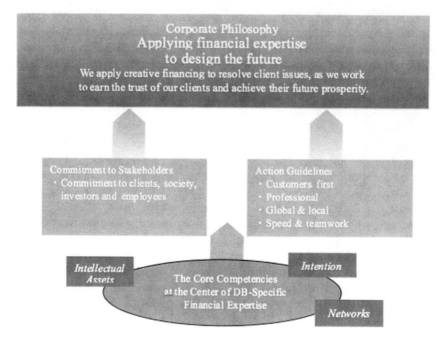

Figure 10.1 Corporate philosophy

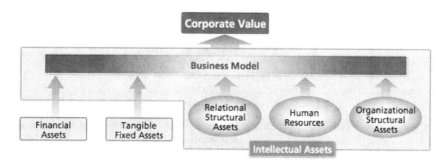

Figure 10.2 Relationships between intellectual assets, corporate models and corporate values
Source: Created by DBJ from Ministry of Economy, Trade and Industry materials

the level of specialist expertise. Furthermore, personnel exchange programs are helpful for their networks.

Finally, concerning SC, DBJ's introduction of new financial methods to Japan and their contribution to creating financial platforms relies heavily on their organizational adeptness, that is, their ability to quickly ascertain emerging issues and deploy appropriate personnel (ibid., 95). This ability, combined with the long-term accumulated financial data and a corporate culture that considers the projects from an economically rational and social viewpoint, constitute DBJ's SC.

Thus, DBJ's report is theoretically well organized and presented in a refined manner. This company is seeking to commit to stakeholders and society in general with a long-term view. Therefore, it is relevant to discuss DBJ's case in relation to the integrated reporting movement. The report discusses the relationship between IC and CSR, concluding that "intellectual assets and CSR are two sides of the same coin" (ibid., 97).

4. FINDINGS FROM THREE FINANCIAL MARKET STUDIES

Three studies of interest regarding the disclosure of IC information from Japanese financial market actors have also been performed by the common Koga-Johanson research group. The first was published in 2010 and was based on a 2004 survey of Japanese analysts' perceptions of IC reporting. The second investigation was also a statistical survey based on data acquisition from lenders in 2008. The last study was a qualitative interview study of four Japanese financial institutions published in 2012.

Study No. 6: Japanese Analysts' Perceptions of IC Reporting in 2004

In 2004, the Koga-Johanson group (Sakakibara et al. 2010) explored current nonfinancial disclosure practices and to what extent these practices were inhibiting a more accurate evaluation of companies. Three hundred fifteen analysts from nineteen securities companies answered a questionnaire on a wide range of issues relating nonfinancial information pertaining to value relevance, degree of use, ease of access to the information and preferred disclosure practices. Some parts of the following text are taken from the study that was published in 2010.

The results suggest that analysts perceive most nonfinancial measures to be value relevant and that the value relevance in general is stronger for small firms than for large firms. Access to IC-related information is generally more restricted than is access to financial information, and for many, IC-measured access to the information is substantially below the perceived value relevance. Overall, access to IC information is somewhat better for larger firms. The results further indicate that HC measures appear to be more accessible in small firms than in large firms, whereas RC measures are more easily accessible in larger firms. The analysis also shows that the lack of access to nonfinancial information restrains analysts' use of the information in their evaluation of companies. The lack of information restricts in particular the use of HC and RC. HC measures such as top management quality, employee participation, satisfaction and training are typically seen as important in terms of firms' performance, and at the same time, these items are difficult to access, even for analysts who evaluate companies. The study has also documented that more experienced analysts, in their evaluation, use HC measures to a larger extent than do inexperienced analysts.

The lack of IC information also suggests that an ordinary investor with only access to public information, limited resources to devote to information gathering and no access to informal contacts with companies may have to guess to a large extent when considering nonfinancial measures in an evaluation. If relevant information were provided on these measures, it would likely have a substantial effect on the use of these measures.

In regard to the question of whether analysts prefer standardized information on IC items and more stringent disclosure practices, the difference among analysts is related to perceptions of the importance of IC as value drivers in companies. Analysts who regard IC factors as important to company performance are also more favorable toward more standardized disclosure practices.

Study No. 7: Lenders' Perceptions of IC Reporting in 2008

In 2008, a committee organized by SMRJ investigated perceptions of IC reporting among 439 Japanese banks. The response rate was 76 percent. The objective was to understand how IC information is used by lenders when judging a borrower's trustworthiness. The results were presented in a conference paper in 2008 (Yosano et al. 2008).

The results from the study revealed that from the lenders' point of view, the trustworthiness of internal corporate information is strongly related to indications of the company's network relations, that is, RC. The lenders have difficulties in judging internal resources (such as human resources, technology and organizational structure), as well as corporate strategy, as isolated data. However, network information is tightly correlated with both internal resources and strategy. This shows that lenders manage to judge corporate value creation by using network information to put other data into context in terms of the company's relation to other businesses and the rest of society. In other words, lenders tend to apply a holistic view in their approach to estimating any single company's value creation. This does not mean that the single measures are uninteresting, just that no single measure is revealing the entire or critical insights needed to make a credit judgment.

Study No. 8: Acquisition and Use of IC
Information for Investment Decisions in 2012

In an exploratory study, the Koga-Johanson group (Holland et al. 2012) sought to increase understanding of how four Japanese financial firms acquired, created and exploited knowledge about IC information for the purpose of investment decisions. The study was originally performed in 2006. The basic idea was to investigate the firm representatives' perceptions of their own organization as a knowledge creating firm. The four cases chosen included one of largest Japanese fund manager firms that was part of a very large financial conglomerate, two medium-sized fund manager firms and a large venture capital company.

All four case firms acted as financial intermediaries and invested savers' or investors' capital in portfolios of company shares or equity stakes. These were designed to provide expected higher levels of return for the suppliers of capital. The case firms shared concepts of their company's investment decision task. This included five major phases: screen/search, appraisal/valuation, buy/hold, monitor/influence and sell/exit.

Company IC information contributed to earnings estimates and company valuation. Impressionistic and emotional information about intangibles contributed to firms' feelings and confidence in their valuation and information use. Both led to investment decisions. Knowledge was an important component of the key interacting and informed contexts used by the firms to make collective sense of these different but complementary types of information in investment decision making. This created opportunities for improved disclosure and accountability between the firms and their investee companies. Common patterns of behavior across the firms were counterbalanced by variety and differences noted in the firms' behavior. These included differences in investment philosophy and "landscape".

The findings provide important insights in how Japanese financial institutions' knowledge creating patterns could limit or progress a common language of communication between companies and markets on the subject of IC. This could impact the quality of corporate disclosure and accountability processes.

5. SUMMARY

Starting with the financial market perspective, analysts (study no. 6) held that there is a lack of IC information and the access to such information is substantially below the perceived value relevance. HC measures appear to be more accessible in small firms than in large firms, whereas RC measures are more easily accessible in larger firms. The lack of information restricts in particular the use of HC and RC. HC measures such as top management quality, employee participation, satisfaction and training are typically seen as important to firms' performance, and at the same time, these items are difficult to access, even for analysts who evaluate companies. If relevant information were to be provided on these measures, it would likely have a substantial effect on the use of these measures. Analysts regard IC factors as important for company performance and are more favorable toward more standardized disclosure practices.

The lenders' perceptions of IC information (study no. 7) deviate somewhat from the analysts' view in that no single measure reveals the entire or critical insights needed to make a credit judgment. HC, SC, technology and corporate strategy are difficult to judge. Instead, lenders try to obtain a holistic picture of the lending company by means of considering the company network (RC).

For the fund management firms (study no. 8), trust and accountability are the key issues. They hold that IC information is important for their decision making process. Impressionistic and emotional information about IC contributes to the firms' feelings and confidence in their valuation and information use. The latter affects accountability between the firms and their investee companies and leads to improved IC disclosure.

To summarize, the three financial market studies commonly indicate that IC is of great importance for Japanese financial market actors, but how do firms respond to these opinions?

The content analysis of the twelve early adopters (study no. 1), most of them big firms, indicates that they hold similar views as the analysts', that is, that SC and RC information are regarded as more important than HC.

The four case firms (study no. 2) had the ambition to use the IC report to achieve advantages in relation to customers and financial institutions. The most important items according to them were the value-creation story, superior technology, alliances and well-recognized people. At a general level, they followed the IAbM structure. The detailed level was totally different from the IAbM guideline. This approach to reporting IC is very close to both the lenders' perceptions of a holistic picture and the fund managers' focus on the overall trust. The four SMEs tried to influence knowledge sharing with their stakeholders in order to create trust and in favor of their businesses.

The 2010 questionnaire (study no. 3) demonstrates that SMEs are more likely to disclose IC information than are medium-sized and big firms. The target audience is both employees and external actors, such as customers and financial institutions. External communication was also the objective for the four case firms in study no. 2. The effectiveness of IAbM reports was said to be highest for employees, followed by financial institutions, clients and trading partners. To promote company values, the firms in the sample held that disclosing strengths, competitive advantage, marketability and management philosophy were the most important issues. This is very close to what the SMEs in study no. 2 also suggested. The same issues were also the most prominent with respect to assuring the report's credibility, whereas the major steps needed to obtain the credibility were "ensuring consistency with management philosophy in developing the story of value creation", "assessing the correlation among data" (company strengths, business plan, etc.) and "obtaining support team cooperation and participation". Even this study demonstrates the importance of trust.

The investigation in 2014 of the three SMEs that have published an IAbM report demonstrates very different motives, effects and difficulties. One of the firms did not have any clear expectation with respect to what they wanted to obtain, whereas the other two were more ambitious. One of these made a thorough revision of its total business. This firm acknowledges favorable effects with respect to clarification of the company's philosophy and business strategy, increase in employee motivation and acceleration of the business transaction with new customers. These SMEs reveal how the IAbM report and the work with it transforms into a *"ba"* (Nonaka and Nishiguchi 2001) for enhancing learning.

The Japanese bank study (study no. 5) is the most recent investigation and very interesting in the way that the integration of the reporting elements, for example, corporate philosophy, management strategy, business model, intellectual assets and corporate data, is very clear. Because even the CSR report is included, it is similar to the ideas of an integrated report. In the same way as networks were regarded by the SMEs (study no. 2) and by the lenders (study no. 6), networks are also important for the bank. Not only RC but even SC is of major importance. The latter refers to flexibility, that is, an ability to quickly ascertain emerging issues and deploy appropriate personnel. Understanding the complete business is at the forefront in this case.

When the eight studies are compared, the overall impression is that IC reporting in Japan has primarily attracted SMEs with the bank as an important exception. This is not to say that IC information is not relevant for medium-sized and large firms, but rather that financial markets obtain their IC information from the latter firms through other channels. All three financial market studies support the proposal that IC information is both interesting and relevant. In particular, RC information, and even SC information, is regarded as being most valuable from firms as well as financial market institutions. Another common conclusion is that it is not the detailed information but rather the holistic view that, from the firm's point of view, creates credibility and that, from the financial market's viewpoint, supports confidence and trust. The IAbM report has a function as a common *"ba"*. For lenders, company networks are highly ranked. So even if there are differences between the eight studies, as well as between the firm studies on one hand and the financial markets on the other hand, the overall impression is that there are clear common interests with respect to IAbM reporting.

6. CONCLUDING COMMENTS

Vollmer et al. (2009) suggest that a closer engagement with sociology would benefit not only studies of behavior at the financial market, but also studies in accounting. This is probably also true for the Japanese context. To better understand the mechanisms behind the issue of credibility and trust, further studies from a sociology of finance perspective appear to be beneficial.

However, most of the research on communication between companies and the financial market has been characterized by assumptions about rational agents and information asymmetry. The point of departure has been that uncertainty about a company's value increases when access to information on that company's intangible resources is limited, which means that the financial market's ability to value companies' assets and debts is a function of the efficiency of the information market. One of the assumptions behind the financial models is that financial market actors are rational, profit-maximizing "economic men". However, the very idea of efficient information markets can be questioned from a social systems point of view (Luhman 1995; Fuchs 2001). Based on a system-theory perspective, Henningsson (2009) seeks to gain insights into how fund managers are affected by social forces when they interpret information about companies' intangible resources. He suggests that fund managers become "cultural observers" when they interpret company information.

In a Swedish study by the Johanson group, the aim was to increase understanding of the role of IC reporting in the interaction between firms and fund managers. Two focus groups were invited to two separate group discussions. One group consisted of fund managers, and the other of heads of communication responsible for investor relations in large companies. The aim of these discussions was to illuminate the differences between the two groups of professionals and their ways of reasoning. The findings reveal a different understanding of what kind of company information is important to the financial market. Whereas the heads of communication wanted to provide a detailed picture of the company, the fund managers reduced the information. Detailed information about employee competence, working environment and sustainability issues was not regarded as interesting unless the issues were considered high-risk factors. Fund managers relied on company management to take care of those matters. Fund managers also developed their own stories about the firms, based on their trust in top management. In this way, they re-create their own social logic whereby complexity is reduced to a question of trust in management.

The two groups held different opinions. This is a reflection of the fact that both groups are representatives of different social cultures who both simplify their surroundings—in this case, the other system. They argue with two different types of systems-blindness and have difficulty seeing the complexity of the other system. Viewed from this perspective, it is not difficult to see that social communication barriers emerge and persist when different systems reinvent and confirm themselves vis-à-vis others.

Fund managers think that the financial market creates a space, a context, adapted to its purpose. This space is created, regardless of whether information is available. The information is not key; the context is. They also think that the conclusions drawn by the financial market are based on history. One knows a company and is thus able to draw far-reaching conclusions based on relatively little information. By creating solid narratives about a company using financial market logic, one does not have to worry about an organization's inherent complexity. Since financial market actors reduce the complexity of company information, this presupposes that they can trust that information.

The Swedish case study and the previously mentioned reasoning underline the importance of mutual trust. The importance of credibility, confidence and trust is also obvious in the eight Japanese studies. Per definition, firms and financial markets represent not only different interests and agendas, but also different social systems. However, IAbM reports appear to have an important role to play in bridging the gap between them. The IAbM report seems to have the potential to support the creation of a place for knowledge sharing, that is, a "*ba*" as Nonaka and Toyama (2005) express it. It seems like the SMEs and the financial markets have recognized that the IAbM can function as a platform for knowledge sharing. However, the "*ba*" is not a stable place. Rather, it is a shared context in continuous motion. The knowledge creation that take place at the "*ba*" needs to be continuously fed, externalized and internalized (Nonaka and Toyama 2005). The IAbM report and the related work with it creates a "*ba*" where the firms', notably the CEOs', subjective tacit and explicit knowledge is externalized into more explicit knowledge. The latter affects, that is, is internalized, by the actors at the financial market. "*Ba*" is not just about sharing subjective or objective kinds of knowledge, but also about sharing emotions. The latter is, of course, always important for learning and was one of the insights that was gained from the study of the Japanese fund management firms. Emotions facilitated learning and supported confidence and accountability.

To conclude, the Japanese IC guidelines, especially the IAbM guideline, seem to have an essential role to play as a complement to financial reporting, especially for SMEs. The eight studies that we have discussed in this chapter also reveal the importance of further studies of how IC reporting contributes to credibility, confidence and trust.

REFERENCES

Brennan, N. 2001. "Reporting intellectual capital in annual reports: Evidence from Ireland". *Accounting, Auditing & Accountability Journal,* 14 (4), 423–436.

DBJ. 2013. Annual report &CSR report.

DBJ. Privatization of DBJ http://www.dbj.jp/en/co/info/privatization.html (accessed in 2014)

Fuchs, S. 2001. *Against Essentialism: A Theory of Culture and Society.* London, UK: Harvard University Press.

Guthrie, J. and Petty, R. 2000. "Intellectual capital: Australian annual reporting practice". *Journal of Intellectual Capital,* 1 (3), 241–251.

Henningsson, J. 2009. "Fund managers as cultured observers". *Qualitative Research in Financial Markets,* 1, 27–45.

Hitachi. 2004. R&D and Intellectual Property Report (in Japanese).

Holland, J., Henningsson, J., Johanson, U., Koga, C. and Sakakibara, S. 2012. "Use of IC information in Japanese financial firms." *Journal of Intellectual Capital,* 13 (4), 562–581.

Japanese Ministry of Economy, Trade and Industry (METI). 2002. *Intellectual Property Policy Outline.*

Japanese Ministry of Economy, Trade and Industry (METI). 2004. *Reference Guideline for Intellectual Property Information Disclosure: In the Pursuit of Mutual Understanding between Companies and Capital Markets through Voluntary Disclosures of Information on Patent and Technology.*

Japanese Ministry of Economy, Trade and Industry (METI). 2005. *Guidelines for Disclosure of Intellectual Assets Based Management.*

Johanson, U., Koga, C., Almqvist, R. and Skoog, M. 2009. "Breaking taboos' implementing
intellectual assets-based management guidelines". *Journal of Intellectual Capital,* 10 (4), 520–538.

Johanson, U., Koga, C., Skoog, S. and Henningsson, J. 2006. "The Japanese
government's intellectual capital reporting guideline: What are the challenges for firms and capital market agents?". *Journal of Intellectual Capital,* 7 (4), 474–491.

Koga, C., Yao, J. and Shimada, Y. 2011. "Kigyo no kyosouyuuisei to chitekishisan-joho no arikata" ("Competitive advantage and intellectual asset information"). In Koga, C. (Ed.), *IFRS-Jidai-no Saiteki-Kaii-Seido (Optimum Disclosure System in the IFRS Age.).* Tokyo: Chikura Publishing Co.

Luhmann, N. 1995. *Social Systems.* Stanford, CA: Stanford University Press.

MERITUM. 2002. *Guidelines for Managing and Reporting on Intangibles.* Madrid: Fundacion Airtel Movil.

New Growth Policy Committee, Industrial Structure Council. 2005. *Interim Report by Subcommittee on Management & Intellectual Assets.*

Nonaka, I. and Nishiguchi, T. 2001. *Knowledge Emergence: Social, Technical, and Evolutionary Dimensions of Knowledge Creation.* New York: Oxford University Press.

Nonaka, I. and Toyama, R. 2005. "The theory of the knowledge-creating firm: Subjectivity, objectivity and synthesis". *Industrial and Corporate Change,* 14 (3), 419–436.

Olympus. 2004. Intellectual Property Report.

Sakakibara, S., Hansson, B., Yosano, T. and Kozumi, H. 2010. "Analysts' perceptions of intellectual capital information". *Australian Accounting Review,* 20 (3), 274–285.

SMRJ. 2008. *Guidelines for Practice of Intellectual Asset-based Management for Small & Medium Enterprises Survey and Research Report on Intellectual Asset-based Finance.*

Sumita, T. 2007. "Japanese program for IC after three years", *Presentation Paper* at World Bank Institute.

Vollmer, H., Mennicken, A. and Preda, A. 2009. "Tracking the numbers across accounting and finance, organizations and markets". *Accounting, Organizations and Society,* 34, 619–637.

Yosano, T. and Koga, C. 2008. "Influence of intellectual capital information on credit risk rating process/criterion and credit conditions-survey analysis of Japanese financial institutions". *Proceedings of 4th Workshop on Visualizing, Measuring and Managing Intangibles and Intellectual Capital.* October 22–24. Hasselt.

Part V
Intellectual Capital in Latin America

11 Innovation and Intangibles
The Challenges of Brazil

Marcos Cavalcanti and
André Pereira Neto

1. INTRODUCTION

Many people were surprised with the result of the 2009–2010 edition of the Global Information Technology conducted by the World Economic Forum. Since 2002, this international entity has presented a ranking of countries that use technology in favor of growth and development. In this edition, Brazil remained in the same position as last time—fifty-ninth place. Ahead were developing countries, such as South Africa, Chile, Costa Rica, Jamaica, Jordan, Kuwait and Malaysia. Other countries have shifted position in the last years. China, which occupied the fifty-seventh place in the previous ranking, now occupies the forty-sixth place.

In this chapter, we will try to analyze some of the motives that explain this underachievement and we will present a few possible alternatives to reverse this trend. Thus, we will identify a couple of dilemmas that must be resolved in order for Brazil to occupy a prominent position in a knowledge-based economy.

2. WHY DOES BRAZIL HAVE FEW INNOVATIVE COMPANIES?

Recent research (PINTEC) has shown that a small number of Brazilian firms are, in fact, innovative. According to the research, 33 percent of companies have declared to do at least one product innovation or innovation of process between 2003 and 2005. However, when data are closely observed, it is clear that less than 10 percent has, in fact, introduced a new product or process into the market. The majority of innovation happened through the acquirement of new machinery or other types of technological updates.

One of the reasons commonly presented to justify this low level of innovation in Brazilian firms has to do with low public investment in science, technology and innovation. Is Brazil underinvesting?

According to figures from the Ministry of Science and Technology, in the last decade, Brazil maintained an average investment in science and technology between 1.3 and 1.6 percent of gross domestic product (GDP). This percentage can be considered low when compared to South Korea (3 percent of GDP), Australia (1.5 percent), Singapore (2.2 percent) and Israel (3.5 percent). However, if the expenditure with full-time researchers is taken into account, the panorama changes dramatically. Brazil invested US$193,000 dollars per full-time researcher in 2000. This is practically the same amount per capita invested by the U.S. This same index is superior to other developed countries such as Canada (US$136,000), Japan (US$153,000), United Kingdom (US$152,000) or Australia (US$118,000). The vast majority of full-time researchers in Brazil work in public institutions of higher education, and some of them in laboratories and research centers that are linked to public agencies and ministries.

What Is the Result of This Investment?

In terms of article publications in international reviewed magazines, Brazil went from 0.8 percent of international output in 1995 to 2.7 percent in 2009. This figure represents the effort of many scientists to divulge their output in international journals, and it corresponds to the productivity criteria established by CAPES (Coordenação de Aperfeiçoamento de Pessoal de Nível Superior) and CNPq (Conselho Nacional de Pesquisa), governmental agencies supporting research. If, however, patent registration is used as an indicator, these results are transformed. In 1999, Brazil registered 126 patents, half of which were recorded by the Chinese. In 2004, this amount increased! Brazil registered one-third of the patents registered by the Indians and one-sixth of the ones registered by the Chinese. In 2009, Brazil obtained 103 patents in the U.S., compared to 196 of Russia, 679 of India and 1,665 of China. Hence, we are registering sixteen times less than the Chinese are!

The problem is not, therefore, low investment in science and technology. To invest around 1 percent of GDP is not that low. The biggest problem lies in the fact that a researcher's productivity is exclusively measured by the quantity of articles published in magazines and assessed by CAPES and not by concrete results for the country's development or for solving severe problems that affect most Brazilians.

In recent years, we have observed sincere efforts of some agencies (CGEE— Centro de Gestão e Estudos Estratégicos and FINEP—Financiadora de Estudos e Projetos) in trying to change this situation by valuing and stimulating the creation of an environment conducive to innovation. This effort, though valid and noteworthy, is insignificant. If we look at the financial implementation of MCT (Ministtry of Science and Technology), we can see that the resources allocated for this purpose are infinitely inferior to those distributed exclusively for academic ends.

The problem is not, therefore, in the lack of investment. Of course, the country could invest more in science and technology, but in our understanding, the main problem is in the quality of this investment. The ultimate end of the governement policy doesn't seems to favor technological innovation, but only the production of scholarly articles.

Second Reason

The second reason for the low level of innovation is the lack of an adequate environment that approximates the different players, knowledge producers, companies and markets. What prevails is a linear vision of the process of innovation. In this model, basic research is carried out in universities, whereas technological development and innovation happen inside the firms. In our understanding, this is a misguided view.

We believe that the process of innovation is not linear. Scholars on the topic have pointed out that "the forms of relationship between research and economic activities are multiple and that the process of innovation isn't linear". Moreover, other authors insist on demonstrating that the direction of development is not necessarily from basic research toward technology; technology does not require scientific advancement, because often, this advancement rides on the success on technology. Therefore, the relation between research and technological advancement is a two-way street. Science contributes to technological advancement, but innovation also contributes to the advancement of science.

The process of innovation is complex, dynamic and nonlinear. It is extremely dependent on an adequate environment that stimulates interaction between companies and research centers and that has adequate financing and legislation, constantly valuing its intellectual capital.

3. OVERCOMING THE INNOVATION GAP: INTANGIBLES AND THE BNDES METHODOLOGY

One of the biggest bottlenecks in this environment has been lines of funding (financing) and a methodology appropriate to the specific characteristics of innovative firms. An innovative firm is intensive in intellectual capital, and all lines of funding and methodologies of company evaluation that existed in Brazil were almost exclusively methodologies that evaluated the company's financial capital and patrimony. The criteria for approval of company funding depended on its presentation of physical (buildings, machinery and equipment) or financial guarantees, which were practically nonexistent in knowledge-intensive companies and intangible capital.

The methodology developed by CRIE (Centro de Referência em Inteligência Empresarial) and the BNDES (Banco Nacional de Desenvolvimento Econômico e Social—presented in another chapter in this book) opened new funding opportunities and contributed decisively to changing the innovation environment in Brazil.

4. FINAL REMARKS

This chapter intended to highlight the fact that Brazil needs to create a more favorable environment for innovation if it wants to position itself competitively in a knowledge-based society. The work developed by the BNDES indicates the path that must be followed to integrate the productive sector with those who do research. Recognizing the difficulties that the country faces in order to move toward a knowledge-based society demonstrates that we need more concrete actions that strengthen the ties between universities and firms, that value the production of knowledge and that are attuned with social, scientific and technological demands.

REFERENCE

PINTEC. PINTEC. http://www.pintec.ibge.gov.br/ (accessed May 15, 2014).

12 Evaluating Intangibles Assets and Competitiveness in Brazilian Firms
The BNDES's Approach

Helena Tenório Veiga de Almeida and
João Paulo Carneiro H. Braga[1]

1. INTRODUCTION

The existence of and the need for development banks (DBs) is an opinion divider. In a market economy, DBs would only operate in the so-called market failures. However, what is the role of DBs in the knowledge economy? From our perspective, and based on the Brazilian Development Bank (BNDES) experience, the knowledge economy demands an important change in the methodologies used by DBs to analyze firms and markets, beyond the traditional understanding of the tangible aspects of these institutions.

BNDES is a large and diversified development bank, with assets of around US$350 billion, average annual disbursements at US$80 billion and a very low delinquency rate (in 2013, 0.02 percent). It was created in 1952 and throughout the decades, its mission has evolved in order to follow the changing path of Brazilian development. Financing infrastructure with a long-term view and setting up complex financial structural projects have been, since 1952, an important role BNDES plays in the Brazilian economy—and this continues today. The financing needs of private firms to expand capacity also constitute a permanent mission. Nevertheless, investment projects and financing models have become very different compared to the beginning of the Brazilian industrialization process. There has been a huge leap from helping the infant industry in Brazil to the current challenge of improving competitiveness in a global economy.

Currently, if firms don't innovate, they are out of the global competitive game. The concept of traditional or commodities industries as low-technology sectors is definitely out of date (Fingerl 2004). All firms must look for new ways of production, marketing, organization and, in a few cases, for new products.[2] Being part of the market game demands the development of competences that lead firms to innovate in a systematic and systemic mode. But, what are these competences? How can they be made dynamic in the sense that they should be flexible enough to follow a changing environment? More importantly, is it possible to value and capture, for planning and decision making purposes, the intangible assets a firm possesses?

BNDES's approach in evaluating intangible assets provides good insight to answering these questions from an external (outside the firm) perspective. Evaluation of intangibles is used at BNDES to amplify knowledge about a client, improving credit decisions and ratings, adding nonfinancial features to traditional instruments such as balance sheets and collaterals. It is stated on an internally developed framework called "Firms' Evaluation Methodology" (*Metodologia de Avaliação de Empresas—MAE, in Portuguese*).[3]

2. BNDES FIRMS' EVALUATION METHODOLOGY

In 2007, the development of an analytical framework began based on Eduardo Rath Fingerl's master dissertation (Fingerl 2004), who also sponsored the initiative. For this purpose, a three-year project was launched, following a series of logical steps: (1) establishing a partnership with a university research team based at the Federal University of Rio de Janeiro Engineering Institute (COPPE/UFRJ) to address intangible assets concepts[4]; (2) introduction of competitiveness and industrial organizational concepts, based on Ferraz et al (1996); (3) internal development of the methodology based on further research on analytical concepts,[5] followed by a debate at "The New Club of Paris" Meeting[6]; (4) workshops to validate the methodology and to define where to apply it first; (5) tests and collegiate validation; (6) training; (7) setting workflows and developing adequate software; (8) executive board approval and (9) setting an improvement and "changing mindset" program.

The main objective of MAE is to provide different areas of the bank (such as areas in charge of planning, loan services, equity investments or credit evaluation) with a single, systematic and operational instrument to assess the intangible capital of a firm. It is also part of the credit rating analysis and loan approval procedures. A second objective is to compile information on nonfinancial aspects necessary to monitor a firm's improvements in time. The periodical application of MAE has resulted in more than an evaluation model—it has become a relational tool that not only strengthens BNDES relation capabilities, but also provides a benchmark for firms to appreciate their performance in time as seen from "BNDES eyes". In short, when defining credit or equity conditions, MAE has become a valuable instrument for sound decisions even if the subject matter is "intangible assets".

The methodology suggests that, when assessing a company demand for funding, the following issues should be taken into consideration: internal intangible assets and competitive strategy, and their consistency with the mode and pattern of competition in the market it operates. The relevant question MAE tries to address is this: Is a given company mobilizing the capabilities and resources that are compatible with the relevant drivers of competition where it operates? BNDES's goal, then, is to bring a competitive and economic dimension to the debate over intangible assets. MAE contributed and became relevant to strengthening BNDES's role as a policy agent in charge of implementing the industrial and infrastructure policies of Brazil.

Intangible Assets and Competitiveness

Traditional credit evaluation tools are generally based on a belief that firms must be assessed individually. Nevertheless, conventional theories are based on the premise that there are representative firms. Other seminal contributions, however, show that there is no such representative firm and introduce other concepts to demonstrate such failure. Coase (1937), Williamson (1979), Penrose (1959) and Nelson and Winter (1982) try to explain the existence of a variety of companies that can be explained also by their hierarchy, growth path, capabilities, skills, rules, routines, etc. As can be easily seen, most of these concepts can be considered intangible assets.

A theoretical concern BNDES has faced since the beginning of its efforts is the prevalence, in the economic debate, of concepts that consider firms the centerpiece of analysis and capabilities and competences as an end in themselves. That is, even in the literature that escapes the simplistic view of conventional theory, there is an implicit assumption of a direct relation between levels of competences and growth of firms. What BNDES's experience has shown is that the dynamic capabilities concept or the intangible assets approach must incorporate a sector-specific approach and take into account the external environment a firm is subjected to in order to arrive at sounder results. For this purpose, when developing the *MAE* methodology, the literature on industrial organization and competitiveness was taken into consideration.

In particular, MAE took in a fundamental concept about competition. That is, competitiveness is "the company's ability to formulate and implement competitive strategies to expand or maintain a lasting and sustainable market position."[7] This approach suggests that competitiveness is the result of individual firms fine-tuning their strategies and being able to mobilize resources that are adequate to the prevailing pattern of competition in a specific market at a given moment in time. Thus, a number of aspects that are not only firm specific must be explicitly taken into consideration, most of them related to the driving forces of competitiveness, as shown in Figure 12.1.

The "firm's internal drivers" (or "business drivers") constitute its intangible assets. Internal drivers are very much influenced by an internal decision process that allocates resources in a given direction. The "systemic drivers" are drivers that are largely beyond the ability of a firm to influence them. The "structural drivers" are represented by the competitive environment at the market level. These can be partially influenced by a given firm as they

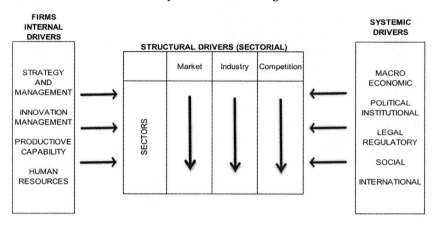

Figure 12.1   Determining driving forces of competitiveness
Source: Coutinho, L. and Ferraz, J.C. 1994. *Estudo da Competitividade da Indústria Brasileira.*
Campinas: Papirus/Unicamp.

are related to the pattern of competition, encompassing the characteristics
of demand and supply, and the influence of incentive schemes and competition regulation.

In order to remain competitive, a corporation must constantly improve
and modify its "routines" and capabilities as the market changes. In this
regard, a firm's strategy and intangible assets must be convergent with the
driving forces required for competitive success: "Companies must seek to
adopt, every time, strategies (expenses to increase productive efficiency,
quality, innovation, marketing, etc.) aimed at enabling them to compete on
price, sales efforts or product differentiation in accordance with the prevailing pattern of competition."[8] The pattern of competition is the set of key
factors for competitive success in the market in which the company operates.[9] At the highest competitive level, a firm would be able to define what
the driving forces of competition are.

MAE Framework

The framework used by MAE suggests that the assessment of a company
should take into consideration its intangible assets, competitive strategy and
consistency with the pattern of competition in a given market. Competitiveness is defined in relation to market specificities, and the firm is expected to
own the strategy and intangible assets required to compete there.

The specification for measuring a group of intangible capitals using the
MAE approach is inspired by other methodologies, such as the new IC Rating model, the Skandia Navigator (Edvinsson 1997; Edvinsson and Malone
1997), the IC-Index (Roos et al. 1998), the Intangible Asset Monitor (Sveiby

1997) and the Balanced Scorecard, or BSC (Kaplan and Norton 1992). The BSC approach was a reference to design evaluation parameters useful to determine BNDES's benchmarks. Porter's strengths, weaknesses, opportunities and threats (SWOT) methodology (Porter 1986) was applied to combine MAE with BNDES's corporate planning process.

Another source of inspiration was the Ricardis Report (European Commission 2006), which presents a list of European initiatives, such as the MERITUM IC Report and the German Intellectual Capital Statement. Another reference was the intellectual capital dynamic value (IC-dVAL model) (Bounfour 2003) and the Italian Association of Financial Analysts (AIAF 2002) score.

In summary, MAE divides the analysis of a firm into two parts: (1) intangible assets as Figure 12.2 shows and (2) competitiveness (systemic and structural drivers), shown before.

These six categories are composed of thirty-six items, such as corporate governance, relationship with clients, innovation management, reputation and sustainability. For each item, there are guiding questions to explore the main aspects that must be addressed and a parameter structure to assess the level of competence on a five-point scale. The assessment is based on the company's competences and on its efforts to reach higher scale levels.

As relevant as the methodology is the process in which BNDES engages with MAE. The methodology was the product of a partnership between the Planning Division, which has the mandate of fostering policies and

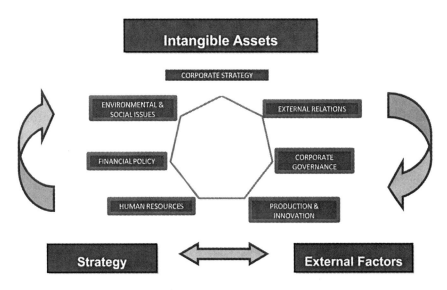

Figure 12.2 MAE: BNDES's firm evaluation methodology
Source: Authors

knowledge management, and the Credit Division, which is in charge of risk assessment with the active collaboration of sectorial specialists.[10] From theory to practice, each MAE exercise is carried out by a multidivision group of experts. The definition of the pattern of competition is carried out by sectorial specialists, based on a list of drivers to which is associated a degree of "relevance". For example, for firms producing pharmaceuticals or airplanes, investments in research and development (R&D) are very relevant, but access to raw materials is not as much. The intangible asset assessment part is a result of a consensual scoring of the thirty-six items that measure the degree of a firm's capabilities.

After the assessment, intangible assets are weighted according to their relative importance to competition. The result is a picture taken in a specific moment that shows the level of a firm's intangible capital development. As the exercise is periodically repeated, it is possible have not only a picture, but a "motion film".

This procedure has strengthened the collective knowledge base of BNDES and the interaction among technical staff. MAE has fostered the intangible assets of BNDES in its capacity to evaluate Brazilian firms for financing purposes.

MAE is used throughout the entire process of corporate financing—from the review and approval of funding, up to the rating measurement—reinforcing the use of nonfinancial indicators. MAE allows the analyst to better understand the client, so as to consider its strengths and weaknesses during the financial support decision, including an appreciation of the potential impact of a specific project (for example, the expansion of the productive capacity of a specific plant) to the competitive position of the whole corporation.

Nevertheless, a word of caution must be given: The product of evaluation is used by each division at its own discretion, given the different mandates they have. In particular, the Credit Risk Assessment Division, for reasons of banking prudence, uses the MAE result independently from operational divisions, with a weighted importance relative to financial analysis.[11]

MAE definitely decreases BNDES's credit risks, but, more importantly, and considering the development nature of the institution, it contributes to the understanding of a corporation's evolutionary trajectory. By doing so, BNDES interacts with firms, and they can discuss and plan further support in the direction of improving intangible assets in order to strengthen its competitive position.

Achievements

MAE has been operational since 2010 for clients with relevant exposure to BNDES and for those operating in high-priority areas. Currently, MAE has been applied to firms responding to 90 percent of BNDES's total risk exposure and for all firms seeking equity support, as well as those participating in special programs, such as innovation and internationalization. Since then, 135 evaluations have taken place, involving 240 employees of different divisions; 52 were carried out in 2013, which reveals an improvement in the internalization process.

Moreover, since 2010, the methodology and workflow have gone through two improvement rounds. On the methodology side, improvements were focused on strengthening the sectorial approach and adding effectiveness indicators to the evaluation criteria. On the process side, the ways the bank does due diligence and deals with the firms were adjusted to facilitate information gathering and the quality of the results. The relation with corporate chief financial officers (CFOs) about financial issues has been improved, and meetings with other clients' teams are carried out (such as R&D, human resources, planning and social responsibility), aiming at analyzing strategy and identifying competences. Procedures for sending forms to be filled in were complemented with interviews and internal rounds for understanding a firm's strengths and weaknesses. However, clients are unaware of this questionnaire method, as it is a bank-classified document.

Those changes resulted in a very positive evaluation by the bank staff: 93 percent of employees found benefits using the methodology in 2013. The greatest benefits were found in sharing information, supporting credit analysis, sharing sectorial information and improving knowledge on firms (100 percent, 92 percent, 92 percent and 98 percent, respectively). This recognition by BNDES staff suggests that collaborative work can generate cumulative knowledge that is much more valuable than divisional or individual knowledges. MAE has introduced a collaborative process and contributed to building a unique corporate competence.

MAE represents a corporate bet in the existing knowledge about clients as an important driver for BNDES to compete in the banking industry and to work as a development institution, collaborating with the country's industrial policy.

3.   CONCLUDING REMARKS

It is a common understanding among bankers that knowledge about their clients is one of the most valuable competitive assets. A good portfolio of diversified clients can ensure a bank's sustainable returns. For DBs, systematic, comprehensive and appropriate knowledge about firms has another dimension beyond ensuring financial returns and low delinquency rates— the capacity to engender a long-term relation to foster investments with a positive impact on development objectives, in the form of competitive, stronger firms or inducing the generation of externalities for society.[12]

In 2010, when the question "In your opinion, what is the most important value for BNDES activity?" was put forward to almost 3,000 employees, the majority indicated the intellectual capital embedded in the competent analysis from staff. This is the core of BNDES's intangible assets: to carry out high-quality analysis and operations with a high degree of effectiveness, including financial, competitive and societal dimensions.

MAE is a contribution in this direction: it is a valuable instrument to evaluate a client's intangibles and to foster BNDES's most relevant intangible asset—adequate knowledge on clients. In summary, MAE has been used as a powerful tool to transform long-standing tacit knowledge into explicit knowledge and individual knowledge in a collaborative process of knowledge building.

NOTES

1. The authors would like to thank João Carlos Ferraz, executive director of BNDES, for the accurate comments and detailed revision, and the comments of Lucas Teixeira.
2. Brazil, for example, is a commodity exporter, but was able to innovate in oil subsea exploration and had great performance in agricultural productivity, due to research in seeds and machinery fields.
3. In 2013, MAE received the "Latin American Association of Development Financing Institutions—ALIDE" Award for Best Technology in Services of Good Practices in Development Banks.
4. Those guidelines can also be found in Deutscher (2008).
5. As theory references, we add Penrose (1959), Sveiby (1997), Teece et al. (1997), Lev (2001) and Cavalcanti, Gomes and Pereira (2001).
6. http://new-club-of-paris.org/
7. Ferraz et al. (1996, 3).
8. Ferraz et al. (1996, 7). The pattern of competition concept that follows is also broadly discussed by the authors.
9. The pattern of competition approach was first developed by Steindl (1952). The author points out that price is not always the best strategy to compete, as firms must compete by innovation, marketing or other efforts, depending on the market's need.
10. BNDES has operational and support divisions. Operational divisions aim at financing firms and are specialized depending on the firm sector and the financing tool. Given BNDES's diversified scope of operations, a very rich and experienced knowledge base exists. Support divisions focus on transversal themes, such as corporate planning, policy design and credit risk assessment, each with a specific knowledge base.
11. As a financial institution, BNDES is subject to regulation by Brazil's Central Bank (BACEN) and to the norms and resolutions of the National Monetary Council (CMN). In addition, its accounts are inspected by the Federal Court of Accounts (TCU), an auxiliary entity to National Congress, while its processes are audited by the Office of the Comptroller General (CGU).
12. Broadly speaking, it is convergent with the notion of "knowledge bank" introduced by the World Bank.

REFERENCES

Bounfour, A. 2003. "The IC d-VAL approach". *Journal of Intellectual Capital,* 4 (3), 396–412.

Cavalcanti, M., Gomes, E. and Pereira, A. 2001. *Gestão do Conhecimento para as empresas: um roteiro para a ação.* Rio de Janeiro: Campus.

Coase, R. 1937. *The nature of the firm.* Economica. New Series, v. 4: 386–405.

Coutinho, L. and Ferraz, J.C. 1994. *Estudo da Competitividade da Indústria Brasileira.* Campinas: Papirus/Unicamp.

Deutscher, J.A. 2008. *Capitais Intangíveis—Métricas e Relatório.* Ph.D. Thesis. Rio de Janeiro: COPPE/UFRJ.

Edvinsson, L. and Malone, M. 1997. *Intellectual Capital: Realizing Your Company's True Value by Finding Its Hidden Brainpower.* New York: Harper Business.

Edvinsson, L. 1997. "Developing Intellectual Capital at Skandia". *Long Range Planning,* 30 (3), 366–373.

European Commission. Ricards. 2006. *Reporting Intellectual Capital to Augment Research, Development and Innovation in SMEs.* Directorate-General for Research.

Ferraz, J.C., Kupfer, D.S. and Haguenauer, L. 1996. *Made in Brazil: Desafios Competitivos para a Indústria Brasileira.* Rio de Janeiro: Campus.

Fingerl, E.R. 2004. *Considerando os Intangíveis: Brasil e BNDES.* Rio de Janeiro: Coppe/UFRJ.

Italian Financial Analysts Society (AIAF). 2002. *The Communication of Intangibles and Intellectual Capital: An Empirical Model of Analysis.* Official Report n. 106. Milan: AIAF.

Kaplan, R. and Norton, D.P. 1992. *The Balanced Scorecard—Measures that Drive Performance,* Boston: Harvard Business Review.

Lev, B. 2001. *Intangibles: Management, Measurement, and Reporting.* Washington D.C.: Brookings Institution Press.

Nelson, R. and Winter, S. 1982. *An Evolutionary Theory of Economic Change.* Cambridge: Belknap Press.

Penrose, E. 1959. *The Theory of the Growth of the Firm.* New York: Wiley.

Porter, M. 1986. *Estratégia Competitiva—Técnicas para Análise de Indústrias e da Concorrência.* 18ª Edição. São Paulo-SP: Campus.

Roos, J., Roos, G., Dragonetti, N.C. and Edvinsson, L. 1998. *Intellectual Capital. Navigating in the New Business Landscape.* Basingstoke and London: Macmillan Press Ltd.

Steindl, J.1952. *Maturity and Stagnation in American Capitalism,* Oxford: Blackwell.

Sveiby, K-E. 1997. "The Intangible Assets Monitor". *Journal of Human Resource Costing & Accounting,* 2, 73–97.

Teece, D., Pisano, G. and Shuen, A. 1997. "Dynamic capabilities and strategic management". *Strategic Management Journal,* 18 (7), 509–533.

Williamson, O. 1979. "Transaction-cost economics: The governance of contractual relations". *The Journal of Law and Economics,* 22 (2), 239–226.

Part VI

Asian versus Western Approaches to Intellectual Capital Reports

13 Varieties of Capitalism vs. Varieties of "Soft Regulatory" Theories

A Discussion on the Case of Intangibles Reporting in Japan and Germany

Laura Girella and Stefano Zambon[1]

1. INTRODUCTION

To study "accounting in organizations and society" (Burchell et al. 1980) is a "resolution" that many scholars have made over the past thirty years. Accordingly, mainly throughout the 1980s, several studies have focused their attention on the investigation of accounting practices in international comparison, casting light upon the potential to discern in this way the similarities and differences that can exist among them in (dis-)similar countries. Based on the observations reached by these works, classification's attempts in terms of influencing factors, such as economic, social, political environments, cultural patterns and regulatory styles, have been formulated by researchers and agencies worldwide (Mueller 1967, 1968; Seidler 1967; AAA 1977; Puxty et al. 1987; Doupnik and Salter 1995). In addition, theoretical frameworks have advanced in this respect (Nobes and Parker 1981; Gray 1988; Gray et al. 1995; Zambon 1996). Recently, this comparative trend has expanded and piqued the interest of scholars in other fields of research, for example, accounting historians, who have advocated for a new perspective on the investigation of accounting history, called comparative international accounting history (CIAH) (Carnegie and Napier 2002). In relation to the Non-financial arena, it is interesting to note that numerous works have examined the adoption of intangibles reporting (IR) in comparison. However, such an innovative device has been mainly examined at a micro (organizational) level in terms of management, measurement and disclosure techniques (de Pablos 2002; Vandemaele et al. 2005; Vergauwen and Van Alem 2005; Bozzolan et al. 2006; Guthrie et al. 2006; Chaminade and Roberts 2010). Few studies have investigated its macro (national) potential in terms of recommending initiatives and implementation processes (Lin and Edvinsson 2010). Even fewer studies have sought to elucidate the theories that can explain the similarities and differences that underlie the decision of constituencies to recommend or adopt this reporting practice and their (successful) efforts. In this respect, Tovstiga and Tulugurova (2009) are able to represent a first attempt, by pointing out the differences that exist among regions and sectors in the impact of intellectual capital (IC) practices, which can be related to "macro" characteristics, such as the economic period, the nature of the competitive environment and the national cultural attributes and attitudes. Nonetheless, this example represents an embryonic observation. In light of the recommendations' actions, which have existed since the 1990s, intangibles reporting practice found at a governmental level in many countries worldwide has relaunched their economic, social and political situations. Indeed, throughout those years, along with globalization and financialization tendencies, the world witnessed a rise in the importance of knowledge-related aspects, such as technological developments, knowledge-intensive services, new business models, etc.

The purpose of this chapter follows from the aforementioned observations. First, it is hoped that the chapter will in some way contribute to the expansion of the debate of IR toward international political and social dimensions. Second, it is hoped that the findings here attained could pave the way for a possible enrichment of intangibles regulatory studies by demonstrating if, and to what extent, accounting "soft" regulatory theories could be adopted, adjusted or confuted in terms of intangibles reporting. To meet these objectives, the chapter examines the possibilities of the existence of IR in terms of rationales, processes and consequences. This path is selected as being closely related to the decision-making mechanisms of governments toward the recommendation of new business practices. In addition, such a path is investigated in two countries that have the same "variety of capitalism", namely Japan and Germany. Notwithstanding the fact that adoption of comparative case studies has been recognized as being problematic vis-à-vis the analysis of individual national systems (Arnold 2009; Power 2009), the reasons that motivate the choice of this method are twofold. First, it enables an investigation of the conditions of possibility that exist in countries belonging to the same varieties of capitalism (Hall and Soskice 2001). In particular, it relates to the participation of various parts of the state in the corporate reporting arena (e.g., the Ministry of Economy, Trade and Industry [METI] in Japan; first the Federal Ministry of Economy and Labour and then the Federal Ministry of Economy and Technology in Germany) and their dissimilar efforts toward the recommendation of intellectual capital reporting (ICR). Second, this focus will also allow us to shed light on the role of the state, which, in the judgment of Hancké (2009), is overlooked in the varieties-of-capitalism approach. Accordingly, the possibilities of interactions in terms of soft regulatory theories and varieties of capitalism in relation to IR will be made visible. Based on the argument proposed, the remainder of the chapter is organized as follows. In Section 2, the varieties-of-capitalism approach is reviewed. Then, political economy, legitimacy and institutional theories are presented in terms of their "soft regulatory" nature and in relation to their adoption of Non-financial practices. Observations about their interactive nature, both in theoretical and practical terms, are drawn. The case studies of Japan and Germany are briefly presented. The chapter also elucidates the similarities and differences in IR recommendation actions in Japan and Germany in terms of varieties-of-capitalism and soft regulatory theories. Finally, Section 8 outlines the synergies that can be created between soft regulatory theories and the varieties-of-capitalism perspective in relation to IR in general.

2. VARIETIES OF CAPITALISM

As pointed out in the previous section, the approach to studying the influence that economic, political and social patterns can exert on the ways in which business practices are adopted and developed in dissimilar nation-states is relatively old. However, it is in the name of the internationalization process that occurred at the beginning of the nineteenth century, that several approaches have been proposed and tested in order to shed light on the interactions, similarities and differences that exist among forms of capitalism. In general terms, Albert (1993) compares the "Rheinish" type of capitalism with the neo-American one. Drawing on his work, Hall and Soskice (2001) propose an analysis centered on the behavior of firms, and especially on their ability to undertake efficient coordination relations with those agencies that constitute the political-economic sphere of a country, such as trade unions, the educational system, customer associations and others. Thus, fundamental to their argument is the acceptance of the Resource-Based View of the firm that sees firms as relational actors, aimed at "develop[ing] and exploit[ing] core competencies or dynamic capabilities understood as capacities for developing, producing, and distributing goods and services profitably" (Hall and Soskice 2001, 6). Putting it differently, firms have to *effectively* engage in various relationships within the economic, political and social environments in order to face transaction costs and principal–agents relationships and to prosper. Effective coordination efforts primarily target five spheres of activity. With reference to internal activities and actors, *vocational training and education* aims at the continual development of employees' skills. Dependent on this, the coordination with and within the *employees'* sphere becomes crucial for the sake of the firm's survival and profitability. Good relationships among employees and between employees and managers can guarantee competencies, skills and information to be constantly provided and maintained within the "organizational walls". With regard to the external environment surrounding the organization, *corporate governance* affects the possibility of financial access and for investors to pursue investments (returns). In *industrial relations*, firms have to coordinate with employees and with their representing association in general to secure acceptable levels of wages and productivity and to face unemployment and inflation problems. Finally, *interfirm relations* relate to a coordination amongst firms, other customers and other companies and to their entrance in processes of technological transfer, research and development (R&D) and, more broadly, of standards settings. Interestingly, the outcomes derived from the five spheres described do not affect just the success of the firms, but the entire economy. However, coordination within the five spheres is not sufficient by itself in explaining the divergent attitudes of countries. The *institutional complementarities* embedded in a system or created from time to time also guide the behavior of firms and of the economy as a whole. As Hall and Soskice (2001) put it, "Two institutions can be said to be complementary if the presence (or efficiency) of one increases the returns from (or efficiency of) the other" (ibid., 17). Consequently, "nations with a particular type of coordination in one sphere of the economy should tend to develop complementary practices in other spheres as well" (ibid., 18).

Based on the nature of the coordination relationships they engage in and of the *institutional complementarities* developed, two distinctive "varieties of capitalism" are advocated. On the one hand, coordination is established through competitive market' forces, and on the other, through synergistic interactions. The *equilibrium outcomes* (Hall and Gingerich 2009, 452) are consequently driven and secured by the presence of market fluidity, connoted by relative prices and market signals in the first case, and by an institutional structure able to provide credible commitments in the second case. This way, although the occurrence of both types of coordination is acknowledged in every country, the predominance of one above the other highly depends on the characterization of the market and the institutional setting. If the market guarantees fluidity and institutions do not support enough credible commitments, coordination would be engaged through competitive markets. This form of capitalism has been called liberal market economy (LME). In contrast, in those nations where the market is deficient and institutions support forms of commitments, coordination would be achieved through synergistic interactions. In this case, the label used to indicate that form of capitalism is coordinated market economy (CME). Examples of countries belonging to the former have been recognized in the literature to be Britain, the U.S. and, in general, most of those characterized by Anglo-Saxon origins. The fluidity and weaknesses that connote, among other things, their employment and industry constituencies, render the relationships within and between organizations and economic, political and social actors almost formal. They are generally based on contractual forms, if not on price systems. Regulation allows hostile takeovers, managers are highly authoritarian, technological transfer is achieved through external personnel as industry associations are unable to provide ad hoc training and, in general, those unemployed invest in wide-ranging skills.

Conversely, a network tendency within organizations (employees and managers) and between organizations and trade unions, industrial associations and regulators delineates the CME scenario. Decision-making processes within the organization permeate all working levels; thus, managers do not act in isolation. Externally, the strong relations with industrial associations allow both employees and unemployed people to benefit from specific training schemes and eventually to take part in technological transfer through interfirm collaboration. Industrial associations play a role also in standards-setting processes. Broadly speaking, the informal exchange of personnel and information among companies permits them to create a reputational aura and secure credit access. Japan and Germany, accompanied by Sweden, Norway, South Korea and others, have been identified in the literature as belonging to this type of capitalism.

A divergent behavior of the two varieties of capitalism is noticed with regard to public policy(-making). For the sake of the inquiry here proposed, the description will focus on the CME system. It has been pointed out earlier that CMEs heavily rely on business coordination based on informal networking. However, although predominant, this attitude cannot be generalized. For example, evidence has been found that firms are not always willing to share sensitive information with governments. Governments are (still) conceived as powerful actors capable of undermining the survival and profitability of firms by using information acquired against them. Consequently, to face this problem, they take advantage (by encouraging and not creating *ex novo*) of the presence of social organizations, such as trade unions and business associations, to recommend or more strongly implement their policies. Indeed, those social organizations benefit on the one hand from an independent attitude with respect to the government, and on the other, they are responsible for their members. This way, firms are more willing to share private information. In addition, the possibilities for monitoring—and, in some cases sanctioning—their members can guarantee coordination with lower transaction costs.

Accordingly, the final scenario displays "producer-group organizations [entering] into 'implicit contracts' with the government to administer the policy, drawing some benefits of their own in the form of enhanced resources and authority" (Hall and Soskice 2001, 47).

To put it differently, public policy becomes a central device for the maintenance of *incentive-compatibility* of the organization of production inputs without which its survival and profitability will be undermined. The incentive-compatibility can take two forms: framework legislation and supporting incentives. The former attempts to guarantee the protection of those principal networks of business coordination. In other words, the state decentralizes its power and delegates it to private bodies, to represent the "new" authorities and secure protection from the state's inference. The latter allows companies to enhance the reliance of their activities and performance upon distinctive institutional comparative advantages.

In the literature, the argument offered by Hall and Soskice (2001) launched the case for several observations and sometimes also criticisms.

Almost concurrently with its emergence, Dore et al. (1999) challenged the existence and perpetuation of this approach. In analyzing the developments through which the main representations of the LME and CME systems—namely Britain and the U.S. on the one hand and Germany and Japan on the other—have traveled, pointing out an admiration that the latter ones are feeling toward the former.

Conversely, Hall and Gingerich (2009) provide support for the adoption of the concept of market-oriented and strategic coordination to elucidate the ways in which the economy performs in dissimilar nations. In accordance with the LME and CME types, Nölke and Vliegenthart (2009) propose a third variety of capitalism, the dependent market economy (DME), which is characterized by the relevance of foreign capital for the relaunch of economic and social systems and is located in post-Socialist Central Europe.

With reference to accounting, Walker (2010) sets forth the case of international accounting standards and argues that an imposition of accounting standards that is mainly derived from stock market mechanisms could be counterproductive toward accounting integration. He suggests the formation of a double set of accounting standards that is able to capture the differences embedded in the varieties of capitalism and especially able to respect them. A first set will be primarily ingrained on the information needs of stock market actors, such as investors and shareholders. A second set will prioritize the information requirements of stakeholders.

3.   VARIETIES OF "SOFT REGULATORY" THEORIES

The theories chosen to analyze the two case studies in terms of regulatory efforts are political economy, legitimacy and institutionalism. The reasons for this choice rely on the fact that these theoretical frameworks are those that in social sciences, mainly in accounting, allow an understanding of the business macrodynamics of a country, in conjunction with its microcontext. In other words, according to these theories, the path toward the adoption of certain (business) practices does not have to be conceived of as only stemming from the coercive nature of public authorities. The capacity of these agencies to render their proposals acceptable and relevant to the interests of other constituencies, especially at a micro level, is also a fundamental aspect. Consequently, the actors that are bearers of the national business interests (in this case, governments) do represent *vehicles* for the achievement of *supra*-national objectives and not the primary addressees.

Therefore, it can be noted that the theories previously mentioned all relate to recommendation processes that originate in "contextual situations". In general and simplistic terms, the origins of the term political economy derive from political, social and economic environments; the origins of legitimacy derive from the societal needs that surround the activities of organizations, and institutionalism finds its roots in the (similar) behavior of entities that face analogous (external) conditions. Stated in another way, it can be said that in relying on these theories, reference is made to "soft regulatory" theories. Indeed, Sisson and Marginson (2001, 4–5) define soft regulation as follows:

> "Soft" regulation tends to deal with general principles, whereas "hard" regulation is concerned with specific rights and obligations;
>
> "Soft" regulation, where it does deal with rights and obligations, tends to be concerned with minimum provisions, whereas the equivalent "hard" regulation involves standard ones;
>
> "Soft" regulation often provides for further negotiation at lower levels, whereas "hard" regulation tends to assume the process is finished—following the French usage, "hard" regulation might be described as parfait or complete and "soft" regulation as imparfait or incomplete;
>
> "Soft" regulation relies on open-ended processes such as bench marking and peer group audit, with monitoring and "moral-suasion" for enforcement, whereas "hard" regulation tends to rely on sanctions;
>
> "Soft" regulation, in as much as it takes the form of "recommendations" or "opinions" or "declarations", might be described as permissive, whereas "hard" regulation is almost invariably compulsory;
>
> "Soft" regulation tends to be concerned with soft issues such as equal opportunities or training and development, whereas "hard" regulation deals with hard ones such as pay and working time.

In other words, "soft regulation" embodies a flexible mechanism through which governments enact lines of actions articulated in concert with their audiences, concerning an improvement in their economic, political and social status and toward which, those impinged possess an arbitrary degree of approval. In addition, following the definition proposed by the European Commission, who define it as "joint opinions, declarations, resolutions, recommendations, proposals, guidelines, codes of conduct, agreement protocols and agreements proper" (European Commission 2000, 17), a similar use can also be advocated here, taking into consideration that the analysis for which they are adopted is based on guidelines.

Following the line of thought proposed earlier, political economy, legitimacy and institutionalism will be reviewed here in relation to Non-financial reporting.

Political Economy and Non-financial Reporting

It has been previously pointed out that political economy is a theoretical approach that stems from contextual situations. Accordingly, it is not surprising that beyond the accounting realm, its relevance has been identified also with regard to forms of Non-financial reporting, such as social, environmental and IC disclosures.

In relation to corporate social disclosure, Ramanathan (1976) is one of the first who recognizes that the firm relies on a narrow, legalistic notion, and then he advocates for a broader definition that is able to capture the social performance of the organization. In this way, he identifies macro- and micro-contexts in relation to which social accounting becomes defined as "the process of selecting firm-level social performance variables, measures and measurements procedures; systematically developing information useful for evaluating the firm's social performance; and communicating such information to concerned social groups, both within and outside the firm" (ibid., 519). Consequently, performance objectives and concepts are also reformulated. In particular, he proposes three objectives, such as the identification and measurement of the net social contribution of a firm, the accordance between corporate strategies and practices on the one hand and society's priorities and individuals' aspirations on the other, and finally an adequate communication of relevant information (ibid., 527). On the concepts' side, he advances social transactions, returns, income, constituents, equity and net social assets. In his view, the combination of these objectives and concepts represents a framework that accounts for the social performance of an organization. In a similar vein, Tinker and Lowe (1980) propose a framework aimed at better illustrating the common terrain that connects the social interest and the indicators of corporate performance. In this respect, they acknowledge that human beings make decisions centered on satisfying terms. Therefore, a system based on the choice of the organization to involve members on the basis of their ability to successfully deal with a "jumpy F-set" (the feasible alternatives acceptable to all participants) is advocated.

Beyond the proposal of "appropriate" frameworks to investigate the field of corporate social and environmental disclosures, several authors also embarked on the "test" of existing theories.

In an attempt to investigate which theory between user utility and political economy has an explanatory power for corporate social disclosure, Guthrie and Parker (1990) find support for the latter one. In their thought, its proactive role enables one "to identify social and political determinants of meanings attributed to social disclosure, recognizes the non-neutrality of the annual report, elucidates the role of social disclosure in legitimizing private sectional interests and existing eco-political arrangements, and [critiques] social disclosures that represent pacification responses to social information demands" (ibid., 173).

To a similar extent, Williams (1999) supports the view proposed by Gray et al. (1996) for the adoption of political economy as a theoretical framework able to illustrate the voluntary economic and social accounting disclosure scenario. Indeed, he points out that the explanatory variables for this type of disclosure are mainly related to cultural and political civil determinants, and not to economic ones. In this respect, it is relevant to point out that a difference between classic and bourgeois political economy has been explicitly depicted in the literature. The Marxian, classical point of view relies on a "materialistic perspective" of human relations. This means that they are mainly based on the modes of production. In other words, the construction of the society, or what has been referred to as "superstructure", is based on economic activities. Given this association, the advancement in terms of technological development of the modes of production leads to an increase in the gap that exists between social classes and, as a consequence, of class struggles. In particular, two main conflicting social classes are identified. On the one hand, there is the so-called proletariat, represented by those performing the highly productive mechanized and socialized production and, on the other hand, there is the bourgeoisie, a minority embodied by those private owners who take appropriation of the surplus value or profit produced.

Chronologically antecedent to Marx, Mills (1909) represents a particular facet of political economy from which the bourgeois perspective arose. Conversely to traditional political economy, he advocates for a "cost-of-production" conception of exchange value that abandons the dichotomy between use-value and exchange-value, and he proposes a study centered on price. This way, he maintains that wealth in the bourgeois society is "given". Indeed, he rejects the labor theory of value and recognizes that all production factors have a proportional share in the formation of value. Consequently, wages are considered as corresponding to amounts deserved by the laborer.

With reference to Non-financial reporting, Gray et al. (1995) summarize the differences between the two approaches in the following way:

> The distinction is crucial because Marxian political economy places sectional (class) interests, structural inequality, conflict and the role of the State at the heart of its analysis. Bourgeois political economy largely ignores these elements and, as a result, is content to perceive the world as essentially pluralistic. (Gray et al., 1995, p. 153)

Adopting this perspective, Arnold (), in commenting on Guthrie and Parker (1990), points out that their analysis of corporate social disclosure (regulation) through political economy lenses suffers from the lack of an examination of the political dimension. In her view, without the acknowledgment of the existence of a variety of theories able to explain the roles and functions of the state, they implicitly agree upon a pluralist perspective of the political economy approach in relation to corporate social responsibility (CSR). This way, their observations can be considered myopic. Similarly, Tinker et al. (1991) contests the view of CSR literature as relying on a static conception of "middle-ground" and demonstrates how its emergence and development are contingent upon social conflicts.

As for IC reporting, a first attempt to link it to the political economy approach has already been carried out by Abeysekera and Guthrie (2005) and Spence and Carter (2011). In the work of Abeysekera and Guthrie (2005), such an approach that "views that accounting is a means of sustaining and legitimising the current social, economic, and political arrangements" [. . .] "appears to be more applicable to intellectual capital reporting", as they recognize a "proactive role" to this type of practice (ibid., 155). In a Marxist perspective, Spence and Carter (2011) advocate for a conceptualization of IC accounting as a device that, on the one hand, permits a "colonisation of the General Intellect", and on the other, enables socialization, depicting in this way an escape from capitalist control.

Although pioneering, the perspectives adopted in the works mentioned represent, in our view, merely one side of the coin (how micro-practices make sense of the "infrastructure"). It could be worthwhile to take this into consideration from a broader point of view, according to which it is of interest to analyze the contextual linkages of IC discourse and practice in their (coupled) process of legitimization and support by means of governmental actions.

Legitimacy Theory and Non-financial Reporting

One aspect of legitimacy theory rests on the connection that is established between organizations and society. By means of this association, it is widely acknowledged that legitimacy is one of the theories that gained prominence within the social and environmental reporting discourse at the firm level. In this respect, one of the pioneering works has probably been the one by Hogner (1982). In more recent years, Robert Gray and Craig Deegan represent the main contributors to this field, exploring the dynamics that motivate companies to release social and environmental reporting (Deegan et al. 2000; Deegan 2002; Deegan et al. 2002). However, a number of studies extended the explanatory power of legitimacy theory in terms of dissimilar types of contextual events in which the company can be embedded. Brown and Deegan (1998) and Aerts and Cormier (2009) also find support for the adoption of this theory with respect to the role of the media. In particular, they note that "press results" largely impinge on the public perception about the company. Answering the call by Sikka (2010) to further investigate the consequences of tax aggressiveness in relation to CSR disclosure, Lanis and Richardson (2013) observe that actions undertaken by companies to minimize or avoid taxes affect public perception, depicting the company as socially irresponsible. Along with the theoretical nuances that this framework offers in terms of dissimilar adoptable strategies (gain, maintain, repair and defense), O'Donovan (2002) explores their practical implications associated with environmental disclosure.

With respect to the investigation of the role of the state as a legitimizing institution toward the disclosure of social and environmental reporting, pioneering efforts have been realized. Patten (1992) provides support for the argument that perceives social disclosure as a means to influence public policy (changes). The lack of quantitative methods in relation to social disclosure leads society to influence public policy in order to be heard. Therefore, companies can act as first movers, publishing social reports in order to avoid public policy shifts. In a more reactive analysis, companies belonging to four industries are found to positively respond to environmental public and policy pressure (Walden and Schwartz 1997). Similarly, support is provided for public policy variables, such as size and industry classification, as explanatory aspects of the tendency of companies to disclose environmental information (Patten 1991). Archel et al. (2009) examine the interplay between organizations and the state, pointing out how strategies toward legitimation are employed by companies and enrolled by the state through a bi-univocal process that leads to the well-being of these two constituencies beyond that of society.

Reconciling these contrasting interpretations, Criado-Jiménez et al. (2008) maintain that a positive association can be established between the volume and quality of social, ethical and environmental disclosures on the one hand and the enforcement of standards on the other. Indeed, an elucidation of the tendency of those companies that persist in a partial disclosure attitude can be explained by the adoption of the impressive management perspective and the related strategies.

Although the broad adoption previously illustrated noted that legitimacy theory does not lack criticism, this investigation is beyond the scope of this chapter. In addition, it is worthy to note how the adoption of legitimacy theory has been predominantly employed within corporate social and environmental disclosure, but no traces are found in the IC/intangibles realms.

Institutional Theory and Non-financial Reporting

It has been recently acknowledged that institutionalism and corporate social responsibility have been streams of research often studied in isolation (Walsh et al. 2003, 877). However, a few attempts have been carried out to let them converge.

In this respect, Campbell (2006) recognizes that CSR activities are employed by those organizations that are imbued in *normative* institutional environments, that is, where mechanisms of monitoring exist. In particular, organizations that adopt this new management practice are those that belong to broader networks, such as business associations, and that actively engage in dialogue with their stakeholders. Indeed, the normative feature that connotes CSR adoption does not correspond to a mere compliance with imperatives or environmental contingencies. Rather, it travels through processes of negotiations and power relations.

From an international perspective, institutionalism is identified as one of the explanatory variables of the existing dissimilar behavior between

U.S. and European companies toward the adoption of CSR practices (Matten and Moon 2008). In fact, national business systems "will play out a rebalancing of corporations' relationships with societal institutions, which we expect to be revealed in changing balances of their implicit and explicit responsibilities" (ibid., 420).

Despite the previous arguments, it is worth highlighting that generalizing exercises cannot be conducted without encountering difficulties. Larrinaga et al. (2002) demonstrate how institutional reforms cannot represent an explanatory variable and, as a consequence, compliance with the disclosure of environmental reporting cannot be guaranteed.

As for intangibles, to the best of the writer's knowledge, no studies have adopted institutionalism as a crucial theoretical framework to elucidate their implementation and dissemination (Moeller 2009).

4. POLITICAL ECONOMY, LEGITIMACY AND INSTITUTIONAL THEORY: AN INTERACTION ATTEMPT

In previous sections, the "soft" regulatory theories applicable to the recommendation of Non-financial reporting have been reviewed in isolation. In this respect, it has been noted that especially after the rise of interest in CSR occurred in the academic arena, several attempts were made to test the theories applicable to it (Mäkelä and Näsi 2010; Cho et al. 2012). This analysis has provided dissimilar results over the years, some of which provide evidence supporting the adoption of legitimacy theory (Hogner 1982; Deegan et al. 2002b; Lanis and Richardson 2013), with some others neglecting its full applicability (Wilmshurst and Frost 2000). Consequently, alternative theoretical frameworks, such as stakeholder theory (Ullmann 1985; Roberts 1992; Van der Laan Smith et al. 2005a, 2005b), have been proposed. Interestingly, in conjunction, a third stream of research started to explore the historical and conceptual developments of these theories. Putting this in a chronological perspective, Gray et al. (1995) analyzed the data on CSR disclosure in the United Kingdom from the 1970s onwards, pointing out that political economy, legitimacy and stakeholders theories have to be seen in complementary terms and not in competitive ones. Indeed, the existing interconnections at the theoretical grounds can enable a better understanding of the nuances of CSR reporting trends.

According to Deegan (2002a), political economy, legitimacy and institutional theories are not to be conceived of as distinct ones. In particular, political economy is seen as giving birth to legitimacy theory in light of the connection between society and organizations that it emerges from. Similarly, legitimacy theory is seen as a part of institutional theory. According to the latter, organizations are expected to conform with external pressures in relation to what is "acceptable" behavior. Concurrently, O'Donovan (2002) recognizes the overlapping nature of the bourgeois political economy, stakeholder and legitimacy theories and calls for further research in order to shed light on their differences. Deegan and Blomquist (2006) maintain:

> Whilst legitimacy theory discusses the expectations of society in general (as encapsulated within the "*social contract*"), stakeholder theory provides a more refined resolution by referring to particular groups within society (stakeholder groups). (ibid., 349–350)

In a later work, Deegan (2007) offers a comprehensive reconstruction of the theoretical path through which legitimacy theory has traveled and he points out a specific schema according to which these connections can be conceived. Political economy, especially the bourgeois perspective suggested by Gray et al. (1996), has to be considered as giving birth to legitimacy theory in light of its pluralistic connotation. In Deegan's words (2007): "It assumes that the views of a reasonably unified and pluralistic society shape the activities of organizations". As illustrated previously, legitimacy theory, in turn, represents the "recipient" of stakeholders theory. Within the broad concept of society, stakeholders theory refers to a specific group of individuals, that is, those directly interested in the life of an organization. Both legitimacy and stakeholders theories rest on institutionalism, by means of the efforts spent by organizations to adapt to social and institutional pressures. The interconnections existing among the theories are represented in Figure 13.1.

According to this, the questions arising from this background are as follows: "What about the other side of the coin of Non-financial information

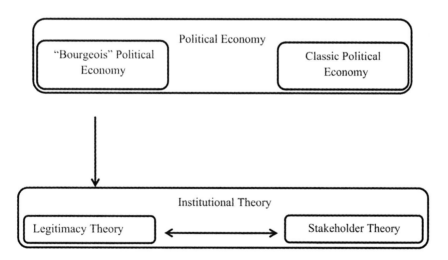

Figure 13.1   Interconnections between political economy, institutional, stakeholders and legitimacy theories as proposed by the CSR literature
Source: Authors' elaboration.

reporting, namely IC/IR?", "Which theory, if any, is able to better capture the multifaceted nature of its recommendation processes?", "Is it possible to capture interconnections with other theories?" As will be elucidated shortly in the next sections, the approaches that describe the recommended actions undertaken by governments in Japan and Germany rely on opposite sides. In the former case, a "top-down" logic, mainly directed by the state, dominates the scene, and in the second one, a "bottom-up" logic governed by companies' consultants finds prominence.

However, in scratching the surface of the theoretical appearance, the glitter and gold of the singular, isolated theories leaves space for substantial interconnections. The "political economy justification" found in the Japanese case cannot transcend both a legitimacy and an institutional dimension. Even if it is acknowledged that the facet of the political economy that better enlightens the Japanese case resembles the "classical" one much more, possible interconnections can still take place. Indeed, the course of action followed by the actors who played a major role in the recommendation of Intangibles Reporting was accompanied by, if not determined by, a lack of legitimacy of the traditional economic system to run the nation-state and, consequently, by an awareness that the institutional environment surrounding this initiative was changed.

Similarly, Germany, whose attitude has been examined in terms of institutional theory, does not transcend the legitimation that the architects, namely the Federal Ministry, the experts-consultants and the moderator found in the promotion of IR. Without the legitimacy conferred first from the Federal Ministry to the experts-consultants, and second, from the

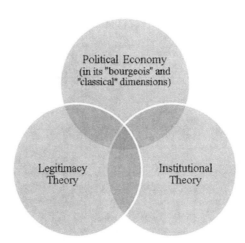

Figure 13.2 Interconnections between political economy, institutional and legitimacy theories as revised by the IR case studies analyzed
Source: Authors' elaboration.

experts to the moderator, the project could have not found a similar company acceptance. Accordingly, the project launched by the state can also be conceived of in terms of political economy, in that it benefited (even if in marginal ways) from the support of government agencies, but especially from its contextual intertwinement. To conclude, it is possible to advocate that the varieties of capitalism do not have to be conceived of as isolated islands in relation to "soft" regulatory theories. What at a first look appears to be a monolithic block, in reality hides possibilities of contributory interrelations (see Figure 13.2).

5. THE JAPANESE CASE

The case of Japan represents a singular episode, as it points out how an "intangibles problem" that at first was mainly depicted as affecting the company level (the ability to use intellectual property in an efficient way and the bad loans problem) has found support and legitimacy at first a macro-economic issue and then as a policy one (Girella and Zambon 2013). Indeed, three guidelines have been formulated and released, first by the government (METI 2005) and then by other governmental institutions (OSMERI 2007; METI 2009).

The first document on Intellectual Asset-based Management (IAbM), published in 2005 by the Ministry of Economy, Trade and Industry (METI), the "Guidelines for Disclosure of Intellectual Assets-based Management (IAbM)", had the aim of introducing mainly to listed companies a corporate management approach based on intangibles resources. The documents that followed—the "Intellectual Assets-based Management Manual for SMEs", published in 2007, and "Keys to Intellectual Assets-based Management Evaluation Finance", published in 2009—were addressed to small and medium enterprises (SMEs) and the potential to improve their access to credit. In particular, the first document was designed to help SMEs base their competitiveness on intellectual assets (IA). In reading the manual, the difficulty of SMEs to access credit is accompanied by the social and economic context that characterized Japan in the past. As a consequence, the growing role played by IA within the economic system has led financial institutions to base their decisions on qualitative information of the company, such as technological capacity and the enthusiasm of top management. As a result, the third document was published relating to financial institutions and how they can support access to credit by companies, especially by SMEs. These documents have been translated into practice by several companies. At present, 200 companies have compiled an IAbM report. Moreover, from as early as 2005, the tendency has been to publish the report, not as an integral part of the financial statement or of other statements (e.g., social reports), but independently.

Such support and legitimacy are not "neutral", but they can be related first to the discernment of intangibles and ICR as a means of disentangling the (more or less transitory) mismatch that the country was witnessing between governmental institutions, globalization and the needs of the business environment, especially SMEs, on the one side, and the accounting information supply and credit access on the other; and second, as a manner to restore them.

It is important to keep in mind that the Japanese business context is highly connoted by an informal relational power among companies and the state. As argued by Dore (1997), Japanese companies belong to the so-called "entity/community view", according to which the actors who participate in the business system constitute a community in the sense that they are "tied together by bonds of mutual interest in the community's fate, obligations of cooperation and trust, the sharing of similar risk" (Dore 1997, 19). Accordingly, it is easier for companies and, in general for associations, to cooperate toward a common interest, as "social relations in which Japanese economic transactions are embedded are achieved" (Dore 1997, 25). This connotation enables the identification of IA both within and without the company.

In this overall picture, the state also played an important role in this sense. Although the American model had a great deal of influence at the beginning of the 1900s in reorganizing the institutional system, several criticisms were aimed at this type of government. These criticisms noted in particular the lack in American thought of an "organic, comparative, or coherent idea of national policy". In fact "Japanese have a 'sense of the state' of the immense importance of collective and civilized action, of wise organization, of social discipline" (Droppers 1907, 111–112). To a similar extent, the role of the Japanese government in relation to business results is relevant, although it presents here another aspect. All the guidelines analyzed, and especially the last one, have to be viewed in light of the reforms that have been implemented since 2000. In that period, which was characterized by a considerable number of reforms, public procurement has been a catalyst in IR and in implementing innovative activities on a national level and in understanding its degree of response in applying these reforms (OECD 2005).

6.   THE GERMAN CASE

The German case represents an attempt to understand how the recommendation of IR can be considered to stem from the claims of expertise of a group of consultants (vis-à-vis the traditional role played by professional bodies or governmental agencies) and the "promotional" course of actions that they undertook, not only in relation to a single company, but also at a national level (in its entirety of companies and professional associations) (Girella and Zambon 2013).

Indeed, in Germany, since 2003, a group of three consultants, as experts, have made their entrance on the national stage to recommend the adoption of ICR in a country considered conservative and prudent in its regulative accounting system. Similar to what was maintained by Christensen and Skærbæk (2010), they have put in action a purification process by which "ideas or things that were considered 'impure', in that they were controversial or devalued, are turned into acceptable and unchallenged concepts of some standing and worth" (ibid., 526–527).

In this respect, the manners through which they captured the attention, not only of the ministry but also of the SMEs, can be considered distinctive ones. Answering the call of the Federal Ministry of Economy and Labour, they launched was initially referred to as a "prototyping idea", aimed at supporting companies in their formulation of ICR. By means of an in-house preparation of the processes through which an ICR can be constructed in SMEs that manifested their interest in adopting such a practice, they formulated an initial guideline. The document was subjected to revisions by the Federal Ministry and was consequently published under its collaboration. Interestingly, in reading and analyzing the document, the expectation that that the government agency was the main promoter and actor in the process of recommending and implementing ICR in companies is mistaken.

Indeed, what has been elsewhere referred to as the "disciplining of scientific experts to conform to bureaucratic modes of action" (Thorpe 2002, 552) did not find justification here. Conversely, the state has, to some extent, been disciplined by the consultants-experts in that their involvement in forming and promoting the guidelines has been minimal and confined to an initial stage. This attitude was likely due to the previous experience by the most important association for consultants in Germany, the Federal Association of German Consultants (*Bundesverband Deutscher Unternehmensberater*, or BDU). Indeed, in the 1990s, this Association sought to achieve a law, linking the right to use the title "consultant" with the standardized qualification that it provided (Groß and Kieser 2006, 79). Nonetheless, this attempt resulted in a failure.

Accordingly, the group of consultants that embraced the IR recommendation process acted independently from the state for the most part, aside from an initial funding involvement. In adopting a rhetorical device centered on "fact-building" or "concrete" actions, the experts-consultants identified and created an ad hoc and *appropriate* figure for the formulation of ICR: the moderator. Such an identity is characterized by the realization of tangible actions and a dependence on its architect (the experts-consultants). Indeed, its "professionalization" is contingent upon the experts. In other words, the experts have been able to embody an "obligatory passage point". They have generated a process comprising a training program, a final examination and a code of ethics, through which a trust system has been established. This way, they also paved the way for "controlling occupational entry or the supply of qualified labour" (Fincham 2006).

7. THE JAPANESE AND GERMAN CASE STUDIES
OF INTANGIBLES REPORTING: SIMILARITIES AND
DIFFERENCES

Drawing on the general observations reported earlier and on the business–
government relationships (Wood 2001) that can foster the recommendation
of certain public policies, the reflections reached through the analysis of
the Japanese and German case studies and the guidelines on IR formulated
and released ("Guidelines for Disclosure of Intellectual Assets-based Management", "Intellectual Assets-based Management for Small and Medium
Enterprises" and "Keys to Intellectual Asset-Based Management Evaluation
Finance") will be expanded upon here. Table 13.1 summarizes the main
findings of these works in terms of (1) time periods during which the guidelines were formulated and published, (2) actors involved in the processes of
formulating and recommending IR and the role they played, (3) addressees
of the guidelines, (4) the context from which the IR recommendation process originated, (5) the connotation that IR assumes in the guidelines and (6)
the effects that followed from the release of the guidelines (demonstrated by
the number of companies adopting IR for both internal and external communication purposes).

Similarities

At a first glance, it is possible to note some common denominators among
the actions undertaken in Japan and Germany with reference to IR recommendation processes. First, the period during which the guidelines were
formulated. In both cases, initial efforts occurred in the mid-2000s. At first,
this tendency can be explained by the fact that it was the period of "major
proliferation" of intangibles discourse. In other words, IC, intangibles and
knowledge management were considered "hot topics" at the time. Indeed,
after the OECD International Symposium held in Amsterdam in 1999, academics and practitioners began to show interest in this subject. In addition,
the European Commission called for research in this field (RICARDIS).
However, the "real" reasons rely more on the presence of countries or better
governments that recommend this reporting practice at a national level. In
other words, the promoters of the recommendation processes in Japan and
Germany referred to similar "soft regulatory" experiences already existing
in other countries. As stated by the director of Research and Strategy Division of International Trade Policy Bureau in Japan in 2003:

> Around that time, I happened to encounter the concept of "intellectual
> capital" originally invented in the Nordic countries. I travelled to Swe-
> den, Denmark and UK in 2003. I had a meeting with Leif Edvinsson
> who is one of the originators of this concept. I also learned that Govern-
> ment of Denmark introduced the bill that encouraged the companies to

Table 13.1 Components of intangibles reporting recommendation in the two countries

Guidelines' Year	Recommending Actors	Addressees	IR Context of Origin	IR Features	Effects
Japan					
2005	Ministry of Economy Trade and Industry (METI)	Large companies	"Lost decade"	IAbM as "growth potential"	Few disclosures
2007	Organization for SMEs and Regional Innovation (OSMERI)	SMEs	"Lost decade" + globalization	IAbM as "further business growth"	271 companies disclose an IAbM Report
2009	METI + OSMERI	SMEs	"Lost decade" + globalization + financialization	IAbM as "Non-financial info"	
Germany					
2004	Group of three consultants + Federal Ministry of Economy and Labour	SMEs	Globalization	ICR as a "comprehensive" device for companies	16 pilot companies
2008	Group of three consultants + Federal Ministry SMEs of economy and technology		Globalization + financialization	ICR as a device that allows "continuity", "more than 1,000 companies success" and a "precise" company's Direct contact with 350 companies indirectly (through moderators) evaluation	

Source: Authors' elaboration.

produce intellectual capital reports and publish a guideline for preparing such reports. In UK, I was informed that debate on the revision of the Company Code was in process. [. . .] Having studied all of these, I decided to take up the concept of intellectual asset as the key concept in the coming White Paper. (Deputy Director-General, Economic and Social Policy, METI, November 2012).

Along the same lines, one of the members of the Arbeitkreis Wissensbilanz (AK-WB) in Germany pointed out that:

It was a bottom-up approach, it didn't start from [scratch], but it was informed by the international experience and we were aware of the problems they encountered. (Owner and general manager, alwert GmbH & Co. KG and "core member" of the Arbeitkreis Wissensbilanz, May 2012)

Interestingly, whether casually or not, most of the nations that formed the basis of this reference, such as Denmark, Sweden and Norway, were those belonging to the same CME category.

A second aspect that is worthy to highlight in terms of similarities relates to the actors that promoted the adoption of IR practices and the roles they covered in these processes. According to the business–government relationships that connote the CME systems, both the Japanese and the German ministries relied on "agencies" to perpetuate their "regulatory efforts". In the former case, METI, after a first attempt in 2005 to recommend the adoption of IR to listed companies, "decentralized" this function to an "external" organization focused on SMEs: the Organization for SMEs and Regional Innovation (OSMERI). This agency, founded in 2005, is an independent administrative organization under the Ministry of Economy, Trade and Industry aimed at "supporting SMEs and regional communities in solving their problems and realizing their dreams, by providing targeted and personalized support measures" (OSMERI web site).

A possible explanation for this shift could be the scarce level of disclosure that the ministry attained when listed companies were targeted. Indeed, as soon as the ministry turned its attention to SMEs and its "intangibles regulatory power" was delegated to OSMERI in 2007 and then to OSMERI and the Intellectual Property Policy Office in 2009, the number of companies that adopted the IAbM Report sharply increased (by the end of 2012, they amounted to 271).

As for the case of Germany, the "decentralization" from the government to external agencies took place from the beginning of the recommendation process. Indeed, the ministry has been the funder of this initiative and most generally the "legitimating entity". No explicit involvement in the procedural aspects has been played by this constituency. Furthermore, as soon as the start-up phase ended and the "IR movement" reached maturity, the government retired its support. The continual promotion and expansion efforts toward the adoption of IR have been undertaken by a group of expert-consultants, and the creation by them of an ad hoc, appropriate figure (the moderator) aimed at helping companies in the preparation of the report. In terms of adopters, these efforts quickly translated into successful results. By 2012, the number of companies that adopted an IR through direct contact with the experts had grown to 350 and the number that had adopted an IR via moderators had grown to more than 1,000. As pointed out elsewhere (Wood 2001), the German government has a constrained power and limited autonomy toward the business environment. Thus, the business environment that surrounds its activities is extremely interiorly coordinated through a high level of information sharing among companies on the one hand and between companies and those associations delegated by the government to run business on the other. Interestingly, the close relationship between the government and the business environment did not encompass other professional bodies and associations. In the Japanese case, although there has been major involvement by the state, the process has been mainly supported by Chartered Accountants, but not, for example, by the Federation of Economic Organizations (*Nippon Keindaren*) and the Japanese Association of Corporate Executives (*Keizay Doyukai*). This attitude can be explained in light of the prime minister's approach that accompanied the birth and evolution of the recommendation process. Although prone to the relaunch of Japan internationally, most of its decisions were oriented toward recovering the traditional Japanese style. By way of contrast, the associations mentioned earlier were more inclined to follow the "innovative" Anglo-American lines of action, where CSR was the fundamental aspect.

Germany witnessed a similar situation. However, the state was the "legitimating" institution and the recommendation process derived from the "substrate" of companies' consultants. No allies were providing additional support (with an exception over the last years for the "German Association for Small and Medium-sized Businesses"—*Bundesverband Mittelständische Wirtschaft*). In addition, an ad hoc association was created by the promoters themselves.

Following these lines of argument, it is possible to generally state that the networking aspect that characterized the CME economies did not find here full justification. In general terms, in both countries, IR and ICR have been conceived of as a means to improve the relationships between the government and SMEs on the one hand, and between companies and the financial system on the other. Put differently, its adoption as aimed at filling a mismatch that occurred between governmental institutions, the business environment, accounting information supply and credit access. These deficiencies were represented in both cases as a cause of globalization and the "financialization" trend that characterized the new capitalistic system.

In conclusion, it can be stated that these two countries, belonging to a CME system according to which "firms depend more heavily on non-market relationships to coordinate their endeavours with other actors and to construct their core competencies" (Hall and Soskice 2001, 8), have shown pitfalls in their main feature, the relational power.

Differences

One of the differences between Japan and Germany lies in the "closure mechanisms" that the promoters of the "Intangibles Project" either actively undertook or passively experienced in their recommendation process. In Japan, it originated *exogenously* (from the external environment toward the promoters), whereas in Germany, it originated *endogenously* (from the initiators toward the external environment). In addition, it is worth noting also that the few allies who decided to be involved in the processes were dissimilar in nature. In Japan, the only professional body included was the Chartered Accountants. Conversely, in Germany, a constituency "interested in supporting Intellectual Capital Statement (or Reporting) in Germany and [promoting] its application also in Europe" was the German Association for Small and Medium-sized Businesses, an independent association in which the needs and opinions of SMEs' converged and that was able to influence, if not lobby for, the political decision-making process.

> The BVMW is a politically independent association which caters for all commercial branches and professions, and represents the interests of small and medium-sized businesses in politics, with administrative authorities, with trade unions and with major companies. Medium-sized businesses—around 3.3 million individual enterprises in all—are the backbone and impulse of the German economy. [. . .] Influence on political decisions affecting economic conditions can only be achieved through the activities of a pressure group. Consequently, the BVMW works hard on a broad spectrum of political levels, starting with local, regional and national levels, and ending with the European Commission in Brussels.
>
> The basis for the political work of the BVMW is the policy statement "small and medium-sized businesses are a mobile force", which combines the most important statements and demands of our association. Together with our co-operation partner associations, we represent more than 150,000 businesses with about 4.3 million employees.

These diverse trends can be justified by a symptomatic awareness of the economic actors that constitutes the networks of the business environment in the two countries where their capitalistic features were changed. Indeed, in Germany, the industry-based economic system, although hit by the occurrence of globalization and financialization, appears—at least in the area investigated here—still to be well functioning, showing the existence of good communication and interaction channels from both within and without the government.

In Japan, this is not the case. The group-based (*keiretsu*) and "convoy" system, in which business is respectively related to the banking system and the state, seems to be under serious reconsideration. Recognizing the definitive role that this system, among others, played in locating the country in the "lost decade" has led to its collapse. As a result, the relationships that the state could count on to influence and to determinate the conduct disappeared.

Accordingly, it is not surprising that the (theoretical) approaches that can be adopted to enlighten the recommendation process of a "new" reporting practice respond to a "top-down" logic in the case of Japan and a to a "bottom-up" one in the case of Germany.

8. VARIETIES OF CAPITALISM, VARIETIES OF "SOFT" REGULATORY THEORIES AND INTANGIBLES REPORTING

In synthesizing the observations reached in the previous sections, the analysis of IR recommendation and implementation processes at international levels poses several challenges on a theoretical ground. First, we look at the "soft" regulatory theories, which are able to better elucidate the underlying reasons according to which governments decide to promote such an innovative practice at a national level. As noted in Section 3, there is a void within Non-financial research of ad hoc theoretical frameworks able to fully explain these behaviors. Accordingly, in our view, the ways through which it is possible to conduct a similar investigation rely on the employment of accounting theories—in particular, where those "soft" regulatory theories that emphasize the macrodynamics of a country intertwine with micro ones. The regulatory frameworks adopted in the two case studies, although different in nature, manifest the possibility of confluence. Despite the fact that the "number" of similarities is larger than the "number" of differences, it is in the name of the (few) existing differences where the diverse attitude that separates the two countries can be explained.

In light of the regulatory and capitalistic similarities and differences that occurred in Japan and Germany in relation to the IR recommendation process, it is possible to conclude that, as contended by Wood (2001), an effective "soft" (added) policy-making is not secured by incentives/sanction mechanisms and an imposition of certain firms' behavior. In contrast, it centers on the formulation and recommendation of firms' attitudes that respect and enhance the institutional settings underlying business coordination. In his words, an effective policy-making is the one "that complements the institutional comparative advantage of their respective market economies" (ibid., 274).

NOTE

1. Although this chapter is the fruit of a common and shared work, Sections 1, 2 and 8 can be attributed to Stefano Zambon and the remaining ones to Laura Girella.

REFERENCES

AAA 1977. *Accounting Review,* Supplement to Vol. 52, American Accounting Association.

Abeysekera, I. and Guthrie, J. 2005. "An empirical investigation of annual reporting trends of intellectual capital in Sri Lanka". *Critical Perspectives on Accounting,* 16 (3), 151–163.

Aerts, W. and Cormier, D. 2009. "Media legitimacy and corporate environmental communication". *Accounting, Organizations and Society,* 34 (1), 1–27.

Albert, M. 1993. *Capitalism vs. Capitalism.* New York: Four Walls Eight Windows.

Archel, P., Husillos Carlos Larrinaga, J. and Spence, C. 2009. "Social disclosure, legitimacy theory and the role of the state". *Accounting, Auditing & Accountability Journal,* 22 (8), 1284–1307.

Arnold, P.J. 2009. "Institutional perspectives on the internationalization of accounting". In *Accounting, Organizations and Institutions: Essays in Honour of Anthony Hopwood.* Chapman, C., Cooper, D.J. and Miller, P. (Eds.), Oxford and New York: Oxford University Press, 48–64.

Bozzolan, S., O'Regan, P. and Ricceri, F. 2006. "Intellectual Capital Disclosure (ICD): A comparison of Italy and the UK". *Journal of Human Resource Costing & Accounting,* 10 (2), 92–113.

Brown, N. and Deegan, C. 1998. "The public disclosure of environmental performance information—A dual test of media agenda setting theory and legitimacy theory". *Accounting and Business Research,* 29 (1), 21–41.

Bundesverband mittelständische Wirtschaft website, http://www.bvmw.de/service/sprachen/gb.html.

Burchell, S., Clubb, C., Hopwood, A. and Hughes, J. 1980. "The roles of accounting in organizations and society". *Accounting, Organizations and Society,* 5 (1), 5–27.

Campbell, J.L. 2006. "Institutional analysis and the paradox of corporate social responsibility". *American Behavioral Scientist,* 49 (7), 925–938.

Carnegie, G.D. and Napier, C.J. 2002. "Exploring comparative international accounting history". *Accounting, Auditing & Accountability Journal,* 15 (5), 689–718.

Chaminade, C. and Roberts, H. 2003. "What it means is what it does: A comparative analysis of implementing intellectual capital in Norway and Spain". *European Accounting Review,* 12 (4), 733–751.

Cho, C.H., Freedman, M. and Patten, D.M. 2012. "Corporate disclosure of environmental capital expenditures: A test of alternative theories". *Accounting, Auditing & Accountability Journal,* 25 (3), 486–507.

Christensen, M. and Skærbæk, P. 2010. "Consultancy outputs and the purification of accounting technologies". *Accounting, Organizations and Society,* 35 (5), 524–545.

Criado-Jiménez, I., Fernández-Chulián Carlos Larrinage-González, M. and Husillos-Carqués, F.J. 2008. "Compliance with mandatory environmental reporting in financial statements: The case of Spain (2001–2003)". *Journal of Business Ethics,* 79 (3), 245–262.

de Pablos, P. 2002. "Evidence of intellectual capital measurement from Asia, Europe and the Middle East". *Journal of Intellectual Capital,* 3 (3), 287–302.

Deegan, C., Rankin, M. and Voght, P. 2000. "Firms' disclosure reactions to major social incidents: Australian evidence". *Accounting Forum,* 24 (1), 101–130.

Deegan, C. 2002. "Introduction: The legitimising effect of social and environmental disclosures—A theoretical foundation". *Accounting, Auditing & Accountability Journal,* 15 (3), 282–311.

Deegan, C., Rankin, M. and Tobin, J. 2002. "An examination of the corporate social and environmental disclosures of BHP from 1983–1997: A test of legitimacy theory". *Accounting, Auditing & Accountability Journal,* 15 (3), 312–343.

Deegan, C. and Blomquist, C. 2006. "Stakeholder influence on corporate reporting: An exploration of the interaction between WWF-Australia and the Australian Minerals Industry". *Accounting, Organizations and Society,* 31 (4), 343–372.

Deegan, C. 2007. "Organisational legitimacy as a motive for sustainability reporting". In Unerman, J., Bebbington, J. and O'Dwyer, B. (Eds.), *Sustainability Accounting and Accountability.* London: Routledge, 127–149.

Deputy Director-General, Economic and Social Policy, METI, November 2012.

Dore, R. 1997. "The distinctiveness of Japan". In Crouch, C. and Streeck, W. (Eds.), *Political Economy of Modern Capitalism.* London: Sage Publications, 19–32.

Dore, R., Lazonick, W. and O'Sullivan, M. 1999. "Varieties of capitalism in the twentieth century". *Oxford Review of Economic Policy,* 15 (4), 102–120.

Doupnik, T.S. and Salter, S.B. 1993. "An empirical test of a judgmental international classification of financial reporting practices". *Journal of International Business Studies,* 24 (1), 41–60.

Droppers, G. 1907. "The sense of the state". *Journal of Political Economy,* 15 (2), 109–112.

European Commission (2000). *Industrial Relations in Europe 2000.* Luxembourg: Office for the Official Publications of the European Communities.

Fincham, R. 2006. "Knowledge work as occupational strategy: Comparing IT and management consulting". *New Technology, Work and Employment,* 21 (1), 16–28.

Girella, L. and Zambon, S. 2013. "A political economy of intangibles reporting: The case of Japan". *Journal of Intellectual Capital,* 14 (3), 451–470.

Gray, S.J. 1988. "Towards a theory of cultural influence on the development of accounting systems internationally". *Abacus,* 24 (1), 1–15.

Gray, R., Kouhy, R. and Lavers, S. 1995. "Corporate social and environmental reporting: A review of the literature and a longitudinal study of UK disclosure". *Accounting, Auditing & Accountability Journal,* 8 (2), 47–77.

Gray, R., Owen, D. and Adams, C. 1996. *Accounting & Accountability: Changes and Challenges in Corporate Social and Environmental Reporting.* London: Prentice Hall.

Groß, C. and Kieser, A. 2006. "Are consultants moving towards professionalization?". *Research in the Sociology of Organizations,* 24, 69–100.

Guthrie, J. and Parker, L.D. 1990. "Corporate social disclosure practice: A comparative international analysis". *Advances in Public Interest Accounting,* 3 (2), 159–176.

Guthrie, J., Petty, R. and Ricceri, F. 2006. "The voluntary reporting of intellectual capital: Comparing evidence from Hong Kong and Australia". *Journal of Intellectual Capital,* 7 (2), 254–271.

Hall, P.A. and Soskice, D.W. 2001. *Varieties of Capitalism: The Institutional Foundations of Comparative Advantage.* Oxford: Oxford University Press.

Hall, P.A. and Gingerich, D.W. 2009. "Varieties of capitalism and institutional complementarities in the political economy: An empirical analysis". *British Journal of Political Science,* 39 (3), 449–482.

Hancké, B. 2009. *Debating Varieties of Capitalism: A Reader.* New York: Oxford University Press.

Hogner, R.H. 1982. "Corporate social reporting: Eight decades of development at US Steel". *Research in Corporate Performance and Policy,* 4, 243–250.

Lanis, R. and Richardson, G. 2013. "Corporate social responsibility and tax aggressiveness: A test of legitimacy theory". *Accounting, Auditing & Accountability Journal,* 26 (1), 75–100.

Larrinaga, C., Carrasco, F., Correa, C., Llena, F. and Moneva, J. 2002. "Accountability and accounting regulation: The case of the Spanish environmental disclosure standard". *European Accounting Review,* 11 (4), 723–740.

Lin, C.Y-Y. and Edvinsson, L. 2010. *National Intellectual Capital: A Comparison of 40 Countries.* New York: Springer.

Mäkelä, H. and Näsi, S. 2010. "Social responsibilities of MNCs in downsizing operations: A Finnish forest sector case analysed from the stakeholder, social contract and legitimacy theory point of view". *Accounting, Auditing & Accountability Journal,* 23 (2), 149–174.

Matten, D. and Moon, J. 2008. "'Implicit' and 'explicit' CSR: A conceptual framework for a comparative understanding of corporate social responsibility". *Academy of Management Review,* 33 (2), 404–424.

METI. 2005. *Guidelines for Disclosure of Intellectual Assets-based Management.*

METI. 2009. *Keys to Intellectual Asset-Based Management Evaluation Finance.*

Mills, J.S. 1909. *Principles of Political Economy, 7th ed.* London: Longmans, Green and Co.

Ministry of Economy and Labour. 2004. *Wissensbilanz—Made in Germany, Leitfaden* 1–52.

Ministry of Economy and Technology. 2008. *Wissensbilanz—Made in Germany, Leitfaden 2.0 zur Erstellung einer Wissensbilanz* 1–68.

Moeller, K. 2009. "Intangible and financial performance: Causes and effects". *Journal of Intellectual Capital,* 10 (2), 224–245.

Mueller, G.G. 1967. *International Accounting Part I.* New York: Macmillan.

Mueller, G.G. 1968. Accounting principles generally accepted in the United States versus those generally accepted elsewhere. *International Journal of Accounting Education and Research,* 3 (2), 91–103.

Nobes, C. and Parker, R.H. 1981. *Comparative International Accounting.* Reddington: Philip Allan (subsequent editions: 1985; 1991; 1995; 1998; 2000; 2002; 2004; 2006; 2008; 2010; 2012).

Nölke, A. and Vliegenthart, A. 2009. "Enlarging the varieties of capitalism: The emergence of dependent market economies in East Central Europe". *World Politics,* 61 (4), 670–702.

O'Donovan, G. 2002. "Environmental disclosures in the annual report: Extending the applicability and predictive power of legitimacy theory". *Accounting, Auditing & Accountability Journal,* 15 (3), 344–371.

OECD. 2005. "Innovation policy and performance in Japan". In *Innovation Policy and Performance: A Cross-Comparison,* 117–146. Paris: OECD.

Organization for Small & Medium Enterprise and Regional Innovation (OSMERI). Japan 2007. *Intellectual Assets-based Management for Small and Medium Enterprises.* Tokyo: OSMERI website, http://www.smrj.go.jp/english/.

Owner and general manager, alwert GmbH & Co. KG and "core member" of the Arbeitkreis Wissensbilanz, May 2012.

Patten, D.M. 1991. "Exposure, legitimacy, and social disclosure". *Journal of Accounting and Public Policy.* 10 (4), 297–308.

Patten, D.M. 1992. "Intra-industry environmental disclosures in response to the Alaskan oil spill: A note on legitimacy theory". *Accounting, Organizations and Society,* 17 (5), 471–475.

Power, M. 2009. "Financial accounting without a state". In Chapman, C., Cooper, D.J. and Miller, P., *Accounting, Organizations and Institutions: Essays in Honour of Anthony Hopwood.* Oxford and New York: Oxford University Press, 324–340.

Puxty, A.G., Willmott, H.C., Cooper, D.J. and Lowe, T. 1987. "Modes of regulation in advanced capitalism: Locating accountancy in four countries". *Accounting, Organizations and Society,* 12 (3), 273–291.

Ramanathan, K.V. 1976. "Toward a theory of corporate social accounting." *The Accounting Review,* 51 (3), 516–528.

Roberts, R.W. 1992. "Determinants of corporate social responsibility disclosure: An application of stakeholder theory". *Accounting, Organizations and Society,* 17 (6), 595–612.

Seidler, L.J. 1967. "International accounting—The ultimate theory course". *Accounting Review,* 42 (4), 775–781.

Sikka, P. 2010. "Smoke and mirrors: Corporate social responsibility and tax avoidance". *Accounting Forum,* 34 (3), 153–168.

Sisson, K. and Marginson, P. 2001. "Soft regulation: Travesty of the real thing or new dimension?". ESR "One Europe or Several?" Programme, Sussex European Institute, University of Sussex.

Spence, C. and Carter, D. 2011. "Accounting for the general intellect: immaterial labour and the social factory". *Critical Perspectives on Accounting,* 22 (3), 304–315.

Sumita, T. 2008. "Intellectual assets-based management for innovation: Lessons from experiences in Japan". *Journal of Intellectual Capital,* 9 (2), 206–227.

Thorpe, C. 2002. "Disciplining experts: Scientific authority and liberal democracy in the Oppenheimer case". *Social Studies of Science,* 32 (4), 525–562.

Tinker, A.M. and Lowe, A.E. 1980. "A rationale for corporate social reporting: Theory and evidence from organizational research". *Journal of Business Finance & Accounting,* 7 (1), 1–17.

Tinker, T., Neimark, M. and Lehman, C. 1991. "Falling down the hole in the middle of the road: Political quietism in corporate social reporting". *Accounting, Auditing & Accountability Journal,* 4 (2), 28–54.

Tovstiga, G. and Tulugurova, E. 2009. "Intellectual capital practices: A four-region comparative study". *Journal of Intellectual Capital,* 10 (1), 70–80.

Ullmann, A.A. 1985. "Data in search of a theory: A critical examination of the relationships among social performance, social disclosure, and economic performance of U.S. firms". *Academy of Management Review,* 10 (3), 540–557.

Van der Laan Smith, J., Adhikari, A and Tondkar, R.H. 2005a. "Exploring differences in social disclosures internationally: A stakeholder perspective". *Journal of Accounting and Public Policy,* 24 (2), 123–151.

Van der Laan Smith, J., Adhikari, A., Tondkar, R.H. and Andrews, R.L. 2005b. "The impact of corporate social disclosure on investment behavior: A cross-national study". *Journal of Accounting and Public Policy,* 29 (2), 177–192.

Vandemaele, S. N., Vergauwen, P. G. M. C., and Smits, A. J. 2005. "Intellectual capital disclosure in the Netherlands, Sweden and the UK: A longitudinal and comparative study". *Journal of Intellectual Capital,* 6 (3), 417–426.

Vergauwen, P.G. and Van Alem, F.J. 2005. "Annual report IC disclosures in the Netherlands, France and Germany". *Journal of Intellectual Capital,* 6 (1), 89–104.

Walden, D.W. and Schwartz, B.N. 1997. "Environmental disclosures and public policy pressure". *Journal of Accounting and Public Policy,* 16 (2), 125–154.

Walker, M. 2010. "Accounting for varieties of capitalism: The case against a single set of global accounting standards". *The British Accounting Review,* 42 (3), 137–152.

Walsh, J.P., Weber, K. and Margolis, J.D. 2003. "Social issues and management: Our lost cause found". *Journal of Management,* 29 (6), 859–881.

Williams, M.S. 1999. "Voluntary environmental and social accounting disclosure practices in the Asia-Pacific region: An international empirical test of political economy theory". *The International Journal of Accounting,* 34 (2), 209–238.

Wilmshurst, T.D. and Frost, G.R. 2000. "Corporate environmental reporting: A test of legitimacy theory". *Accounting, Auditing & Accountability Journal,* 13 (1), 10–26.

Wood, S. 2001. "Business, government, and patterns of labor market policy in Britain and the Federal Republic of Germany". In Hall, P.A. and Soskice, D.W. (Eds.). *Varieties of Capitalism: The Institutional Foundations of Comparative Advantage.* Oxford: Oxford University Press, 247–274.

Zambon, S. 1996. *Profili di Ragioneria Internazionale e Comparata* [Comparative in International Accounting]. Padua: Cedam.

Part VII

Trends and Challenges for Intellectual Capital Reports

14 Trends and Challenges of Future IC Reporting

Experiences from Japan

Jun Yao and Erik Bjurström

1. INTRODUCTION

Intellectual capital (IC) has come of age and undergone a series of transformations through a number of different actors. The initial ground-clearing and visionary contributions from Scandinavia and the U.S. (Skandia 1994; Brooking 1996; Edvinsson and Malone 1997; Sveiby 1997; Stewart 1998; Roos 1998) paved the way for both a more intellectually explorative journey of its classification, definitions and meaning (Jeny and Stolowy 2000; Gröjer 2001; MERITUM 2002; DMST 2003) and practical evidence of the virtues and flaws of the concept (c.f. Chaminade and Catasús 2007). In hindsight, it is clear that the IC concept has become established as an essential expression of the need to capture and communicate value in the modern business context and that this need cannot be isolated to specific countries or regions, but has become a global endeavor. One of the most impressive records of sustainable policy commitment and academic research efforts into the development and use of IC measures can be found in Japan, particularly through the long-term support of the Japanese Ministry of Economy, Trade and Industry (METI).

However, although the Japanese efforts have resulted in an impressive array of reporting initiatives, explorations of IC concepts and evaluation of its consequences, the evolution of reporting practices has not been without difficulties and challenges, as we will see in this chapter. Elucidation of these difficulties or challenges may highlight what should be improved in the guidelines and policies and contribute to the diffusion of IC reporting in the future. Therefore, we propose that these findings should be seen as a rich body of experience through which IC concepts, measurements and reporting initiatives could be further discussed.

The structure of the chapter is as follows. First, we introduce a more theoretically inspired reflection of the general challenges of capturing the complexities of IC in reporting models and synthesize IC measurement through strategies and business models from a Japanese perspective on strategy. We then turn to empirical findings as we account for the recent trends in Intellectual Assets-based Management (IAbM) and explain the reasons behind the trends. Then, we address suggestions for an integrated reporting model and its challenges. Next, we raise the issue of quality in IAbM reports and problematize its criteria. Finally, we sum up our findings in a discussion about the value of the Japanese experience and its contribution for the further development of IC.

In the Japanese context, instead of IC, the term intellectual assets (IA) is often used to describe the same business resources. Therefore, in our discussion, IC and IA are used interchangeably.

2.   DIFFICULTIES IN PREPARING THE IC REPORT

> There are not more than five musical notes, yet the combinations of these five give rise to more melodies than can ever be heard. . . . In battle, however, there are not more than two methods of attack—the direct and the indirect; yet these two in combination give rise to an endless series of maneuvers.
>
> Sun Tsu (in Clavell), 2013.V.

A Neat Report Model vs. a Complex Value-Creation Process

Academia has almost reached an agreement on the classification of IC into three categories: human capital, relational capital and structural capital. However, combining them to create value is a dynamic and complex process. Just as a few basic elements combine to create innumerable variations in Sun Tzu's thought, so do the three types of IC form the basis for countless variations. To effectively evaluate and report IC, dozens of models and approaches have been developed. Among these models and approaches, the Balanced Scorecard, Skandia IC model, Value Chain Scoreboard, MERITUM Guidelines and METI guidelines, to name a few, are among those well known and often used in preparing IA reports. Under this model, various components of intangible assets or IC are identified and indicators and indices are generated and reported in scorecards or as graphs. The IAbM model is one of them, containing (1) management philosophy, (2) past to present, (3) present to future and (4) IA description and indicators. The design of indicators largely follows the MERITUM guidelines.

These models and guidelines can actually create a more comprehensive picture of an organization's health than financial metrics can, and they can be easily applied at any level of an organization (Sveiby 2010). However, none of the models is preferred over the others. A common feature of these models is that they are neatly structured, whereas the value creation of IC is dynamic and complex. First, IC can be used in multiple ways at the same time. For example, technology or know-how owned by one staff can be used in other departments by sharing the knowledge. On the other side, the activities of a firm may produce several IA simultaneously (Itami and Roehl,

1987). Second, no single asset, but rather a combination of assets, forms competitive advantage and creates value for the company. The relevance of IC for value creation lies not in the stocks of IA components or individual elements, but in the flows that happen between the various elements that exists in the black box of the company (Ricceri, 2008). To know what is in the black box is tough, if not impossible, for both managers inside the company and stakeholders outside the company. Hence, there may be a missing link in the current balanced scorecard models.

The Missing Link: Strategy and Business Models

Realizing the missing link has moved reporting guideline setters toward what Ricceri (2008) called the third wave of knowledge management, that is, the tendency to incorporate strategization within the management of IC. However, both proper strategy formulation and execution are needed to link IC to performance. A good strategy formulation provides guidelines for coordinating activities so that the firm can cope with influences of the changing environment, hence adopting a holistic approach, integrating considerations of both the external environment and internal resources (Itami and Roehl 1987). However, as Dumay (2012) noted, focusing on winners' strategies is not enough to know the causal link between IC and value creation, as losers' strategies have often been the same as the winners', just executed differently. Strategy implementation, that is, undertaking activities and utilizing IC to conduct innovation, also means that different combinations will result in different corporate performances (c.f. Ricceri 2008). For example, the same staff, if working in different organizational cultures, will have different motivations and different behaviors. An environment that encourages innovation will spur the renewal of products or business models, whereas an organization whose structure discourages innovation may hinder the renewal process even with the same equipment and staff. Therefore, it is difficult to causally link IC to value creation.

The business model is a relative new and increasingly popular concept (George and Bock 2011) also used to connect IC and corporate value. In practice, the business model is often used interchangeably with strategy or described as how an organization makes money, how the company is structured and how it delivers its product or services and how a company adds value at different stages of its operational process (Black Sun 2012) or as the firm's value-creation mechanism (Markides 2008). The International Integrated Reporting Council (IIRC) notes that it is often seen as the process by which an organization seeks to create and sustain value (IIRC 2013). George and Bock (2011) found five different views on the business model: as organization design, organization narrative, opportunity facilitator, innovation form and transactive structure. In the IC reporting context, it would mean a Resource-Based View of dynamic capabilities that links the firm's distinctive competencies to organizational aspirations and outcomes

(Eden and Ackermann 2000). Although both business model and strategy can be used to link IC and corporate value, George and Bock (2011) argue that a business model is the organization's configurational enactment of a specific opportunity, whereas strategy is the process of optimizing the effectiveness of that configuration, including the potential to change the configuration, alter the underlying opportunity or seek out new opportunities. Consequently, if a business model represents the present, strategy should tell about the future.

Getting the Point of Japanese Management Style and Reporting

Although the METI guideline borrowed many of its ideas from Western reporting models like the MERITUM guideline, it is questionable whether it showed enough consideration of the Japanese style of knowledge management. Japanese companies are said to have different style of IA management (Uchida and Roos 2008). If this is true, then there should be different types of management theories, appraisal methods and the optimal ways of intellectual resources disclosure, respectively. Some researchers criticize the top-down approach for guiding IC reporting, indicating that more research on what works (and does not work) in specific organizational contexts from a bottom-up perspective to understand how IC performs toward value creation is required (Mouritsen 2006; Dumay 2012). So, management of IA in the Japanese context may be important for companies. To understand the different style of management might help us understand the difficulty in preparing the Intellectual Asset-based Management (IAbM) report from other perspectives.

Uchida and Roos (2008) have distinguished the Western style of intellectual resources management from the Japanese style. The former was labeled *strategy rationality* style, whereas the latter was described as *resource rationality* style. The IA management with strategic rationality has a goal based on external environment analysis and pursuits and utilized necessary intellectual resources according to the strategic goals. This is a strategic execution focus and is considered an indirect management of intellectual assets. In contrast, the Japanese style of IA management, which features resource rationality, chooses its optimal activities based on the company's internal resources. Its focus is on strategic formation. And it is a direct management of intellectual assets. Sometimes, Japanese companies are criticized for a lack of strategic views from the Western perspective of strategy, which is based more on the analysis of external competition and environment. The strategic formulation of Japanese companies is more internally oriented. Instead of comparative value, some Japanese companies have a propensity for pursuing absolute value, which is regarded as the essence of innovation (Nonaka and Katsumi 2004). For example, Honda, the second largest automobile maker, develops automobiles based on its own concepts instead of benchmarking its competitors. These kinds of Japanese companies try to differentiate themselves from others with unique intellectual resources that only exist within their own companies. The unique intellectual resources may be specific knowledge, know-how, corporate culture, network or the decision making mechanism that is generated and accumulated with the development of the company. Some intangible resources may be gained through specific business activities or experiences. So these IA are labeled with the name of the company.

Consequently, the Western strategy of rationality built into much of the IA reporting seems to sit ill with the Japanese resource rationality, and there may be other things to be learned from the Japanese experience than would be expected from a Western perspective.

2.   RECENT TREND OF IABM REPORTING IN JAPAN

Almost a decade has passed since METI compiled the first guideline for IA reporting in 2005. In the three years since 2005, other institutional measures and complementary guidelines have been created to promote the preparation and disclosure of IA reporting by specific companies, such as venture companies and small and medium enterprises (SMEs) or companies in a specific region (Kansai Area) or prefecture (Kyoto Prefecture).

Table 14.1 shows the guidelines and policies to promote intellectual asset-based management and reporting that were created by different levels of authorities.

As a part of an action plan of Kansai Intellectual Property-NET, METI Kansai bureau produced a practical guide for the intellectual assets-based report for SMEs as well as venture capitals. It is based on the idea that disclosing more IA information will help eliminate the information gap between these companies, especially the research and development (R&D)– intensive venture companies and financial institutions.

To promote the awareness of intellectual asset-based management and disclosure of IA reporting, Kyoto prefecture (2008) created its own *Chie management evaluation and certification system* (Chie means intelligence or knowledge in Japanese). When used here, it refers to the technology and know-how that cannot be registered as intellectual property, such as patents. It also includes other intangible business resources that bring about corporate value, such as human resources, customer base and brand. In other words, Chie equals the strength of companies, and the Chie management (which is called intellectual asset-based management by METI) is regarded as a management tool that helps companies increase sales and profits. The certified model company can utilize a specific long-term financing system that offers a maximum loan of 560 million yen. To be certified as a Chie management model company, companies should prepare a

Table 14.1   Measures and guidelines to promote IAbM reporting

	Authorities	Guidelines and policies
Country level	Ministry of Economy, Trade and Industry (METI)	Guidelines for Disclosure of Intellectual Assets-based Management
	Organization for Small & Medium Enterprises and Regional Innovation, JAPAN	Guidelines for Practices of Intellectual Asset-Based Management for Small and Medium Enterprises; Intellectual Asset-Based Management Manual for SMEs; Revision of Manual for Intellectual Asset- based Management report
Regional level	Kansai bureau of Economy, Trade and Industry (covering Osaka, Kyoto, Hyogo, Nara, Shiga, Fukui and Wagayama prefecture)	Report on Intellectual Asset-Based Management SME and Venture companies and Strategic Information Disclosure
Prefecture level	Kyoto Prefecture	Promotion System of Chie Management, Guidebook for Chie Management Report

Chie management report (IAbM report). In preparing the Chie management report, companies can refer to the Chie management navigator and guide-book provided by the prefecture. However, it is up to the applying company to determine whether they will disclose their Chie report. This provides SMEs with great motivation to produce an IA report.

We may then ask how effective these policies are in stimulating the management and reporting of IA. Based on our analysis, four trends are demonstrated in the following paragraphs.

1. Despite the government's various efforts to encourage IAbM reporting, though there is some progress, the result is not so exciting. According to the latest data, of all 297 disclosing companies, 198[1] are located in the Kansai area. Kyoto and Osaka are the two cities that show great passion in promoting IAbM reporting. After slowly climbing for seven years, the number of companies reporting declined after 2011 on the country level. The publicly disclosed reports of Kyoto SMEs even kept decreasing after a short increase in 2009 (Figure 14.1).
2. Although an upward trend can be observed generally, there is fluctuation in the number of IAbM model companies certified by Kyoto prefecture. The number on the y-axis represents the number of IAbM reports and Chie reports. (Figure 14.2). Furthermore, compared to an increasing number of certified companies, the reporting companies

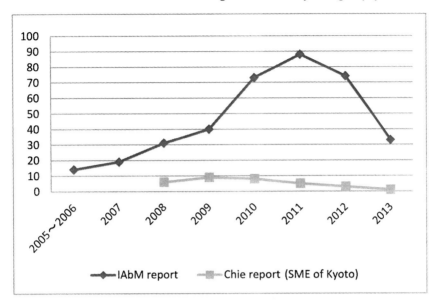

Figure 14.1　Trend of IAbM reporting in Japan

didn't increase. This may be explained by the fact that the evaluation and certification system does encourage companies to figure out
the way they utilize IAs and prepare Chie (IAbM) reports. However,
fewer companies would really want to disclose the report to the general public for reasons such as the avoidance of leaking confidential
business information to competitors. However, because information
asymmetry is the main motive for METI to encourage IA reporting,
it is not always driving the decision of firms to disclose information
on IC (Brüggen el al. 2009). Some of the companies only distribute
their IAbM report to customers or employees or other related parties
(METI Kansai 2010).

3. According to the dynamic view of IAs, organizations must develop
their strategic resources and renew these to achieve congruence with
a changing environment. This is known as dynamic capability (Ricceri 2008). According to a survey of sell-side analysts, the disclosure
of IAbM time-series information illustrates the story of the company
in the long run that helps analysts evaluate the potential of the company (METI 2007). Thus, continual disclosure of IA information is
helpful to users. However, a majority of companies gave up reporting only after their first year try. Figure 14.3 shows the companies'
continual reporting practices. The companies that quit, especially
large companies, instead disclose their IA information in their annual
reports or intellectual property report. There is very little research

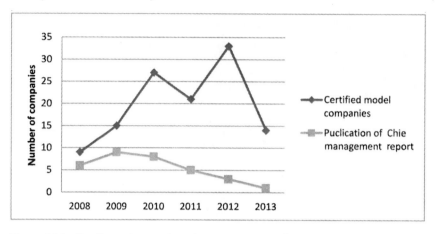

Figure 14.2   Intellectual assets-based management and reporting in Kyoto

based on content analysis of IA information in Japanese companies' annual reports. However, research on corporate social responsibility (CSR), corporate governance and risk information disclosure reveals an increase in the disclosure of information on human resources, structural resource and relationship resources of the company.[2] But there is still a lack of systematical disclosure from the IA management perspective.

4. The fourth feature is the different reporting format of small and medium-sized nonpublic companies and large public companies. Companies may choose to increase intangible assets information disclosure by inserting a section in the annual report, or a description in the securities report, or other information media. Companies may also prepare an independent report. When looking at the scales of the companies that have disclosed independent IAbM reports, we find that about 95 percent are small and medium-sized nonpublic companies. Large companies seem to prefer incorporating IA information in the annual report or other reports like the CSR. Very few large companies adopted the IAbM model in disclosing their intangible resources.

Summing up recent reporting practice in Japan reveals a great challenge for the general acceptance and diffusion of IA reporting, and there is different reporting pattern for large companies and SMEs. According to the METI investigation, there are quite a lot of expected merits to disclosing the IA report for both Japanese companies and financial institutions. Disclosure of IC information is regarded as a win-win strategy for companies and users of the information, such as financial institution, employees and customers. Table 14.2 reveals the perceived advantages for both companies and corporate assessors.

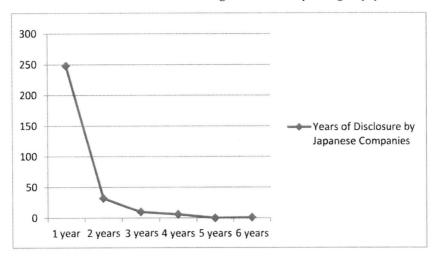

Figure 14.3 Years of disclosure by Japanese companies

Table 14.2 Perceived Advantages for IAbM Reporting

Advantages for companies	Advantages for financial institutions
(1) Increase of corporate value	(1) Improvement of accuracy of analysis of corporate value
(2) Optimal distribution of managerial resources	(2) Assessment of risk in corporations
(3) Easy procurement of funds	(3) Spotting corporations with high growth potential
(4) Improvement of employees' motivation	
(5) Enabled re-investment in intellectual assets	

(Adapted from METI 2007, chapter 2)

However, compared to the soaring CSR reporting by listed companies in Japan during the last decade, the reluctance of large companies and uncertainty in SMEs' interests in disclosing the IA report spurred us to think about what is behind that. What are the barriers that prevent the reporting of IAbM by the business community? Much research has been done on the role of IC reporting in the interaction between firms and fund managers (Johanson et al. 2009; Holland and Johanson 2003). But fewer efforts have been made to analyze the difficulties and challenges faced by preparers of IA reporting that may tell us why IC reporting still stays at low levels.

Furthermore, the clear difference in the reporting format between large companies and SMEs reflects a natural selection of companies with different scales and complexities. How to disclose IA information in an IA report or in other forms of reports is also a highly relevant problem for these companies. The reporting model is always evolving, especially the new global trend of integrated reporting, which is strategy focus and takes into account that IC has attracted a lot of attention from leading companies all over the world. Whether these new models solve the challenges or problems faced by large companies as well as SMEs needs to be discussed.

3.   THE NEW MODEL

For large public companies, because the format of the securities report is fixed, there is less flexibility for them to organize information according to the idea of knowledge management. That may be one of the reasons why the disclosure in the securities report tends to be boilerplate. Because the annual report is more flexible and voluntarily disclosed, it can be creative and incorporate anything that companies think critical and relevant for users' assessment or decision making. However, not all companies have annual reports. What the annual report should be depends on the idea of the companies that design them.

Since 2009, a new reporting instrument, integrated reporting, was proposed and promoted by IIRC, an organization that oversees the creation of a globally accepted international integrated reporting framework. The integrated report is supposed to be adaptable to all kind of companies, large, medium or small, listed or unlisted, revealing their value creation over time and related communications regarding aspects of value creation. The governance, risk management, innovation, sustainability, CSR and other perspectives of the company are connected. Various capitals, financial, intellectual, human, social and relational capital and other nonfinancial capitals, are regarded as both input and output of the value-creation process and should be incorporated in the reporting. From this point of view, the integrated report seems to be a carrier of IA information. To discuss the possibility and way of reporting IA in the integrated report, several points should be carefully investigated.

Holistic Approach or More Focused Report

First, IIRC announced that the integrated report should target a variety of users, with investors given the highest priority. In its framework, it declared:

> The primary purpose of an integrated report is to explain to providers of financial capital how an organization creates value over time. An integrated report benefits all stakeholders interested in an organization's ability to create value over time, including employees, customers, suppliers, business partners, local communities, legislators, regulators and policy-makers. (IIRC 2013)

However, Japanese public companies and nonpublic companies differ in the purposes of reporting IA. For nonpublic companies, customers, employees and other stakeholders are not inferior to financial capital providers. For example, for customers, the technological advances or the know-how of the skilled staff or on-time production system increase their confidence in the product and services they receive. For employees, being aware of how important a role they play in the value-creation process and how they grow within the organization may help them to be prouder of their job and increase job satisfaction. So instead of value creation per se, the process and attribute of IAs fills users' information needs. Because nonpublic companies do not have the obligation to reveal everything, they often choose to disclose information for particular users instead of to general public for particular purposes.

Although theoretically, an integrated report can also provide useful information to stakeholders other than the financial capital providers, for nonpublic companies and small and medium-sized companies in particular, a more focused report seems more reasonable from both the perspective of the targeted user and cost consideration. To know how Japanese companies disclose IAbM information, the author did some content analysis of all the reports disclosed on the web site of the Intellectual Assets-based Management Holder of METI.[3] According to the analysis result, the average length of the disclosed IAbM report is only twenty-three pages. In contrast, a holistic approach to reporting might be more suitable for public companies because they are required to disclose more information. An integrated report is more likely to fill in the information gap between companies and the public. On the other hand, if the IAbM report is just used for internal management purposes, a more holistic report may be more helpful to improve value creation and sustainability.

Inconsistent Definition of Value

The core of the IA theory is *value*. IA attracted the attention of academia, practitioners and policy makers because of the increasingly important role of IA in value creation. IA is regarded as value drivers, corporate performance drivers and companies' core abilities that need to be strategically managed (Bose and Oh 2004; Edvinsson 1997). IA or IAbM reporting are justified based on the logic that the disclosure of such information helps financial capital providers understand how value is created. Here, the value is obviously the one defined in the finance theory and connected with future cash flow.

However, the value concept in the integrated report is broader to include value to itself and value to others, which refers to stakeholders and society at large. Although the two aspects of value are interrelated, the latter is less connected with financial return in the short run. In the long run, the *value to others* is also expected to be turned into value to itself. People may argue that the value in IAbM reporting also contains a long-term point of view. So, they are not essentially different from the IIRC definition. However, there is a lack of research on the link between the companies' social value and financial value. Moreover, from a reporting perspective, the difference in the core concept may lead to a different reporting structure and model. The financial result-focused *value* is a clear objective in IA reporting, whereas the broader *value* seems to lack focus and a clear destination. IIRC describes that "value created by an organization over time manifests itself in increases, decreases or transformations of the capitals caused by the organization's business activities and outputs" (IIRC 2013, P11). On the other hand, it described capital "as stock of value that are increased, decreased or transformed through the activities and outputs of the organization" (ibid., P12). These descriptions are confusing. To design the IA report, a more careful definition of value needs to be taken into account.

Inconsistent Understanding of the Integrated Report

According to the author's interview with one of the pilot companies,[4] the manager said that in his opinion, the integrated report is not one report, but a summary of all the other reports. It shows the connection of different perspectives of the company and gives the user an overall picture about what kind of company it is. This may represent a few companies' opinion. By analyzing the reports declared by Japanese companies to be integrated reports, we found that the length of report varied from 222 pages to 21 pages. The integrated report was either a usual annual report, which is often over one hundred pages, or a summary of a business report, which may be quite short with only dozens of pages. In cases where the integrated report is treated as just a summary, then a more detailed report on IAbM is needed for users who want this. If an integrated report is a complete report full of details, then how IA is incorporated is the greatest challenge.

Currently, some companies disclose human resources information in the CSR report, whereas others put this information in the innovation section of the annual report. Some disperse information in different sections of the annual report with no focus and no strategic connection of different components, whereas others have a clear propensity for R&D disclosure or a technology focus. From a resource- and strategy-based view of organization, strategically managed IA and reporting IA information contribute to corporate value creation, and these two aspects are interrelated (Ricceri 2008). In this sense, the IA report is based on a systematic view that reveals the interaction of different components of IA, and the dynamic value-creation process is helpful for companies to learn about its own sustainability and for outsiders to evaluate the company.

The ambition of the IIRC is to make the integrated report the corporate reporting norm and for integrated thinking to be embedded within mainstream business practices in the public and nonpublic sectors (IIRC 2013). If this occurs, the diffusion of integrated thinking and reporting is anticipated to increase IA disclosure because it clearly incorporates IC in the framework. However, as shown, broadening the scope of reporting doesn't seem to reduce the challenges of packaging complex realities into neat models, but rather multiplies it.

4. THE QUALITY OF THE IC REPORT

As a communication tool, how effective the IAbM report conveys information and how useful the information is to users are essential issues. Yet, in the Japanese guidelines, there is no such section prescribing the quality criteria to guide the reporting. Some researchers think that quality is a proxy of quantity. Many empirical researchers, especially those adopting content analysis, usually examine the IA disclosure using quantity as the proxy. However, many other researchers think quantity is not a satisfactory proxy. The quality of the reports depends on several factors, including both the quantity and the quality of the information, for example, the richness of information (Beretta and Bozzolan 2004). How do we decide what kind of quality the report should have? First of all, the quality of the IA report should be assessed from the users' point of view. In order to explore the desirable characteristics of IAbM information, METI conducted a survey of analysts and fund managers. Twelve characteristics were listed for the respondents to choose from. There is variety in the choices for different types of assessors (the sell-side or buy-side analysts, institutional investors, venture capital fund manager or rating institution's analysts). The following four characteristics—association with corporate value, creditability, easy to understand and comparability—are considered most desirable.

1. Link with corporate value. As discussed in earlier sections, the causal link between IAbM information and future corporate performance and value is a great concern for most information users. "The improvement of business value, in particular, how it links with performance and how much effect it has, should be specified" (METI 2007, P29). Value relevance is considered the most desirable characteristic of information.
2. Easy to understand. Understandability is the second most critical characteristic required by information assessors. Many analysts believe that it is hard to incorporate IAbM information in the assessment of corporate value because this information is technical and abstract. Thus, the IAbM information should be described by avoiding terms that are too technical and too abstract. A survey result reveals that getting the image of the report even with a practical manual is one of the greatest difficulties in preparing the reports (METI Kansai Bureau 2010). Even in SMEs' IAbM reports, attempts to show the interaction between different IA as well links between IA and sales or profits often

result in complex figures. Within the figures, dozens of lines with different colors make it very difficult to understand. It is a challenge for users to figure out what really counts.
3. Comparability. Information users not only want to view the absolute value of a corporation, but also its relative position. That is why they want IAbM information to be comparable with financial information. Some respondents said "it is desirable that the disclosure format is stylized to a certain degree so that the comparison within the industry becomes possible" or "it is desirable to enable the comparison" (METI 2007, P30).
4. Credibility. Credibility is a principle for any information disclosure. According to METI's survey, there were opinions that the "forecast of a corporation and its actual condition differ widely in many cases" and "[it is desirable that] the credibility of information is objectively assured by third party assessment and the authority and actual record of the assessment of such third party assessment institutions are clearly indicated with other corporations in the same business category" (METI 2007, P31).

Then, here is the question: Are these four characteristics the right criteria for reporting? For example, the "link with corporate value" principle represents those who care about corporate value most. If the target readers of the report are customers or employees, the focus on value relevance from a finance theory perspective may not have the highest priority. Another example, the logic that "comparability" is a necessary attribute, seems to be that because users want them to be so. However, the necessity and possibility of comparability depend on how the information is used. If the users use it like financial information, then comparability is indispensable. But if the IAbM report is just used to form a whole picture of the company, to gain confidence instead of detailed calculations as revealed in some former research (Johanson et al. 2009), comparability might not be a necessity.

Unfortunately, no research has been done to justify these principles. The survey is no more than a pioneering attempt. The approach is not scientifically strict, nor is the survey sample large enough. Although stockholders are the most important users of large companies, for many SMEs and venture companies, customers, banks, employees or other related parties are more important targeted users. Furthermore, some qualities seem to be in conflict with each other. For example, from the perspective of information users, according to a survey concerning the desirable disclosure format of IAs, only 12.3 percent of respondents who are fund managers think that IA should be systematically disclosed in the business report, whereas 29.9 percent, the largest portion of respondents, prefer IA to be included in the financial statements. 25.3 percent respondents prefer a qualitative description, and 17.5 percent prefer quantitative information to be disclosed in the securities report. The other 19.6 percent would rather quantitative IA information be disclosed in the note of financial statements (Yao 2010). Information in the financial statements is considered more understandable and credible than nonfinancial information in other reporting media. However, there is a lack of an agreed-upon method to measure IA that prevents recognizing these assets in the financial statements. Moreover, the connection of IA to value is complex, so making the report easy to understand and credible is a great challenge. Therefore, more research studies on other users' perspective of what good quality is are desirable.

The conceptual framework of the International Accounting Standards Board (IASB) and the Financial Accounting Standards Board (FASB) seems to be a good example that regards investors as the main information user, yet taking into consideration other users' needs and requirements. It provides guidance regarding generally accepted notions of information quality that the financial statement preparers can refer to (IASB 2010). Because the IAbM report is a kind of business report that contains mainly nonfinancial information, this framework may not provide a sufficient foundation to assess information quality. However, the process of creating and updating the framework gives us many hints when considering quality criteria for nonfinancial information.

More recently, IIRC has released a new version of the framework providing guiding principles to "underpin the preparation and presentation of an integrated report, informing the content of the report and how information is presented" (IIRC 2013, P17). The seven principles are as follows: (1) strategic focus and future orientation, (2) connectivity of information, (3) stakeholder relationships, (4) materiality, (5) conciseness, (6) reliability and completeness, and (7) consistency and comparability. The first and third principles ensure that the information is relevant to users. The other principles highlight IIRC's considerations about how to keep the quality of reports at a high level. The IASB's and IIRC's guidelines, especially the former, are all based on vast theoretical and/or empirical studies, as well as numerous investigations to justify and test the logic of these principles. The same efforts should be made to improve the criteria or principle setting for the IAbM report. Hence, although IC and its related reporting frameworks have come of age, we still seem to be in the beginning of its progress and we still have questions on the most fundamental levels as to the very criteria for quality, progress and success. In other words, there is time to reflect upon the ideas and norms behind reporting and how they may interact with the development of reporting practices.

5.   WHAT CAN BE LEARNED FROM JAPAN?

The account of the Japanese experience with IC reporting is hardly a traditional success story. Nevertheless, throughout the last decade, Japan has shown to be one of the most eager promoters of IC development and is still making considerable efforts both in terms of policy development and research on IC issues. From a Western view, this would certainly look like a failure and whoever financed its development would likely consider its abandonment. From the promoters' perspective, the strategy to develop and implement IC reporting seems not so successful. Without doubt, in the Western world, the initial enthusiasm about IC and the knowledge economy rapidly turned into doubts and disappointments as the new economy didn't meet its high expectations. However, this is not a neutral or self-evident perspective of the development of IC reporting. What can be learned from Japan is perhaps not only the concrete experience of trying to implement IC reporting, but to an even greater extent, the more fundamental questioning of our attitude to IC, reporting and strategy in itself.

There is no doubt that the Japanese government, policymakers, intermediaries, companies and researchers still struggle to get IC reporting right, and are trying to reconcile the demand for neat reporting models with the complex realities in the processes of value creation. However, what has become clearer during this journey is that the Japanese business context refers to another practice and different fundamental perspectives, not only to reporting itself, but also to its underpinning in the very views of what strategy is about. Hence, it is not self-evident that strategy in terms of elaborate planning and business models in terms of static arrangements for value creation is the answer to the question of how to design reports that can really make sense of IC and its deepest character. As an alternative to Western strategy rationality, the Japanese context and experience point to the possibility of a more fundamental resource rationality that implies an understanding of IC as something more and something in its own right that goes beyond the structured plans and static models in Western strategic thinking.

There is not enough evidence to suggest that this is the very reason behind the challenges in the somewhat disappointing present trends in Japanese IC reporting. Although some progress is being made, there are also fluctuation, backlashes and reluctance on the part of companies to continually track their IC to renew their strategic resources. The exact reasons for these trends are matters for further research, but factors that probably play some role may be the interest to keep internal secrets in the company, a lack of interest to solve problems of information asymmetry and specific factors for large public companies, nonpublic companies and small- and medium-sized companies.

It doesn't seem likely that the present development of integrated reporting will be able to do much about this in terms of the technical side of merging data into one single model. As shown, holistic ambitions may serve some companies better than others, and especially when considering the resources, abilities and interests of small and medium-sized companies, focused reports still seem more likely. Furthermore, the broadened scope of integrated reporting will hardly lessen the challenges of reconciling different stakeholders' interests and views on fundamental notions of value and what an integrated report should be. However, by creating a broader movement, integrated reporting may have a better chance to push reporting practices forward.

Then, the big remaining question is where IC and its related reporting practices should go. A tempting idea is a report that links IC to corporate value, is credible, is easy to understand and allows for comparability. However, who knows how and when it could be obtained, how much effort it would take, and whether the answer lies in the analytical perfection of reporting technique or in the gradual evolution of reporting practices and expectations into something that is both useful and feasible. As mentioned, the Western approach to IA reporting seems to sit ill with the Japanese resource rationality, and there may be other things to be learned from the Japanese experience than would be expected from a Western perspective, notably that strategy isn't necessarily about exactly where you are going, but rather, about what resources are needed to move your ambitions forward in whatever direction seems desirable when you know more about future possibilities. Hence, such a genuine resource-based view on strategy would rather embrace than curse the uncertainties involved in the development of IC reporting, as in any human endeavor.

Based on its experience, Japanese companies should perhaps be more prone to adopt IA reporting. However, this may also become a cause of companies' ignorance of the importance of IA reporting. Because Japanese companies take IA management for granted, it is difficult for them to realize the management of IA. It is hard for them to realize that behind everyday operation there is some logic behind which they can find their real strength and competitive advantages. That is why some companies that disclosed an IA report said that by preparing the IA report, they gained a new understanding of their core ability. The IA report, rather than being a pure communication tool, plays an important role in helping companies revalue their intellectual resources. On the other hand, the third wave of knowledge management specified by Ricceri (2008), in the authors' opinion, is more like a combination of the Western and Japanese style that incorporates stakeholder, technology, competition analysis and internal resource analysis. It not only includes strategy formulation, but also strategy execution. Some successful companies like Toyota show a good example of strategization combining external considerations (comparative value achieved by competitive advantage) and internal considerations (absolute value achieved by utilization of internal intellectual resources). But for most companies that keep a strong future formed in the historical and cultural context, it is a good start to analyze their management style before preparing the report.

The scorecard approach does simplify the way we understand each component of IA, but not the complicated mechanism of value creation. The majority of models do not address the important issue of IA dynamics. They are too neat or simplified to provide guidance on how to identify and visualize them. We cannot blame the simplicity of models, because this is how they simplify complex phenomena and clarify the most essential part to save us from complete ignorance or from becoming completely lost before these phenomena. However, the lack of connectivity between different components hinders our further understanding of the interaction of IA components. The simplicity of the static model may have caused difficulties for companies in preparing IA reports. In particular, when a company has many business segments and a complex structure, the inability of the simplified reporting model to demonstrate the value-creation process of IA becomes more obvious.

Nonaka and Takeuchi (1995) explained the Japanese view on knowledge as a dynamic process of justifying a personal belief toward the truth. In similar vein, from a Japanese perspective, a reporting model is not necessarily a solution waiting to be implemented, but rather a prototype for thinking in the process of realizing of a sometimes unclear but convincing potential. This view is typically hard for a Western mind to embrace. An even more fundamental challenge to the future development of IC management and reporting lies perhaps in the Japanese idea of a resource-based view and its most fundamental consequences—namely, that we may not be able to reduce uncertainty by establishing strategy as a plan where no predictability is to be found, and that we may not be able to reduce the complexity of real-world value creation by proclaiming an abstract idea of a generic business model. In a world where uncertainty and variance should be embraced and exploited rather than only eliminated or wished away, management may rather be a matter of growing competences than instructing people what to do. It is noteworthy that when Toyota originally was talking about "respect for people" (Sugimori et al. 1977 p. 557), it wasn't only about having a happy working life, but rather about the respect for the human capacity for adaptation and development, which in turn allows for more distributed systems of intelligence.

NOTES

1. http://www.kansai.meti.go.jp/2giki/network/vbnet_ic.html (accessed March 20, 2014).
2. For example, the survey by Keizai Doyukai (2011) Yao (2010).
3. There are 272 reports available from METI Intellectual Asset-Based Management Holder. http://www.jiam.or.jp/CCP013.html (accessed March 25, 2014).
4. The IIRC has initiated a pilot program to promote integrated reporting. Over one hundred companies from around the world have joined the program. The company the author interviewed is the one that joined the program.

REFERENCES

Beretta, S. and Bozzolan, S. 2004. "A framework for the analysis of firm risk communication". *The International Journal of Accounting*, 39 (3), 265–288.
Black Sun. 2012. "The business model—the missing link for twenty-first century companies?". http://www.blacksunplc.com/corporate/pdf/the_business_model_the_missing_link_for_twenty_first_century_companies.pdf (accessed March 20, 2014).

Bose, S., and Oh, K.B. 2004. "Measuring strategic value-drivers for managing intellectual capital". *The Learning Organization*, 11 (4/5), 347–356.

Brooking, A. 1996. *Intellectual Capital: Core Asset for the Third Millenium*. London: Thomson Business Press.

Brßggen, A., Vergauwen, P. and Dao, M. 2009. "Determinants of intellectual capital disclosure: Evidence from Australia". *Management Decision*, 47, 233–245.

Chaminade, C. and Catasús, B. 2007. *Intellectual Capital Revisited—Paradoxes in the Knowledge Intensive Organization*. Northampton, MA: Edward Elgar.

DMST. 2003. *Intellectual Capital Statements: The New Guideline*. Danish Ministry of Science, Technology and Innovation.

Dumay, J.C. 2012. "Grand theories as barriers to using IC concepts". *Journal of Intellectual Capital*, 13 (10, 4–15.

Eden, C. and Ackermann, F. 2000. "Mapping distinctive competencies: A systemic approach". *Journal of the Operational Research Society*, 51, 12–20.

Edvinsson, L. 1997. "Developing intellectual capital at Skandia". *Long Range Planning*, 30 (3), 366–373.

Edvinsson, L. and Malone, M. 1997. *Intellectual Capital: Realizing Your Company's True Value by Finding Its Hidden Brainpower*. New York: Harper Collins.

George, G. and Bock, A.J. 2011. "The business model in practice and its implications for entrepreneurship research". *Enterpreneurship Theory and Practice*, 35 (1), 83–111.

Gröjer, J-E. 2001. "Intangibles and accounting classifications: In search of a classification strategy". *Accounting, Organizations and Society*, 26, 695–713.

Holland, J. and Johanson, U. 2003. "Value-relevant information on corporate intangibles-creation, use, and barriers in capital markets: Between a rock and a hard place". *Journal of Intellectual Capital*, 4 (4), 465–486.

IASB. 2010. *Conceptual Framework for Financial Reporting 2010*, International Accounting Standards Board.

IIRC. 2013. *The International IR Framework*. The International Integrated Reporting Council.

Itami, H. and Roehl, T.W. 1987. *Mobilizing Invisible Assets*. Harvard University Press.

Jeny, A. and Stolowy, H. 2000. "Classification of intangibles". *HEC Accounting & Management Control Working Paper No. 708/2000*.

Johanson, U., Koga, C., Almqvist, R. and Skoog, M. 2009. "'Breaking Taboos': Implementing intellectual assets-based management guidelines". *Journal of Intellectual Capital*, 10 (4), 520–538.

Keizai Doyukai. 2011. "CSR in the age of globalization" (in Japanese). http://www.doyukai.or.jp/policyproposals/articles/2010/pdf/110404a_02.pdf (accessed March 20, 2014).

Kyoto Prefecture. 2008. "Practical guidance on Chie management report" (in Japanese). http://www.pref.kyoto.jp/sangyo-sien/documents/1227854577732.pdf (accessed March 20, 2014).

Kyoto Prefecture. 2008. *Guidebook for Chie Management Report*.

Markides, C.C. 2008. *Game-Changing Strategies: How to Create New Market Space in Established Industries by Breaking the Rules*. New York: Jossey-Bass.

MERITUM. 2002. *Guidelines for Managing and Reporting on Intangibles*, Madrid Fundacion Airtel Movil.

METI. 2007. *Perspective of Intellectual Assets-Based Management Reports and Empirical Analysis and Research of Disclosure—Disclosure of "Strength" and Dialogue with Stakeholders*.

METI Kansai Bureau. 2010. *Research on the Evaluation and Certification Method of Intellectual Asset Management Report* (in Japanese).

Mouritsen, J. 2006. "Problematising intellectual capital research: Ostensive versus performative IC". *Accounting, Auditing & Accountability Journal,* 19 (6), 820–840.

Nonaka, I. and Katsumi, A. 2004. *The Essence of Innovation* (in Japanese). Nikkei BP.

Nonaka, I. and Takeuchi, H. 1995. *The Knowledge-Creating Company: How Japanese Companies Create the Dynamics of Innovation.* Oxford University Press.

Ricceri, F. 2008. *Intellectual Capital and Knowledge Management: Strategic Management of Knowledge Resources.* Routledge Advances in Management and Business Studies: Routledge.

Roos, J. 1998. *Intellectual Capital: Navigating in the New Business Landscape.* New York: New York University Press.

Skandia. 1994. *Visualizing Intellectual Capital in Skandia, Supplement to Skandia's 1994 Annual Report.*

Stewart, T.A. 1998. *Intellectual Capital: The New Wealth of Organization.* Crown Business.

Sugimorl, Y., Kusunokl, K., Cho, F. and Uchikawa, S. 1977. "Toyota production system and kanban system materialization of just-in-time and respect-for-human system". *International Journal of Production Research,* 15, 553–564.

Sveiby, K.E. 2014. "Methods for measuring intangible assets". 2010. http://www.sveiby.com/articles/IntangibleMethods.htm (accessed March 20, 2014).

Sveiby, K.E. 1997. *The New Organizational Wealth: Managing and Measuring Knowledge-Based Assets.* Berret-Koehler Publishers.

Uchida, Y. and Roos, G. 2008. *Intellectual Capital Management for Japanese Firms* (in Japanese). Chuokeizai-sha, Inc.

Yao, J. 2010. "Investment risk and relevance of intellectual capital information" (in Japanese). *Journal of Accountancy,* 178 (4), 71–81.

15 Trends and Challenges for Intellectual Capital

Eunika Mercier-Laurent

1. INTRODUCTION

According to Youriev (2014), the roots of intellectual capital go far back in history. In the twentieth century, the term human capital was reintroduced by economist Theodore Schultz (1961). He considers the investment in human capital crucial for the economic development and that education is a key contributing factor. Later, human capital evolved to "intellectual capital" in an aim to cover larger field including patents and documents. The Organization for Economic Cooperation and Development (OECD) has been involved in defining a general methodology for measuring intangible investment since 1989 (OECD 1996).

Globalization changed the game of economic development. Intellectual capital has become an important asset, and its assessment and management have become priorities for the knowledge economy. For over a decade, intellectual capital has been a hot topic of conversations, conferences, magazines, scientific journals, books and reports around the world. However, companies and organizations are still measuring their success in terms of financial capital and return on investment (ROI).

This chapter presents key references related to the evolution of human capital, gives some elements of economic and environmental context and mentions current efforts in measuring intellectual capital. It is followed by a presentation of a method and tools to manage this wealth differently and to stimulate a reflection on the role of this capital in the knowledge economy and in innovation ecosystems, including education and training in real time and its use as a means of creating shared wealth.

2. SOME SELECTED ELEMENTS OF THE STATE OF THE ART

The issue of intellectual capital is complex. It involves various fields such as management, psychology, economy, sociology, health, intellectual property rights and recently, sustainable development. Intellectual capital forms the basis of the successful development of companies and countries. Such a development requires the right way to manage intangible wealth in connection with tangible wealth.

Numerous publications provide a multidisciplinary view of the subject. According to Theodore Schultz (1961), Nobel awarded economist education is most important in the managing of human capital. Economist Gary Becker (1964) considers education, training and health to be the major investments in human capital.

Edvinsson (1997) points out the role of intellectual capital in the modern economy, and the OECD (2001) points out the role of human capital in the well-being of nations.

According to Dixon (2010), training, capacity building and learning are key enabling factors for sustainability, which is seen as the long-term ability of individuals and organizations to produce innovation as a reaction and adaptation to changes in external conditions. It is the link between opportunities, projects, addressing the real needs and building capacity or empowerment that ensures useful learning, innovation and an economically efficient process. Training supports the development of all phases of the project life cycle (situation analysis, forecasting, planning, implementation and evaluation/measurement of impacts). Trained persons develop skills and produce methods, information and knowledge required for the success of the project. Training, combined with the development and implementation of projects on the local level, allows (1) increasing and mobilizing human and social capital, (2) developing new activities and (3) creating interactions leading to collective dynamics and to the invention of new rules and standards (institutional capital) needed to integrate new activities in the formal economy.

Folke et al. (2003) propose to develop an "adaptive capacity". The concept has been used in biology and in the context of climate change, but can be applied to a much broader range of issues. Adaptive capacity developed in poor countries is extremely important to be successful in the twenty-first century. Persons able to adapt and to solve problems using individual and collective knowledge, as well as solutions from the past that work for the current challenge, are able to survive and even lead in global dynamics (Mercier-Laurent 2011). The viability theory of Aubin (1991) may be useful to control the balance of the ecosystems, based on human capital as the engine. It offers a framework to conceive, and control, dynamical models of all kinds, including social phenomena. In this theory, systems that, stated in general terms, undergo a Darwinian evolutionary, self-transforming process must at the same time maintain themselves, that is, keep complying with viability constraints (we want that for such systems that we value and want to stay into existence). Yet, critical to the ability of an entity to maintain itself is the number of available paths of transition at a given stage.

According to Savage (1990), the fifth generation of managerial methods has to consider knowledge as an asset. This statement has been enhanced by

Amidon (1997). *To know* is the opposite of the *to have* attitude cultivated in the world today and focuses exclusively on quick business. From an education point of view, the most important thing is to learn how and what to learn.

These few references cover a large spectrum of human and intellectual capital themselves and the roles they play in economic development and the well-being of nations.

3.   ECONOMIC AND ENVIRONMENTAL CONTEXT

The current economic situation in developed countries and intensive industrialization in Asia generate new problems and needs—among them, the industrial decline and unemployment in developed countries, exodus from regions to towns and the urgent need to protect the planet. China has become the world's factory because it provides the cheapest work. Goods travel all around the globe, generating pollution. Asian people are also studying abroad to increase their intellèctual capital and sometimes bring it back to their respective countries.

In Europe, the emphasis is on education, and innovation is seen as a magic wand to renew industry. Despite the recommendations of the Lisbon Treaty, the impact of education and innovation is still not measured in terms of job creation and economic development of the regions and countries.

The intensive industrialization at the beginning of the twentieth century did not taken into account the impact of these activities on the planet (Lenkowa 1969; Eckholm 1976). The recent alerts point out the extreme emergency (Arthus-Bertrand 2009). The sustainable development and corporate social responsibility movements focus on the use of local resources. Although companies are concerned about carbon and recently about their water footprint, they are less concerned with raw materials and do not seem concerned with biodiversity. In reality, they still do not manage the human capital; the local skills and know-how are not taken into consideration because of the lack of a holistic approach. Consequently, skilled people are traveling is the consequence of ignorance and not managing the local competency. Despite a ubiquitous information and communication technology, these movements remain significant and are increasing.

Appropriate management of human capital and education of knowledge cultivators will certainly bring about a contribution to the protection of the planet's ecosystem. This challenge is among the most important of the twenty-first century. It is vital to understand, know and manage intellectual capital in connection with other tangible and intangible assets of companies and other organizations, of cities, regions and countries using a combination of holistic and system approaches (Mercier-Laurent 2011).

4.   KNOW AND MANAGE HUMAN CAPITAL

Although some thinkers state that human capital is the most important asset, only a few are measuring and managing it. A person does not go into a store if they do not know how much money they can spend, but companies and policymakers seems to ignore the fact that in order to avoid going bankrupt. We need to manage human capital in the function of the vision for the future and associated strategy. Companies and politics should know the "amount" of human capital they have to plan the future development in connection with their vision and strategy.

The most important barrier to managing intellectual capital is ignorance. Another one is a way of thinking. It is not uncommon for a person with a high position in a company to be afraid of hiring a specialist that is more skilled than they are. A multifaceted perspective of skills will certainly facilitate the decision of the most suitable person to hire.

There is a plethora of databases, even big data, that are still built using traditional information processing methods, with a very limited number of codes for professions,[1] taking into account only traditional ones. Pole d'Emploi (National Center for Employment) and other public initiatives in France are supposed to help people find jobs, but their efficiency is very low, because they are not using the right methods and tools.

With the quick progress of technology and artificial intelligence, computers are able to process natural languages instead of codes. This open programming approach allows the inclusion in real time of new professions that appear every day.

There are several valuable reports about intellectual capital containing key information and complex charts, both electronic and paper based. They are very useful to know the current status, but they are static.

For someone looking for local know-how, it is not easy to find quickly the right person. Some social networks, such as Viadeo in France or LinkedIn, are trying to connect talents and those who are looking for them. Google is certainly among the most efficient search engines, but its business model introduces an important "noise" (and intellectual pollution) due to the advertisement system management.

Know What We Have

The concept of "knowledge trees" was introduced by Autier and Levy (1992) and implemented in tools such as Ginko (Trivium) and Selva (Ligamen), offering graphic representations of individual and collective skills as a tree.

Figure 15.1 illustrates the skills of eleven people: the trunk represents common knowledge, branches the specialties and the leaves the unique skills. Such an image provides information on everyone's ability and helps to decide if the unique skills represented by the leaves are strategic.

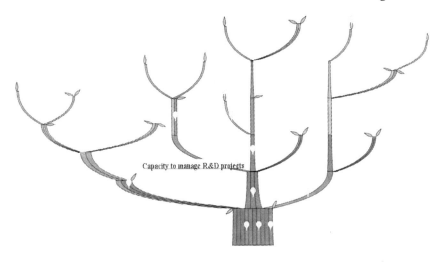

Figure 15.1   Example of a knowledge tree created using the Ligamen software
Source: http://www.ligamen.fr

The far right of the trunk, as well as the triple branch, indicate the position of a person in a group. Such visualization facilitates the identification of skills and helps to detect a lack in relation to a required profile, which can be filled by training. Thus, we can build the competency tree of a company or a region and reason backwards: What projects can we achieve with such intellectual capital? We then need to search for the skills in a neighboring region or "rent" them from a partner.

In the international context, and within a networked enterprise, it would be better to manage skills on the regional, national and international levels. This intangible wealth can grow through continual learning by interacting with the environment, according to corporate strategy.

Managing skills is a complex problem, requiring foremost a good reflection of the way to describe and display these skills in relation to a clearly defined strategy. Some questions to consider:

- Who is better able to define their skills than the people themselves, on the condition that they do not under- or overestimate their abilities?
- What are the essential skills for companies, both now and in the future?
- What role can the skills play in the organizational strategy?

The training department is also involved, because it is in charge of making this capital grow. It is involved for now, because in the global knowledge management approach, all knowledge cultivators are constantly learning. The training department could be a guardian for the transmission and preservation of the essential knowledge and know-how of those retiring, especially when this is the knowledge of a long life and is a strategic product for the company (Ermine 2009). Collaboration between several professionals is vital for optimized managing of the skills.

Find the Right Profile

When we know what we have and what we are looking for, an artificial intelligence technique—case-based reasoning (Kolodner 1993)—could be very helpful. The built-in analogy engine works by matching demand (I am looking for) and offer (base of existing skills and know-how) to find instantaneously the profile we want, if such a profile is registered. If not, a set of similar profiles that could be adapted to the expected ones by training is proposed to the user. We can imagine a world knowledge base including a talent bank equipped with such an engine.

The various methods of measuring the value of human capital of a company, city, region or country provide the information on what we have. But it is certainly useful to know what can be done with this information for future development, what new activities and companies may be created. This purpose is illustrated in Figure 15.2.

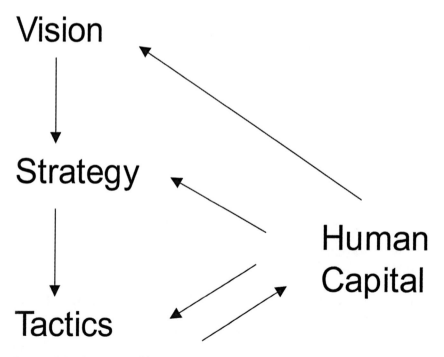

Figure 15.2   Dynamics of human capital

Companies, cities and regions need to elaborate a clear vision for the future. At this point, the skilled persons able to envision it are needed. This vision will be "translated" into corporate strategy and tactics (actions to achieve the strategic goals). The growing intellectual capital of professionals working on accomplishing various tasks and the new knowledge and capacity should be taken into account at a strategic level. It may also influence the vision.

5. WHAT ARE THE CAPACITIES FOR THE FUTURE?

Today, the educational system produces the traditional professionals. Many of them face difficulty in finding a job in their region or country. The most audacious travel for a job and change their country, language and continent. They have to adapt to new conditions and to a new culture.

As mentioned before, our future depends on our capacity to adapt, to detect opportunities and to gather necessary skills and knowledge and to transform them into economic values in balance with ecosystems. It also depends on the rapidity of our decision making, on our risk-taking ability in a dynamic environment and on our ability to use the computer, regardless of its form, as an intelligent assistant. The latter facilitates innovation without boundaries between fields (out-of-the-box thinking).

Facing the affluence of information and solicitations, a new skill is required—innovation know-how. This is the art of finding and exploiting strategic information and of gathering momentum and developing the knowledge and skills essential to the success of this enterprise, which is innovation in its entirety.

These skills are numerous—from the management of ideas and people to the implementation and commercialization of products or services. Existing training courses prepare specialists of atomic components for this process; very few of them consider innovation as an ecosystem.

Although Europe has a long tradition of innovation since the industrial era, globalization has changed the odds. Factors such as the slowing down or the obsolescence of some sectors and the emergence of others, as well as the relocation of activities, influence active knowledge and skills. The lack of interest in scientific studies expressed by youths will lead to a shortage of engineers. Some skills are disappearing with retirements, which are sometimes accelerated by the economic crisis. Knowledge capitalization approaches are saving part of the strategic and "sensible" skills, but these initiatives are quite rare and are often initialized too late. The European document "Putting Knowledge into Practice" (European Commission 2006) specifies that the lack of skills, notably in the fields of sciences, engineering and information-communication technology (ICT), is a challenge for European education. Another publication, "Innovate for a Competitive Europe" (European Commission 2004) advises companies to learn how to transform the absorbed knowledge into action. Such an innovation dynamics combines the knowledge and skills in value creation. Kolding et al. (2009) describe the skills we need to acquire to face the post-crisis era in Europe. The authors are convinced that the ICT skills are the most important, but they did not mention what approach to ICT and to computer programming should be used.

Some skills for today and that will be useful for the near future are presented in Table 15.1. This table illustrates also the leap necessary for the educational system. Companies' training departments need to focus on transforming today's capacities, which are good for an industrial economy, to those that are essential for a knowledge economy. The progress from left to right in this table can be measured using, for example, the trees of knowledge software or any other that may help.

Table 15.1 Contrasts in managerial roles

Industrial Economy		Knowledge Economy
Functional title	**Focus on**	**New role**
Enterprise Manager	Planning, organizing, staffing, leading or directing, and controlling an organization (a group of people or entities) or effort for the purpose of accomplishing a goal.	Leader, visionary and strategist, Focus on dynamic governance, sustainable success manager, stakeholders, strategic alliances
R&D	Managing research and development projects	Manager of the e-co-innovation dynamics
Human Resources Manager	Managing human resources, training and lay-off	Talent miner and optimizer, Manager of the Intellectual Capital
Marketing Manager	Market study and customer relation	Opportunity hunter Risk taker
Communication Manager	image	Image, Links maker
Corporate Social Responsibility Manager	Image, environmental impact, recycling, CO_2 emission	e-co-innovation, minimizing the impact and packaging, nature inspired design
Project Manager	Managing tasks and people, reporting	Facilitator of the collective intelligence and creativity able to motivate and valuate

(Continued)

Table 15.1   (Continued)

Industrial Economy		Knowledge Economy
Functional title	Focus on	New role
Practitioner of the *faster*, *cheaper*, *better*	Manager of delocalization, cheaper workers finder	Practitioner of the e-co-innovation culture
Financial	Estimation of ROI (return on investment)	Measuring the capacity to innovate and the of tangible and intangible benefits and values
Computer user	Planning, reporting, scoring	Master of ICT (intelligent and creative technology), able to take the best of technology

Source: Mercier-Laurent E. 2011. *Innovation Ecosystems*. New York: Wiley.

6.   IC IN THE FUTURE

To build a sustainable future, we need more than databases, reports and dashboards; we need a disruptive innovation in the way we build, evolve, maintain and manage human capital.

We need a new educational system, with the ambitious task of changing mentalities and values, to educate a culture of knowledge cultivators and to increase imagination and creativity. The main challenge of education is to teach how to learn, the curiosity, adaptability and capacity of solving problems with limited resources and to undertake and succeed collectively. This education is based on exchanges, on listening and respecting others' opinions—an education for all, to learn from nature, from the past and from differences, in which technology and means of communication have a significant role to play.

We need to use the power and "intelligence" of computers and other connected devices. When programmed using "knowledge thinking", they can bring significant help in storing, updating, displaying, matching and finding relevant elements of human capital.

We need to create synergy between educational programs and local needs, as well as a dynamic vision for the future.

New metrics could be boldness, imagination, associations (making links), the capacity to find and use the appropriate knowledge, mental flexibility, knowledge and ecosystem thinking, and the capacity to transform ideas into value and to envision the future. The estimation of (5 dimensions) 5D impacts of resulting activities—economic, technologic, cultural, social and environmental—could be added to measure the progress.

Such a wise management of intellectual capital, supported by electronic "intelligent" assistants and appropriate measure of progress, is essential for the development of companies, regions and countries.

NOTE

1. For example, all information services are coded 721Z.

REFERENCES

Amidon D.M. 1997. *The Innovation Strategy for the Knowledge Economy*. Boston: Butterworth.
Arthus-Bertrand Y. 2009. "Home". https://www.youtube.com/watch?v=jqxENMK aeCU
Aubin, J-P. 1991. *Viability Theory*. Boston: Birkhauser.
Autier M. and Lévy, P. 1992. *Les Arbres de Connaissances*. Paris: La Découverte.
Becker G.S. 1964. *Human Capital: A Theoretical and Empirical Analysis, with Special Reference to Education*. Chicago: University of Chicago Press.
Dixon P. and Gorecki, J. 2010. *Sustainagility. How Smart Innovation and Agile Companies will Help Protect Our Future*. London: Kogan Page Publishers.
Eckholm E.P. 1976. *Losing Ground. Environmental Stress and World Food Prospects*. New York: Norton.
Edvinsson L. and Malone, M.S. 1997. *Intellectual Capital: Realizing Your Company's True Value by Finding Its Hidden Roots*. New York: Harper Business.
Ermine J-L. 2008. *Mémoire de Projet et accès à L'information, Accélérer L'innovation par une Meilleure Capitalisation des Expériences Acquises*. Paris: ICC.
European Commission. 2004. *Innovate for a Competitive Europe. A New Action Plan for Innovation*. Brussels: European Commission.
European Commission, 2006. "Putting knowledge into practice: A broad-based innovation strategy for the EU" Communication from the Commission to the Council, the European Parliament, the European Economic and Social Committee and the Committee of the Regions of 13 September 2006.
Folke C., Hahn T., Olsson P. and Norberg J. 2003. "Building resilience and adaptive capacity in social-ecological systems". In Berkes F., Colding J. and Folke C. (Eds.), *Navigating Social-Ecological Systems*. Cambridge University Press, 352–387.
Kolding M., Ahorlu M. and Robinson C. 2009. *Post Crisis: E-Skills Are Needed to Drive. Europe's Innovation Society*. IDC White Paper.
Kolodner J. 1993. *Case-Based Reasoning*. Morgan Kaufman.
Lenkowa A.1969. *Oskalpowana ziemia*. Warsaw: Omega, Wiedza Powszechna.
Mercier-Laurent E. 2011. *Innovation Ecosystems*. New York: Wiley.
OECD. 1996. *Measuring What People Know. Human Capital Accounting for the Knowledge Economy*. Paris: OECD.
OECD. 2001. "The well-being of nations. The role of human and social capital, education and skills". http://www.oecd.org/site/worldforum/33703702.pdf
Savage C. 1990. *5th Generation Management: Integrating Enterprises through Human Networking*. Washington: Digital Press.
Schultz T. 1961. *Investment in Human Capital*. New York: W.W. Norton and Company, 1–17.
Youriev A.M. 2014. "History of human capital". http://www.yuriev.spb.ru/polit-chelovek/human-capital-resource.

Contributors

Abdifatah Ahmed Haji holds a master's of science in accounting from the International Islamic University, Malaysia. His research interests are in the areas of corporate disclosure and governance. He has published papers in peer-reviewed international academic journals such as *Journal of Intellectual Capital, Journal of Human Resource Costing & Accounting, International Journal of Disclosure and Governance, Humanomics, Asian Review of Accounting, Managerial Auditing Journal* and others.

André de Faria Pereira Neto has a master's of science in history from the Universite de Paris (Sorbonne Nouvelle) (1985), a doctorate in public health from the University of the State of Rio de Janeiro (OFRJ) (1997) and a postdoctoral fellow in health sociology from the University of California, San Francisco (2006). He is a researcher of the Casa de Oswaldo Cruz (Oswaldo Cruz Foundation—Fiocruz) and of the National School of Public Health, where he coordinates the "Internet Lab, Health and Society" (LAISS). He is a professor of the graduate program in information and communication in health offered by the Institute of Communication and Scientific and Technological Information in Health (ICICT) and Master on Business and Knowledge Management (MBKM) offered by UFRJ.

Antonio Lerro is a senior research fellow in management engineering at the University of Roma. He is also a lecturer in innovation management at University of Basilicata in Italy. His research interests focus around innovation and technology management and policies. Antonio received his degree in economics from the University "Tor Vergata" in Rome and his PhD in management engineering from the University of San Marino. He has been a visiting research fellow at the Cranfield School of Management, UK, and at the Centre for International Competitiveness of the University of Wales Institute Cardiff, UK. He is a regular speaker at national and international conferences and has authored or co-authored more than forty publications.

Chitoshi Koga is a distinguished visiting professor, PhD, Faculty of Commerce, Doshisha University and professor emeritus, Kobe University, Japan; president, Japan Intellectual Asset-based Management Association (present); and head and member of the board for a number of Japanese academic organizations. Among his research interests are intellectual capital management, measurement and reporting. He has various publications in several academic books and journals in English and Japanese, including several joint papers in the *Journal of Intellectual Capital*.

Erik Bjurström is an associate professor with a focus on management control at Hedmark University College, Norway, and innovation management at Mälardalen University, Sweden. He worked as a controller, analyst and consultant in several positions before entering into academic research, earning a PhD from Uppsala University in 2007. His research interests are broad and cover different but overlapping fields, such as intellectual capital and integrated reporting, especially in networks and different cultural contexts, business and intelligence (including methodology) in an ill-structured world, and control doctrines and alternative notions of control.

Eunika Mercier-Laurent is an associate researcher with Université Lyon. Among her research topics are knowledge and innovation management systems, artificial intelligence methods and techniques for innovation and complex problem solving. She teaches knowledge and innovation management at engineering schools and universities. Chair of the IFIP Knowledge Management Group, she organizes AI4KM conferences and serves as an expert for national and European research programs. Prof. Mercier-Laurent is president of Innovation3D, International Association for Global Innovation, among E100 experts of Entovation Intl. and a member of the New Club of Paris. She has authored over ninety publications. Her last book, *Innovation Ecosystems*, was published in 2011 by Wiley. More information can be found at http://innovation-ecosystems.eu.

Giovanni Schiuma is director of the Innovation Insights Hub at the University of the Arts, London. He is also a professor at Università della Basilicata (Italy). He has held visiting teaching and research appointments at the Cranfield School of Management, Graduate School of Management, St. Petersburg University (Russia), Cambridge Service Alliance— IfM University of Cambridge (UK), University of Kozminski (Poland), University of Bradford (UK) and Tampere University of Technology (Finland). Giovanni has authored or co-authored more than 150 publications, embracing intellectual capital management, performance measurement and management, and organizational development. He serves as editor-in-chief of the journal *Knowledge Management Research and Practice* and as co-editor-in-chief of the international journal *Measuring Business Excellence*.

Giustina Secundo, MSc, is an assistant professor in management engineering at the Department of Innovation Engineering of the University of Salento (Italy). Her research is characterized by a cross-disciplinary focus, with a major interest toward areas such as human capital creation, intellectual capital management in universities, management development and knowledge management in new product development. These research activities have been documented in about ninety publications, including book chapters, international journals and conference proceedings. Her research appeared in the *Journal of Intellectual Capital, Knowledge Management Research & Practices, International Journal of Innovation and Technology Management,* and the *Journal of Management Development.* She managed a research and education project focused on high-tech entrepreneurship and entrepreneurial engineering in collaboration with leading Italian aerospace companies and Dhitech (An Italian high-tech district). She has been a lecturer on innovation management and technological entrepreneurship at the Faculty of Engineering of the University of Salento since 2001. She's also a lecturer on knowledge management and innovation management in undergraduate programs and higher education programs (master's and doctorate).

Helena Tenório Veiga de Almeida is the head of the Brazilian Development Bank's (BNDES) Planning Area Department. She graduated from the Federal University of Rio de Janeiro with a master's degree in macroeconomics and an MBA in executive management. At BNDES, she was in charge of the implementation of the methodology for intangible assets evaluation and of the innovation policy.

Jessica Y.T. Yip graduated with a BSc. in logistics engineering and management (Hons.) from The Hong Kong Polytechnic University, and is pursuing her PhD studies at the same institute. She is an assistant officer of the Knowledge Management and Innovation Research Center and workshop tutor of the MSc. subject in organizational learning theory and practice. Jessica has accumulated five years of practical field experience in conducting knowledge management projects in different organizations, such as the Mass Transit Railway Corporation, Hong Kong China and Gas Corporate Limited, and Gold Peak Manufacturing Ltd. She was also appointed a facilitator for the Food and Agriculture Organization, United Nations (FAO-UN) in a three-day workshop on knowledge management.

João Paulo Carneiro H. Braga is a manager at the Brazilian Development Bank's (BNDES) Planning Area. He is an economist who graduated from the Federal University of Rio de Janeiro with a master's degree in innovation and industrial organization. At BNDES, he implemented the BNDES Methodology for Intangible Assets evaluation and works with issues such as competitiveness, nonfinancial analysis and industrial policy.

Johnathan Mun, PhD, is the founder/CEO of Real Options Valuation, a consulting/training/software development firm specializing in strategic real options, financial valuation, Monte Carlo risk simulation, stochastic forecasting, optimization and risk analysis. He has created eighteen advanced analytical software programs in quantitative risk and decision analytics, authored twelve books and is currently a professor at various universities globally (Naval Postgraduate School, University of Applied Sciences in Switzerland/Germany). He had consulted over 300+ multinationals from 3M, Airbus, and Boeing, to BP, FASB, Microsoft, Northrop Grumman, Pfizer, state of California and the U.S. Department of Defense. His PhD is in finance and economics from Lehigh University.

Jun Yao is currently an assistant professor of the College of Business Administration at Ritsumeikan University. She is also one of the advisory board members of the Japan Intellectual Capital Management Association. She got her bachelor's degree from Shanghai International Studies University, China, and master's degree and PhD from Kobe University, Japan. She has wide interests in the area of accounting and management, including intellectual capital, management control, risk management and corporate governance. She has several papers published in academic journals in Japan. She won the Academic Award from the Japan Institute of Certified Public Accountants in 2014.

Karl-Heinz Leitner, PhD, is senior scientist at the Austrian Institute of Technology and teaches innovation management at the Technical University of Vienna. His main research interests cover changing research and development (R&D) and innovation processes, strategic management, research policy and the valuation of intellectual capital. He has been involved in a number of research and consultancy projects related to the introduction of intellectual reporting systems for various public and private organizations. His research has been published in *Management Accounting Research, Higher Education, R&D Management* and the *Journal of Intellectual Capital,* among others.

Laura Girella is currently a postdoctorate research fellow at Ca' Foscari University of Venice (Italy). She got a master's degree in business economics and a PhD (Doctor Europeaus formula) in economics (major in business economics and management) from the Department of Economics and Management of the University of Ferrara (Italy), discussing a thesis titled "Soft Regulating Intangibles Reporting in Japan and Germany: Rationales, Processes and Consequences". Her main research interests include intangibles and intellectual capital measurement and reporting, integrated reporting and its development and public policies in relation to accounting and nonaccounting practices.

Marcos Cavalcanti has a PhD in computer science from the Université de Paris XI, Orsay, France. He is a professor at the Federal University of Rio de Janeiro (UFRJ) and director of CRIE—the Business Intelligence Institute of UFRJ. He is editor of *Revista Inteligência Empresarial* (a Brazilian business intelligence magazine). He wrote the books *O Conhecimento em Rede* (*Knowledge Networks*) and *Gestão de Empresas na Sociedade do Conhecimento* (*Managing in the Knowledge Era,* the best-seller book on knowledge management in Brazil. He is coordinator of the Master on Business and Knowledge Management (MBKM) and MBA on Web Intelligence and Digital Ambiance (MBKM). He is a member of the board of the New Club of Paris.

Markus Will, born in 1975, is head of the Fraunhofer IPK Project Office, Brazil, and senior researcher in the area of strategic management at the Division Corporate Management of Fraunhofer IPK, Berlin. He completed an apprenticeship in business administration, holds a master's degree in communication sciences and a doctoral degree from the Technical University, Berlin. He was responsible for the German federal IC-initiative "Wissensbilanz—Made in Germany" and the European Union's pilot project "InCaS. Intellectual Capital Statement—Made in Europe". Markus is a lead trainer at the Fraunhofer Academy and member of the board of the German association for intellectual capital management.

Nazli A. Mohd Ghazali, PhD, is an associate professor in the Department of Accounting, International Islamic University, Malaysia. She received her bachelor's and master's degrees from Lancaster University, England and a PhD in accounting and finance from Strathclyde University, Scotland. Her research interests are in the areas of disclosure, corporate governance, corporate social responsibility, risk management and ethics. She has published papers in the *Journal of International Accounting, Auditing and Taxation, Corporate Governance: The International Journal of Business in Society, Social Responsibility Journal, International Journal of Commerce and Management, International Journal of Business Governance and Ethics, International Journal of Disclosure and Governance, Managerial Auditing Journal, Asian Review of Accounting and Journal of Intellectual Capital* and others.

Pirjo Ståhle is a visiting professor at the Aalto University School of Engineering, Research Institute for Measuring and Modeling for the Built Environment. Her main areas of expertise are the measurement of intellectual capital and knowledge and innovation management. Pirjo moved to her current position from the University of Turku Futures Research Centre, where she served as professor from 2004 to 2013. More information on her is at www.stahle.fi.

Rongbin W.B. Lee is currently the Cheng Yick-Chi Chair of Manufacturing Engineering of the Department of Industrial and Systems Engineering and the director of the Knowledge Management and Innovation Research Center of The Hong Kong Polytechnic University. Professor Lee is the chief editor of the *International Journal of Knowledge and Systems Science* and co-editor of the *Journal of Information and Knowledge Management Systems*. He has pioneered research and the practice of knowledge management in various industrial sectors in Hong Kong, which include manufacturing, trading, public utilities and health care. Prof. Lee and his team have launched Asia's first online MSc. program in knowledge management. His research interests include manufacturing engineering and strategy, knowledge management and intellectual capital management.

Sladjana Cabrilo, PhD, is an associate professor at the University Educons, Serbia. Her teaching and research areas are knowledge management, intellectual capital, innovation and change management. Her current interests focus on IC measuring and reporting as well as IC-based innovation gap assessment. Dr. Cabrilo's rich experience includes participation in scientific and industry-related projects, publishing more than sixty academic articles, books and book chapters, lectures and presentations worldwide, and awards for research excellence. She is a member of the New Club of Paris, committee member of the ECIC and a consultant of the Regional Chamber of Commerce (Serbia).

Stefano Zambon, PhD, is Chair of Accounting and Business Economics at the University of Ferrara, Italy. He has held visiting appointments in universities on four continents. Stefano has more than one hundred publications in books and international journals in management and reporting of intangibles, international financial reporting and accounting theory and history. He was a coordinator of the 2003 EC study on the measurement of intangible assets and was a member of the 2006 EC Expert Group that prepared the study "RICARDIS". Stefano has been an invited keynote speaker at OECD, United Nations, European Parliament, European Commission and French, Chinese and Japanese government events on intangibles. He was a founding member of the Global Network "World Intellectual Capital Initiative" (WICI), and in 2013, became a member of the EC Expert Group on IP Valuation. Since April 2014 he has been president of the Collège des Experts de l'Immatériel of the French government.

Sten Ståhle is a freelance analyst specializing in business intelligence and measurement of intellectual capital. He has contributed to several academic and corporate research programs on intangible capital measurement and has many scientific publications on the subject. More information on him can be found at www.bimac.fi.

Susana Elena, PhD, is a scientific fellow in the Knowledge for Growth Unit at the Institute for Prospective and Technological Studies (IPTS), a Joint Research Center of the European Commission, and an associate professor at Loyola University (Seville, Spain). Her work focuses on higher education institutions, intellectual capital, knowledge management, innovation policies and management and governance of public organizations. Her research has been published in international journals such as the *Journal of Intellectual Capital, Foresight Journal,* and *Perspectives: Policy and Practice in Higher Education.* She has been involved in numerous European projects and has been part of several scientific committees for international conferences and in European expert groups.

Tadanori Yosano is associate professor at the Graduate School of Business Administration at Kobe University in Japan. His fields of interest in research include accounting for intangibles and intellectual capital reporting. He is a member of the New Club of Paris, and received the Pricewaterhouse Coopers Award for the "Best Junior contributor to the Development of Intangibles and IC theory and Practice" at the 4th European Institute for Advanced Studies in Management Workshop on "Visualizing, Measuring, and Managing Intangibles and Intellectual Capital", 2008.

Thomas J. Housel, PhD, specializes in valuing intellectual capital, knowledge management, telecommunications, information technology and value-based business process reengineering. He is a tenured full professor (U.S. Naval Postgraduate School) and received his PhD from the University of Utah, has authored two books and was featured in a *Fortune* cover story, *Investor's Business Daily,* numerous books, periodicals and academic journals. He has conducted more than eighty projects within the U.S. Department of Defense (Army/Navy/Marines), and more than one hundred projects in the private sector. Previously, he was a research fellow for the Center for Telecommunications Management and an associate professor at the Marshall Business School (University of Southern California).

Ulf Johanson, PhD, is professor emeritus at Mälardalen University, School of Business, Society and Engineering. He is the author of ninety scientific articles, books and book chapters in accounting, human resource costing and accounting, governance and management control, as well as capital market communication. These texts have specifically addressed intangible resources, for example, competence, health, human capital and intellectual capital. On occasion, he has contributed to policy development, for example, with respect to managing and reporting intangibles and working environments.

Wolfgang Baer, PhD, has extensive experience in computer systems, software development and managing the business of state-of-the-art prototype products. He ran a multimillion-dollar simulation laboratory for the U.S. Army, integrated intensive real-time video battlefield simulation and rapid terrain database creation algorithms into battlefield knowledge systems and previously worked at Ford Aerospace on meteorological communication satellites and started a computer graphics simulation company. His PVNT software pursues unmanned aerial vehicles' mission control, cognitive vision interpretation and interoperability standards. His PhD in physics is from the University of California at Berkeley, and he holds a research position at the U.S. Naval Postgraduate School.

Zilvinas Martinaitis, PhD, is a reader at Vilnius University and a partner at Visionary Analytics—a Vilnius-based policy advisory group. His work focuses on the development of research and HE monitoring and evaluation systems and analysis of the interactions between education and labor market systems.

Index